The Positive Power of Imagery

The Positive Power of Imagery

Harnessing Client Imagination in CBT and Related Therapies

Tammie Ronen

WILEY-BLACKWELL

A John Wiley & Sons, Ltd., Publication

Wiley-Blackwell is an imprint of John Wiley & Sons, formed by the merger of Wiley's global Scientific, Technical, and Medical business with Blackwell Publishing.

Registered Office
John Wiley & Sons Ltd, The Atrium, Southern Gate, Chichester, West Sussex, PO19 8SQ, UK

Editorial Offices
The Atrium, Southern Gate, Chichester, West Sussex, PO19 8SQ, UK
9600 Garsington Road, Oxford, OX4 2DQ, UK
350 Main Street, Malden, MA 02148-5020, USA

For details of our global editorial offices, for customer services, and for information about how to apply for permission to reuse the copyright material in this book please see our website at www.wiley.com/wiley-blackwell.

Library of Congress Cataloging-in-Publication Data

Ronen, Tammie.
  The positive power of imagery : harnessing client imagination in CBT and related therapies / Tammie Ronen.
    p. cm.
  Includes bibliographical references and index.
  ISBN 978-0-470-68303-3 (cloth) – ISBN 978-0-470-68302-6 (pbk.)
  1. Imagery (Psychology)–Therapeutic use.   2. Cognitive therapy.   I. Title.
  RC489.F35R66 2011
  616.89′14–dc22

                                                                    2010038086

A catalogue record for this book is available from the British Library.

This book is published in the following electronic formats: eBook 9780470979969; Wiley Online Library 9780470979976

Set in 9/11pt Plantin by Aptara Inc., New Delhi, India.

Printed in Malaysia by Ho Printing (M) Sdn Bhd

1   2011

To Michael,

Through living with you, I have learned what happiness and flourishing mean. Being with you continually reinforces my own personal positive power and my optimistic outlook toward the future.

Contents

List of Tables	*xiii*
Acknowledgments	*xv*
About the Author	*xvii*

PART I THEORETICAL BACKGROUND **1**

1 Introduction: On Becoming a Therapist **3**
Who Am I and What Am I Doing? (The Emperor is Naked; The
  Wingless Bird) 4
How Can I Do What I Plan to Do? (The Ladder; Having a Dream) 6
Swimming Against the Tide: How Can I Remain Positive? 8
How Can I Best Do What Needs to Be Done? (Discovering
  Creativity and Guided Imagination) 10
Overview of the Book 12

2 Thinking Like a Cognitive-Behavioral Therapist **15**
The Basic View Underlying CBT 15
Traditional Behavioral Therapy 17
The Transition to an Approach Integrating Cognitive Therapy 17
The Integration of Cognitive and Behavioral Therapies 18
Self-Control Models: An Offshoot of Integrated CBT 20
Constructivism Enters the Scene 21
Mindfulness Becomes Part of CBT 22
Major Tenets and Processes of CBT 24
Skills-Directed Therapy 32
Summary 34
Practice: Guidelines for Developing the Client's Profile 34

3   On Being a Positive Therapist   **37**
    Becoming a Recognized Theory and Therapy   38
    The Positive View of Clients and Therapeutic Processes   38
    Defining Positive Psychology   41
    Positive Psychology and Happiness   42
    Subjective Wellbeing   44
    Training in Positive Psychology   47
    Summary   51
    Practice: Guidelines for Applying Positive Psychology Exercises   51

4   Creativity: Who Needs It, and for What?   **55**
    What Is Creativity?   57
    Creativity and Emotion   60
    Creativity, Genetics, and Intelligence   62
    How Can One Promote Creative Action?   63
    Who Are Creative People?   65
    Creative Psychotherapy and Creative Psychotherapists   66
    Noncreative Imagery in Therapy   69
    Techniques to Facilitate Therapists' Creativity   70
    Summary   71
    Practice: Guidelines for Activating One's Creativity   72

5   Applying Developmental CBT with Children   **73**
    The Unique Nature of Childhood   73
    Characteristics of Childhood Disorders   75
    CBT with Children as Distinct from CBT with Adults   76
    Applying CBT with Children   77
    Considering Developmental Components   78
    Summary   85
    Practice: Guidelines for Applying CBT with Children   85

PART II   THE POSITIVE POWER OF IMAGERY   **89**

6   Major Concepts Regarding Imagery   **91**
    Perspectives on the Major Concepts   91
    Imagery and Memory   93
    Historical Uses of Imagery   94
    Imagery   95
    Types of Imagery   96
    Pros and Cons of Working with Imagery   100
    Summary   103
    Practice: Guidelines for Increasing Therapists' Own Ability to
        Elicit Memories   104

7   Using Imagery in Psychotherapy: How, Why, and What For?   **107**
    What Kinds of Therapies Can Integrate Imagery, and for Which
        Client Problems?   107
    Overcoming Resistance to or Anxiety about Imagery Work   110

The Major Benefits of Imagery Use in Psychotherapy 111
Dangers of Working with Imagery 119
Summary 121
Practice: Guidelines for Therapists and Clients to Foster Imagery
in Therapy 121

8 Using Metaphors in Therapy **123**
What Are Metaphors? 123
Metaphors and Emotions 124
The Role of Metaphors in Therapy 125
Client- and Therapist-Generated Metaphors 132
Summary 135
Practice: Guidelines for Therapists Beginning Metaphor Work 135

PART III PREPARING TO APPLY THERAPY
THROUGH IMAGERY **137**

9 Getting Ready to Start: Relaxation **139**
Preliminary Preparations 139
Meditation 140
Relaxation 141
Types of Relaxation Techniques 143
Summary 147
Practice: Guidelines for Therapist Self-Relaxation Exercises 147

10 Basic Guidelines for Conducting Imagery Therapy: From
Setting to Termination **149**
Preparation of Therapist, Setting, and Client 149
Pre-Imagery Exercises in Eliciting Images 151
Pre-Imagery Practice of Client Relaxation, to Set the Stage for
Generating Images 153
Bringing Up Images and Describing Them 154
Facilitating New Coping Skills Through Imagery 159
Ending the Imagery Work Phase Within the Session 160
Follow-Up to Imagery Work: Reflection, Interpretation, and
Meaning Making 163
Assigning Homework 165
Summary 166
Practice: Guidelines for Summarizing Knowledge and Skills
Needed for Conducting the Session 166

11 Adapting Relaxation and Imagery to Children **169**
Applying Relaxation to Diverse Childhood Disorders 169
Adapting Relaxation Techniques to Children's Needs and Abilities 170
Case I: Dianne's Television Phobia and Anxieties 171
Case II: Ronnie's Stuttering 172
Case III: Daniel's Test Anxiety 173

Applying Imagery Techniques with Children   174
Summary   176
Practice: Guidelines for Adapting Relaxation and Imagery to
   Children and Young People   177

**PART IV   USING IMAGERY WHILE ASSESSING AND
          TREATING CLIENTS**   **179**

**12 Using Imagery for Assessing Clients Throughout the
    Treatment Process**   **181**
Imagery Integration into Assessment   181
Assessment in Different Treatment Phases   184
Targets for Conducting Assessment   186
Summary   195
Practice: Guidelines for the Main Questions Directed at Each
   Assessment Target   195

**13 Applying Imagery to Treat Past Events (Fears,
    Trauma, Posttrauma**   **199**
Treating Distressing Past Events   199
Imaginal Exposure Followed by *In Vivo* Exposure   201
Imaginal Exposure Instead of *In Vivo* Exposure   204
Imagery as a Way to Elicit Memories and Remember
   Forgotten Material   207
Using Imagery for Cognitive Restructuring of Past Trauma   210
Summary   214
Practice: Guidelines for Choosing Between Options   214

**14 Imparting Assessment and Awareness Skills for Changing
    Present Behavior**   **217**
Imparting Skills for Self-Assessment   218
Imparting Skills for Assessment of Relationships   221
Imparting Skills to Increase Awareness of Internal Stimuli   227
Imparting Skills for Changing Automatic Thoughts   231
Summary   234
Practice: General Guidelines   234

15 Imparting Skills to Improve Present Coping   **235**
Skills for Coping with Performance and Test Anxiety   236
Preparation Phase: Learning and Memorizing Materials Through
   Visualization   236
Execution Phase: Alternative Positive Images, Gradual Exposure,
   Humor, and Role Reversal   238
Eliciting Positive Images During Stressful Performance Situations   239
Implementing Gradual Exposure to the Feared Situation   240
Using Humor and Role Reversal to Gain Control and Confidence   242
Skills for Improving Social Relationships   243
Skills for Initiating Social Contacts   244

Assertiveness Skills (Learning to Say No)   247
Summary   250

16   Imparting Skills for Developing a Positive View of the Future   251
Planning the Future   253
Facilitating Positive Emotions and Sensations   255
Increasing Happy Relationships   259
Summary   262

17   Imparting Skills to Help Children Change: Further Guidelines and Case Illustrations   263
Treating Young Children   264
Treating Children in Middle Childhood   267
Treating Adolescents   271
Summary   274
Practice: Guidelines for Imparting Skills to Children   274

PART V   NOTES AND CONCLUSIONS FOR IMAGERY THERAPISTS   275

18   Helping Therapists Help Themselves   277
Skills for Self-Supervision   278
Skills for Learning to "Get Rid" of Difficult Things and
    Continue Toward the Future   281
Skills for Focusing on Your Own Positive Abilities as a Therapist   282
Skills for Planning Future Therapeutic Processes   285
General Skills for Helping Yourself   286
Summary   288

19   Summary: Limitations, Dangers, and Future Directions   289
Limitations: Is Imagery Therapy Evidence Based?   291
Are There Dangers in Applying Imagery Therapy?   294
Last Words   295

References   *297*

Index   *313*

List of Tables

Table 6.1 Chart for measuring ability to create images   105
Table 9.1 Chart for monitoring self-relaxation   148

Acknowledgments

Thanks. . .

. . . To Dee B. Ankonina, my friend and editor, who has been editing my professional work since its early days. Working with you turns even the difficulties into joy. Like the assessment exercises I suggest in this book, if I asked myself *"If you could not write your own books, who would you trust to write them?"* I believe that Dee could!

. . . To my students and clients, who challenge me to be creative and continually develop new methods for facilitating happiness, and who trust me as I put my wild ideas and imagery exercises into practice.

. . . To Darren Reed and Karen Shield, my editors at Wiley-Blackwell, who were brave enough to let me produce this nonroutine book.

About the Author

Tammie Ronen is a professor at the Bob Shapell School of Social Work in Tel-Aviv University, where she is in charge of Child Clinical Studies. She is the Head of the Renata Adler Memorial Research Center for child welfare and protection. She is the previous head of the school and the past president of the Israeli Association of Behaviour and Cognitive Therapies. She has written many books, articles, and chapters in the area of cognitive-behavioral therapy, child therapy, and positive psychology. She is well known as an international lecturer and a supervisor.

Part I
Theoretical Background

1

Introduction:
On Becoming a Therapist

The present book is an outcome of my self-guided, personal journey toward becoming a therapist. My journey has been rich and variegated, peopled along the way with a broad range of clients of all ages from diverse ethnicities and cultures, suffering from various disorders, and bringing with them different life experiences, gaps in motivation for change, and, of course, a richness of abilities, skills, and resources. As I worked with these clients along my personal and professional path to becoming a mental health practitioner, some experiences helped me craft my choices about where I should go next as a therapist; from time to time, my path deviated from the main roads to encounter sudden detours, obstacles, and hazards; and eventually, some clients and some of my work gradually began to seem like familiar signposts on roads traveled daily.

As I look back at roads I already traveled as I grew and developed as a therapist, the memories come to me mainly as pictures. Some are snapshots – actual, colorful, visual pictures that I see in my mind's eye – like a certain client's proud facial expression, or a couple's body language as they shout fervently at one another. Some are metaphorical; that is, I can hear or see a story playing itself out in images with hidden meanings – like the vision of a wild animal family interacting against the backdrop of a natural landscape as a mental metaphor I created while treating a certain family. Some pictures more resemble abstract art, like a complex image I envisioned for the interrelationships between the components of the human psyche.

Indeed, as I survey those landscapes and experiences on my road to learning this profession, the most striking discovery is how replete with imagery my journey has been. In this book, I hope to open up a vivid album of all my travels up to this point in time, and to share with my readers the fascinating pictures and memories I have been privileged to see, feel, and sense, and how I learned to navigate and draw on countless images to help my clients and myself over the years of my career. The current volume is a crucial milestone in my journey, because here I hope to assemble some key highlights of my travels and some insights I reached

The Positive Power of Imagery: Harnessing Client Imagination in CBT and Related Therapies,
First Edition. Tammie Ronen. © 2011 Tammie Ronen. Published 2011 by John Wiley & Sons, Ltd.

that shaped my therapeutic work over the years, all related to the world of images and pictures, and to the meaning of imagery.

As a means for helping readers enter into this world of imagery, in the next sections of this chapter I will share some more details about my own journey toward becoming a therapist. Over time, my metaphorical picture of myself as a therapist has gradually blended several main orientations or entities. I see myself as a cognitive-behavioral therapist, as a skills trainer, as a structured and goal-directed practitioner, as a positive therapist, and as a creative therapist. I found that these entities merged well into one united approach for working with imagery. First, in this Introduction, I will share how I myself developed and harmonized these entities during my long journey toward becoming a therapist who uses cognitive-behavioral intervention in a creative way in light of positive psychology theories. Then, the book will focus on each of the basic entities and will guide readers in how each entity may be relevant to their therapeutic work, and in how to integrate them through metaphors and images.

Who Am I and What Am I Doing?
(The Emperor is Naked; The Wingless Bird)

I never made a conscious decision to become a cognitive-behavioural therapist. As I graduated from my School of Social Work, I began working in a psychiatric hospital and, later on, in a mental health community center. At that time, despite my license to practice, I felt completely inadequate. I was terrified that everyone would find out that I, like the emperor in *The Emperor's New Clothes* (Andersen, 2004), was actually naked – no skills, no ability, and just parading around as if I were a genuine professional. I felt I had no inkling of what therapy really was or how to conduct it.

I had many proofs for that self-perception. I attended many staff meetings where I never understood the language. The discussions used complicated, abstract concepts to analyze the therapeutic process, which everyone except me seemed to understand. In those meetings, I found that I was concerned about different notions from the rest of the staff. Rather than focusing on my own emotions and internal processes, I was preoccupied with what was happening with my clients. I thought my clients were the center of therapy. I was talking more about facts and goals and less about processes. I wanted to focus on what I needed to teach and what the client needed to learn. I was talking here and now, and also looking at the future, not so much at the past. I so much wanted to help my clients, and I had so many ideas, but I felt different. I thought that there must be some locked away secret of therapy, and that everyone knew the secret except me. How could I unlock the deep box and find the hidden secret of what it meant to conduct therapy? I felt like a bird without wings. Aching to fly, I hoped that one day I would find a mother bird or father bird who would finally understand my different way of thinking about therapy, and that maybe it could be a beginning of a new family...

4

Meanwhile, I focused on imparting the skills they needed to my clients, helping them change, drawing with them, helping them map out where they wanted to go in life, aiding them in looking for their own goals, and trying to improve their subjective wellbeing. I knew that what I was doing was not "therapy" – but this was all I knew how to do. So, as a wingless, naked bird, I did the best I could.

Two of my teachers at the university finally swooped in to help me make the move toward behavioral therapy (at that time I was not yet a cognitive-behavioral therapist). I was already treating clients when I met the first of these teachers, Dr. Yair Abraham at the School of Education of Tel Aviv University. I was a graduate student and soon became his assistant. He introduced me to behavioral therapy. Israel was (and still is) very psychodynamically oriented, and I had never studied cognitive-behavioral therapy (CBT) formally. When I discovered that my employer was a behavioral therapist, I thought: "Well, that makes some sense because he seems to be a very organized, structured person and I'm not. He can follow precise instructions and I can't. I'm a very flexible, intuitive person so behavioral therapy must not be for me."

As I started working with him, I also began visiting his clinic and watching him treat clients using cognitive-behavioral methods. I saw how helpful and effective his work was for his clients. As a result, I told myself: "Well, I may not be a behavioral therapist, but I think it would be okay and even easy to treat children who wet their beds using behavioral methods under his supervision. It is fast, effective, and makes sense." So, I began writing my master's thesis with Dr. Abraham on enuresis and treating children with nocturnal enuresis using cognitive-behavioral therapy. Soon enough, I realized that in a relatively short time I was able to help many children overcome their bedwetting, and even become more independent and confident. I gradually saw more and more clients and eventually became an expert in this area. Still not grasping my identity, I told everyone: "You know, behavioral therapy is a very good technique for treating nocturnal enuresis in childhood." Although I was nowhere near ready to fly, I began to feel like some feathers were growing stronger on my naked, birdlike body.

Beginning to acknowledge that this behavioral approach to therapy had some merit, I started reading every book I could find on behavioral therapy and cognitive therapy. I wanted to fully understand the theory behind my practice and to learn the techniques' rationales to see if I wanted to adopt them more. And all that voracious reading reached a pinnacle one day, as I looked in the mirror (before I learned from Michael Mahoney how to work properly with mirrors in therapy) and it dawned on me: all those years, all that time, I had considered myself to be a naked, wingless bird, when what I had been doing naturally had actually been to practice CBT all along. This approach just fitted who I was! It matched my way of life: the way I planned my day, the way I thought positively, the way I used reinforcement, the way I changed my thoughts, the way I used self-talk. It was strange how much of this approach I used daily. Looking in the mirror, I finally recognized the image facing me: I really was a therapist! I knew what therapy was. I was a cognitive-behavioral therapist. I felt my wings actually extending and growing larger and more powerful. Suddenly I understood that I was ready to fly. After that, as I began to feel good enough about my work to believe in myself as a therapist, I began flying high.

Thus, having arrived at cognitive-behavioral therapeutic work through a back door, serendipitously, I first recognized one entity within my self-identity, that of "A Cognitive-Behavioral Therapist." One of the first things I did then was to seek out other people with whom I could collaborate, talk, and explore this new identity. Eventually, Dr. Abraham helped me establish the Israeli Association for Behaviour Therapy, and I finally felt my wingspan spread. Once my internal bird discovered this flock of colleagues who felt like I did, treated clients like I did, and lived like I did, I truly began to soar. My early experiences made me invest great efforts in preventing my students from suffering the horrific fear of being emperors without clothes. I insisted that my students come watch me conducting sessions – either through video, a one-way mirror, or direct observation of therapy – or be my co-therapist in sessions. I was determined that they should understand what I did not: that every individual therapist must unlock the box and find his or her own solutions. Equally, I was willing to show them some of the secrets I had found.

By that time, I realized that I had indeed found my "therapist's identity." I finally knew what was important for me in conducting therapy. I knew that therapy for me is a combination of educational and therapeutic processes, where my role is to guide, teach, and supervise clients in the process of change. I also discovered that it is extremely important for me to ensure that what I apply with a client is an effective, provable method for change, one that really works.

Later on, I met Professor Yochanan Wozner at the School of Social Work, who became my doctoral supervisor. He was (and still is) one of Israel's traditional behaviorists. He has devoted much time and effort to investigating the efficacy of treatments, assessments, and evaluations. His academic courses strongly influenced my later insistence that I apply evidence-based therapy.

So, my new identity was that of a teacher who teaches clients how to help themselves change by applying effective skills and techniques. I started introducing myself as a teacher in helping people change. I thought that "teacher" was the right concept for me, because I strongly emphasized the importance of skills acquisition. I wanted to educate clients in what to do and how best to do it. I was not yet sure what exactly I needed to teach or how best to teach, but I knew that I was a teacher.

How Can I Do What I Plan to Do?
(The Ladder; Having a Dream)

As a very goal-directed person, even back then, each time I met a new client I found it difficult to start therapy unless I first discovered what that client wanted to achieve at the end of therapy. This meant that I, together with my client, needed to have a vision of him or her in the future. This is how I work to this day. The client and I must collaborate together to address questions like: How will this client act or be when we reach the end of the process? How will we know that the time has arrived to end therapy? What reasons will there be? What will signal the differences in the client?

I learned that an effective way to trigger discussion of this vision of the future was to ask my clients to make a drawing of how they wished to look at the termination of therapy. Only after this initial drawing was completed would we start talking, drawing, or thinking about how the clients looked in the present, about the gaps between "now" and "later," and about what they felt was missing in order to reach that future vision.

In response to my requests to look ahead and envision their future, my clients used to ask: "How can I possibly know what the future will hold?" And I used to answer: "If this is your life, you have to think about what you want it to be. You must run your life, not let your life run you. You should maneuver it, not just go with the wind. You need to have a dream in order to realize that dream!" Thus, two main metaphors emerged from these clarifications to my clients, reflecting who I came to be as a therapist. The first metaphor was the lyrics from "Happy Talk," a song from the old musical *South Pacific*: "You got to have a dream. If you don't have a dream, how you gonna have a dream come true?" (Rodgers & Hammerstein, 1949). Following this metaphor, with all my clients we began by relating to their dreams. Clients need to relate to their dreams as something that can wait for them in the future, something that is worth working toward.

For example, when I treated a teenage girl who had dropped out of high school, spent most of her time on the streets, and showed delinquent behavior, we discovered that her dream was to become a scientist at the university. Of course at the time, in her current life situation, this dream seemed stupid and unrealistic to her. But we used it as a stepping-stone for creating hope and learning about working toward goals, or as the top rung on a ladder she would like to climb from her present place on the bottom rung. We started by outlining how she could try to make her dream come true, step by step. As her first goal, we decided she needed to complete her high school studies. With my support, she was able to sign up for evening classes and complete her matriculation examinations. As she experienced this success, she felt emboldened to attempt to undertake higher education. It was not easy. She did not become a university professor, but she does work today in a government laboratory and feels very proud that she achieved a profession.

As mentioned regarding the previous client, the second metaphor I began to use with my clients was the ladder, a symbol of climbing up step by step to reach one's dream. The ladder became an important part of my treatment room. With children, I brought in a real ladder for them actually to climb up, see how the top rung felt, and fall back before ascending once again. With adolescents, drawing ladders on paper could help them measure and monitor their progress. With adults, a metaphorical ladder became an integral part of therapy. Clients planned where they wanted to be at the end of therapy and then started climbing up, while I was busy teaching them the skills needed for that climb. As they worked to change their identified thoughts and behaviors, the clients could evaluate their progress using this metaphorical ladder, assessing when they fell a rung or two,

7

or when they skipped upward quickly and easily, thus helping them gain self-awareness and confidence.

For example, in our large-scale national project to reduce aggression and increase self-control skills among at-risk Israeli adolescents (see Chapter 2), small groups meet for a series of 12 sessions with two co-therapists (Ronen & Rosenbaum, 2010). During the first session, all students receive pictures of a ladder and are asked to note where on the ladder they would like to be at the end of therapy and how they envision that place. Many adolescents draw themselves on the top rung, explaining that up there they would have many friends and would have no problems with their teachers. Then the students are asked to draw themselves where they are presently, at the beginning of the treatment. They usually put themselves either on the ground or on the first rung, explaining that right now they continually fight and argue with parents and teachers, and have few friends. We use the ladders in each session, to check where they would like to climb to and what they need to be able to climb there. The group sessions focus on giving these adolescents the skills needed for achieving these goals.

Thus, using such metaphors as dreams and ladders, at this stage I not only knew who I was, a cognitive-behavioral therapist, but I also recognized two other entities within my self-identity. I had become a "Structured Therapist," a practitioner who works systematically toward achieving goals while planning and mapping out the process of therapy, and assessing and evaluating the outcomes. I had also become a "Skills Trainer," who based therapy on teaching, training, and applying specific, relevant skills that were tailored to clients' needs and aimed to improve clients' functioning in particular areas that we continually identified and updated.

Swimming Against the Tide: How Can I Remain Positive?

At this point in my career, I drifted with the tide, trying to do what supervisors at the local public mental health center expected of me, but concurrently I started receiving supervision in CBT and found myself using it more and more in my daily work.

To my great fortune, during my Counselling studies at the School of Education (in addition to my degree in Social Work), I was lucky enough to study with Professor Zipora Magen. Unlike most researchers of that period who were concentrating on pathology and problems, she was investigating happiness among adolescents. As I studied in her class and listened to her positive psychological orientation, I felt I had found not only a kindred spirit but a whole new way of looking at the world of the human psyche and its treatment. I realized for the first time that I was not alone. There were other people out there, albeit a minority, who, like me, were looking for clients' strengths rather than their weaknesses.

At that time, I took a deep breath and dived into my positive therapeutic orientation with sudden confidence. I started swimming against the tide – doing what I believed in, working in the way I thought was right despite others' questions and criticisms. The epitome of this turn I took was my therapy with Ayelet, an anorexic client. Her story can be read in the book we wrote together: *In and Out of Anorexia: The Story of the Client, the Therapist and the Process of Recovery* (Ronen & Ayelet, 2001). Ayelet claimed that out of her total of 12 therapists over the years (11 before coming to me), I was the only one who could help her because they all saw only the sickness and focused on the pathological diagnosis, whereas I saw her soul and found her strengths. Nevertheless, the positive approach I used to treat Ayelet received not only much attention but also much criticism.

Throughout her therapy, I tried to show her that she was strong rather than weak, creative rather than crazy, and that her fantasies were a good way to start designing a new world rather than simply staying trapped in familiar, ineffective patterns of behavior. For example, when Ayelet first entered my room saying, "I'm not sure if you'll agree to treat me. I'm a weak, terrible person," I answered, "I think you are a very strong person. Being in and out of five different hospitals from age 14 to 18, sometimes in isolated rooms, and staying sane – that means you are very strong. I would probably go crazy!" When Ayelet described her feeling of being alone and deserted ("I feel now like somebody standing on one side of the ocean, on the distant shore, talking about someone who has been left behind;" Ronen & Ayelet, 2001: 187), I knew I had to build a bridge for her, to let her cross the water and feel she could be heard by others.

However, out of all my books, this one received the worst critical reviews. I was blamed for being overly optimistic and for focusing on positive aspects that were unrealistic rather than treating the "real problem." My critics foretold that my positive stance would not last long, because with such a difficult, serious diagnosis, Ayelet would certainly return soon to anorexia. I was also blamed for breaking all of the "rules" of therapy: I worked with Ayelet's parents and boyfriend too, rather than insisting on meeting with her only; I saw her when needed rather than once a week at a fixed time; I permitted her to phone me between sessions, and so forth.

Nine years have passed since that book's publication, and 12 years since we terminated therapy. Ayelet is married and has a steady relationship with her husband, whom she met during exercises we conducted to practice social skills. She is a mother to two children and a very good special education teacher. I believed in her – and am happy I did so. My positive psychology orientation helped her express positive emotions, believe in herself and her own virtues, use her skills and strengths, and thereby improve her quality of life.

So, I began to recognize another clear entity within my self-identity, that of a "Positive Therapist." I was an optimist, doing what is now called "positive psychology" long before it got that name. I had uncovered another part of myself as a person and as a professional: I fully believed that humans are strong, capable, and only need to learn the "how to" of finding strengths within themselves. I found that this positive approach buoyed clients, supporting and encouraging them to delve deeply into themselves and render the needed change; moreover, this approach improved the client–therapist rapport and relationship, leading to further progress on the client's part.

I now had found my road, and I knew where I wanted it to lead. I now had found my dream, which was the first step in making it come true. I also now knew what the top rung of my ladder looked like: maintaining my own positivity and optimism while making my clients happy. As I progressed toward this new goal time after time with different clients, I succeeded more and more in climbing to the top rung of that ladder.

How Can I Best Do What Needs to Be Done? (Discovering Creativity and Guided Imagination)

I already understood that I was a CBT therapist, working in light of positive psychology, and that I was interested in facilitating change among my clients, wishing to focus on strengths, abilities, and skills. By now I also realized that my clients and I had to define goals and climb the ladder we designed together, each time, until reaching those goals. CBT offered a broad range of techniques to help clients change, but I found myself still looking for the best, most effective therapeutic solutions to apply with each client. I knew words were not enough; they could not always do the job. I wanted to actually train and teach clients in whatever they needed to climb their ladder, giving them opportunities to practice those skills. But which techniques were optimal? I thought that if I myself could find the hidden secrets of conducting therapy, my clients would be able to do so as well.

I never thought of myself as a creative person. As a child at school, we had art classes, and my drawings and sculptures always came out very ugly. I hated those classes. As a student at the university, I attended some classes in creativity. I came out very frustrated: They all wanted me to redesign a house from four matches, find a new solution to make a rectangle, and think "outside the box." I could never do it. So, I figured that creativity was not for me.

Two events in my life brought about a change in my thinking about creativity. The first event happened one summer 26 years ago. I was driving with my two daughters, Efrat, age 4, and Anat, age 1. In those days, children were not strapped into car seats or even seatbelts. Efrat was sitting behind the empty passenger seat when a car unexpectedly swerved in front of me. I slammed on the brakes and Efrat's little body rammed into the empty seat beside me, which broke and folded forward. I heard screams and saw lots of blood. I drove quickly to the hospital, where I learned that she needed stitches immediately, but could not receive general anesthesia because she had just eaten. The surgeon told me that local anesthesia would necessitate multiple injections in and around the wound which would themselves be painful; therefore, he suggested that I hold her, tell her not to move, and they would start stitching.

I explained the situation to Efrat and she lay down quietly. When it was over, the doctors gathered around us and asked how it was that she didn't say a word, or cry, or yell. Efrat replied by telling a story. She said that she had imagined she was Wonder Woman (her favorite television series at that time; Fitzsimons,

Marston, & Ross, 1975–1979) and, as such, she flew to help other people overcome their problems during the procedure. She claimed that she didn't feel anything. She still has a V-shaped scar on her cheek today. I was amazed by the natural manner in which she used imagination to overcome the frightening situation, and this incident prompted me to start reading material about self-control, imagery, and metaphors. In these tools, I found the answer to my search. I knew that these "secrets" would pave the way for me to help people change.

Then, a few years later, a second personal event gave me deep insight into the power of imagination for myself. I was about to finish my PhD studies when I went, for the first time, to present a lecture at a conference in Oxford, England. It was a world conference on cognitive therapy. At that time, I chaired a two-year program for specializing in CBT, and my PhD supervisor, Professor Yochanan Wozner – one of the earliest founders of behavior therapy in Israel – as well as five of my students came with me to the conference.

My presentation was scheduled to follow several impressive British lecturers, all wearing formal suits and speaking English that I did not always understand, in a large auditorium. I saw my supervisor go pale and apologize, intimidated: "Tammie, I had no idea what I was thinking! How did I think of exposing you to this situation? How can you present your talk after these people? I am so sorry." Until that moment, I had been feeling excited, but now I started feeling sick. My stomach hurt and I fought the impulse to burst out of the auditorium and run as far away as possible.

I knew that I needed to help myself discard the panicky sensations I was experiencing. I tried to reassure myself and, automatically, I did: I imagined I was giving the most wonderful lecture of the entire conference. I imagined how the audience was so enthusiastic that as I finished, they all bowed in ecstasy and admiration, and then I was invited to tour the world, presenting my work everywhere. I became famous...

With this image in mind, I started giving my talk, and I felt so confident that I didn't even use the written lecture I had prepared, but rather talked spontaneously, as I usually do when I lecture in my mother tongue. The only thing that disturbed me as I finished my lecture was that although people applauded and some came up to speak with me, nobody actually bowed down or invited me on a world tour!

I didn't know how I was spontaneously able to apply creative imagination to calm my tensions and set up success, but it immediately associated in my mind with my earlier observations of Efrat's creativity and my study of metaphors, images, and self-control. It was on this day that I began to recognize the final entity within my self-identity, that of a "Creative Therapist." I learned at first hand how imagery can be useful and render change. I learned personally how important and powerful a tool it is. I already knew that thinking positively is better than thinking negatively, and now I knew that from then on, I could best help my clients as follows.

I would apply positive, structured, yet creative CBT for helping people change. I would be a cognitive-behavioral therapist who teaches clients how to achieve their goals while imparting skills to them using a structured, positive way of thinking, using creative modes that go beyond words, especially imagery and metaphors, and helping the clients bring their lives back to order and make the most out of them. This book will present all of these components in unison.

And last but not least, I want to share with you how I started writing with such openness about my way of doing therapy. For many years after developing my multifaceted therapist identity, I thought that my way of conducting therapy was routine for CBT specialists. I suppose I believed that the route I traveled during my professional development was similar to that of many others. Then, around 18 years ago at a conference, I met Michael Mahoney, who became a close friend of mine and my husband's. At the time, I was writing mainly scientific articles about theory or about the efficacy of intervention packages. We started meeting Michael at conferences, and he came to visit us in Israel and during our sabbatical in the United States. We used to talk a great deal about therapy, and sometimes we even role-played therapies. Michael Mahoney was the one who urged me to "stop writing theory and start writing what you really do." It is hard for me to write this book knowing that he is not around any more for me to share ideas, show him what I wrote, and consult with him. I really miss him and know that this book could be better if he were here to comment on it. I hope I will be able to write what he thought I could. He will always be a positive part of my creative therapy.

Overview of the Book

This book is divided into five parts. In the first part, I relate the basic theories that serve as the foundation for developing imagery therapy. First, I describe CBT and skills-directed therapy (Chapter 2). This was not easy for me, because I have written several whole books on CBT; therefore, shortening it all into one chapter was an enormous challenge. However, in this chapter I try to focus mainly on thinking like a cognitive-behavioral therapist, to provide a grounded theory for applying imagery therapy, and I present guidelines for constructing therapy and leading it toward well-defined goals.

I continue by presenting a short review of positive psychology (Chapter 3). Positive psychology is a new name, and the popular focus today on positivity is relatively new, too. However, many people have been working toward subjective wellbeing, happiness, and positivity long before national and international associations for positive psychology came into being. In this chapter, I attempt to present some of the main concepts and issues involved in positive psychology theory, especially those that readers will find relevant to imagery therapy.

Next, I dedicate a chapter to creativity (Chapter 4) – another issue that could be a topic for an entire book in itself. I focus on what creativity is and why it is important for therapists, clients, and the process of therapy. In contrast to most of the existing literature on imagery therapy, this book does not mainly supply readers with fixed techniques or images to apply. Rather, I wish to challenge therapists to learn the skills for creatively designing personalized exercises to match each client's specific needs, problems, and personality.

I added a chapter on child therapy (Chapter 5), because imagery is certainly an excellent and natural choice for working with children. Most of this book deals with applying imagery as part of CBT interventions in general, without specifying clients' ages. However, many techniques require certain adaptations when applied to children; hence, this chapter discusses developmental considerations for applying imagery with children and adolescents.

The remainder of the book concerns imagery, accompanied by many case illustrations (with all names changed for anonymity) and practical guidelines. In Part II, I introduce basic concepts regarding imagery and metaphors in therapy and guidelines for their use in sessions with clients. Chapter 6 surveys the basic concepts of imagery, images, and imagination, including discussion of different ways for using imagination and its pros and cons in therapy. Chapter 7 focuses on how to use imagery in therapy, relating to various therapies' ways of incorporating imagery. Chapter 8 describes metaphors, differentiates between working with imagery and with metaphors, and discusses ways for applying metaphors in daily work with clients.

Part III involves the preparations recommended for applying imagery therapy. In this part, Chapter 9 focuses on relaxation, Chapter 10 outlines guidelines for creating and utilizing imagery along the process of treatment, from setting to termination, and Chapter 11 specifies adaptations of relaxation and imagery for children and adolescents.

The core part of the book, Part IV, presents imagery therapy itself, describing and illustrating this creative, structured way of intervening with clients. First, Chapter 12 focuses on assessment. I propose some important components for using imagery to facilitate the efficacy of assessment. The next four chapters categorize clients' problems into past, present, and future, while focusing on techniques for skills acquisition. Chapter 13 describes imagery therapy for treating problems related to clients' past traumatic experiences. Chapters 14 and 15 focus on imagery therapy to impart skills for coping with the present: overcoming fears and anxiety, increasing awareness of internal stimuli, and improving performance skills. Chapter 16 relates to the future: imparting positive thinking, gaining strengths, and future planning. Chapter 17 specifies applications of imagery therapy to children. All of these chapters provide case illustrations and examples to demonstrate specific techniques that can be applied via imagery.

The last part of the book, Part V, offers concluding thoughts. Chapter 18 focuses on the therapist, suggesting unique self-help techniques for therapists to design their own imagery training. I end the book with Chapter 19, which surveys the advantages and limitations of imagery therapy and suggests directions for imagery therapy to progress in the future.

I hope you enjoy the book as much as I enjoy doing imagery work, and I trust that you will find it useful in helping you gain the courage to apply imagery consistently in therapy, thereby utilizing its positive power to harness client imagination in CBT and related treatments.

2

Thinking Like a
Cognitive-Behavioral Therapist

This chapter will outline the history and basics underlying multimodal CBT, which includes cognitive, behavioral, constructivist mindfulness, self-control, and skills-training components. The major CBT tenets and processes will also be described.

The Basic View Underlying CBT

Modern CBT is a multimodal therapy that integrated traditional behavioral therapy with cognitive therapy, constructivist therapy, and, later on, mindfulness. Neimeyer (2009) described this changing or multimodal nature of therapy as a process where

> every emerging perspective repackages the wisdom of earlier thinkers, adds its own insights and innovations, draws on other streams of thought ... and then propounds this complex mixture as in some sense a valid reflection of "reality." (Neimeyer, 2009: 1)

Try to imagine each of these four components – behavioral, cognitive, constructivist, and mindfulness – as a metaphorical human being.

Behavioral therapy derives from learning processes, emphasizing that people learn behaviors through systematic processes based on classical conditioning, operant conditioning, and social learning. Thus, the metaphorical figure representing behavioral therapy could be an obsessed old man who continually keeps measuring, assessing, and making decisions. He wears glasses, thinks a lot, takes measurements all the time, and verifies that everything is in its correct place. He could fit the image of a scientist in an exact science. Although he does use a computer, he also walks around with a pencil to take notes.

The Positive Power of Imagery: Harnessing Client Imagination in CBT and Related Therapies,
First Edition. Tammie Ronen. © 2011 Tammie Ronen. Published 2011 by John Wiley & Sons, Ltd.

In contrast to behavioral therapy, cognitive therapy views behavior as the outcome of thinking and emotional mediational processes. Thus, cognitive therapy could be imagined as a tall, middle-aged, sophisticated man, wearing glasses, carrying his laptop everywhere, looking at his handheld organizer to check things, raising hypotheses, thinking, and rechecking. His room is overflowing with books, machines, scanners, computers, cameras. He keeps talking and arguing, and always asks about the link between thoughts, emotions, and behavior. Like the behavioral man, the cognitive fellow views himself as a scientist and talks "facts."

A third party comes on the scene: constructivism. Constructivist therapy derives from the beliefs that humans are the designers of their own reality, and that people's conceptions and conceptualizations of reality influence their problems. Constructivism may thus be illustrated by the figure of a woman who looks like an artist, speaks in a soft, musical voice, and keeps raising doubts, talking about emotions and feelings, questioning, and using intuition. She carries a poetry book to read and even writes her own poems.

The fourth component of CBT, mindfulness, derives from the belief that problems can be changed once clients gain more awareness of their own thoughts, feelings, emotions, and bodily sensations. Mindfulness can be seen as an old Hindu man who talks slowly, asks more than he says, sits on the floor, and practices meditation and mirroring. He seems to be highly content and profoundly self-aware.

Could you see all four of these figures merging together? They themselves wouldn't believe it possible that they could integrate into one entity; however, they are presently becoming an integrative model that combines all four components – behavioral therapy, cognitive therapy, constructivism, and mindfulness – under the one umbrella of CBT. Increasingly, CBT is now being seen as an integrated multimodal therapy whose conceptual strength, research basis, and broad therapeutic repertoire of techniques have placed it at the forefront of existing treatments (Rosner, Lyddon, & Freeman, 2004).

Importantly, CBT is a dynamic mode of intervention, subjecting itself to a constant process of change whereby therapists continuously modify their thinking and adapt and update their methods. CBT's primary role – helping people change – can only be realized by combining new theoretical knowledge with empirically tested interventional approaches that account for the cultural, social, economic, and political transformations typifying modern life (Clark & Beck, 1999).

A more apt metaphor for today's CBT might be the metaphor of a phenomenal tennis player. The game is continually changing, with new challenges, dynamic tempos, and varying ball velocities and curves. The player needs to move quickly from one position to another to meet the ball wherever it lands and to persistently lift it up and volley it back.

Looking at this concept of a tennis player, CBT can be viewed as making continual efforts to adapt itself to clients' changing lives. Life is conceived as an ongoing experience to which human beings are exposed. Those experiences require people to open themselves up, to explore and experiment with new realities, and continually to pursue the process of learning as well as an ongoing process of change following that learning (Mahoney, 1991, 2003). Inasmuch as human behavior continuously undergoes a process of change, people are always able to render changes to their thoughts and behaviors (Clark & Beck, 1999).

The dynamic nature of CBT can be understood by reviewing its development over the last 70 years, as it progressed and evolved from behavioral therapy alone to an integration of behavioral and cognitive therapies, and then gradually added constructivist and mindfulness components.

Traditional Behavioral Therapy

Basic behavioral theory had already started developing at the beginning of the twentieth century. Its origins lie in the idea that learning and conditioning processes can lead to abnormal reactions in behavior and emotion (Salkovskis, 2008).

Classical conditioning focused on stimulus and response (Pavlov, 1927; Wolpe, 1982). Pavlov's study of dogs' digestion depicted the connection between food (stimulus) and salivation (response). Classical learning principles soon became the basis for explaining human habits, behaviors, and disorders and the source for developing relaxation training and desensitization techniques (Wolpe, 1982). The latter are still considered an important contribution to the treatment of anxiety disorders. Yet, these concepts – stimulus, response, conditioning – were used to analyze behavior without relating to the person as a human being.

Very soon, the proponents of basic classical conditioning were joined by those of operant conditioning. Operant conditioning assigned a specific role to the environment, focusing on the ability to modify a behavior by changing its consequences (Skinner, 1938). This learning mode linked behaviors and outcomes, highlighting techniques such as positive and negative reinforcement, extinction, and punishment. Behavior eliciting positive outcomes will continue, whereas behavior eliciting negative outcomes will be eliminated, decreased, or made extinct. More complex learning programs such as contingency contracts, token economies, and exposure techniques pinpointed the need for environmental change (Hughes, 1993).

The main focus of behavioral therapy was learning, rather than history or life events. Therapists were interested in understanding how clients learned to behave as they did, and what kind of learning clients lacked if they were to change their behavior.

The Transition to an Approach Integrating Cognitive Therapy

By the end of the 1960s, a third kind of learning, social learning, had emerged, further pinpointing the environment's role in conditioning behavior. This approach employed constructs such as modeling, environment, and observation (Bandura, 1969), underscoring the links between stimuli and responses;

behaviors and outcomes; and expectancies, behaviors, and environments. Bandura demonstrated that learning can occur as a result of observation and in the absence of reinforcement either to the model or to the learner. His social learning theory and his notion of vicarious (observational) learning provided the basis for conceptualizing the person–environment relationship as a reciprocal process of influence. People started to become perceived as active participants in their own learning.

Bandura's (1977, 1997) work on self-efficacy served as a bridge between traditional behavioral therapy and modern cognitive therapy. At the time, behavioral therapy was criticized for its exclusive focus on overt behaviors and its reliance on classical and operant learning models that, while important and useful, had limited clinical value and could not supply an adequate solution for emotional problems (Samoilov & Goldfried, 2000). Bandura identified the role of expectancies and self-efficacy as an important part of behavior. He viewed these concepts as central to the process of self-regulation. Research began to focus directly on the alteration of covert rather than overt behavior, and on the role of cognitive processes in different populations. Based on accumulated knowledge and developments in basic cognitive science, researchers began to focus more and more on the growing evidence that thoughts and emotions play a crucial role in change processes (Samoilov & Goldfried, 2000).

Just like behavioral therapy, cognitive therapy was not interested in clients' history as an interpretation of their behavior, but rather in order to understand clients' process of developing automatic or dysfunctional thoughts.

The Integration of Cognitive and Behavioral Therapies

Although the behavioral, overt focus of traditional behavioral therapy differed considerably from the cognitive, covert nature of cognitive therapy, the two approaches began to combine into one unified entity. What first emerged from this amalgamation already contrasted with purely behavioral treatments because the latter had not considered cognitions as important explanatory variables and had not previously identified cognitions as a specific target for change (Butler *et al.*, 2006). Gradually, as interest increased in the role of cognition and as the work of Ellis and of Beck (see below) received a broader audience, behavioral therapy progressively transformed into modern CBT.

Ellis (1973) developed the idea of irrational thinking as the main source of human disorders. His theory of rational-emotive behavioral therapy became a central one in cognitive therapy. Ellis conceptualized disturbance in general, and emotional disorders in particular (such as depression, anxiety, anger, guilt, and so forth), as an outcome of basic irrational, illogical beliefs. He delineated a wide range of frequent irrational beliefs, such as the belief that things must inevitably happen in a certain way without any personal control, or the attitude that a particular event is horrific and catastrophic. Concentrating on the cognitions of people with emotional disorders, Ellis pinpointed their tendency to view events as unbearable or extreme, as well as their tendency to exaggerate or overgeneralize when thinking about problematic events and feelings.

At the same time, Beck started developing his cognitive model for depression (Beck, 1967, 1976). Beck conceptualized disorders as problems arising from normal emotional processes, and therefore recommended that therapy should be directed toward shifting distorted patterns of thinking into more helpful patterns (Salkovskis, 2008). Thus, through the work of both Ellis and Beck, thinking was pinpointed as central to disorders' etiology and maintenance. As behavioral theory evolved into CBT, its focus became multidimensional, addressing changes not only in overt actions but also in covert behavior, such as imagery, thoughts, and emotions. In his foreword to the book *Oxford Guide to Metaphors in CBT* (Stott *et al.*, 2010: vii), Beck described CBT as

[a] set of therapeutic interventions that aims to help patients learn to solve current problems and change dysfunctional thinking patterns that contribute to maladaptive emotions and behaviours.

The work of Beck and his colleagues on depression demonstrated the clinical utility of mediation models for human behavior. In cognitive mediation, thoughts can transform or mediate negative feelings, thereby preventing undesired behavioral responses, or, alternatively, encouraging desired behavioral reactions. Because the mediation process is crucial for understanding human behavior, cognitive theory has emphasized how people structure their world (Beck, 1976; Beck, Emery, & Greenberg, 1985). A person's cognitions (verbal or pictorial "events" in the stream of consciousness) derive from attitudes or assumptions (schemata) developed from previous experiences (Alford & Beck, 1997; Beck, 1999a; Clark & Beck, 1999). From birth, individuals start to develop their personal schemata. These schemata derive from life experiences, individual character, and environmental components, thus creating a personal repertoire for coping with life events. This repertoire reflects a person's basic belief system and can be noted in that individual's automatic self-talk. People tend automatically to interpret similar events and circumstances in a similar way. Such interpretations are responsible for creating clients' problems due to inappropriate expectations, self-statements, and attributions. Mediation of these cognitive activities becomes the main focus of therapy. Change processes in therapy derive from attempts to convert irrational, automatic, or maladaptive emergent core schemata into more rational, mediated, or adaptive beliefs and thought processes (Rode, Salkovskis, & Jack, 2001; Ronen, 2003b). Cognitive theory underscored these activities as important in understanding and predicting psychopathology and psychotherapeutic change.

Cognitive theories highlighted concepts such as memory, thoughts, emotions, imagery, and information processing as the main contributors to human development (Case, 1991, 1992; Demetriou, Shayer, & Efklides, 1993; Halford, 1993). Obviously, cognitive theories considered cognitions to be the key to psychological disorders. According to the cognitive approach, cognitions encompass the most important links in the chain of events leading to disordered behavior and psychological dysfunction (Powell & Oei, 1991). Within this chain of events, thoughts, feelings, and behaviors are causally interrelated. Cognitions constitute the function that involves inferences about one's experiences, about occurrences, and about control over future events. Therefore, the identification of thoughts and images must be targeted as the key element responsible for information processing and interpretation.

As a result of theoretical deliberation concerning the interrelations between thoughts and behaviors, emotions also came to the forefront of discussion for cognitive scientists. The way one processes information influences the emotions that are elicited, which in turn are responsible for activation of the behavior, and vice versa. Awareness of emotions is therefore also crucial in order to learn how affects derive from thoughts and lead to behaviors (Salkovskis, 1996a,b).

Self-Control Models: An Offshoot of Integrated CBT

Self-control models integrate basic traditional behavioral methods (reinforcement, charting, assessing) with cognitive components (identfying automatic thoughts, linking thoughts to emotions and behaviors) to help people help themselves. Self-control models share a basic view of human behavior as goal-directed, as continually undergoing a process of change and development, and as associated with interactive factors that influence the process of self-regulating behavior (Kanfer & Schefft, 1988; Kenneth, Worth, & Forbes, 2009; Rosenbaum, 1990, 1998a, b). Self-control is conceived as a learned repertoire or set of skills that are needed when one faces difficulties, when obstacles need to be overcome to achieve goals, when new behaviors need to be learned, when choices need to be made, or when habitual response sequences are interrupted or prove ineffective (Kanfer & Schefft, 1988; Kenneth, Worth, & Forbes, 2009; Rosenbaum, 1990, 1998a, b, 2000). Attaining control of oneself is defined as achieving the ability to cope with stress, pain, or disturbing emotions; delay temptation; and establish goal-directed criteria and targets for conducting one's own life as it changes and unfolds over time (Rosenbaum, 2000). Self-control skills are linked with verbal competencies, evolving during the stages of infancy and childhood and leading up to adulthood: first the child is directed by others' talk, then he or she learns to use self-talk aloud, and finally the capacity emerges for silent self-talk (thoughts).

Self-control training is anchored in the claim that skills acquisition is the most crucial component of any CBT (Kenneth, Worth, & Forbes, 2009). In such training programs, clients are active participants who must learn how to look at their own irrational thoughts, stop their automatic thoughts, change them into mediated ones, start an internal dialogue, and search for alternative behaviors (Beck, Emery, & Greenberg, 1985; Copeland, 1982; Meichenbaum, 1979, 1985; Ronen, 1997, 2004). Hence, the main goal of self-control treatments is change through skills acquisition (Ronen, 1997; Ronen & Rosenbaum, 2001, 2010; Rosenbaum, 1990).

Constructivism Enters the Scene

With the emergence of constructivism and mindfulness, those components entered the mainstream of CBT as well. In the early 1950s, with Kelly's (1955) work, constructivism became part of psychotherapy, although constructivist theory is generally attributed to Jean Piaget, who articulated learners' mechanisms for internalizing new knowledge through processes of accommodation and assimilation (Piaget, 1969, 1977). Kelly (1955, 1969) opposed the notion that stimuli and responses lead people, suggesting that humans are complex systems characterized by concurrent multidirectional changes. Unlike computers, people actively anticipate the world and the actions of others.

Constructivist therapy's conceptualizations of self-representation and self-organization gained considerable attention in the 1990s. According to the constructivist view, people possess the capacity to create principles and attach meanings to their behaviors, thoughts, emotions, and imagery, and thus to operate using symbolic linguistic constructs that help them navigate in the world without contacting it in any simple, direct way (Neimeyer, 2009). The ability for self-organization is thus considered vital to understanding human development (Mahoney, 1991; Thelen, 1993). Constructivism is interested in people's subjective construction of the world rather than the objective, external, "real" world, emphasizing the human mind's active, form-giving nature (Neimeyer, 2009).

According to constructivism, just as scientists organize knowledge, all people act as scientists, organizing their experiences (whether in reality or imagery) in ways that create meaning in their lives. Knowledge comprises the main way for humans to regulate their perceptions of environmental events (Guidano, 1995). Continuous comparison and organization of ongoing life experiences elicit knowledge about similarities and contrasts. One's construction system varies and changes as one successively anticipates events and construes their replications. This knowledge is key to one's ability to organize, make sense, and give meaning to unfolding life experiences, the developing self, and the changing world. Knowledge is progressively shaped and changed in response to challenging environmental pressures (Guidano, 1995). This means that every person provides an idiosyncratic "map" of the world and his or her place within it at any given time (Neimeyer, 2009). Therefore, when directing intervention, therapists examining such "maps" should closely consider that people are continually undergoing a process of change and will continue to change in the future (Cull & Bondi, 2001). Due to these constant fluctuations and developments, therapy should also attend to strengthening the sense of oneness inherent in selfhood structures (Guidano, 1995).

In constructivism, people are seen as responsible for creating their own realities by constructing, reconstructing, and construing their life events and by attributing personal meanings to their experiences (Mahoney, 1991, 1993, 1999). Thus, problems can be understood as determined by the way people construe their experiences (Kelly, 1955), and the focus is on how one subjectively interprets such events and how this specific interpretation gives rise to particular emotions and behaviors. As Neimeyer (2009: 20) stated: "We are our constructs."

Viewing each individual as a unique architect, the personal construct intervention advocates first attempting to understand the client, and then creating an intervention appropriate for that one human being (Raskin, 2002; Swell, 1996). Constructivist therapists reframe human distortions and errors as merely reflecting the way people construct and organize their lives, which could be seen to have both strengths and weaknesses (Neimeyer, 2009).

The main contribution of constructivism to CBT lies in the importance of the emotional associations to the basic constructs (Samoilov & Goldfried, 2000). The way in which a particular individual understands feelings is of paramount importance. Research into emotion pinpointed the fact that symptoms often persist despite extensive self-understanding at the rational/logical level (Greenberg & Safran, 1989; Teasdale, 1993). According to the constructivist approach, affect does not exist as an entity separate from cognition, and vice versa (Neimeyer, 1995; Swell, 1996). Emotions are inseparable from the cognitions that play a central role in behavior, and together they constitute the core of change processes (Swell, 1996).

Emotion in constructivism also encompasses a crucial part of relationships. People live in a constant process of making sense of the emotions they feel, the emotions others feel, and how those emotions interact with each other. The self is viewed as a dynamic component that keeps changing during life experiences. Greenberg and Goldman (2008) described the self as a multiprocess, multilevel organization emerging from interactions experienced over the life span. They suggested that the self is crucial for understanding, accepting, and eliciting emotion in humans.

In sum, constructivism as well as basic CBT emphasizes the dynamic, changing nature of humans through the life span, where people actively (not passively) lead their lives to desired places. Considering that clients should be active and responsible for their own realities, the constructivist therapeutic orientation upholds the concept that clients must take on an active role in the therapeutic process (Kincheloe, 2005; Raskin, 2002; for more details, see Chapter 12). The treatment process must thus enable not only clients' but also therapists' culture, values, and background to become an essential part of the dynamic interplay between clients, therapists, and tasks while shaping meaning (Neimeyer & Raskin, 2000; Raskin, 2002). Both clients and therapists should develop an awareness of each other's viewpoints and then look to their own beliefs, standards, and values.

Mindfulness Becomes Part of CBT

The first wave of behavioral therapy focused on systematic applications of learning theory in the early 1960s, suggesting positive outcomes and reliable procedures to enable effective therapy (Hayes, Strosahl, & Wilson, 1999). Through the second wave, cognitive therapy arrived, underscoring memory and mental representations and thereby instigating a shift into CBT. The third wave is now ongoing, incorporating features such as dialectical philosophy, mindfulness, acceptance, relationship, and spirituality (Koons, 2007). Over the last decades, mindfulness techniques have become well integrated into the process of intervention in general, and into CBT in particular (Hayes, Follette, & Linehan, 2004).

Mindfulness at its most basic is awareness in the present (Koons, 2007). According to Jon Kabat-Zinn (1994: 4), developer of mindfulness-based stress reduction, "mindfulness means paying attention in a particular way: on purpose, in the present moment, and nonjudgmentally." This awareness attends fully to the observer's ongoing experiences of thoughts, emotions, and sensations. Kabat-Zinn (2005: 25) stated that mindfulness is:

> openhearted moment-to-moment, non-judgemental awareness ... optimally cultivated through meditation rather than just through thinking about it ... often described as the heart of Buddhist meditation...

In the broader view, mindfulness is a psychological intervention designed to reduce distress. Clients receive skills training in defusing and decentering, aimed at reducing their experiential avoidance and allowing them to turn toward and accept distressing thoughts and feelings as a point of departure for working within them, in effect developing a different relationship to them. Hayes, Follette, and Linehan (2004) suggested mindfulness as an alternative model to the cognitive mode, where the focus of processing is at the level of representation and not on specific discrepancies. The main focus of mindfulness is not on overcoming but rather on accepting; it focuses on "being" rather than "doing."

Looking at the training, Segal, Williams, and Teasdale (2002) suggested that mindfulness presents therapists with a way to teach clients to stay with and accept themselves the way they are, rather than trying to jump in and solve the problem. By purposely standing back to see what it feels like to see the problem through the lens of "no reactivity," therapists bring a kindly awareness to the difficulty. Clients can thereby clearly see their problems and identify the needed steps for addressing them more skillfully.

The emphasis in therapy lies on training clients to be fully present and attentive to the content of moment-by-moment experiences, whether pleasant, unpleasant, or neutral. Therapists encourage clients to let go of the idea that all problems are fixable or changeable, instead teaching them to stay close to the mental struggle by finding a calm place from which to observe their thoughts and emotions.

A major goal of mindfulness is to be in touch with internal stimuli, to increase awareness, and to teach clients a way to surrender to the body's basic wisdom (Mahoney, 1991). This purpose can be achieved through meditation. (For more details on meditation, see Chapters 9 and 14.)

Mindfulness helps clients make first-order changes, such as letting go of ruminative thinking, accepting that certain thought patterns are likely to emerge and recur during a depressive episode, and overcoming anxiety (Germer, 2005). Bogart (1991) reviewed different forms of meditation that have been developed over the years and showed how they affect physiological, cognitive, and psychological states in novice and experienced practitioners.

Mindfulness as part of CBT started with treating specific disorders, such as the work of Kabat-Zinn (1990) to reduce anxiety and distress, the work of Segal, Williams, and Teasdale (2002) to cope with depression, and the work of Marsha Linehan (1993a,b) on borderline personality. It was extended to include applications with a large range of clients and disorders (Hayes, Follette, & Linehan, 2004).

Segal, Williams, and Teasdale (2002) as well as Hayes, Follette, and Linehan (2004) related to mindfulness as an integration of the CBT elements developed by Beck (1976), with the component of mindfulness developed by Kabat-Zinn (1990). Both emphasize skills acquisition and both aim at changing distorted thoughts, reducing stress, and increasing the ability to cope. The main difference lies in the fact that, unlike CBT, in this view of mindfulness there is little emphasis on changing the content of thoughts; rather, the focus lies in changing awareness and relations to thoughts, feelings, and bodily sensations. However, this approach does advocate decentered views such as "thoughts are not facts" and "I am not my thoughts."

Mindfulness is now being practiced as part of many therapies, with a wide range of clients and disorders.

Major Tenets and Processes of CBT

This section describes the major tenets and processes of CBT, including its view of clients and human experience; assessment and the assessor's role; the therapeutic process and setting; techniques, the therapist's role, and therapeutic relationships; and the efficacy of intervention.

CBT's view of clients and human experience

In modern integrated CBT, clients are seen as both architects and scientists, thus placing the human being rather than the pathological response or diagnosis at the center of therapy (Rosenbaum & Ronen, 1998). As architects or scientists, clients are not mere receptors of treatment, but rather need to collaborate actively with therapists and be their own active change agents, once they acquire the appropriate skills and resources.

The concept of the client as an architect underscores human beings as responsible for creating their own lives and experiences (Kelly, 1955; Mahoney, 1993). Like architects who design their own homes, deciding where to put each object and how the house should look, clients as architects are actually responsible for designing the meaning of their own lives. This notion proposes that problems are caused not by a life event itself, but rather by the person's interpretation of that event, which elicits specific emotions and behaviors (Beck, 1976; Clark & Beck,

1999). Often, clients seeking therapy can be likened to prisoners of their own meaning-making and design, as described by Israeli poet Yehuda Yanai (1971, p. 36, free translation):

> Man builds his own prison with his own hands. He is the guard, he is the prisoner; there is no place there for anyone else, anywhere. From his own prison he will not run away.

The second notion, viewing clients as scientists (Kanfer & Schefft, 1988), highlights the empirical scientific basis of CBT, as well as its core as a self-help method. Through therapy, clients learn that they can act as scientists, carefully observing their own behaviors, emotions, and thoughts; learning to raise hypotheses about their own behavior; and assessing data to make decisions about change. Clients learn to establish targets, expectations, and goals for change systematically. They learn to observe their strengths, resources, and support systems carefully, thus discovering themselves to be strong, capable human beings. They are continually asked to find proof for their beliefs or assumptions. All along the therapy, clients as scientists learn to seek empirical knowledge, data, and outcomes about the self and the environment.

Both notions -architect and scientist- emphasize the active roles played by clients, the relationships and mutual interplay between clients and therapists, and the scientific nature of the process of therapy that necessitates raising hypotheses, checking their accuracy, and assessing progress.

Assessment in CBT

CBT has replaced the traditional medical approach to diagnosis with an ongoing collaborative assessment process, which continues between client and therapist not only prior to treatment, but in fact throughout the course of therapy, relying on a continuous series of questions and inquiries (see Chapter 12). The CBT assessment process is an ongoing one because therapists begin assessing clients in intake sessions, continue in each and every therapy session, and evaluate outcomes at termination and follow-up – in a collaborative effort created by therapists as learners and by clients as active agents for change.

CBT therapists are uninterested in broad definitions or labels such as "social anxiety," but rather detail how specific anxiety problems manifest themselves as distress in a particular client's life, for example, as fears of going out, avoidance of social activities, rapid heartbeat or high blood pressure in social situations, and so forth. Therefore, rather than giving interpretations and excuses for situations by asking "Why?" at each time-interval along the therapy, a detailed profile is continually developed by asking questions such as: How are you behaving today? What disturbs you regarding this behavior? How do you behave when you face the thing you are afraid of? What would you like to change about your behavior, thought, or emotion? In what way does this thought affect your emotion? For practice in designing such a profile, see the Practice section later in this chapter, as well as details in Chapter 12.

Clients are further assessed for the cause-and-effect links between the reported behaviors and their thoughts, emotions, and environment. Thus, in line with the underlying CBT approach that concentrates on contemporary determinants of behavior rather than on early life events or client histories, assessment throughout the therapeutic process focuses on the *What?* and *How?* and not on the *Why?* Therapists attempt to determine: *How* does the client learn to act this way? *What* maintains the behavior? Therapists ask clients questions such as: *What* do you think influenced your behavior in the past? *What* interferes with you trying to overcome your problem now?

Emphasis on contemporary rather than past determinants of problems implies that therapists often cannot explain specific disorders' etiologies, yet nevertheless can help clients change. I remember many years ago at the Bethlem-Maudsley Psychiatric Hospital in London, I heard Professor Isaac Marks explicating this CBT approach to a client:

> We cannot explain how you came to develop your disorder. It might take scientists many years to uncover why this happens. But, we do already have effective techniques for helping you overcome it, if you learn and practice them.

In ongoing treatment sessions, each session usually begins with assessment directed toward several main issues:

1. What changes or progress occurred in the client's situation, thoughts, feelings, or behaviors since the last session?
2. Which methods/techniques were useful in achieving those changes?
3. Were the client's expectations and goals appropriate to the situations he/she encountered and to his/her responses?

Clients are also asked to assess and evaluate their progress on a weekly basis. This ongoing pattern of regular self-assessment teaches clients to attend to small changes, in line with the CBT tenet that large changes occur through many small steps (Kanfer & Schefft, 1988). This initial assessment in each session examines changes, methods, and goals while revealing evidence of the therapy's efficacy, allowing for reinforcement of changes achieved, pinpointing factors that do and do not lead to progress, and enabling the establishment of realistic targets for the next session. Assessments of the treatment's outcomes at termination and follow-up are described separately below.

The assessor's role

CBT emphasizes that therapists act as participant-observers who play an active, influential role in shaping the assessment process, along with their clients. The assessor's own personality, appearance, past experiences, and theoretical framework are all seen as potent factors that facilitate (or hinder) the entire assessment process (Mahoney, 1991; Ronen, 2003b). Such factors influence how clients and assessors relate to one another, what information is shared, how the assessment data are understood or contextualized by the assessor, and whether or not clients experience significant learning or change during their assessments (Finn & Tbnsager, 1997).

With children, the rapport established between assessor and child especially influences outcomes of assessment. Children are more willing to share information, collaborate better, and express a larger range of emotions when they feel good with the assessor and trust him or her (Ronen, 1993, 1997).

An important role for the assessor is to help clients leave their assessment process with new experiences or new information about themselves that subsequently assists them in making changes in their lives. Therefore, the assessor's primary role is to be sensitive, attentive, and responsive to clients' needs and to foster opportunities for self-discovery and growth throughout the assessment process. In many ways, the goals of the therapeutic assessor parallel the aims of therapy itself – being committed to helping people confirm, challenge, and change how they act, think, and feel about themselves (Finn & Tbnsager, 1997).

The therapeutic process and setting

If CBT is defined as cognitive mediation of symptoms and dysfunctional behaviors, then improvement can be produced by modifying dysfunctional thinking and beliefs (Butler *et al.*, 2006). The specific features necessary for effective CBT may be an issue for debate; however, strong consensus suggests that the therapeutic process and the kind of atmosphere and therapeutic relationships established are crucial.

Especially because CBT offers no single technique or method for achieving change, a heavy responsibility lies on the shoulders of therapists to generate a successful therapeutic process. Therapists must design the optimal intervention for each client, based on the client's unique personality, strengths, resources, interests, and motivation for change and on the nature of the referred problem (Ronen, 1997; Rosenbaum & Ronen, 1998). Therefore, interventions vary from one client to another. Deliberations concerning the treatment of choice are very important, because therapists continually make decisions in one or another phase of the treatment process. They must continuously deliberate and ask themselves: What is the best intervention with this specific client, with that specific problem, in this specific situation (Paul, 1967, 1993; Ronen & Ayelet, 2001)? In other words, to make effective decisions about the treatment strategies of choice, therapists must undertake a very careful, continuous assessment process that attempts to analyze clients' needs, skills, and abilities at that time in the treatment process and that taps into therapists' knowledge about the specific problem and potential therapeutic techniques. The same problem could be treated differently as a result of therapists' and clients' ongoing decision making related to clients' current personal, environmental, and behavioral considerations: Is the problem currently the focus of treatment still relevant, or have other, new problems emerged that should take precedence? Are the techniques being used suitable for this client at this time? Is the client progressing at a reasonable pace?

Regarding the CBT setting, no rigid rules predetermine treatment location, session frequency, or therapy duration. These, too, encompass part of decision-making processes regarding the treatment of choice for each client. Therapy generally transpires in the clinic, but may utilize outdoor walks or nature settings for exposure exercises, for learning to observe elements in the environment, or for practicing skills. Therapists may shift to a basketball court, for example, to promote a child's motivation or practice new skills in a concrete context (Ronen, 2003a).

Likewise, the therapeutic setting is not limited to time sequences (once weekly, for example), but rather is scheduled based on clients' training and achievements. Treatment sessions can reduce in frequency as clients progress. Phone calls can provide between-session contact. Homework assignments are considered integral to most CBT interventions, in order to exercise, practice, and apply knowledge from the intervention setting to natural environments (Ronen, 2008). Therapy terminates not when the problem decreases but when clients prove their ability to maintain and generalize achievements to other settings and problem areas.

Techniques, therapists, and relationships

Often, CBT is misconceived as a collection of "magic tricks" that therapists perform to resolve human disorders and maladaptive behaviors. In actuality, CBT advocates the selection of intervention strategies with a high probability of success; sequential steps that match available skill levels; clear, relevant means of monitoring progress; opportunities for practice; and maintenance and follow-up periods (Gambrill, 2006). CBT therapists need dynamic thinking, considering that no single correct interventional approach exists for treating the diversity of clients encountered. As described above, therapists must continually make decisions about adapting available techniques to clients, problems, and current situations. Moreover, therapists must also be continually aware of the impact that therapist-related factors can have on decision making, such as therapists' service setting, abilities, knowledge, and skills.

CBT therapists regularly use a large variety of techniques. Joyce (1980) viewed the appropriate use of techniques as a ritualized method of human relatedness and communication, or as a stylized language for expressing and exploring the ongoing narratives of life processes. CBT is not only a talking process but also an experiential and practical course (Ronen, 1997; Rosenbaum & Ronen, 1998). Creative indirect techniques such as imagery, metaphors, drawing, or sculpting can assist therapists in helping clients overcome difficulties encountered during verbal treatment, in facilitating clients' ability to surmount obstacles in therapy, and in identifying effective treatments to meet clients' specific life goals. Different available techniques have different aims, helping therapists illustrate problematic areas to clients, clarify processes, or render specific changes. Behaviorally-based techniques include taking records, reinforcement, exposure, and relaxation. Cognitively-based techniques include changing automatic thoughts to mediated ones, linking thoughts to emotions and behaviors, using rational arguments, and posing Socratic questions. Typically, constructivist techniques include writing poetry, mirror time, and stream of consciousness. Mindfulness techniques include the use of meditation, concentration, and attentional focus.

In trying to characterize the main techniques and intervention style in modern CBT, Rosenbaum and Ronen (1998) pinpointed seven basic features:

1. Therapy as a meaning-making process, which helps clients develop new and often more complex meanings for what they define as problems.
2. Systematic and goal-directed therapy.
3. Focusing on practicing and experiencing rather than "talk therapy."
4. Collaboration between client and therapist.
5. Focusing on clients rather than problems.
6. Facilitating change processes by therapists.
7. Empowerment and development of clients' independent functioning.

CBT therapists' role has changed over the years. Therapists in the past were conceived as being in charge of the entire intervention process, from planning to method selection to pace. Whereas most of the literature in the 1960s and 1970s suggested effective procedures for therapists' intervention, the 1980s saw more attention given to therapists' role as an educational, therapeutic trainer and to an increased focus on the process of therapy. In the 1990s, therapists were seen as enabling experiences and providing a safe setting for practicing skills. Safran and Segal (1990), for example, underscored the client–therapist relationship as a vital feature in the CBT process.

Today's CBT interventions have become a collaborative educational process aimed at teaching, practicing, and applying new skills, knowledge, and coping strategies, and offering an experiential setting. Viewing the therapy process as educational highlights the client–therapist interaction; it is easier to learn from someone with whom we have a good relationship, who is a good model, and when the atmosphere is pleasant. Likewise, viewing therapy as collaborative pinpoints the fact that without trust, good relationships, and mutual understanding, it is difficult to activate clients' efforts. Treatments now focus significantly more not only on behaviors and cognitions, but also on emotions. CBT now targets emotional processes and methods for helping clients let go of control and accept and live with problems, rather than continually trying to overcome them.

To summarize the cognitive-behavioral therapist's way of thinking, Kanfer and Schefft (1988) suggested six rules for supervising therapists:

1. *Think behavior*. Rather than concentrating on clients' problems, making assumptions and interpretations regarding their causes, the CBT therapist defines problems in terms of behavior rather than insecurities, anxiety, or similar constructs. Action is the main dimension on which interchanges in therapy are focused.
2. *Think solution*. Frequently, non-CBT therapists devote more time to thinking of difficulties and problems than to finding solutions. A full problem description requires knowledge, not only of the current situation or state, but also of a more desirable future end-state and some indication of how to achieve it.

29

3. *Think positive.* Just as therapists help clients think positively and focus on small changes and positive forces rather than on difficulties, therapists must aspire to positive thinking, too. In line with the positive psychology orientation, CBT reinforces positive outcomes and strengthens any strategies, plans, or actions that make these outcomes more likely (Seligman, 2002). Therapists should not focus solely on reducing problems and overcoming difficulties, but rather should pinpoint clients' strengths and virtues (Seligman *et al.*, 2005). Furthermore, this orientation also helps people feel happy, flourish, feel satisfied with life, and improve subjective wellbeing. This shift toward positive thinking reflects the human wish to lead more productive and fulfilling lives, and to identify and nurture talents (Joseph & Linley, 2006). Keyes *et al.* (2008) added that happiness incorporates both an ability to achieve subjective wellbeing by expressing positive emotions and also an ability for positive functioning.

4. *Think small steps.* Although clients are usually interested in major, significant life changes, extreme changes are difficult to achieve. Targeting small, gradual changes reduces fears, motivates clients, and helps therapists observe and pinpoint difficulties. An accumulation of many small changes constitutes one large and significant change.

5. *Think flexible.* Sheldon (1987) accused therapists of falling in love with the methods they use, arguing that this precludes them from asking questions about effectiveness or from negotiating the best methods for particular clients. Flexible, creative therapists modify traditional interventions to adapt themselves to clients' specific needs. Gambrill (2006) suggested that therapists should look for disconfirming evidence (which points to alternatives), try to understand other people's points of view, use language carefully, watch out for vivid data, move beyond the illusion of understanding, complement clear thinking skills with knowledge, and ask about accuracy.

6. *Think future.* Many therapeutic approaches focus on the past and its role in clients' present. CBT challenges therapists to think toward the future, predicting how clients will cope and how they themselves would like to be different or better in the future.

Mahoney (1991) depicted therapists' role as helping clients explore and experience themselves and the world in different ways. He suggested that these new modes of exploration challenge ordinary, familiar patterns and consolidate embodiment, emotion, feeling, sensing, and thinking into one entity.

Efficacy of intervention

CBT is one of the most extensively researched and evidence-based forms of therapeutic practice, achieving intervention efficacy in a relatively short time (Butler *et al.*, 2006). Over the years, thousands of research studies and CBT applications have investigated various clients, problem areas, and disorders. It is beyond this book's scope to cover all of the successful therapies using a CBT approach, but I will mention several practices that have been proven effective.

Depression was one of the earliest foci of the CBT model, where Beck (1967) started his applications. The efficacy of CBT for depression has been studied widely (Segal, Williams, & Teasdale, 2002). Recent applications of CBT to depression showed its advantages for youths as well as for adults. Studies demonstrated that involving parents in therapy as change agents for their children reduced depressed young people's use of medications and other services, lowered their overall treatment costs, and possibly increased their speed of improvement (Weisz *et al.*, 2009).

Another area in which CBT has long proven its efficacy is anxiety disorders. In a meta-analysis that reviewed 56 studies of anxiety among adults, CBT was effective in all pretest–posttest effect sizes for disorder-specific symptoms, suggesting that CBT for adult anxiety disorders is effective in clinically representative conditions (Stewart & Chambless, 2009). In their work on posttraumatic stress disorder, Foa and Rothbaum (2001) found that CBT reduced the severity of the disorder, helped clients cope better with various traumatic events, and improved their wellbeing. The efficacy of CBT was also demonstrated for obsessive-compulsive disorder, intrusive thoughts (Clark, 2004; Salkovskis, 1999), panic disorders, and agoraphobia (Salkovskis *et al.*, 1999).

With adults, anger, hostility, and violence were also treated successfully by CBT, confirming its ability to help people reduce their disorders and adjust to society (Beck, 1999b). In a controlled study using CBT, children and adolescents successfully reduced aggression and increased self-control (Ronen & Rosenbaum, 2010).

In recent years, many research studies have shown CBT's efficacy for schizophrenia and personality disorders (Beck, 1999a, b; Beck, Freeman, & Davis, 2003), borderline personality disorder (Linehan, 1993a, b), and emotional disorders (Segal, Williams, & Teasdale, 2002). Brown *et al.*'s (2004) clinical trial for patients with borderline personality disorder resulted in significant and clinically important decreases in measures of suicide ideation, hopelessness, depression, number of borderline symptoms, and dysfunctional beliefs, at termination and at 18-month follow-up.

Significantly, Butler *et al.* (2006) conducted a large meta-analysis combining 16 meta-analyses of 9995 participants in 332 studies and 16 disorders. They studied depression among adults and adolescents; anxiety disorders, including generalized anxiety, panic, social phobia, obsessive-compulsive, and posttraumatic stress disorders; and a range of other disorders and problems, including schizophrenia, bulimia, childhood internalizing disorders, sexual offenders, chronic pain, marital distress, and anger. Findings suggested that CBT is highly effective for most disorders, such as adult and adolescent depression, panic disorders, social phobia, posttrauma, and childhood internalizing disorders. For other disorders such as bulimia and schizophrenia, Butler *et al.* reported impressive improvements, but CBT was not efficacious for sex offenders. In addition, as expected, inasmuch as CBT involves modifying thoughts and maladaptive distortions as well as applying skills to use in the environment, the outcomes persevered in the long run.

CBT is now the treatment of choice for adults as well as children and adolescents for behavioral, emotional, and personality disorders, applied as individual therapy, family therapy, and group therapy

Skills-Directed Therapy

As a primary example of today's integrative, multidimensional interventions in CBT, I will next briefly describe a model we have developed for empowering children, increasing self-control, and decreasing aggression (Ronen & Rosenbaum, 2010). The skills-directed therapy (SDT) model focuses on imparting self-control skills to diverse clients. The basic belief underlying the SDT model is that well-adjusted behavior results from the ability to apply appropriate skills for coping with the present challenges one faces. Therefore, therapy aims to assess needed skills and supply clients with skills that are lacking.

Skills are defined (Merriam-Webster, 1965: 815) as: "The ability to use one's knowledge effectively and readily in execution or performance" or "a learned power of doing a thing competently." A skilled person is someone who has undergone "training in a particular occupation, craft, or trade."

The integrative SDT approach to help clients change (Ronen & Rosenbaum, 2010) combines basic CBT together with a positive psychology orientation that focuses on strengths and merits, in conjunction with constructivist ideas and art techniques. The model emphasizes the need to assess each client to determine which skills the client performs and executes competently, which skills the client lacks, how the deficient skills influence the client's behavior, and how best to design the client's training to impart the needed skills through teaching and practice.

The SDT model was first applied to the problem of enuresis (Ronen, Wozner, & Rahav, 1992) and then extended to various childhood and adolescent disorders (Ronen, 1993, 1997, 2003a), subsequently being applied comprehensively to enuresis and aggression (Ronen & Rosenbaum, 2001, 2010). Recently, SDT has been employed with adults as well, aiming to provide adult clients with self-control skills and also with self-help methods to facilitate their future independent functioning. Enhancing self-help skills enables clients to maintain treatment outcomes, continue treating themselves in daily life after being successfully treated by therapists, generalize and transfer their basic learning, and facilitate self-change.

The structured SDT model contains four nonhierarchical modules that can be used interchangeably throughout the treatment process:

1. *Cognitive restructuring.* This first module aims to teach clients that behavior can be changed and that change depends on clients themselves (Beck, 1999a; Beck, Emery, & Greenberg, 1985). Therapists elicit clients' cognitive restructuring by increasing their self-efficacy about their ability to achieve change (Bandura, 1997), as well as by utilizing redefinition, changing

attributional styles, and reframing clients' present functioning (Beck, Emery, & Greenberg, 1985; Kanfer & Schefft, 1988; Meichenbaum, 1979). Techniques include Socratic questions and paradoxical examples. For clients to learn how to improve functioning, this module accentuates skills and strengths, guiding clients to look at what helps them cope and survive, and to discover what helped them overcome other previous problems. The goal of therapy is defined not as reducing disorder but as improving subjective wellbeing and happiness.

2. *Problem analysis.* This module trains clients to observe the links between the brain, body, and final problematic behaviors. Therapists teach clients to notice the links between thoughts, emotions, and behaviors and to observe links between cause and effect (Beck, 1967; Ronen, 1997). Therapists use rational analysis of these processes, employ written materials and anatomical illustrations of the human body, and help clients accept responsibility for behaviors by learning to change the brain's commands. Clients practice identifying automatic thoughts and using self-talk and self-monitoring to change unmediated thoughts into mediated ones. Focus is directed to analyzing positive emotion and how it is linked to clients' functioning; clients need to learn what can increase happiness and what happens once they feel happy (how they look, what they do, and what they think about once happiness is attained).

3. *Attentional focus.* This module aims to increase awareness of behavior and internal stimuli, raise sensitivity to the body, and teach how to identify internal cues related to specific problems (Bandura, 1997; Mahoney, 1991, 1995). Therapists use relaxation, concentration, and self-monitoring to promote achievement of these targets. Emphasis is placed on emotion. Clients learn to identify positive affects as well as negative affects, to express emotions, and to understand how emotions relate to thoughts and behaviors.

4. *Self-control practice.* This module trains clients in self-control techniques such as self-talk, self-evaluation, self-monitoring, thinking aloud, and problem-solving skills (Barrios & Hartman, 1988; Brigham *et al.*, 1979; Ronen, 1997). In the first stage of general skills training, therapists assign various kinds of practice assignments. Practicing includes using self-instruction, both in the sessions and in homework assignments. Through practice, clients learn that as confidence grows, chances of success also increase (Bandura, 1997). Self-control techniques taught via this module for changing automatic behaviors to mediated ones include physical as well as emotional exercises such as resisting temptation, self-talk, self-reward, problem-solving, and imagery exercises (Meichenbaum, 1979; Ronen, 1997). Clients practice specific exercises to increase happiness and improve subjective wellbeing.

In a controlled study comparing the SDT model to a control group, SDT was successful for reducing aggression among adolescents (Ronen & Rosenbaum, in press). Also, the outcomes showed that those adolescents who reduced aggression were those who had acquired self-control skills.

Summary

Alford and Beck (1997) summed up what characterizes modern CBT as an integrative therapy: its unifying theoretical framework within which validated clinical techniques may be properly incorporated. In this integrated CBT, the central pathways to psychological functioning or adaptation consist of people's meaning-making cognitive structures (schemata), referring to interpretations of given contexts and the contexts' relationships to the self.

Today's CBT constitutes a holistic way of life, a way of thinking and perceiving human functioning and needs, and a way of operating within the environment – to achieve the most effective means for accomplishing one's aims (Clark & Beck, 1999; Salkovskis, 2008). It is a scientific approach to human behavior, relying on empirical data, and underscoring the interaction that exists between behavior and environment; therefore, change can be achieved by changing either the environment or the individual. Modern CBT addresses the entire spectrum of human functioning, pinpointing various components relating to (i) the individual – such as inner thoughts, beliefs, personal constructs (deriving from constructivism), awareness of internal emotions and physical sensations (deriving from mindfulness), imagery, and the major links between thoughts, emotions, and outward behaviors (deriving from cognitive therapy); (ii) the human–environment interface – such as the importance of relationships and the view of behavior as dependent on reinforcement (deriving from basic behavioral therapy); and (iii) all their interrelations. Moreover, both the subjective and the objective receive a central focus in the interplay between clients, therapists, and therapeutic tasks.

During the last decades, the use of CBT has grown and been extended to a large range of populations as well as a gamut of emotional and behavioral disorders (Baumeister & Boden, 1998).

Practice: Guidelines for Developing the Client's Profile

As described above in the section on assessment, a detailed profile of the client should be continually developed at different time-intervals along the therapy. In keeping with the underlying CBT approach that emphasizes contemporary determinants of behavior rather than historical life events, the client's profile should continually focus on the *What?* and the *How?* and less on the *Why?* It should provide information on the client's problem(s) and environment; how that problem(s) is demonstrated in the client's way of thinking, feeling, and behaving; and the client's view of the future – by carefully identifying objectives of therapy, target behaviors, and appropriate methods for measuring change.

When constructing behavioral profiles, therapists can ask clients a series of questions (Ronen, 2003b):

About the present

- How do they behave (think, feel) now, in the present, while facing the problems at hand?
- What disturbs them about these problems (behaviors, thoughts, emotions)? Why do they wish to solve these problems?

About the past

- How do they explain their behaviors (thoughts, emotions)? How did they learn to react in this way?
- What prevented them from overcoming the problems? (For example, for internalizing problems: What will happen if they dare to do what they are afraid of doing? How do they know this is what they will feel?)
- What made them happy in the past, before the problem started?

About the future

- How do they wish to behave (think, feel) in the future, when therapy terminates?
- What needs to be different in order for them to be happy and to attain/maintain subjective wellbeing?
- What do they think they can do differently when they face difficulties?
- What would improve if their problems were solved?
- Who (in the family, social environment) can help them fight the problem and feel better?
- Who would they like in the future to be involved in their life and in maintaining their subjective wellbeing?
- How will you, the therapist, be able to know that a problem is over?

3

On Being a Positive Therapist

Long before the name "positive psychology" came into being, I thought of myself as a positive therapist without knowing how to give this entity a name. For me, being a positive therapist meant believing in human beings' strengths and virtues, believing that people can change, and consistently focusing on positive transformations instead of pathology reductions. I used to tell the children who came to me for therapy that I was a teacher of happiness and that I wished to help them become happy, or at least happier. When people used to say, "There is no such thing as happiness, only happy moments here and there," I would reply, "I am a happy person and I have a happy personality and a happy life, although I do experience moments and sometimes even days of sorrow." I explained that this differentiation was a matter of the perspective you choose to take on life.

A frequent metaphor I use in therapy is that of an angel or genie coming to fulfill three wishes. After discussing the wishes that my clients would request, I inquire: "Will these wishes' fulfillment make you happier? How? What will they bring to your life that you do not have now?"

I heard an apt metaphor about happiness many years ago when attending a ceremony in a Reform Jewish temple in the United States. Rabbi David Meyer told a story about his young son who for months excitedly anticipated the Passover holiday, because he had heard of the Jewish tradition where children search for the *afikoman* that is hidden during the Passover feast. When the feast arrived, he suddenly turned to his father, admitting that despite his months-long wait, he now realized that he actually had no idea what object he needed to find. He didn't know what *afikoman* was (a broken piece of unleavened bread or matzo).

It seems as if happiness is the same: something that remains distant, that we are looking for although we are not sure what it is. Happiness is usually mentioned in relation to the future (we anticipate being happier if we achieve something or acquire something) or in relation to past experiences ("I was so happy when we were together" or "I was so happy before I became sick"). However, happiness is very rarely described in relation to the present. Think for a moment how often

The Positive Power of Imagery: Harnessing Client Imagination in CBT and Related Therapies,
First Edition. Tammie Ronen. © 2011 Tammie Ronen. Published 2011 by John Wiley & Sons, Ltd.

you actually say to yourself, "Oh, I am so happy now. I just want this to last for ever." A good exercise is to start telling yourself "I feel happy" every day – in the present tense!

Becoming a Recognized Theory and Therapy

For decades, therapists focused almost exclusively on mental illness, adopting a disease-based model of client functioning that almost completely overlooked individual strengths, virtues, and areas of wellbeing, focusing instead on pathology, weaknesses, and deficits (Magyar-Moe, 2009). During the last decade, a major shift occurred from focusing on pathological characteristics to focusing on individual differences and diversity in coping with such disordered responses. This shift reflects the human wish to lead more productive and fulfilling lives, and to identify and nurture talents (Joseph & Linley, 2006).

In his presidential address to the American Psychological Association (APA), Martin Seligman (1999) and his colleagues resolved that the APA should initiate change and asked psychologists to return to their roots and focus more on positive psychological aspects related to understanding problems in living (Seligman, 2002; Seligman & Csikszentmihalyi, 2000). They highlighted the effectiveness of positive psychology as a tool for decreasing distress, such as depression (Seligman *et al.*, 2005).

Since Seligman's presidential address, the positive psychology orientation has blossomed enormously and led to the publication of many books and research studies in this area. Joseph and Linley (2006) pointed out that positive psychology did not begin in the late 1990s. Rather, this approach has existed for decades and might even be traced back to the origin of psychology itself. Researchers have always been interested in the positive aspects of psychology: emotion, subjective wellbeing, coping. However, establishing the International Association for Positive Psychology gave it the formal legal basis for operation.

The Positive View of Clients and Therapeutic Processes

Positive psychology values subjective experiences and investigates the field of subjective wellbeing, contentment, satisfaction, hope, optimism, flow, and happiness (Joseph & Linley, 2006; Seligman & Csikszentmihalyi, 2000). Csikszentmihalyi (2002) defined flow as the positive aspects of human experience, "joy, creativity, the process of total involvement with life" (2002: xi), and stated that flow is when "people can learn to control inner experience [and] will be able to determine the quality of their lives which is as close as any of us can come to being happy" (2002: 2). As yet, there is no clear explanation of why, but it seems as if negative thoughts, emotions, fears, and anxieties come automatically to people, maybe as warning signals, whereas most individuals need to learn and undergo training in how to become positive. This is where creativity and imagery come into play. Imagery is one of the most effective tools in helping people view themselves as happy and in trying to attain skills to become happy. The ability to be positive broadens the mind and can expand a person's range of vision (Fredrickson, 2009).

Fredrickson (2009), in her book *Positivity*, stated that positivity is fragile. It is the dream one holds for the future. Asserting that negativity pervades people's self-talk and judgments of the self and others, Fredrickson suggested that compared to negativity, positivity looks pale and weak. Yet, she also asserted that positive emotions do not depend on how one thinks ("I think I am happy"), but rather on how one senses events and ideas as they unfold, and on whether one allows oneself to take a moment to find the good in oneself and others. She stated that all human beings have the power to turn positivity on and off for themselves. Although people often move back to negativity, they can learn to focus attention on positivity, thus learning how to return to positivity more easily and more often.

Human beings' complex physical immune system maintains a balance between two competing needs: the need to recognize and destroy invaders such as viruses and bacteria, and the need to recognize and respect the body's own cells (Gilbert, 2005). Likewise, humans' psychological immune system may protect them from invading feelings and thoughts of hopelessness and unhappiness, while respecting the psyche's need for comfort, hope, and joy. Just as good nutrition, regular exercise, avoidance of toxins, and so on are important for maintaining a healthy physical immune system, it is possible to work toward building and strengthening the psychological immune system by accepting the fact that sometimes things do not proceed the way we wish, by exercising positive thinking, expressing positive emotion, feeling gratitude, and so forth – thus facilitating happiness.

Clients suffering from mood disorders offer an opportunity to gain greater understanding about the development of negative affects and the suppression of positive ones. When treating such clients, I try to emphasize the existence of positive feelings alongside their suffering. I do ask them about their bad moods. However, I also ask them to think about their positive emotions and discover circumstances conducive to those emotions' expression. In an imagery exercise aiming to strengthen depressed clients' "psychological immune system," I describe the following:

> Imagine you work in a hospital as a nurse or doctor. The hospital is full of people who are sick – with bad moods and depression – and came to get cured. Because you work in the hospital, you need to ensure you won't catch their illness. So, just as people get immunized annually against seasonal influenza, you need to take something now to protect you from infection by bad moods and depression. What would help improve your immune system? Help you fight against falling ill with the bad-mood sickness?
>
> Often this exercise produces answers like "a good mood," "love," or the people the clients love as preventive solutions. I can then ask clients to recruit the first-aid tools they have identified as protection from slipping into negative moods.

Although we do not always know why and how negative emotions start, we do know that positive emotions can be useful for decreasing negative ones, so another good exercise is to prepare a list of positive events that can increase and facilitate positive emotions. This list can be used as an antidote when feeling bad, or even routinely as a preventive, everyday medicine. For example, how about trying each morning as soon as you get up to think of one good thing that creates a good feeling and trying to start the day feeling good?

When my daughter Anat was young, I once inquired about her recent English test score. She replied, "I didn't tell you yet because I'm waiting to get my terrible mathematics grade first. Then I'll tell you about both, so you won't be angry at my terrible math grade any more because you'll be happy at my good English grade." I liked this method of preparing good things to coincide with the bad, and for many years as a mother, when I came back home from work, I applied it. I wouldn't listen to my children's complaints before they had something good to report also; then we would deal with both.

Attempts to help clients focus on positive functioning may seem in vain when those clients suffer from posttraumatic stress disorder, anxiety, or loneliness. Such clients may not feel capable of picturing themselves without their difficulties, or of looking forward to a dream or positive goal. They may repeat, "Those good things will never come true for me." When therapists feel helpless in the face of such deep pessimism and dark moods, imagery exercises may create the necessary change.

After several weeks of treatment, a 42-year-old client with posttraumatic stress disorder due to a severe car accident was improving, but complained he'd lost his joy and happiness. To help him see himself as happy again, I used an imagery exercise that asked him to imagine a time that couldn't possibly seem real to him, 100 years from the present, at age 142.

THERAPIST: "Can you see yourself as happy when you are 142?"
CLIENT (mocking): "I won't be alive in 100 years."
THERAPIST: "Well, then it can be easier to imagine yourself happy in some magical time in the future."
CLIENT (cynically): "Well, it's not real, but, yes, at age 142 I might be happy."

Only then could we start working on what characterized this 142-year-old happy person. Over several sessions, I was able to adapt the picture to a 120 year old, then a 100 year old, and eventually a 42 year old, discussing what he could actually do now to become happy.

So, for me, being a positive therapist has always meant seeing beyond clients' problems and illness, and unearthing clients' strengths using creative methods. I consistently try to use these strengths as leverage for making the changes necessary to help clients. I value the strength of this psychological approach, even when it is extremely difficult. Using the metaphor of therapist as tennis player (see Chapter 2), even when the ball hit to me is very low, near the ground, I try to return it as high as possible.

A prime example might be when I asked Ayelet, my client with anorexia (described in Chapter 1; Ronen & Ayelet, 2001: 66), to add colors to her drawing of herself as the black, sad soul bird (Snunit, 1985; see Chapter 6), even if those colors were very faint. Likewise, when Ayelet said she fell into a big black hole of emptiness, I took a ladder and went down the well to show her there was a way out (Ronen & Ayelet, 2001: 174). I believed that discovering Ayelet's abilities for positive thinking and positive emotions would lead to significant change.

Defining Positive Psychology

So, what is positive psychology? It is not being optimistic, nor is it being naïve. It is not viewing the world through rose tinted glasses to avoid seeing problems or disorders. It is not the New Age wave of looking only at love and light.

There are many definitions of the concept. Mainly, they all share an emphasis on positive psychology as the scientific study of optimal human functioning, to better understand and apply those factors that help individuals and communities thrive and flourish. The general definition of positive psychology is the scientific enterprise that focuses on understanding and explaining happiness and subjective wellbeing and accurately predicting factors that influence such states (Carr, 2004). Sheldon and King (2001: 216) defined positive psychology as "nothing more than the scientific study of the ordinary human strengths and virtues." Seligman and Csikszentmihalyi (2000: 5) defined it as "the values of subjective experiences: well being, contentment, and satisfaction (in the past), hope and optimism (for the future) and flow and happiness (in the present)." Similarly, Gable and Haidt (2005) defined it as the study of the conditions and processes that contribute to the flourishing or optimal functioning of people, groups, and institutions. As can be seen, all the definitions accentuate the links between positive psychology and happiness, subjective wellbeing, and virtues.

An important concept regarding positive psychology is "positivity." This notion refers to turning or shifting attention to what is positive, inside and outside. Fredrickson (2009) stated that positivity comes in many shapes and sizes and encompasses more than mere physical pleasure or a vague sense of happiness. Rather than relating to happiness, she used the term positivity to describe 10 forms of positive experience that can make an affirmative difference in people's lives: joy, gratitude, serenity, interest, hope, pride, amusement, inspiration, awe, and love. The ability to relate positively to the world renders an effect on one's mind, body, and actions.

Fredrickson (2009) also enumerated six important facts relating to positivity:

1. Positivity refers to feeling good. Letting positivity into one's life occurs through thoughts, emotions, behaviors, increasing one's number of minutes of feeling good, and enabling oneself to feel better.

2. Positivity changes how the mind works. People are accustomed to thinking about, finding, and reacting to negative things, but as we increase awareness about positive issues we start revealing more and more positive things around us. It is a matter of training to learn and code the positive and give it at least as much attention as we give the negative.

3. Positivity transforms the future. Just as behavioral therapists focus on outcomes that can change human behavior; just as cognitive therapists focus on changes that can occur when one modifies interpretations of an event; just as constructivist therapists emphasize that it is the person who gives meaning to life and actually creates experiences – positive psychologists believe that by looking for positivity we introduce more positivity into our lives; by paying more attention to it we change ourselves and our future.

4. Positivity puts the brakes on negativity. Fredrickson (2009) gave as an example how negativity can spike blood pressure but positivity can calm it. A good metaphor for positivity could be that of a fortress. If the fortress walls are high enough and strong enough, they can prevent our enemies from entering and harming us. In other words, strongly anchored feelings of positivity may protect against feelings of negativity that try to infiltrate consciousness and wellbeing. This metaphor suggests that people should invest a great deal of effort in strengthening those walls – in nurturing positivity – to protect themselves.

5. Positivity obeys the notion of a tipping point. That is, outcome studies have shown that positivity is not linear. Multiple, multivariate effects relate to how positivity works on our mind, body, and soul.

6. It is possible to increase one's own positivity. This simple tenet has led to the development of many guidelines for exercises to increase positivity.

Positive Psychology and Happiness

In her studies of subjective wellbeing, Ryff (1989) asked what constitutes positive psychological functioning and how it relates to happiness. She suggested that many facets of life can be linked to positive psychology, particularly subjective wellbeing and happiness. To distinguish components of happiness, she emphasized that to feel happy one needs to achieve personal wellbeing, emotional satisfaction, and good environmental relationships.

Indeed, most of the positive psychology literature is linked to happiness. The Dalai Lama, spiritual leader of the Tibetan people, explained that the very purpose and notion of life is to seek happiness (Dalai Lama & Cutler, 1998). He suggested that happiness is an achievable goal with a clear path leading toward it. Not only can we reach happiness, we can measure and assess it.

The concept of happiness is often connected to the notion of control. Human beings come into the world with a passion for control, and if they lose their ability to control things they become unhappy, hopeless, and depressed. The desire to control is so powerful, and the feeling of control so rewarding, that people often act as though they can control the uncontrollable (Gilbert, 2005). In positive psychology, people undergo training to look at themselves and assess what control really means to them. They learn that by gaining control of their own feelings and happiness (rather than concentrating on controlling the environment), they can increase positive feelings and feel better.

Positive psychology has also strongly connected happiness to coping (Ben-Shahar, 2007). Keyes *et al*. (2008) suggested that happiness incorporates two abilities: achieving subjective wellbeing by expressing positive emotion and achieving positive functioning (toward both oneself and one's environment). Research showed that helping clients focus on their happiness assisted them in gaining a sense of mastery, connectedness, and self-acceptance, which directly led to happiness (Biswas-Diener & Dean, 2007).

Gilbert (2005) differentiated emotional happiness from moral happiness and judgmental happiness. Emotional happiness, in contrast to the other two, is related to feelings, not actions. This common feeling arises from satisfying life experiences. However, moral and judgmental happiness relate to thinking; knowing that one conveys positive, acceptable, moral behavior makes one feel happy.

Research has identified two factors as crucial for enhancing happiness or positivity: subjective wellbeing and social support, which encompasses personal, social, and familial relationships (Biswas-Diener & Dean, 2007; Keyes, 2006; Keyes & Ryff, 2000; Ronen & Seeman, 2007; Sarason, Sarason, & Pierce, 1990). Subjective wellbeing will be elaborated in the next section. Regarding social support, research has demonstrated its importance for increasing coping and happiness feelings in two ways: via a direct main effect and an indirect buffer effect. Directly, feeling support from others boosts one's sense of value, self-efficacy, and self-evaluation (Cohen & Wills, 1985). The indirect buffer effect refers to the decreased negative outcomes of stress when one experiences social support (Antonucci & Akiyama, 1994).

As described above, many researchers emphasize the importance of happiness as a way to help people live better lives. Like Keyes *et al*. (2008), and Ben-Shahar (2007), and Biswas-Diener and Dean (2007) reported that happier people also live longer, are more likely to marry, have better marital longevity, and have more close friends and casual friends. Moreover, just being happy is actually beneficial not only as a tool but also in and of itself, acting as important psychological capital that can be spent while working toward other goals (Biswas-Diener & Dean, 2007). In her study comparing happy and unhappy people, relating to their thinking and behavior patterns, Lyubomirsky (2007: 23) identified several attributes characterizing happy people:

- They devote a great amount of time to their family and friends.
- They are comfortable in expressing gratitude for all they have.
- They are often the first to offer help.
- They practice optimism when imagining their futures.
- They try to live in the present.
- They do regular physical exercise.
- They are deeply committed to lifelong goals.

- They do experience crises, but their secret weapon lies in the poise and strength they show in coping.

Although happiness is individual, we expect happy people to know when they are happy. Nevertheless, I find that people often take their happy feelings for granted, stop noticing them, disconnect from their sources of happiness, and experience distress. They then mourn their lost past happiness. To avoid this chain of events, people should self-observe, chart, measure, and talk about happiness, thereby expanding awareness of its existence and helping see themselves as happy. According to Lyubomirsky (2007), happiness can to some extent be influenced by training. She claimed that 50% of happiness relates to one's "set point," referring to one's biological genes and potential heritage, and an additional 10% is related to circumstances, but the 40% that relates to intentional activity can respond to training.

It is important to note that happiness is a subjective issue. What makes one person happy differs from what makes another person happy, and sources may change over time. Therefore, therapists should first uncover the specific nature of the particular client's happiness before working toward achieving it. Imagery offers one good way to learn what makes clients happy:

> *Try to recall a memory of yourself being happy. Now focus on yourself then, being happy. What do you see? Can you let the feeling of happiness fill you more and more? Can you sense the happy feeling in different parts of your body? Can you describe yourself as a happy person? What do you look like? How are you standing? Can you recall other situations when you were happy? Is this a familiar feeling for you? Could you increase the happiness?*

Sometimes people have difficulty thinking of themselves as happy. Training in uncovering concrete manifestations of happiness, both external and internal, can help the client unravel how happiness feels and remember events that led to the desired feeling.

Subjective Wellbeing

Like the case for positive psychology, attempts to study this field's major concepts, such as subjective wellbeing, also raised multiple definitions. Over the years, researchers have mainly approached subjective wellbeing using two major conceptualizations and measures. One focused on life satisfaction as a cognitive index or component of subjective wellbeing, measuring people's evaluations and declarations about their life quality, including expectations, comparisons to others, and other cultural aspects (Keyes, 2006; Shmotkin & Lomranz, 1998). The second focused on positive and negative affects, defining wellbeing as the balance between the two (Ryff & Keyes, 1995). Many studies resolved these contradictory measurement trends by integrating the cognitive and emotional components and examining subjective wellbeing through a combination of positive affect, negative affect, and general life satisfaction (Ronen & Seeman, 2007).

A third index of subjective wellbeing (beyond the two aforementioned indices of mental adjustment) is that of physical adjustment (Keyes, 2006; Keyes *et al.*, 2008). Niven (2000) stipulated that happy people must take care of basic physical needs such as eating on time, sleeping enough, and exercising before they can take care of their emotional and social wellbeing. Similarly, Csikszentmihalyi (1966) described creative, happy people as finding time to exercise and care for themselves physically.

A challenge facing researchers studying the elusive concept of subjective wellbeing was to determine what it really means to be well psychologically. Ryff and Keyes (1995) were able to show the efficacy of Ryff's (1989) multicomponent model of subjective wellbeing, suggesting that a person with high levels of wellbeing functions well in all six personal and environmental components:

1. *Self-acceptance* – a central feature of mental health as well as a characteristic of self-actualization, optimal functioning, and maturity.
2. *Finding purpose and meaning in life* – the belief that one has a sense of directedness and intentionality that leads one's life.
3. *Continuous personal development and growth* – the ability to try to accomplish potentialities, open up to experiences, and function fully (Mahoney, 1991, 2003).
4. *Self-determination or independence* – self-regulation of behavior. Rosenbaum (1990, 2000) suggested that acquisition of self-control skills enables people to overcome difficulties, cope with distress, and live better lives.
5. *Mastery* – the ability to choose or create environments that match one's physical conditions and to manage these surroundings masterfully.
6. *Establishing positive meaningful relations with others* – the ability to develop trusting interpersonal relationships, love, express emotion, and be in touch with others.

These components of subjective wellbeing relate not only to internal personal aspects – feeling good, accepting oneself, and developing as a human being – but also to interpersonal aspects – having positive emotions toward one's surroundings and meaningful interrelations. People with a high level of subjective wellbeing were found to think more actively and openly, report a greater sense of control over their lives, cope better with stressful situations, and set themselves more life goals, rather than merely letting themselves be carried wherever life takes them (Keyes & Ryff, 2000; Veenhoven, 1991).

Regarding the emotional aspects of subjective wellbeing, positive and negative affects as well as their ratio have been widely studied. Positive affects include happiness, satisfaction, joy, energy, relaxation, and so on (Keyes, 2006). According to Fredrickson (1998, 2009), positive emotions broaden momentary thought–action repertoires, resulting in a higher likelihood of pursuing a wider range of thoughts and actions. In other words, when people feel positive emotions, they are able to see more possibilities. This broadening effect is essentially the opposite of what happens when people experience negative emotions (Magyar-Moe, 2009). Negative affects include sorrow, fear, worry, anger, disgust, hate, guilt, and so on (Bradburn, 1969). According to Fredrickson (1998, 2009), negative emotions narrow momentary thought–action repertoires.

The balance between positive and negative emotions has been a source of great interest for researchers. Studies showed that high rates of subjective wellbeing occur when low rates of negative emotion coincide with high rates of positive emotion (Bradburn, 1969; Shmotkin & Lomranz, 1998). Shmotkin and Lomranz emphasized that it is not one's experience of negative emotion that determines one's distress but rather one's inability to express more positive emotion than negative emotion. This capacity to experience more positive than negative emotion was conceived as the ability to "flourish" (Fredrickson & Losada, 2005). A key predictor of human functioning, flourishing means living optimally and experiencing the good things in life, such as personal growth, generativity, and resilience (Keyes, 2002). More specifically, Fredrickson and Losada (2005) hypothesized that, to flourish, the ratio of positive feelings/sentiments to negative feelings/sentiments needed over time is 2.9 to 1. In other words, for each negative affective experience, one must experience three positive affective experiences. As the ratio dips below 2.9 to 1, flourishing becomes less likely and problems may arise. Fredrickson and Losada found this ratio to hold true for individuals, marriages, and business teams. Furthermore, positive to negative affect ratios up to 11.6 to 1 will promote flourishing; however, ratios beyond 11.6 to 1 may lead to its disintegration (Fredrickson & Losada, 2005).

Fredrickson (2009) contrasted upward spirals of wellbeing with downward spirals of depression. When people have negative experiences and therefore negative affects, they begin to experience tunnel vision that often leads to negative, pessimistic thinking. In turn, this negative thinking leads to more negative affects, which can spiral downward very quickly. In contrast, positive emotions take the blinders off, allowing people to see more possibilities and think more optimistically. Those who experience positive emotions are more likely to experience upward spirals of wellbeing regularly, which are enjoyable in and of themselves. In turn, they cope better and are more resilient in the face of life's adversities (Fredrickson, 2009).

Thus, within subjective wellbeing, a flourishing emotional state (high positive affects and low negative affects) is related to assessing and accepting oneself as content and satisfied with life (the cognitive component), as well as to having a positive environmental support system (the interpersonal component). To further unravel the role of personal and environmental resources in explaining subjective wellbeing, I undertook a series of studies together with some colleagues, which all highlighted the moderating effect of such resources on adolescents' wellbeing (Hamama, Ronen, & Rahav, 2008; Ronen & Dweik, 2009; Ronen & Seeman, 2007). For example, we examined 567 Israeli adolescents facing the expected threat of Iraqi rocket attacks with chemical warheads, conducted immediately before the United States attacked Iraq in the 1991 Gulf War (Ronen & Seeman, 2007). The findings showed that adolescents' self-control skills and social support, jointly and separately, moderated the link between their fear of war and their subjective wellbeing. That is, adolescents with high self-control and high social support demonstrated high positive affect and low negative affect, as well as high overall life satisfaction compared to adolescents lacking these resources. Furthermore, adolescents expressing strong fears about the possibility of war required both these important resources in order to achieve high subjective wellbeing and cope with their fears.

Empirical studies on the advantages of positive psychological assets like subjective wellbeing offer numerous issues to consider. Mainly, research showed that by using exercises to increase positivity or happiness, people can feel stronger and can feel good – an experience found to have physical and mental health benefits. Moreover, personal and environmental resources were found to explain subjective wellbeing, suggesting that positive affects and experiences may help in gaining better social connections and social supports. The research supporting positive psychology models suggests that training interventions are warranted to apply this approach more widely.

Training in Positive Psychology

At the first World Conference on Positive Psychology, held in Philadelphia in June 2009, the state-of-the-art presentations clarified beyond doubt that positive research and applications are currently being undertaken in all walks of life internationally. These include the realms of education, business, organizational consulting, marriage counseling, interpersonal relationships, parenting, athletics, coaching, and more.

Wright and Lopez (2002) recommended that, in order to apply positive psychology exercises, therapists themselves should first believe that all clients have both strengths and weaknesses as well as both opportunities and destructive forces in their environments. They also suggested that the prominent guidelines for mental health professionals, as outlined in the *Diagnostic and Statistical Manual of Mental Disorders* (*DSM-IV*, American Psychiatric Association, 1994), be amended to incorporate a clearer emphasis on clients' strengths and resources rather than dealing primarily with clients' weaknesses.

A broad range of strategies and exercises have been suggested for incorporating positive psychology into therapeutic work with clients (Magyar-Moe, 2009). Biswas-Diener and Dean (2007) suggested that helping clients focus on existential challenges such as mastery, connectedness, and self-acceptance can be an important and fruitful route to happiness, especially if clients practice exercises for eliciting positive outcomes (Duckworth, Steen, & Seligman, 2005; Seligman, Rashid, & Parks, 2006; Seligman *et al.*, 2005). Most of the suggested exercises promote awareness of strengths and virtues, increase positive expressions toward the immediate environment and even strangers, and pursue happiness through various means (Keyes & Haidt, 2002; Lopez, 2008; Lyubomirsky, 2007; Magyar-Moe, 2009). Such exercises may focus on teaching daily skills for self-assessing and writing down important strengths, performing nice acts for others, expressing positive emotions toward oneself and others, and so forth.

Lyubomirsky (2007) designed five "hows" for happiness exercises, under the assumption that everyone can learn to be happy, but not everyone knows how to sustain happiness in the long term. The first "how" suggests creating many experiences of little happy moments, not necessarily the ultimate happiness but rather numerous minor events and emotions that elicit happy feelings. One can facilitate such happy moments through mindfulness, by observing oneself and identifying those objects, people, and events that increase positive emotions. These moments may be a nice sunset, good food, or an enjoyable meeting with someone.

The second "how" relates to optimal timing and variety of actions. Lyubomirsky suggested that people identify the best time to accomplish their goals, practice their sports activity, or talk with others. Allowing oneself to devote time to important activities comprises an important step toward augmenting happiness and experiencing happy moments. At the same time, one should find various options for increasing happiness, trying to apply diverse actions to accrue different routes leading to happy feelings.

The third "how" focuses on social support and relationships. People cannot be happy alone – they need to share happiness more than they share sadness. Consider how often crying occurs naturally when a person is alone; people often even seek out a quiet space to cry in private. But how often do people express happiness alone? Do dancing, singing, and shouting out for joy feel right when there is nobody to share them? I have observed this clear social distinction between emotions repeatedly over the years, in treatment groups and workshops I have conducted around the world.

For example, in a movement exercise for emotional expression, I ask a group of people to imagine they are walking in the Land of Sorrow and then in the Land of Happiness. Regardless of their nationality or culture or clinical status, people express emotions in exactly the same direction, albeit at different intensities, thus supporting the crucial role of social relations when experiencing positive emotions. When they imagine themselves in the Land of Sorrow, people walk around very slowly, become increasingly sad, and eventually find it difficult even to move. They bend down, fold up within themselves, emit no voice, and connect with no one. When I ask them to move to the Land of Happiness, the change is remarkable. People straighten up, smile and laugh, and, most perceptibly, they start looking at one another, vocalizing, speaking, and touching each other. Happiness thus increases social relationships, whereas sadness decreases them. Happiness creates the need to share those moments much more than sadness does.

The fourth "how" involves motivation, effort, and commitment. Just as negative thoughts come automatically but need work to change them into mediated positive thoughts, happiness does not come automatically (see the section describing automatic and mediated thoughts in Chapter 2). To find happy moments, people need to work hard, look for opportunities, and use situations to their advantage.

The fifth and last "how" concerns habituation. Nothing changes by merely doing it once. People need to make a habit of searching for happy moments, practicing happy events, and allowing themselves to enjoy those times without guilt. Repetition and rehearsal will increase the chances that such opportunities will arise again.

In her book *The How of Happiness,* Lyubomirsky (2007) also suggested three additional sets of exercises for increasing happiness, based on common myths about this emotion:

- Based on the myth that *"happiness is here,"* people commonly believe that happiness is an entity that exists somewhere out there and must be found. In fact, happiness exists inside us; therefore, the first set of exercises aims to help people find the happiness that is already inside them using awareness, imagery, and mindfulness exercises.
- Based on the myth that *"happiness doesn't come without change,"* people commonly believe that happiness requires changing their life circumstances. They often say, "I'd be happy if I could only change this or that – buy a new perfume or clothes, eat this food that I'm not supposed to eat, etc." Therefore, exercises aiming to refute this myth should help clients (i) accept their current lives and find happiness within them ("Focus on your feeling right here and now and see if you can find happiness within you") and (ii) acknowledge that although change is desirable, the search for happiness needn't wait for it ("You're right, there is that goal you wish to achieve, but see if right now, right here, you can find something small, not a major issue, that might help you feel better").
- Based on the myth that *"happiness is either all or nothing,"* people commonly believe that they can be either happy or unhappy, and can do nothing to change that fate. In fact, inasmuch as happiness can be facilitated in various ways, many exercises like the five "hows" mentioned above can be applied to dispel this myth.

For therapists trying to strengthen their clients' ability for happiness and positivity, the most difficult part may be enabling clients to recognize and experience such feelings in the present. People who cannot seem to experience current events as happy may nevertheless be able to remember and even dwell on happy events that they experienced in the past. For example, in therapy a client may claim, "I was so happy with him! Why did it have to end?" or "Those were the days. If only my miserable life today was like it used to be." In contrast, how often do clients come and say "I am so happy with him now" in the treatment room?

Gilbert (2005) suggested that people may also find it easier to think about good things in the future than in the present. When daydreaming about the future, clients tend to imagine themselves as achieving and succeeding rather than as fumbling or failing. Therefore, thinking about the future can be a pleasurable place to start practicing. This future thinking was described earlier in this chapter in the case of the 42-year-old client with posttraumatic stress disorder who could not picture himself happy again unless he was imagining himself in 100 years' time. Gilbert even implied that thinking about the future can be so pleasurable that sometimes people would rather think about it than actually get there.

Constructivist therapy offers a broad spectrum of exercises for helping clients explore themselves and their emotions, such as mirror time and following the affect trail. Mirror time teaches clients to spend time looking in a mirror and quietly focusing on themselves, their bodies, and their emotions, trying to explore themselves and enhance emotions they feel about themselves (Mahoney, 1991; Neimeyer, 2009). Such usage of mirrors can help clients examine themselves more objectively as well as subjectively, leading to greater self-acceptance and self-appreciation. Mirrors appear widely in this context in fictional literature, which substantiates the culturally embedded role that mirrors play in providing a source of information and self-reflection about one's beauty (e.g., in the Snow White fairytale; Grimm & Grimm, 1932) or about one's assets and flaws, as in the first book in the Harry Potter series by J. K. Rowling (1997). In *Harry Potter and the Philosopher's Stone*, the Mirror of Erised shows "only the deepest desire of our hearts," meaning that it reflects what is desired but absent from the characters' current lives. Thus, Harry sees himself with his dead parents for whom he yearns; and his friend Ron sees himself as an older, successful Captain of the Quidditch team, thus finally achieving his desired success and popularity. Only the wise and contented school headmaster, Dumbledore, sees himself as he is, showing his innate happiness. As can be seen, many of the suggested exercises for eliciting happiness can actually be part of mindfulness therapy or constructivism, trying to emphasize the need to accept rather than change, find meaning in one's life, and increase awareness of internal stimuli.

Another constructivist exercise for emotional exploration, suggested by Neimeyer (2009), comprises the metaphor of following the affect trail. This affect trail refers to signs of significant emotion. By asking the client to focus on that emotional trail and watch where it leads, much can be learned about the emotion experienced. We can follow our clients as they lead us along their affect trails and discover what direction the trails go in, and what unique emotions the clients face while leading us down their trails. Are there any surprising new feelings that clients were unaware of before? Are there any emotions that clients would like to embrace, keep, and enlarge? There might also be some difficult emotions – can clients face those and embrace them too? How does it feel to meet all those emotions?

Another simple exercise consists of the habitual utilization of positive word choices, which can significantly contribute to positive feelings. My youngest child was 7 when we first visited Australia. Soon we noticed that his most frequent activity had become jumping and shouting "I'm happy" (in the very few words he knew in English at that time). I soon found myself joining him occasionally, jumping up and down and yelling that I was happy too. I noticed that as I joined him more often, he started shouting about his joy even more frequently. I also realized that when I loudly exclaimed how happy I was, I found myself feeling happier. Soon enough, we all started using the language of happiness: We invented songs about how happy we were, we talked "happily," and we felt our happiness increase. Later, in anticipation of a subsequent trip to Australia, we found ourselves becoming happy even before our flight; we had developed expectations of being happy, so it was even easier to find that feeling when we arrived. Very soon we learned that measuring happiness ("How happy did this whale watching make you?"), expecting happiness, stating our expectation that we were going to be happy ("How great it is to know we are now going to be happy for two whole months"), and talking happiness ("It's just so happy to be happy!" or "I am so happy you are happy") made us happier. Observing happiness, pinpointing it, and making space for it strengthened this emotion.

Summary

Since the positive psychology movement started, it has become part of many theories and a large range of professions and areas of intervention. There is common agreement now that humans do not need to suffer in order to learn new knowledge and that joy and happiness are important for wellbeing. Positive psychology has become part of education and commerce; we can see trends toward positive learning milieus and positive business strategies. I believe that the future holds many more domains to which positivity will become integral.

Practice: Guidelines for Applying Positive Psychology Exercises

These practice exercises aim first to help therapists apply the exercises on themselves and then to help them facilitate clients' happiness by teaching them to find their own strengths, express positive emotions toward themselves and others, and relate to positivity in the past, present, and future.

The past

Asking clients to look at their contentment and satisfaction in the past is usually the easiest exercise with which to start, because people tend to feel nostalgic when reminiscing about the past. Ask the client:

Every day this week, try to elicit and practice:

- *An image from the past in which you can see yourself being happy.*
- *One positive emotion you used to experience in the past.*
- *A memory of yourself from the past, having fun with somebody.*

The future

After looking at the past, it is easier to look at the future and find some hope and optimism. Ask the client:

Every day this week, try to picture yourself:

- *Being happy in the future. Focus on your face and try to see what you look like when you are happy.*
- *Accomplishing something that is important for you in the future. Try to see the area in which you succeed.*
- *Expressing a positive emotion to someone in the future. See what emotion you express and how it was for you.*

The present

The most difficult exercises attempt to help clients express flow and happiness in the present; therefore, they should be practiced last. All or part of these six exercises can be delivered in any sequence.

Find your own strengths and virtues

- *On every day of the first week, find 2 minutes to look at yourself in the mirror and tell yourself why you like what you see.*
- *On every day of the second week, write down one strength or virtue that you find in yourself.*

Express positive emotion

- *On every day of the first week, write down at least one positive emotion you sensed during that day.*
- *On every day of the second week, write down one positive emotion you expressed toward someone else that day.*
- *Every day, try to notice when you are happy, even if you feel that way only for a moment or only for a very minor reason. Tell yourself "I am happy."*

Express gratitude

- *On every day of the first week, write down one thing in your life for which you are grateful.*
- *On every day of the second week, express gratitude toward someone else for something.*

Help others

- *During the first week, do something good for yourself every day.*
- *During the second week, do one good thing for someone else every day.*

Happiness

- *During the first week, keep a chart of your happiness score for each day on a scale of 1–10.*

- *During the second week, keep a chart of the kinds of positive feelings you felt every day and try to increase their number.*

Flourishing

During the upcoming week, each day close your eyes, look at your day as if it were a movie playing in a cinema, and ask yourself:

- *What is going right for me today?*
- *What made me happy today?*
- *What was positive in my day?*

4

Creativity:
Who Needs It, and for What?

Imagine that you, a therapist, have just finished reading my book. You have learned how to apply imagery therapy with clients. You are now eager to start applying it and you decide to start by using an exercise you have read here that aims to obtain better information about your client's social relationships. Now, let's see: what exercise are you going to design for your client?

You certainly just used your imagination to bring up an image; in fact, you invented one because you haven't really read this book yet. So, you used imagery. You might have done this for the first time so it is novel, at least for you. Is it also creative?

The definition of creativity is diverse and complex. Some say that creativity involves mostly doing something for the first time, in a new way (just like you tried to design an imagery exercise). This definition would say that the act of trying to apply something new that you haven't tried before is creative. Examples of this approach are abundant in collections of modern art. If we see a painting of an all-black canvas with one white spot in the middle, or a pair of trousers hanging as an exhibition on the museum wall, we might think: Why is that there? Who decided it is art? What is so special about it? Although we might say, "Well, I could create that same artwork," the fact is that we were not the ones who created it. Part of the reason that this artwork is hanging in the museum is the fact that while we merely claim we could make the artistic piece, the artist on display actually did make it, and for the first time, and therefore he or she deserves the credit for it.

Another definition of creativity focuses on the creative acts' outcomes. Many start-up companies work diligently on impressive products and attractive services with powerful potential, but only a minority actually sell to international high-tech giants for an enormous profit. We usually hear about the successful ones whose investments of time, money, and effort paid off. Thus, outcomes cause us to view the companies as creative. Likewise, in the case of your imagery exercise for assessing your client's social relationships, if you succeeded in hearing a

The Positive Power of Imagery: Harnessing Client Imagination in CBT and Related Therapies,
First Edition. Tammie Ronen. © 2011 Tammie Ronen. Published 2011 by John Wiley & Sons, Ltd.

different viewpoint or information you didn't expect to obtain from your client – that is, you achieved good outcomes – then that imagery exercise would be considered creative.

A third emphasis in evaluating what constitutes creativity involves the creative work's social value. Was your imagery exercise socially valuable – would society appreciate it? In line with this approach, a start-up company that invented new medical equipment to facilitate easier and safer surgery would probably achieve social recognition and value beyond its successful financial outcomes. Accordingly, this company's venture should be considered as creative. The link between social value and outcome means that products that are not socially appreciated will not be called creative. For example, we would never refer to Hitler as creative, although he developed novel, different ways to kill people.

Imagery and metaphors as part of creative therapy meet all three criteria of the creative process: novelty, outcomes, and social values. First, imagery therapy is creative because new images and imagery techniques must be adapted to each client's specific needs, thus opening up novel channels for achieving change. Second, a major indication for applying imagery in therapy is to facilitate change during an impasse; thus, imagery is used to improve the efficacy of treatment outcomes. And third, social value is achieved when creative use of imagery helps clients become an integral part of society, adjusting and adapting to social norms and goals.

The human imagination enables its users to produce countless creative acts. This book will focus on such creativity through creative modes of therapy using imagery. Let us take an example of creative imagery that can help both the therapist and the client appreciate the slow process of working with a particularly uncommunicative client:

> *Imagine your client donned so many layers of clothing that you can hardly see him. You can barely hear anything he is saying. You are the first person he is trusting to bare his soul and see him from the inside by unraveling the layers that cover his real self. Each piece of clothing that he peels off enables you to see him more and more clearly. He lets you get nearer his true skin and soul.*

This illustrates a way to mobilize a therapist-generated imagery exercise as a creative psychotherapeutic tool. This exercise is creative because it is new for the particular client, it is outcome-oriented because it effectively helps the therapist self-supervise and the client understand the situation better, and it has social value because it fosters work toward change in both partners in the therapeutic relationship.

Negotiating between what is available to the therapist on the outside and what lies inside is an intriguing challenge for therapists, especially in working with difficult clients. Other images can powerfully convey this gap between what is hidden and what is exposed in therapy. For example, Ben, a 6 year old with selective mutism who did not talk to me in therapy, explained his feelings by drawing himself once as a very big child and writing "This is me from the outside" (how everyone else sees him) and once as a very small encircled figure, writing "This is me from the inside" (how he really thinks and feels about himself) (Ronen, 2003b: 88–89). Thus, diverse creative images can help therapists unlock different clients' inner secrets and then use that new understanding to personalize ways to enhance behavior and achieve wellbeing.

Creative therapy, for me, is not a self-contained theory or a structured mode of intervention. Creative therapy as advanced in this book constitutes a way of thinking. It mobilizes therapists' flexibility to adapt, invent, or adjust techniques until they discover the best means for helping a specific client change. It also offers means for identifying each client's unique characteristics, interests, hobbies, and natural skills, to optimally facilitate that client's learning and expression of diverse thoughts and emotions. Creative therapy, therefore, is the best route for adapting CBT to clients' developmental stage and individual needs.

What Is Creativity?

Unlike many phenomena in science, there is no single, authoritative perspective or definition of creativity. And like many phenomena in psychology, there is no standardized measurement technique for assessing creativity.

Societies' perceptions of creativity have changed throughout history, as has the term itself. The ancient Greek concept of art (*techne*, the root of "technique" and "technology"), with the exception of poetry, involved not freedom of action but subjection to rules. In Rome, this Greek concept was partly shaken and visual artists along with poets were viewed as sharing imagination and inspiration (Wikipedia, 2009a). Although many terms in modern usage are rooted in ancient Greek or Roman culture, neither had a word that directly corresponded to the word "creativity." Nevertheless, their art, architecture, music, inventions, and discoveries provided numerous examples of what today would be described as creative works.

An old word in Christianity, *creatio*, came to designate God's act of "creation from nothing." *Creatio* thus took on a different meaning than *facere* ("to make") and ceased to apply to human functions (Wikipedia, 2009a). Weisberg (1993) stated that understanding creativity is a challenging task, not only because creative thinking occurs in diverse domains, but also because a complex set of psychological and social forces contributes to it.

In its broadest definition, creativity can be viewed as the quality or ability to create or invent something. Therefore, creativity is often replaced by the word "originality." From a scientific perspective, the products of creative thought (sometimes referred to as divergent thoughts) are usually considered to have both originality and appropriateness.

Creativity can be viewed as a mental and social process involving the generation of new ideas or concepts, or new associations between existing ideas or concepts. Creativity is fueled by the process of either conscious or unconscious insight. Weisberg (1993) explained creativity as a process of logical thinking that uses rules of inference to produce new knowledge. Each thinking rule is dependent on the other and facilitates the new ideas as an outcome of previous knowledge.

Guilford (1950, 1967) drew the distinction between convergent and divergent products or thoughts. Convergent thinking involves aiming for a single, correct solution to a problem, whereas divergent thinking involves the creative generation of multiple answers to a set problem. Divergent thinking is sometimes used as a synonym for creativity in the psychology literature.

As described above, an alternative conception of creativeness is as the simple act of making something new. Thus, creativity is constructing and appreciating crafted transformations; in other words, making a living out of the transformational imperative in human beings to create something new (Feldman, 1988). The primary criterion for calling a given product creative is its novelty, at least for the individual producing it. Mahoney (2003) described creativity at work simply as the courage to take risks and pursue a noncustomary direction. Sometimes, this implies a major departure from what was known at that time (Weisberg, 1993).

Usually, we remain creatures of habit, stuck in our old, known, familiar behavior patterns that lead us to repeat the same routines over and over, which often helps us function smoothly and cope less anxiously. To facilitate my university students' willingness to open themselves up to the creative mindset, to the need for risk-taking and new experiences (Mahoney, 1991), I often perform a set of simple but effective exercises:

> *I first ask students to move from their regular seats in class elsewhere and look anew at the classroom experience.*
>
> *Next, I ask them to observe themselves walking over to an unfamiliar part of campus and eating lunch in an unfamiliar cafeteria, trying to focus on how they walk, talk, and feel in a strange environment.*
>
> *In both these exercises, students report feeling completely different from usual, and they realize that they behave differently in familiar and unfamiliar environments.*
>
> *Their homework assignment was to do one new thing daily, like bathe rather than shower, ride buses instead of cars, drive along another route to campus, or dress differently.*

Doing something new is not necessarily synonymous with creativity. Yet, daring to face unfamiliar experiences is an important first step leading to creativity. One should be willing to overcome nervousness or fear about changing old customs and dare to attempt something novel.

It is often useful to distinguish explicitly between creativity and innovation. Creativity typically refers to the act of producing new ideas, approaches, or actions, whereas innovation is the process of both generating and applying such creative ideas in some specific context. In organizational contexts, therefore, innovation often refers to the entire process by which an organization generates creative new ideas and converts them into novel, useful, and viable commercial products, services, and business practices. In contrast, the term creativity is reserved to apply specifically to the generation of novel ideas by individuals or groups, as a necessary step within the innovation process. For example, Amabile (1996, 1998) suggested that innovation begins with creative ideas, whereas creativity by individuals and teams is only a starting point for innovation. Thus, both words relate to novelty and go hand in hand, but creativity is a necessary yet insufficient condition for innovation. To be innovative, one must be creative to stay competitive.

Another appropriate definition of creativity is as an "assumptions-breaking process." Creative ideas are often generated when one discards preconceived assumptions and attempts a new approach or method that might seem unthinkable to others. However, the product's novelty is insufficient; it must be of value or must meet the situation's cognitive demands. Many of our best-known creative artists – musicians, painters, and writers – were not appreciated in their lifetimes but only attained recognition much later, after death. Before being recognized, their works were not accepted as creative, but were deemed as "crazy," "strange," or "unworthy." Someone else needs to evaluate creative work, to assess it and declare it worthy, before it can be accepted as such.

Along the same line of thought, Mihalyi Csikszentmihalyi (1966) proposed a provocative reconceptualization of the concept of creativity, emphasizing the role of societal value judgments. His theory presented a cyclical process: an individual produces some new work; however, to be considered creative, that work must be examined by others and accepted as valuable. Therefore, creativity requires not only novelty or cognitive importance, but also socially recognized value.

As mentioned above, while some relate to creativity based on novelty, originality, or social values, others emphasize its outcomes or products. Yet, transformational creativity does not have to be evidenced by an artistic product. Rather, evidence for its presence can be found in the processes of self-creation, an applied creativity that tackles the never-ending negotiations of life: family, friends, associates, career, personal style, inner experiences, and general behavior (Carlsen, 1995).

Whether we emphasize novelty, innovation, outcome, or social value, we can see that creativity is not a fixed behavior that stays constant and stable over time. Creativity varies throughout the life cycle (Csikszentmikhhalyi, 2000), increasing from childhood as one matures, reaching its peak by adolescence, and then starting to decline (Carrigan, 2007). Donald Winnicott (1971) observed that the most creative children were those who played within a certain radius of their mothers. He claimed that within this circle of creativity – a space in which children can take risks and experiment, fall and stand up again, fail and succeed – they feel secure and safe in the presence of a person who loves them unconditionally. Ben-Shahar (2007) stated that adults are capable of higher levels of abstraction than children; therefore, they do not always need to be in physical proximity of near loved ones to be within the circle of creativity. Creativity for Ben-Shahar derives from adults' knowledge that they are safe and secure. In therapy, therapists can dare to become creative once they feel secure and confident in their own skills.

Cohen (2000) developed a stage theory of mid- to late-life creativity, depicting ordinary people who are more creative than others in their everyday lives. He asserted that around age 50, people with creative minds enter a reevaluation phase, in which they reflect on past accomplishments and formulate new goals. He claimed that at this stage people take more risks and tolerate their own failures better; hence, they can be more creative.

Creativity changes not only through the life span across groups of people, but also at different stages within the individual. Changes in the conditions surrounding a person, whether situational, cognitive, or emotional, can affect creativity.

Creativity and Emotion

Creativity is an activity rooted in the right hemisphere of the brain, which also contains emotion. Pink (2005) stated that we are entering a new age in which creativity is becoming increasingly important, and we should therefore encourage and foster right-directed thinking, representing creativity and emotion, over left-directed thinking, representing logical, analytical thought.

Creativity has been strongly linked to emotional states – to an openness to new ways of seeing, an intuition, an alertness to opportunity, a liking for complexity, or a challenge to find simplicity, independence of judgment, a willingness to take risks, or an unconventionality of thought that allows odd connections to be made (Carlsen, 1995). Layard (2005) suggested that people have always recognized a link between artistic creativity and extreme emotional experience, even mental instability. Layard's study of 291 world-famous people showed that creative writers were more likely to have suffered from depression than the population at large. However, some studies claimed that it was not the creativity that directly caused their distress or vice versa, but rather that these depressed writers were more sensitive and therefore could be more creative.

According to Isen, Daubman, and Nowicki (1987), positive affect has three primary effects on cognitive creative activity. First, the existence of positive affect makes additional cognitive material easier and more available for processing, thereby increasing the number of cognitive elements available for association. Second, exploring positive affect leads to defocused attention and a more complex cognitive context, thus increasing the breadth of elements treated as relevant to the problem at hand. Third, positive affect augments cognitive flexibility, increasing the probability that diverse cognitive elements will in fact become associated. Together, these processes lead positive affect to have a positive influence on creativity.

While Isen, Daubman, and Nowicki (1987) highlighted the contribution of positive affect to the development of creativity, other theorists suggested that negative affect leads to greater creativity. In a study of 1005 individuals from over 45 different professions, Ludwig (1995) found a significant correlation between depression and level of creative achievement. In a later study, Ludwig (2002) examined the personality characteristics, childhoods, and mental stability of six kinds of rulers to pinpoint the chief predictors of later political success. He suggested that highly creative individuals and their relatives exhibited a higher incidence of affective disorders (primarily bipolar illness and depression) than in the general population.

Certain external circumstances often seem conducive to creative thoughts and initiatives. We may sense that specific situations or the presence of other people provide a muse or inspiration, or that a particular location lends itself to creative yearnings. However, not only external triggers but also internal features like a restless urge to express feelings or convey some idea differently may play a facilitative role in creativity. As an illustration of the power of emotional factors, let me share an experience from my family's travels in Australia one cold winter.

We rented a houseboat without possessing much skill in sailing it. On the first evening, we readied ourselves to moor the boat for the night on a deserted, dark, bush-filled shore of the river, with kangaroos jumping all around. My husband maneuvered the boat close to the embankment and tried to keep it there as I jumped ashore with my 11-year-old son and we attempted to moor the boat to a tree. However, my husband lost control, and the boat started moving downstream. My son and I were stranded ashore. We stood in the dark, with no coats for warmth, watching the boat float away into the distance. We were alone in the bush, and we knew no one could hear us or pass by.

These were our external circumstances. Internally, we could have become frightened or stressed; we could have cursed or screamed. However, we both remembered that, for us, being in Australia meant we were happy (see Chapter 3). My son and I decided that if we'd been served lemons, we would just have to make lemonade. I can't say if our positive thinking emerged from our trust that my husband would find a solution, from our confidence in Australia's safety, from our happy moods associated with our travels there, from my need to protect my child, or all of the above. Whatever the sources of our positive emotions, we started telling jokes, laughing, and making up silly songs about our father/husband who wanted to maroon us on a desert island. For three hours we walked through the bush, until my husband was able to return with help and find us. When he approached us and saw how much fun we were having, he couldn't believe his eyes. We were happy rather than stressed, and we felt it had been a very positive experience. We sang out our newly invented songs to him, proud of our creativity during those hours.

This illustration shows that creativity can serve as a means for enhancing positive emotions even in difficult situations. It can be manifested as action, like drawing or sculpting, and it can be manifested as changing thoughts or emotions and as finding new solutions to tricky situations.

In sum, although a link has emerged between emotions and creativity, its direction for affecting individuals remains unclear. In other words, no one can yet state that positive emotions lead to better creativity; or vice versa, that negative emotions stir up creative acts; or both.

Creativity, Genetics, and Intelligence

The psychology literature has attempted to examine intelligence and creativity to determine if both are part of the same process (the conjoint hypothesis) or if they represent distinct mental processes (the disjoint hypothesis) (Guilford, 1950, 1967; Wallas & Smith, 1926). Citing the "threshold hypothesis," Torrance (1974) claimed that high intelligence is a necessary but insufficient condition for high creativity. He suggested that creativity and intelligence will correlate in the general population, but not due to the effect of the most highly intelligent subsample. However, there are no results to prove this hypothesis.

In the past, creativity was viewed as a matter of genius, pointing to creative achievements as the result of extraordinary individuals employing extraordinary thought processes (Weisberg, 1993). This view explains the origin and development of creative works by postulating special thinking processes that allow individuals to "break the set" – break away from the habitual and the ordinary. This view conjectures creative people's different levels of thinking, sensitivity, and mental processes. Three assumptions underlie the search for the psychological characteristics behind creative genius. The first assumption is that genius is a measurable psychological characteristic or trait. Second, any personal characteristics unique to creative individuals, whatever they turn out to be, are assumed to be causally related to creativity. The third is that the quality of "possessing genius" is assumed to be a permanent, or at least a relatively permanent, characteristic of the individual (Weisberg, 1993).

Based on these assumptions, many people mentioned throughout history (Mozart, for example) were considered to be born geniuses. Even as little children, their genius was clear to their environment, and therefore their achievements were seen as unique to geniuses' special characteristics. This assumes that creativity is an inborn trait depicting some rare individuals (e.g., Einstein, Picasso, Freud) who are recognized inspirations and influences on the entire world. This view also assumes that creativity cannot be taught or acquired; most of us will not produce creative inventions that change the planet.

However, an examination of some of the innovators responsible for the striking medical and high-tech start-up achievements over recent decades indicates a different picture. We often hear people comment about these innovators, "I can't really say that he seemed different from anyone else at school or at university. No one could have predicted his extraordinary success." The issue of individual differences points to the fact that all creative processes are not of the same degree of importance (Weisberg, 1993), suggesting that the genius view of creativity is a myth. Feldman (1988) upheld that each individual's life is a unique creation, and that this uniqueness is in dialectical interaction with the universal. This tenet indicates that any human being can potentially create in a unique way.

Accepting the fact that creativity can be learned and acquired by a wide range of people has led to questions such as: How is a creative work produced? and What are the psychological characteristics of creative people? Human beings can perform many sorts of activities creatively, ranging from painting to cooking to studying the origin of the universe. A set of skills, talents, and motivations seems necessary, but, most of all, years of work and persistence activate creativity. In fact, underlying some of the most extraordinary inventions we can find ordinary thought processes, the ability to persevere in conducting lengthy and systematic laboratory studies, and the capacity to accept feedback and utilize it constructively.

Csikszentmihalyi (2000) proposed that creativity can be increased if one sets one's mind to doing so. He even suggested some means for consciously boosting creativity: trying to be surprised by something every day; trying to surprise one other person every day; trying to write down surprising experiences every day; spending time in creative settings that are stimulating; and so forth.

How Can One Promote Creative Action?

When I teach courses in the use of imagery in therapy, I often ask my students to try implementing a creative technique with their clients. They feel very self-conscious when they start out. The notion of attempting to create or develop something on their own seems very obscure to them. To encourage them, I explain that copying what someone else did, even if we adapt it to our own purposes, can have many deficiencies compared to developing something directly based on our own needs and knowledge. For example, by asking leading questions, I urged a social work student of mine to find a creative solution to his resistant adolescent client's refusal to cooperate in treatment.

For three weeks, the client would come to therapy, sit down, and refuse to talk. He also refused the therapist's offers to use drawings, games, or imagery. Then, out of despair, my student suggested going outside the clinic, and for the first time, the client agreed. They went to the backyard, and for the first time my student saw a sparkle in his client's eyes. From then on, therapy was conducted outside the clinic, in the garden, while weeding, planting, and watering the garden.

In what way is such a therapeutic decision creative? It is creative in the sense that the routine, regular way of treating this particular adolescent boy did not work. Even the traditionally creative psychotherapeutic methods – imagery, games, movement therapy – were rejected by the client. My student had to "think outside the box," by stepping outside of his routine and looking for something new and different that might help overcome this impasse. Focusing his thoughts on what would establish an effective relationship with the client rather than on what therapists and clients usually do together helped my student create real change.

Many thinkers, researchers, and artists have given considerable thought to the creative process. Linus Pauling, an American scientist who was awarded the Nobel Prize for Chemistry, was asked at a public lecture how one creates groundbreaking scientific theories. He replied that one must endeavor to come up with many ideas –much like "brainstorming" – and then discard the useless ones (Wikipedia, 2009b). Carlsen (1995) described creativity as a human process that transforms the bits and pieces of experience into new patterns of significance and personal understanding. In other words, it is the capacity to go beyond old solutions, to transcend conventions, and to step into the uncharted terrain of novel thoughts and ideas.

Ward (2003) claimed that empirical evidence proves that incubation aids in creative problem-solving, in that it enables "forgetting" of misleading clues. Absence of incubation may lead the problem-solver to become fixated on inappropriate problem-solving strategies. Ward's work disputes the earlier hypothesis that creative solutions to problems arise mysteriously from the unconscious mind while the conscious mind is occupied on other tasks. Thus, creative ideas do not fall from the sky or come from nowhere.

Graham Wallas and Richard Smith, in their work *Art of Thought* published in 1926, presented one of the first models of the creative process. They emphasized that, indeed, becoming creative is a process. First, one needs to make preparations for doing the work. This means focusing on a problem and exploring the problem's dimensions. Next comes the incubation stage, which enables one to internalize the problem into the unconscious mind and stay with it. Third, one needs to get intimate with the problem, and to gain a "feeling" that a solution is on its way. Only then is it time for illumination or insight, where the creative idea bursts forth from its preconscious processing into conscious awareness. Last is the stage of verification, where the idea is consciously verified, elaborated, and then applied.

Markova (1996) examined creativity as a process in which one uses symbolic language, like thinking kinesthetically by functioning through the hands, skin, and muscles. Rather than using the eyes and the ears, which convey words and sounds, such thinking enables utilization of pictures, colors, and sensations. This permits movement from the conscious to the subconscious to the unconscious and back again.

Many of the most important innovations of recent decades resulted from persistent hard work and from continuity with the past. Weisberg (1993) suggested that even the most creative work is based on what was done before, because people deal with new situations based on what they did in similar past situations. New knowledge, therefore, can extend past steps taken in a similar direction or can shift a similar step in a new direction.

As we can see, although creativity can be an outcome of perseverance and hard work based on past achievements, it also necessitates the courage or the wisdom to break old routines and pursue a new direction. A good example would be Alexander Fleming's invention of antibiotics, which resulted from work he had thrown into the garbage because he thought it was spoiled.

Who Are Creative People?

Many researchers have tried to describe the essence of creative people. Barron (1988) viewed the creative person as someone who challenges assumptions; someone who dares to question what most people accept as truth; who recognizes and creates new patterns, sees new paths, and makes new and unusual connections in bringing together ideas. This person takes risks and produces daring new ideas; seizes the chance to take advantage of the unexpected; and constructs networks to form associations between people for an exchange of ideas. Such a process-based definition suggests the uniquely human facility to take bits and pieces of experience and transform them into new meanings and inferences. This capacity enables the person to transcend prior solutions and limits and to open up to the here-and-now of novel conceptions and notions (Carlsen, 1995).

May's (1975) work added some personality features to the composite of creative people. Creative people must possess the courage to create, wisdom and integrity that triumph over ignorance and despair, and sufficient caring for the generations, their culture, and their world to help them overcome narcissistic preoccupations. In addition, Hurwich (1992) and LeClerc (1992) studied characteristics of older creative people and found that they were able to experience life as meaningful, hold optimistic perceptions of health, maintain close relationships, continue to grow, live in the present, and practice spiritual development.

Csikszentmihalyi (1966) claimed that, in order to be creative, a person must internalize the entire system that makes creativity possible. Therefore, creative people are remarkable in their ability to adapt to almost any situation and to make do with whatever is at hand to reach their goals. He viewed creative people as characterized by paradoxical attributes, along the lines of the following ten paradoxical dimensions. Creative people:

1. Possess great physical energy but also can be quiet and rest.
2. Tend to be smart, yet also naïve.
3. Can combine playfulness and discipline.
4. Alternate between imagination and fantasy on the one hand, and a rooted sense of reality on the other.
5. Harbor opposite tendencies on the extroversion–introversion continuum.
6. Are remarkably humble and proud simultaneously.
7. Can escape the rigid dichotomy of masculine versus feminine behavior.
8. Are rebellious and independent, but also internalize their cultural context.
9. Are often passionate about their work, but can also be objective about it.
10. Are open and sensitive, which exposes them to suffering and pain yet also to much enjoyment.

It seems that the main characteristics of creative people present a mix of paradoxical and diverse skills rather than excellence in any one extreme trait. This means that we human beings are complex creatures. Exposure to a diversity of activities, challenges, and emotions rather than focusing on one particular one enables a sense of development and creativity.

Creative Psychotherapy and Creative Psychotherapists

Psychotherapy is a complex profession subject to diverse trends. Therapists are consistently asked to accomplish two conflicting tasks. On the one hand, they must apply critical thinking and evidence-based practice that is well documented and empirically tested (Gambrill, 2007). On the other hand, they must be creative, innovative, and flexible (Ronen, 2003a, b). During the last decades, more appreciation has emerged for the merit of integrating into therapy not only methods that rely solely on well-documented data concerning the client's problem or demographic features, but also methods that capture the therapist's mind and soul. The shift between these two diverse trends is not easy to achieve and necessitates high-level professional skills. Using imagery and metaphors, therefore, is a good way to help the professional therapist flexibly apply creative modes of intervention within effective treatment settings, especially for conducting nonverbal, indirect therapy.

In the same vein, for therapists to be creative, apply novel techniques, and facilitate change using various modes, Sheldon (1987) suggested that they should always think and rethink and never accept things as they are. He blamed therapists for conducting "love relationships" with their clients instead of "business relationships." Those who fall in love stop asking questions and simply accept their love object as is, whereas in business relationships we question and reconsider, even when things are presented as facts. We wouldn't trade in our old car for a new one, adding significant money to the deal, just because we like the salesperson, for example. We may not even buy the same model of car we had before, although we were satisfied with it. Instead, we will check the market, compare prices, determine which new cars are available, and try to make the most informed, rational decision possible. Likewise, therapists should conduct a business relationship in the sense that they continually ask whether yesterday's decisions still hold up today, whether the specific techniques selected are adequate for the specific client right now.

Like Sheldon's (1987) recommendations for continual reevaluations in keeping with a "businesslike" approach, Safran and Segal (1990) proposed that therapists should be open and receptive to the patterns of the moment rather than attempting to impose their own will upon it. They emphasized the importance of therapists' open state of mind, as in the following Hindu notion: If one can suspend one's attempts to force things to happen and be receptive to the patterns of the moment, one will be able to respond to them completely, spontaneously, and creatively. This implies that spontaneity is a key component in applying creative psychotherapy. However, it is important to emphasize that spontaneity and creativity can only be applied by trained, skilled therapists who are expert in the process of therapy, in human change processes, and in appropriate means for helping clients change. Safran and Segal also warned therapists to avoid developing detailed and elaborate preconceived formulations, which could blind them to new developments taking place in the session itself. Instead, Safran and Segal recommended that therapists should devise only a very general formulation about the client's core cognitive processes, keeping this blueprint at a fairly formal level and revising it in an ongoing fashion in response to new, emerging information.

Applying good therapy means that the therapist is not a technician following prescribed rules and guidelines, but rather an artist who can implement diverse media flexibly in different contents (Ronen, 2003a). The therapist needs to empower the individual client by identifying his or her positive ability for change and conveying awareness of that ability to the client via whatever creative means is necessary. Harnessing the specific client's positive forces can be a good way to facilitate treatment outcomes, but it is also a modeling process for teaching clients to focus on their strengths rather than on their problems, and thereby to learn how to change their future functioning. A creative psychotherapist is one who can adapt the treatment process to the client's unique and individual needs, using the modes, strategies, and techniques that can best suit the client's way of thinking or designing a new intervention from which the client can learn and benefit the most. However, much of what we call creativity is intuitive and tacit (Mahoney, 2003). For example, when treatment with a 4 year old for chronic constipation, withholding, and toilet avoidance showed no progress, I instinctively asked the boy to come with me to the toilet:

As we were walking down the corridor toward the toilet, he clung to my trousers, and as I entered the door he paled, grabbed my leg, and held tight. Although his parents had assured me he had no fears of the toilet, and he had never mentioned it in the treatment room, outside the door of the toilet he said he was afraid of the monster who lived in there. After that breakthrough, we moved the treatment to the corridor outside the toilet. We started playing "as if," imagining that there was a monster there, talking about what the monster ate and how it lived. I brought bread to throw in the toilet to feed it. We fed it and called it, but it never came. So, we realized there was no monster, because monsters do not resist food. Gradually, he agreed to enter the toilet, take off his pants, and empty himself.

The creative responsibility for change is shared between the therapist who proposes new experiences, and the client who needs to try them (Ronen, 1997, 2003a). Creative modes of intervention are also fitting when trying to help unblock clients' resistance to growth and change. Mainly, creative therapy offers the power to restore the empathetic communication between therapist and client. Rothenberg (1988) suggested that by functioning creatively themselves, therapists thereby also initiate and facilitate their clients' engagement in creative work.

Creative intervention has traditionally been related to the use of art therapies – movement, drawing, music, sculpturing, and so forth – which have customarily arisen from specific needs that were difficult to meet through verbal treatment methods. Art therapies are usually seen as appropriate for expressing feelings that are difficult to articulate verbally, for accessing the interrelationships between soma and psyche (Schaefer, 1999), or when working with special populations for whom verbal conversation cannot suffice (e.g., young children, clients with autism, etc.). McNiff (1992) described art therapy as a therapy of soul, which extends to every life situation:

> Life does imitate art, as evidenced by how we change in response to images. One of the most well-known creative modes of psychotherapy is art therapy, which takes us into the primary sources of sacred and psychological experience if we allow the shamans and spirits to emerge once again from images and imaginations. (McNiff, 1992: 38)

Every art form is a dramatic enactment. Stories are continually being told, bodies are always in motion. Mahoney (2003: 182) claimed that "most techniques leave us the act of creation – the spontaneous generation of novel expression of life activity." Experience with art materials helps us to see how the flourishing imagination embraces diverse faculties. We learn to follow expression in its varied movements. In art therapy, the environment of the room transforms as clients begin to interact creatively with their pictures. When this shift occurs, the tone of feeling immediately changes, imagination enters the room, and an unconscious sense of sacred spectacle, affect, and support from others is established (McNiff, 1992). Like others, McNiff believes that creativity necessitates risks:

> Nothing will happen unless a person begins and risks failures, and there will be constant failures and restarts and changes of directions along the way, all of which are essential to the emergence of something fresh and surprising. (McNiff, 1992: 34)

McNiff suggested that embracing the soul's debased expression as manifested in the images of art and dreams involves a shift in consciousness that transforms psychotherapeutic values.

Carlsen (1995) proposed that a creative therapist is one who is called on to compare and contrast the differing ways in which a client can make the world cohere, rather than one who avoids this demand. The task is to help clients create order out of personal chaos; that is, to help them transform personal confusion and pain into a more meaningful, fulfilling life plan. She added that the challenge for psychotherapy is to encourage creative enjoyment of the questions and the growing, and to avoid any fixed conclusions about what life is about. Therapists can point clients toward the creative preparations, incubations, illuminations, and verifications that can lead to new insights that interrupt and transform old systems of meaning (Langley & Jones, 1988).

As we saw in Chapter 2, Mahoney (1991, 1995) described creative psychotherapists as helping clients explore and experience themselves and the world in different ways. These new ways challenge ordinary, familiar patterns and consolidate embodiment, emotion, feeling, sensing, and thinking into one entity. He claimed that the creative psychotherapist views each client as unique, understands that the particulars of each life are never the same as another, and acts flexibly in response to the client, thus modeling the creation of novelty. Mahoney (2003: 182) stated:

> Novelty, once again, is necessary for all learning and development, and the best way to teach clients how to risk new experiences is for the therapist to do just that in front of their client's very eyes and when they may least expect it.

There are many ways to elicit creativity in therapy in light of all these principles for creative modes of intervention and the characteristics of creative psychotherapists. There are also many books addressing art therapy, music therapy, movement therapy, and so forth, using drawing and sculpting and other media as creative modes of therapy. The focus of the present book, however, is using imagery in therapy as a promising springboard for eliciting creativity among therapists and clients. Nevertheless, it should be noted that imagery is not necessarily a creative process of therapy.

Noncreative Imagery in Therapy

Both in therapy in general and in CBT in particular, imagery is often employed in a manner that is not especially creative, but rather is very similar to other modes of therapy. Like other techniques such as redefinition, cognitive restructuring, role play, or self-talk, imagery can be used very effectively in a structured, repeated way to achieve well-defined goals, even if those applications are not creative. For example, simple imagery exercises may be utilized in therapy to help a client recall some recent memories, such as simply imagining that it is morning and she is eating her regular breakfast meal (e.g., "Focus on your plate and describe what you are eating"). There is nothing new, novel, or different in imagining what she ate. Also, there is nothing artistic about this way of applying an imagery exercise.

Another example of noncreative imagery would be assisting clients in overcoming test anxiety (see Chapter 15). We can ask clients to close their eyes, see their notebook in front of them, and try to focus on what is written there, to recall the material they studied. This type of imagery can be very fruitful in assisting clients to remember materials they have learned despite their anxiety, but it is not creative.

Similarly, when desensitization is employed to help clients overcome a fear of dogs, imagery can be an effective technique, but that does not signify that it was a creative mode of intervention. A dog desensitization process could start with the client imagining himself walking down the street hearing a dog in one of the nearby houses, could continue with the client imagining himself getting closer to the dog, and eventually the client would imagine even holding the dog.

Thus, an exercise can be helpful but not creative. It can be creative but not helpful. It can use imagery but not be creative. Or it can encompass all of these components and be imagery that is both creative and helpful.

Techniques to Facilitate Therapists' Creativity

Inasmuch as nowadays we believe that creativity can be learned rather than being inborn, and that creative intervention can facilitate client change, it is important to train therapists in various techniques for achieving creative thinking. The first step in creative thinking is to try to flow, to leave traditional thinking behind and try to think differently. Creative thought is assumed to involve attacking a problem from a new direction, which implies cognitive flexibility (Weisberg, 1993). Therefore, an important step toward creativity is the phase of brainstorming, which includes ruling out criticism, welcoming freewheeling, wanting quantity, and improving and complementing suggestions (Weisberg, 1993), as explained in more detail below. Weisberg presented a table of methods for increasing creativity, such as making lists, questioning assumptions, listing attributes, producing analogies, allowing for incubation, and problem-solving. Other guides for creativity include skills such as breaking out of old patterns or ways of thinking, keeping options open, suspending judgment, thinking broadly, departing from scripts, taking fresh perspectives, and using tricks. Weisberg offered four basic rules to govern any brainstorming session:

1. *Criticism is ruled out.* First one must raise any and all ideas that come to mind, without trying to judge them or decide if they are good enough. Criticism can kill any good creative application, and should not take place at the beginning of the process. Rather, criticism should be applied only once the need arises to make decisions about applications of the ideas raised.
2. *Freewheeling is welcomed.* Weisberg suggested that it is easier to tame down than to think up; hence, as many ideas that are as wild as possible should be elicited.
3. *Quantity is wanted.* More people means that more ideas are generated, and thus the more chances there are of finding a good idea. Furthermore, gathering people who differ socially, culturally, demographically, occupationally, or in other characteristics increases the likelihood of generating a larger quantity of ideas.
4. *Combination and improvement are sought.* It is sometimes easier for people to reflect on how to better somebody else's idea than to elicit their own new ideas. So, while trying to elicit creativity, address both options. Ask and invite new ideas but also comment and reflect on others' ideas, trying to improve and enlarge them.

In light of his ten paradoxical characteristics of creative people (see above), Csikszentmihalyi (1966) proposed that training in the excessive investment of attention to selfish goals could enhance personal creativity and energy. First, nobody can be creative while suffering from hunger, cold, or pain. Second, one needs to wake up every morning anticipating a specific goal. If people do things right, these goals can become enjoyable. Habits, a fixed schedule, and discipline should thus protect creativity. As mentioned above, Csikszentmihalyi emphasized, for example, the importance of trying to be surprised by something every day, as well as trying to surprise someone else daily, and of keeping records of these surprises. He also focused on the importance of "flow" for increasing happiness. Another suggestion was to look for personality traits and try to shift between paradoxical ones, such as openness and closedness.

Many methods of teaching creativity have been developed over the years. It is beyond the scope of this book to describe in detail all of the possible means for improving creativity. However, I do hope that I have at least been able to present the flavor and significance of creativity and the creative process as an important and integral part of therapy. The case studies presented throughout this book illustrate how creative thinking can be incorporated into clients' CBT to design the most effective interventions for change.

Summary

Creativity in this book relates to both therapists and to clients. Therapists are asked to be attentive to clients, to be creative, to be flexible in their thinking, and to elicit different ways for facilitating clients' change processes. Clients are asked to be creative in letting themselves use different modes, skills, and techniques such as play, paint, sculpture, imagery, and so forth, and in mobilizing all of these in order to learn and change.

I propose that a good therapist must be a creative one, who can conduct classic, traditional therapies when these meet the client's best interests, but who can also be creative when needed and who continuously seeks out, invents, and finds new ways to facilitate change. This is not merely for the sake of doing something novel, but to harness the positive power of his or her own capabilities for the best interests of the client.

While in the past we saw creativity as essential for artists, we are now aware of the important contribution of creativity in all areas of life. We now expect people to be creative in whatever they do: whether they cook, bake, write, sell, research, raise children, or sculpt. We believe that people should be creative employees, creative students, creative lecturers, creative parents, and creative therapists.

Creativity helps people look for new alternatives, discovering the best in themselves and leading to more effective solutions.

Practice: Guidelines for Activating One's Creativity

- Take 20 minutes for yourself, without anyone around, and let yourself relax by practicing any method you choose – yoga, meditation, or relaxation.
- When terminating the exercise, think of three positive things about your past 24 hours, regarding yourself, your interaction with other people, your environment. Are these positive emotions and interactions that you recall familiar to you? Is there a way to feel things differently or do things differently, not routinely?
- Spend a few moments each day thinking about your daily routine, considering such incidents as going to work, preparing food, taking a shower, doing shopping, working with your staff, talking to people, and so forth. How happy are you with your daily routine? Can you also invent something new or creative in that routine?
- Ask yourself: If I knew I would have to do the same things in the same routine over and over again for the next 100 years, would I continue doing them?
  - If the answer is yes, then reinforce yourself for what you are doing.
  - If the answer is no, then take a good look at yourself and think: What would I do differently?
- Try to do one thing differently every day. Start from small things like putting on your clothes in a different sequence, arranging your food in another way, using a different route to get to work, talking to people differently or to different people than usual.
- Reflect on these small changes by looking at your life again. Does it look the same? Does the change have any meaning? Does it make you feel different?
  - If the changes are perceptible and meaningful, continue doing those things you enjoy and try to maintain them.
  - If not, see what other changes you can make.
- Measure your happiness every day on a scale of 1 (totally unhappy) to 10 (totally happy), and see if you can bring a happier atmosphere into your life. Is there anything new, different, or creative you can add to increase your happiness?

5

Applying Developmental CBT
with Children

The main core of this book refers to applications of imagery therapy with adults. Nonetheless, imagery plays a unique role in therapy with children, warranting some specialized attention and explanation.

Adults need to be taught how to use imagery, whereas every child naturally uses the language of imagery. Children imagine that their toys are alive and communicate with them, talk to themselves, and play with imaginary friends. In fact, during healthy childhood development, children must learn to use imagery to internalize their self-talk. This natural accessibility to imagery among children makes it an excellent therapeutic method for this population.

This chapter presents unique attributes of childhood that therapists should consider when designing children's imagery therapy, especially CBT. Throughout the book I add brief instructions on adapting specific techniques to children, and in Part IV I devote a separate chapter to imagery therapy with children.

The Unique Nature of Childhood

Child therapy differs from adult therapy in many respects. One major difference stems from the very nature of childhood development. Children are continually "moving targets," continuously changing. Any parent can easily bear witness to the challenge involved in "keeping up" with children's often surprising new behaviors and thought patterns, which suddenly seem to appear as children enter new developmental stages; and, just as importantly, the subtle changes that children naturally reveal over time, necessitating adjustments from the family.

These dynamic developmental phenomena evolving during childhood hold important implications for therapy. Very often, what seems to be a problem at one point in time spontaneously disappears without any intervention. As far back as the 1960s, Levitt (1963) found an approximate 73% improvement rate among children who did not receive treatment. On beginning therapy, parents

The Positive Power of Imagery: Harnessing Client Imagination in CBT and Related Therapies, First Edition. Tammie Ronen. © 2011 Tammie Ronen. Published 2011 by John Wiley & Sons, Ltd.

often claim that the original problem reported during the assessment or intake period had already resolved itself but another problem suddenly arose in its stead. Thus, the very fact that children continuously and rapidly change as they grow frequently complicates the diagnostic and assessment process (Schaefer, 1999; Schaffer, 1990). Child therapists face difficulties in deciding about the need for any therapy whatsoever, or the need to target specific referred problems. Such decisions should be based not only on general knowledge regarding spontaneous recovery for the specific difficulty area, but also on the pace and development of the specific child's problem hitherto: What is the probability of the problem disappearing? Will it remain stable, improve, or worsen?

With children, it is insufficient and even inadvisable to look merely at their problems or symptoms as a means for assessing the severity of their distress. For one, different children may present the same symptoms for different reasons. For example, crying, anxiety, and fear of separation may be one girl's way of keeping her parents nearby, one boy's way of expressing fear of darkness at night, and another child's response to being abused. We therefore need to "look beyond the problem" to assess and treat children. An excellent way to "see beyond the disorder" is also to see beyond words, and therefore techniques such as metaphors and imagery come into play as an invaluable part of assessment and intervention.

Children's actions and behaviors stem from complex interactions between their developmental status, family processes, environmental influences, and individual characteristics (Kazdin, 1988, 2000; Ronen, 1997). Thus, child therapists must unravel and make sense of a host of developmental and environmental complexities that could affect therapy, beyond the regular issues – the referred problem and the client. The metaphor of a puzzle can describe child therapy. Each puzzle piece derives from a different area, such as sociology of childhood, developmental psychology, behavioral norms, family processes, and so on. Only the correct combination of all those pieces can result in optimal therapy for children.

An important piece of the puzzle for child therapists must always be supporting the child's motivation to begin therapy and to collaborate with the therapeutic process. Unlike adults, children have an immature ability to conceptualize time, delay gratification, and cope with short-term difficulties in order to reap long-term benefits. Consequently, children simply refuse to continue to cooperate in therapy if they fail to find the experience interesting and beneficial. Therapists, therefore, must consistently direct their knowledge and techniques toward arousing children's curiosity, ambition, and challenge. In this regard, I suggest that therapists who treat children need to be artistic – in their capacity to be flexible, creative, and interesting. Such "artistic" attributes in therapists can challenge children to remain and participate fully in treatment (Ronen, 1997, 2003a, b). Therapists who work well with children demonstrate an intrinsic talent that manifests itself in liking and enjoying children and in a natural affinity for understanding and creatively communicating with young minds and spirits. Of course, child therapists also clearly need to be scientists, who have also mastered a range of different strategies and methods within verbal and nonverbal therapy, in order to translate diverse concepts and techniques successfully to each child's personal level of understanding and to foster cooperation, adherence, and compliance.

Many factors seem to mediate children's coping with their problems, including age, gender, and individual differences. Research into problematic childhood behaviors has not yet provided a solid body of evidence-based outcome studies that sufficiently addresses these factors. For example, most of the 230 different techniques for treating children identified by Kazdin's (1988, 2000; Kazdin & Weisz, 2003) meta-analysis were never empirically investigated, and only a few were found effective. Schaffer (1990: 21) suggested that

> the view of childhood will need to be modified from time to time as new findings are uncovered but [it] is not dependent on any one specific study or set of studies and instead reflects the general thrust of knowledge currently available about children's development.

Characteristics of Childhood Disorders

Children's disorders relate to all areas of life, starting at a young age with educational problems that involve eating, toileting, sleep, and discipline, or with developmental problems such as pervasive developmental disorder, attention deficit/hyperactivity disorder, Asperger syndrome, autism, and so on. Childhood disorders may also concern emotional problems such as anxiety, depression, and stress, or social problems such as loneliness and social phobia (Ronen, 2007).

Although many childhood problems naturally disappear, they deserve assessment and, if necessary, treatment, because they comprise a critical predictor of adult mental health problems (Kazdin, 1993). Thus, some problems disappear, but others may develop into problems in adulthood.

Four different goals were identified regarding children's disorders (Mash & Terdal, 1988; Ronen, 1997): decreasing unwanted behaviors, increasing desired behaviors, removing anxieties, and facilitating development. Each of these aims targets one of the four main groups of children commonly referred for treatment.

The first group of childhood disorders relates to acting-out, externalizing problems such as aggressiveness, delinquency, negativism, disobedience, hyperactivity, or impulsivity (Durlak, Fuhrman, & Lampman, 1991; Kazdin, 2000; Kendall, 2006). Such children act without thinking or planning and lack careful information-processing. They have difficulty tolerating frustration, delaying gratification, and keeping attention on target (Barkley, 1997; Kazdin, 2000; Kendall, 1993, 2006; Kendall & Braswell, 1993; Ronen, 1997, 2003a). Therapy for these children should aim to decrease their undesired behaviors (Achenbach, 1985; Mash & Terdal, 1988) by training them in problem-solving skills and changing their impulsive thinking and behavior.

The second group has received less attention in the literature: children referred for acting-in, internalizing problems such as anxiety, depression, somatic complaints, and social loneliness. These disorders' main feature comprises fear of new and unknown experiences and of disturbing or disconcerting emotions, leading to avoidant behaviors. Characterized by emotional dysfunction, these children demonstrate low self-confidence, self-acceptance, and self-esteem. Kendall

(1993, 2006) pinpointed such children's distorted thinking, where they miscon-strue and misconceive social situations. Thus, interventions with these children should aim to increase specific desired behaviors – social skills, self-concept, self-evaluation, self-confidence – by challenging them to do more. The focus lies in experiencing and practicing, using mindfulness techniques, learning self-acceptance, and identifying their strengths and virtues (Achenbach, 1985; Mash & Terdal, 1988).

The third type – children suffering from anxiety – demonstrates avoidance and regression caused by fears, anxieties, and trauma. Unlike the second group, these children's difficulties do not stem from overly high expectations, low self-evaluations, and distorted thoughts, but rather from overwhelmingly anxious feelings. In therapy, they need to acquire a wider repertoire of coping skills and to practice exposure assignments for trying out new experiences (Kendall, 2006; Kendall *et al.*, 2008).

For the last group of children, whose development needs to be facilitated due to their immaturity, treatment should promote the acquisition of new skills such as refraining from or ceasing to cry, restraining oneself in various situations, or taking on responsibilities. Treatment for this group should offer practice in new tasks and provide new models for change, both for the children themselves and for their environments.

In sum, knowing the aim of therapy with a specific child in light of the referred problems will enable better selection of intervention settings and techniques.

CBT with Children as Distinct from CBT with Adults

As applications of CBT with children have progressed, the field has developed differently from that of adults. CBT with children has become an umbrella term for different treatment techniques offered in many different sequences and per-mutations. CBT applications thus far have not adequately converged to provide a comprehensive compilation of assessment and treatment techniques address-ing multiple components of prevalent childhood disorders such as attention-deficit/hyperactivity or anxiety disorders.

Research evidence suggests that CBT comprises an effective treatment for children with externalizing behavior problems such as disruptive, attention, and conduct disorders (Kazdin, 1988, 2000, 2005; Kendall, 1993, 2006; Kendall & Braswell, 1993; Southam-Gerow & Kendall, 2000) and with inter-nalizing problems such as anxiety, depression, and fears (Harrington *et al.*, 1998; Kendall *et al.*, 2008; Southam-Gerow & Kendall, 2000). However, Durlak, Fuhrman, and Lampman (1991) proposed that CBT is mainly effective with children 11 years and over. Grave and Blissett (2004) recently asked whether young children possess the needed skills to benefit from CBT.

As I have suggested previously (Ronen, 1997, 2003b), I propose that rather than asking whether children can benefit from CBT, we should ask: How best can CBT be adapted to render the needed benefits for various children? What is the most effective CBT application with children of different ages, problems, and environments? Along the same lines, the question asked here is not whether children can be treated by using imagery, but rather how children can best benefit from imagery therapy applications.

Applying CBT with Children

The dynamic nature of childhood and adolescence necessitates treatment flexibility, adjustment, and adaptation. CBT with children, adolescents, and families must adapt basic cognitive-behavioral principles to children's developmental needs and abilities (Herbert, 2002; Kazdin, 2000; Kendall, 1993, 2006; Ronen, 2007, 2008). Just like adults, children can be active partners in decision making concerning the therapy's aims, the establishment of criteria for target behaviors, and the kinds of techniques to be used (Ronen, 1998a,b). They can understand the rationale underlying needed techniques for behavior change and can take responsibility for their practice and application.

Children can be partners for learning if material is explained in simple, concrete words they can understand (Ronen, 1997). Children who don't understand terms such as schemata or unmediated thoughts should nevertheless be able to address all the needed aspects of these concepts if therapists explain them simply, as in the following examples:

- *Automatic behavior*. Therapists can teach children that the brain sends commands to the body just like military commanders send commands to their troops. This metaphor can guide children in pinpointing specific commands their brain is sending them (e.g., to disrupt class, to fear elevators), followed by attempts to learn how to change those commands.
- *Self-assessing behavior change*. Therapists can use a ladder, asking children to observe how high they have climbed since starting therapy.
- *Changing automatic thoughts*. Using a river metaphor, therapists can say that the river is now flowing in one direction, but we want to change its flow to the other direction, asking children to generate ideas about how this could be accomplished (e.g., building dams).
- *Predicting outcomes*. Therapists can ask children to imagine that a magician could fulfill their wish to become something or someone different: What/who would they like to become?
- *Change processes*. Therapists can use the metaphor of building a house to help children understand how change requires many steps and levels of new skills.
- *The need for training and practice*. Talking about the need to train, practice, and work toward improving athletic, skateboarding, or rollerblading skills provides apt metaphors for practicing and training in social skills.

Over the last decade, impressive progress has occurred in CBT applications with children, resulting from several trends. First, social processes elicited interest in children's abuse, neglect, and distress, which, in turn, triggered interest in developing effective interventions. Concurrently, research outcomes pinpointed the lasting effects of childhood disorders such as loneliness, depression, and aggression, and their impact on adults' social adaptation. Also, the notion of linking cognitive, emotional, social, and developmental components with information-processing models and with the basics of adult CBT permitted the formation of a unified theoretical framework for working with children. Another important development consisted of the emergence of studies about emotions and about the role of therapeutic relationships, which are crucial for child therapy. All of these trends, together with the recent call for evidence-based therapy and the emphasis on outcome studies, goal-directed treatment, and data-based knowledge, have enabled new and groundbreaking applications of CBT with children (Thyer & Kazi, 2004).

Thus, accepting that CBT can certainly be made effective for children, we return to the question of identifying the most effective ways to apply CBT with children of different ages, problems, and environments. To this end, next I present developmental components to consider when adapting therapy to children.

Considering Developmental Components

Over the course of their development, children undergo many changes in how they think, feel, and behave. Concurrently, familial, social, and cultural norms within children's immediate environment also influence how they behave and how they may benefit from intervention. Theoretical understanding and available basic research on development indicate that specific processes and opportunities may emerge at different ages and stages of development, and differentially for boys and girls. These occur in domains such as cognitive comprehension, exposure to new experiences, establishing relationships, and perceiving and expressing emotions (Davies, 1999; Herbert, 2002; Kazdin, 1993; Ronen, 1997). Research on cognitive development, peer influence, and transition periods (e.g., transferring schools) suggests that children need different sorts of interventions to achieve change (Kazdin, 1993, 2000).

Therefore, adaptation of CBT to children must consider several components: cognitive development (age and gender), information processing, language acquisition, emotional and social development, and familial components.

Cognitive components

The consideration of cognitive development is crucial for understanding and treating childhood disorders (Crick & Dodge, 1994; Davies, 1999; Kazdin, 1988; Shirk & Russell, 1996) and plays an integral role in applying imagery therapy. For some researchers, such as Jean Piaget (1969, 1977), children's ability to change is a matter of cognitive development. Those who rely on Piaget's theory have focused on age as the most important component in determining children's capabilities and functioning, with stages of development as the main window into children's ability to understand the world. Others, such as Lev Vygotsky (1962), agree that age is essential for change, but underscore the influence of environment, especially as responsible for learning processes related to language development, which is crucial for human communication and interaction. Bandura (1969) and his followers chiefly highlight the role of social learning and social influences in determining children's development. This view focuses on society's different expectations of children that elicit various demands and reinforce specific behaviors; thus, society's behavior influences how children develop.

Piaget is the most influential researcher in children's cognitive development. He claimed that intellectual development proceeds in a stepwise, ordered manner in response to experiences (Piaget, 1969, 1977). Individual differences and the social and physical environment all influence the age at which children achieve certain cognitive activities, but not their order or content. Specific age is less important than the order and progress of learning (Vasta, Haith, & Miller, 1995). For example, Piaget emphasized that children cannot possibly perform "concrete" operations before undergoing some sensorimotor preparation. Learning cannot change skills' order but can facilitate their acquisition. Piaget defined four major stages of cognitive development enabling classifications of children's thinking and charting of their progress: sensorimotor, preoperational, concrete operational, and formal operations.

The identification of children's cognitive skill level is therefore imperative for CBT therapists to adapt therapy to children's developmental needs (Ronen, 1997, 2006, 2007, 2008).

Age as a mediator in child therapy

Age is inseparable from cognitive stage, although children mature differently, revealing developmental gaps. Age is a crucial criterion in determining when a behavior previously considered normal becomes maladaptive. For example, every infant and toddler urinates while sleeping, but bedwetting becomes a problem if it continues after age 4 or 5 years. Likewise, every infant cries at night and suffers from nightmares, but sleep problems only become problematic if persisting into childhood. The same goes for fear of separation, lack of self-control, aggression, and shyness – natural behaviors during the first three years of life but problematic if still exhibited at age 6. As children grow, they are gradually expected to gain control of the bladder; learn that their parents always return and stop crying when parents leave; gain self-control and self-evaluation skills; develop assertiveness; and learn to communicate and negotiate verbally instead of crying. However, dysfunctional behavior cannot be assessed solely in relation to chronological age. One can often expect discrepancies between a child's chronological, emotional, cognitive, and behavioral ages (Sahler & McAnarney, 1981). Such incongruities create a challenge for the therapist attempting to assess and diagnose an individual child referred for therapy.

For example, younger children exhibit limited appreciation of time; therefore, distant goals and long-term benefits seem incomprehensible, whereas short-term gratification and displeasure are vivid in comparison, shaping the design of treatment objectives. Older children have already acquired abstract thinking; therefore, they can understand concepts such as changing automatic thoughts into mediated ones and practice this skill, whereas younger children necessitate other means, such as metaphors and simple explanations.

Age is crucial for the entire process of therapeutic planning and delivery, starting from the decision as to whether or not to treat a child, proceeding with the decision about who should be treated, and continuing with the selection of the treatment method. Children develop different roles at each childhood age/stage, requiring a specific treatment plan best suited to facilitating the new roles emerging then (Forehand & Weirson, 1993). For example, when children are young and dependent on caregivers, therapy usually has primary prevention aims (i.e., preventing future risk and reducing disorders' incidence; Graham, 1994) and comprises counseling and supervising parents in educating and rearing their children. As children start school, therapy has secondary prevention aims (i.e., educational-therapeutic assignments that prevent existing problems from worsening and reduce disorders' duration; Graham, 1994) and addresses children within their natural environments (parents, teachers, friends). Approaching adolescence, therapy has tertiary prevention aims (i.e., solving an already existing problem, preventing future risks, and imparting skills for decreasing its frequency) and addresses the children themselves. In adolescence, therapy covers rehabilitative activities and reduces the disability arising from an established disorder (Graham, 1994).

Outcomes suggest that different CBT techniques be considered for children of different ages. Young children can enjoy more behavioral or cognitive techniques based on simple, concrete instructions (such as self-talk). Older children can benefit more from cognitive therapy techniques like changing automatic thoughts, rational analysis, and cognitive restructuring.

Gender as a mediator in child therapy

Basic cognitive and social learning research indicates that biological elements (genes, hormones) set the process of sex differentiation into motion, but that environmental conditions, information-processing models, and parental influences maintain this process and lead to gender roles (Vasta, Haith, & Miller, 1995). Several factors may explain gender differences, such as social norms or variations in maturation processes. On the one hand, girls as a group mature more quickly than boys, so one can expect fewer disorders with an important developmental component among them. On the other hand, role-taking influences girls by allowing them to talk more freely about anxieties and fears than do boys; hence, anxiety reports are usually higher among girls (Kazdin, 1988, 2000; Ronen, 2008).

Gender influences development and has an impact on how behavioral dysfunction develops as well as how therapists assess behaviors and treat them. For example, in general, patterns of play and social relations differ between boys and girls (Raviv *et al.*, 1990). Girls are tied more to one or two significant friends of their own age and sex, while boys play in large, same-sex groups. Girls find it more difficult to make new friends than do boys. Also, aggression may appear in young boys' play but is less frequent in young girls. Thus, sex mediates social relationships, predicts social adjustment to new environments to some degree (Raviv *et al.*, 1990), and contributes to assessment and intervention processes.

Gender's influence increases as children enter the adolescent stage, acquiring specific gender roles; studies pinpoint greater differences between the sexes as children mature. For example, in research on moving to a new house, girls reported more stress (loneliness feelings, sadness, confusion) compared to boys (Raviv *et al.*, 1990).

The CBT approach to gender-role development focuses not so much on sociobiological differences between sexes as on the gender schemata that each child develops. Children's attributions of specific behaviors to only one sex (e.g., girls don't usually play football) may influence therapists' choices of technique (e.g., selecting football game metaphors to teach boys how to assess the skills needed for success, but preferring other metaphors for girls who hold this attribution about football). Basically there are "masculine," "feminine," and "androgynous" schemata, each of which can be held by children regardless of their gender. "Androgynous" schemata may be most adaptive to the norms and mores of Western society, because they enable children to accept both "feminine" and "masculine" parts of their personality. The role of the CBT therapist is to discover children's gender schemata and help them develop healthy and functional gender schemata.

The role of information processing

The information-processing approach has become very useful in guiding developmental and clinical psychologists' research on children's problem-solving, memory, reading, and other cognitive processes. Findings from numerous studies linked specific aspects of processing cues with specific behaviors such as aggression (Crick & Dodge, 1994) or social skill deficits (Dodge *et al.*, 1986; Waldman, 1996). However, social information-processing models posit that such relations are overly simplistic, contending that every action involves multiple processing operations. In line with such models, studies highlighted multiple processing steps to predict behavior (Dodge & Price, 1994).

Research underscored that the way in which children process information has a critical impact not only on how they behave but also on how they think and feel, and therefore must comprise a main feature in intervention design (Crick & Dodge, 1994). CBT therapists should therefore gain knowledge on how children process information at various ages, to enhance therapists' comprehension of children's normal behavior and maladjustment.

Dodge's model of social information processing contains four basic steps (Crick & Dodge, 1994; Dodge & Pettit, 2003): (i) encoding the information that is gathered; (ii) representing this information and interpreting it; (iii) looking for possible responses to the situation at hand; and (iv) selecting a response. That is, children focus on and encode particular cues in a social situation; then, using these cues, they construct interpretations of the situation; then, they access possible responses to the situation from long-term memory, evaluate those responses, and select the most favorable one for enactment. The four-step model presumes that children possess limited capabilities and past experiences while facing a social situation (Crick & Dodge, 1994).

This model successfully predicted children's social adjustment and may contribute considerably to understanding how cognitive development and language acquisition influence children's behavior (Ronen, 2007, 2008).

Acquisition of language skills

In contrast to Piaget (1969, 1977), who emphasized the individual child's constructs and knowledge, developed through actions, as the main component enacting on the child's world, Vygotsky (1962) viewed language as most crucial for development. Vygotsky claimed that children's continual interaction with the environment is reflected in and mediated by language development (Cole & Wertsch, 2005). For many years, linguistic development was widely studied in child cognitive development research (Casasola & Cohen, 2000; Oller, Cobo-Lewis, & Eilers, 1998).

Vygotsky's (1962) and Luria's (1961) theories explain how language evolves and how in time children acquire language skills. Mischel (1973) described children's ability to shift from being directed by adult external control to individual internal control as a matter of internalizing self-talk. Children move from talking aloud to internal self-talk, which actually constitutes a state of self-control that enables them to use cognitive thinking, stop automatic negative thoughts, and start using mediated dialogue (Ronen, 1997). Thus, the ability to use language, the skills to interpret, understand, and accept what others say as well as the child's ability to express him or herself, are major and necessary skills for applying therapy with children.

Emotional development

Recent years have brought a dramatic increase in interest in emotions' role for therapy in general, and for CBT in particular. Emotions are no longer considered a "byproduct" or "outcome" of the mainstays of CBT; that is, of cognitions or behaviors. Rather, emotions are increasingly considered a necessary and integral human function. For instance, until recently CBT therapists generally focused on teaching aggressive children to control behaviors such as hitting (e.g., using self-talk or imagination), but therapy did not usually focus on feelings of frustration, anger, and helplessness that underlie and elicit aggressiveness. More and more, today's therapists are integrating affects into treatment plans.

Emotions play a major role in childhood disorders' development, maintenance, and resolution (Crick & Dodge, 1994; Power & Dalgleish, 1997; Wells, 2000). Power and Dalgleish (1997) emphasized that emotional disorders relate to the interaction between life events and cognitive features such as self-esteem.

Treating emotions necessitates, first of all, assessment of emotional skills that children possess, emotional skills that children lack, and means for enhancing the acquisitions of the skills that are lacking. Inasmuch as emotions are not changed by merely talking about them with children, imagery and metaphors encompass a major tool for treating feelings.

Children are frequently referred for psychotherapy because of problems with emotions, and many childhood disorders can be viewed as involving difficulties with the experience, expression, or regulation of affects (Shirk & Russell, 1996). To help children cope with, experience, and express emotions, therapists should understand emotions' role in general behavior and in skill acquisition, maintenance, and change processes. Through development, children are increasingly able to demonstrate signs of emotions, talk about emotions, comprehend emotional constructs, understand situations that elicit emotions, induce emotions in themselves and others, recognize emotional cues, and integrate successive or simultaneous emotions (Terwogt & Olthof, 1989).

The emergence of emotional expression is primarily guided by biological processes, but is subsequently tied to cognitive learning and influenced by social environments (i.e., learned through modeling and reinforcement processes). Like other modes of development (age, gender development, and cognitive development), emotions also develop in stages, from diffuse, intense emotional states in infancy, to a rudimentary awareness and discernment of some affects, to a capacity to regulate some emotions, and gradually to a more mature differentiation between subtleties in affective experience and increased levels of control.

Emotions are elicited through the development of an attachment to significant figures from the first few months of life; through the second year when specific attachment bonds become clearest and fear begins to emerge as a dominant emotion, including wariness of strangers and protests at separation; and up to the age of 11 years and higher, when children are already more likely to attribute emotional arousal to internal causes rather than to external events (Thompson, 1989). Thus, with growing age, children not only develop a broader range of emotional concepts, but also increasingly appreciate the psychological dimensions of emotional experience, which helps them interpret their own emotional experiences in more sophisticated ways. This new perceptiveness fosters more accurate interpretations of the direct emotional displays of others and increases children's competence at inferring emotions in others when direct cues are lacking (Thompson, 1989).

Studies have also illuminated how emotions that emerge early begin to grow in sophistication and scope throughout the childhood years, contributing to knowledge about others and oneself (Thompson, 1989). Before children gain the ability to feel empathy for others, it is difficult to train them in cognitive techniques involving problem solving or checking alternative solutions, which necessitate discerning what others feel and what others might do. Helping the child understand emotions is a vital part of CBT, involving the identification of internal cues, differentiating between thoughts and emotions, and learning how emotions elicit behavior.

The way children accept and understand others' emotional cues and their own emotional responses can be a primary impetus for children's behaviors toward their peers. The fact that children's behavioral responses (e.g., anger, aggressiveness, patience) are directed by their emotions highlights the important role of treatment in teaching children to understand their emotional responses as a cue for learning about their internal thoughts, sensations, and wishes. Socialization aims to modify the fixed relations between situations and children's emotional reactions to those situations, by enhancing children's sensitivity to internal stimuli (Terwogt & Olthof, 1989). In this way, emotions can be simulated, and emotional reactions can be withheld or acted out more or less deliberately in keeping with social mores and expectations.

Social development

Schaffer (1990) emphasized that social development stems from early attachment, self-awareness (self-concept, self-esteem, self-emotion), and socialization with parents, siblings, and environment. Social development therefore encompasses the acquisition of skills relating to *behaviors* (participating in the environment and learning social competencies), skills relating to *thoughts* (accepting and understanding social norms and rules, and thinking it is important to be part of society; comprehending what another person may be feeling or thinking), and skills relating to *emotions* (feelings of belonging, empathy). Social experiences and social interactions critically influence children's ability to become an integral part of society and to develop self-concept, self-identity, and self-control (Harter, 1983; Ronen, 2003a).

CBT relates to social skills, prosocial values, positive communication, self-efficacy, and social efficacy as crucial for human adjustment to society (Bandura *et al.*, 2001; Gambrill & Richey, 1988; McGinnis & Goldstein, 1997). Studies also highlighted social support as an important resource for children's coping with life distress (Baumeister, 1999; Schaffer, 1990).

Social development is an outcome of children's process of learning how to be social, how to take others' perspectives into account, and how to acquire social skills and prosocial behaviors and values. Experience encompasses a major part of this process. New circumstances and developmental changes contribute to the need to develop social abilities (Davies, 1999).

Familial components

Whenever a child is concerned, parents or caregivers must be involved. CBT has always focused on treating children within their natural environment (Bandura, 1997). Parents play a vital role in the development, continuation, and resolution of their children's disorders. The interpersonal role of the child's pathology is inseparable from the familial influence that helped elicit this pathology. Research has underscored this link between parents' problems and those of their children (Kazdin, 1988, 2000). This link manifests itself not only in terms of parents' history and frequency of disorders, but also their belief systems and behavioral development. Research outcomes, for example, presented a correlation between parents' self-control and children's self-control, and also between parents' lack of self-control and children's high frequency of disorders.

Among their other roles, parents are not only responsible for children's learning and normal development, but are also important change agents, facilitating children's ability to change (Webster-Stratton, 1993, 1994). Parents act as role models and direct trainers, both of which hold significant implications for children's skills acquisition (Webster-Stratton, 1993, 1994).

At the youngest ages, children are more affected by their immediate environment, namely their parents. As children grow, external events become more and more influential, reflecting children's burgeoning interest in their surroundings. The child and the child's experiences should therefore be conceptualized by the therapist in terms of the impact of specific environmental experiences on the specific child of a specific gender who has a specific problem at a specific developmental stage.

Summary

Davies (1999) claimed that interactions between different domains throughout development create increasing complexity. While examining one particular domain of development, such as cognition, it becomes nearly impossible not to observe how that cognitive development interacts with other domains such as emotional and physical development. Thus, school-age children are not merely more advanced than preschoolers, but fundamentally think, communicate, behave, and see the world differently from younger children. As children grow and mature, the brain makes new capacities available and is responsible for the timing at which changes occur. However, the way they occur depends, too, on the environment that shapes children's development. Davies asserted that thinking in terms of stages and ages tends to limit appreciation of the multiple changes that transpire across many areas of functioning.

Therapy with children challenges therapists, but can elicit effective outcomes if therapists design treatments based on child development components, adapting the theory of CBT to children's needs, and exploiting effective tools such as art, play, metaphors, and imagery.

Practice: Guidelines for Applying CBT with Children

Regarding cognitive stage, check:

- Can the child sit still, listen, and concentrate?
- Does the child's developmental stage enable verbal therapy?
- Can the child understand abstract concepts?

Regarding age components, ask:

- How old is the child?
- Is the behavior normal for the child's age?
- What techniques are most appropriate at this age?

Regarding gender, assess:

- To what extent does the behavior characterize the child's gender?
- In what way is this technique suitable for the child's gender?

Regarding information-processing, check:

- Is there distortion in the child's way of coding or interpreting information?
- Is it important to change the child's information processing to solve the problem?

Regarding emotion, assess:

- Can the child express emotion?
- If so, in what ways?
- Are there new emotions that the child needs to learn to express?

Regarding the environment, check:

- Is the problem characteristic of the child's environment?
- What role does the environment play in the problem's development and maintenance?
- Does the child have support from family and/or peers?

Regarding the problem, ask:

- Has the problem recently emerged or become aggravated?
- What is the probability of the problem disappearing?
- Will the problem remain stable, improve, or become worse?

Regarding the child, assess:

- Does the child have motivation for therapy, or should play therapy be implemented to establish motivation?
- Does the child have verbal skills, or should art, music, dance, or play therapy components be implemented?

Regarding therapeutic decisions, ask:

- Which technique is most suitable to help this individual child with this specific problem?
- Which technique(s) could best help you achieve your aims?

Remember:

1. Young children can benefit more from nonverbal therapy, while verbal therapy can be applied from middle childhood.
2. Children with higher cognitive skills can benefit more from verbal therapy.
3. Especially for emotional change, imagery and metaphors are more effective than verbal therapy alone.

Part II

The Positive Power of Imagery

6

Major Concepts Regarding Imagery

The second part of this book is related to the concepts of imagery with which therapists need to become well acquainted in order to use imagery in therapy. In the current chapter, I first discuss the common concepts in this area, trying to clarify the differences between imagination, images, imagery, and memory, as well as the advantages and disadvantages of using imagery for therapy.

Imagination, imagery, and images are often used interchangeably, causing confusion and difficulty in differentiating one from the other. In general, this book will refer to imagination as the subject, imagery as the process of eliciting images, and images as the pictures or sensations themselves.

Imagery is a critical feature of all effective human communication in general, but plays a special role in psychotherapy (Singer, 2006). Although images remain difficult to assess, Lang (1977) asserted that psychotherapists should learn about how the brain processes and stores images, to enhance the understanding of psychopathology and to employ imagery therapy effectively.

Perspectives on the Major Concepts

Although the notion of imagery may be considered as different from that of imagination, some view images as the product of the faculty of imagination – as the function of evoking and creating images – and therefore consider images to be a part of imagination (Assagioli, 1965). Assagioli categorized imagination as a synthetic function because it can operate at several levels concurrently – at the sensory level as experience, at unconscious levels of feeling, sensation, and intuition, and at the conscious levels of the mind as thinking. These can be known or readily summoned from memory, or they can be outside the individual's awareness.

The terms "imagery" and "fantasy" are often confused or used interchangeably. Imagery is usually a broader, more overarching umbrella concept than

The Positive Power of Imagery: Harnessing Client Imagination in CBT and Related Therapies, First Edition. Tammie Ronen. © 2011 Tammie Ronen. Published 2011 by John Wiley & Sons, Ltd.

fantasy (Hall *et al.*, 2006). Hall *et al.* attempted to explain this mixture of concepts by claiming that images are internal representations of perceptions of the external world, in the absence of external experience, whereas fantasy is a series of spontaneously created internal representations that may be fantastical, bizarre, or unlike any previous experience of reality. Often people refer to fantasy as something intentionally created, whereas imagery spontaneously occurs without conscious involvement.

In the past, images were sometimes viewed as fantasies waiting to become conscious (Assagioli, 1965). Nowadays, using information-processing models, images are conceptualized as a way in which the mind processes information. When talking consciously about events, people generally utilize cognitive filters to present those events in ways that avoid painful memories or distressing associations. However, as Lazarus (1977) noted, when talking about events while using imagination, it is possible to reach many realities that are physically absent and to deal with internal feelings and sensations that are otherwise difficult to touch on.

Traditionally, imagination is seen as giving a picture to a thought. Some also regard imagination as abstract thought, or internal quiet self-talk. People start imagining as soon as they acquire language and, from then on, they begin attributing meanings to things.

Images have been conceptualized in two ways (Lang, 1977). One defines sensory images as primary products of external observation, which are stored in the brain as primitive, nonreducible units, having a fundamental representation. According to this viewpoint, images are perceptual entities present in the brain's storage centers, to be accessed as is done by therapists. The other conceptualizes the brain not only as a silo storing information, but as a processor of knowledge; therefore, images are not merely sensed pictures and sounds, but also incorporate crucial information that the brain has processed and associated with this perceived information. Thus, images act more as a functionally organized set of propositions constructed through an unconscious dialogue between newly perceived information and associated prior knowledge or attitudes. Old information stored in the brain can influence new, incoming information, resulting in new, different knowledge. This means that the experience of the image itself arises out of "constructive" processes and should be treated like any other information available to therapists about their clients.

Imagery, according to Zohar and Marshall (2000), constitutes a different language from that of the brain; it is the language of the soul (imagery) and the heart (feeling and emotion) – human beings' spiritual intelligence. Accordingly, clients' longing for meaning gives rise to symbolic imagination, to the evolution of language, and to the extraordinary growth of the human brain. Hume (1912) described this unique nature of images in the early twentieth century, asserting that imagery is less about force and vivacity and more about sensation, passion, and emotion. Lazarus (1977) also related to imagery as the eye of the soul.

The current book proposes that imagery is an important tool in therapy, opening a window for both clients and therapists into how clients perceive information from past events, present experiences, and future expectations, and to explore associated thoughts and feelings. People make sense of their complex world by forming scripts and by bringing up and reshaping memories (Singer, 2006). By directing images to past memories, especially traumatic ones (see Chapter 13), clients can learn to control them and change them (Foa, Keane, & Friedman, 2000; Foa & Rothbaum, 2001). Contemporary images can target skills acquisition, interpersonal coping, and increased awareness of internal stimuli (see Chapter 14). Images of the future may facilitate coping and establish hope (see Chapter 16) (Fredrickson, 2009; Lyubomirsky, 2007).

Due to individual differences and cultural influences, people vary in their capacities to form vivid images and in how they make sense of experiences and memories. Some can conjure up perfectly distinct images that clearly resemble actual events, whereas others cannot (Lazarus, 1977). Some people do not spontaneously rewind or fast-forward their memories, whereas others take time to analyze, reflect on, and relate systematically to every detail. Some convey their experiences employing only concrete verbal language, whereas others regularly focus on images, emotions, and memory during their descriptive talk (Singer, 2006). Some refer to images only through memory, whereas others also attend to the images they experience in visions and to images as symbols and metaphors.

These variations were noted as early as 1883, when Galton asked scientists to chart the images in their dreams and visions for a week. While some claimed that they could recall no images at all, others recalled frequent, logical, clear images. Surely, working with imagery will initially yield better results for those who easily bring pictures into their mind's eye.

Imagery and Memory

An image is conceptualized as a mental picture of something not actually present (Lazarus, 1977). Singer (2006) related to the human imagery system as reflected in relatively concrete or specific memories, whether past memories or "future memories" appearing as daydreams. Any discussion of visions, imagery, and images must involve the role of memory, which is a prerequisite for these, as seen from the following two exercises:

> *Think of your breakfast today. Can you see the food? Can you see yourself eating it? Can you smell it? See the colors?*
> *Think of your route home from work. Can you describe it to someone? Do you need to map it out in your mind before describing it?*

While trying to report the content of your meal or your route home, you need to bring up the picture – the memory – in your mind's eye in order to explore it.

Even such casual memories, but particularly emotionally laden memories, may be distorted and certainly should be viewed as subjective rather than objective versions of reality. People are usually overconfident about their memories, regarding them as completely accurate. However, memories are influenced by multiple factors, especially by emotional states experienced during their creation (see Chapter 13).

For example, I remember myself at age 3 crying because I didn't want to stay at nursery school. I remember the teacher showing me a big black telephone and warning me that she would call the police if I kept crying. Later, my grandfather said that he would accompany me to school for the next few days so that I wouldn't cry. I can describe the old black telephone in detail. But is this a "real" memory based on fact, or was I told the story so often, and loved the idea of my grandfather's rescue so much, that I adopted it as my own "memory"? This book contends that it is unimportant whether a memory is authentic or a personal myth. Either way, I treasure this memory because it is part of my history and childhood, and I have few memories of my grandfather. Neither is it a traumatic memory for me, despite the crying and fear of the police. My subjective memory involves pleasant feelings that my grandfather loved me.

This anecdote shows that stories, photographs, and events that occurred after the original memory all influence memories that clients present to therapists. Imaginal reality is always situated in an actual experience, a specific image, an immediate reality (McNiff, 1992). Yet, when working with memories in therapy, therapists should relate to what clients bring to the therapeutic process at that particular time – what clients subjectively remember from that reality, regardless of its objectivity. The notion of subjectivity also means that therapists can creatively use imagery for many purposes with a large range of clients and problem areas.

Historical Uses of Imagery

Imagery has been part of many forms of psychotherapy for decades (Shorr, 1974) and seems to play a role in nearly all proliferating new psychotherapeutic techniques today (Singer, 2006). As early as the psychoanalytical method, imagery was brought into play to achieve several purposes. One aim was to elicit concentration by focusing on certain evocative scenes. Another aim was to facilitate the expression of emotion. Also, imagery was considered a powerful tool influencing unconscious drives and fantasies in evolving the early memories that are crucial for increasing one's awareness (Freud, 1958).

Jung (1958) expanded the notion of unconscious processes in human motivation. He was the first to advocate the use of "active imagination," where clients reenact their dreams and fantasies through vivid imagery and then are led to dialogue and interact with symbolic images. Jung thought that therapists must examine how clients use and tell their life stories. He viewed spiritual, mystical, and creative elements of the unconscious as the core of therapy, and developed techniques for employing cultural archetypes or symbols.

Emphasizing definite differences in people's capacities to form clear and vivid images, Lazarus (1977) recommended that therapists should look at how clients bring up and describe images and at the extent to which these images represent symbols of what they experience in daily life.

CBT, and especially constructivist theories, suggest that human beings are motivated to make sense of their complex world through perceptual and reflective processes and through the formation of schemata, scripts, and prototypes (Singer, 2006). Moreover, human beings are motivated to undertake the continuing retrieval, rehearsal, and reshaping of memories.

Many forms, techniques, and directions of intervention have been proposed for imagery usage in therapy. In the present book, I focus on using imagery as a therapeutic technique in psychotherapy (see Chapter 7). However, to clarify the specific contribution of imagery in therapy, I next clarify some of the common definitions and distinctions between various kinds of imagery, and the differences between mental imagery, active memory, symbolic imagery, and guided imagery.

Imagery

The term "imagery" refers to all of the senses involved in creating a mental picture of something that is not actually present. Most prominently, human beings tend to visualize, but imagery may connect to the sense of hearing, touch, smell, proprioception, and so on (Battino, 2007). To illustrate this gamut of senses, in my university classes I ask students to close their eyes and bring to mind a memory of a nice vacation. After this exercise, without giving further instructions, I ask them to share this aloud with the class. The diversity of senses pervading students' images is impressive, including odors – "I can still smell the wonderful corn on the cob"; tactile sensations – "The strong feeling of the sun on my skin was so wonderful"; and sounds – "The first thing that came to me was the loud crash of waves breaking on the beach and it was so powerful." Nevertheless, the great majority of students automatically respond to this exercise with pictorial memories, seeing describable pictures before their eyes: "Oh, the blue water against the white sand is so beautiful, especially in the sunset."

Thus, it is important to identify the senses that work best for each individual. For example, like most people, my pictorial memory dominates; therefore, during school tests I could visualize my study materials, remember that I'd summarized a particular topic on the upper-right side of the page and circled it in red, and thereby bring it into my working memory. Other students may study better tactically, recalling through writing, whereas others may prefer auditory learning.

Imagery is also the word commonly used to explain the mechanism of introducing images into therapy, including those steps necessary for imagery work. This book describes many methods for volitionally generating images, accessing images, and working with images in myriad ways that are often goal-directed and controlled; but traditionally, imagery was considered to be an uncontrolled, spontaneous, and automatic occurrence, with images simply "popping up" in the mind. However, imagery is under the person's control even when it arises spontaneously, without awareness. In therapy, people can learn to change spontaneous images or to create new, different images volitionally. Therefore, therapists should consider imagination as within clients' responsibility and full control.

Such spontaneous imagery often appears in culturally iconic stories of dreams and visions. A case in point is the human testimony about imagery that pervades biblical stories. There, imagery often appeared as dreams, daydreams, visualizations, or prophecies. For example, in the Book of Genesis, Abraham's wife Sarah saw angels presaging that she would give birth in a year; Jacob dreamed about angels ascending and descending a ladder; Joseph saw the moon and sun bowing down to him; and the Pharaoh of Egypt dreamed about fat and thin cows. All of these images foretold the future, reflecting the belief that dreams carry specific messages from God.

Another case is that of adolescent fantasy books about characters like Percy Jackson (Riordan, 2009) or Harry Potter (Rowling, 1997), where both nighttime dreams and daydreams convey important messages or hints to help the hero solve problems or anticipate the future.

Dreams – an important source of human imagery – are the product of the dreamer's internal world, but maintain an essential continuity with waking thought processes (Freeman & Boyll, 1992). In studying typical dreams of psychiatric patients, Beck and Ward (1961) found that dream themes manifested characteristics of patients' waking disorders (e.g., unpleasant dream content in patients with neurotic-depressive reactions; Beck, 1967). Rosner (1997) presented dreams as an efficient method for working with clients from within the framework of cognitive and constructivist theories.

Several interventionists have attempted to show that dreams and other imagery are not uncontrollable phenomena. For example, Doyle (1984) tried to determine the extent to which dreamers can learn to control their dreams by recording their dreams and performing skills-training sessions. Outcomes showed that clients trained in restructuring strategies did learn to control their dream content in a pleasurable direction. Also, Hall *et al.* (2006) suggested that imagery can be acquired and that clients can learn how to make use of imagery. They asserted that when people are asked to relay their dreams and spontaneous images, they develop greater awareness and start remembering more of these images.

Types of Imagery

Battino (2007) differentiated several kinds of imagery: mental imagery, receptive imagery versus active memory, and concrete versus symbolic imagery, as well as guided imagery.

Mental imagery

Mental imagery is an experience that, on most occasions, significantly resembles the experience of perceiving some object, event, or scene, but that occurs when the relevant object, event, or scene is not actually present to the senses (McKellar, 1957; Richardson, 1969). Mental imagery is a critical feature of all effective human communication, but plays a special role in psychotherapeutic processes (Singer, 2006).

Lazarus (1977) stated that through the proper practice of mental imagery, one can achieve an immediate sense of self-confidence, develop more energy and stamina, and tap one's mind for numerous productive purposes. Common examples of mental images include musicians' mental visualization when listening to songs, "seeing" the notes as well as hearing their tonal qualities; book readers' mental images of the characters and their physical surroundings; or writers' images of their upcoming works. Many people are familiar with the experience of generating vivid mental images of characters from a book they have read, only to feel disturbed later when the movie produced from that book portrays a very different set of images.

I personally often see mental images when writing my books: I may be cooking or listening to the radio when suddenly I see a mental image of a chapter written in front of my eyes, helping me get started. Or, when I debate with myself about how to present a lecture at an upcoming conference, I sometimes can suddenly see myself standing on the podium and giving the lecture, and that mental image lets me know the crux of what I want to convey and how the lecture should sound. This kind of mental imagery is not something I make up "out of thin air." Rather, it is based on my preexisting knowledge about the theme I want to talk or write about and on my continuous thinking and rethinking about that theme. At a specific time, when all the pieces are ready, they come together in my vision and guide me on how to proceed.

Once mental images are envisioned, they can be associated and compared with other mental images, and can be used to synthesize completely new images. Some therapists believe that this process of image comparison, revision, and synthesis allows people to form useful theories about how the world works based on likely sequences of mental images, without having to experience events and outcomes directly (Mahoney, 1991).

Receptive imagery

Receptive images are those that simply pop up and are thereby received by the mind, not volitionally created by the mind. They just appear or spontaneously form in the conscious mind (Achterberg, Dossey, & Kolkmeier, 1994). Daydreams can be categorized in this group. This kind of imagery often occurs just before falling asleep, or on awakening, when brain activity is at lower levels. Images from the past or the future may simply appear, as in the biblical visions and stories, Harry Potter's premonitional dreams, and clients' dreams of traumatic accidents. These images reflect what disturbs the person or what the person fears in the future, but they pop up without planning and are often extremely realistic, therefore frightening the dreamer.

A problem often encountered in therapy occurs when anxious clients experience a receptive image, like a vision of themselves failing or suffering, and they interpret that vision as a true magical sign or message that should direct their behavior. For example, a 36-year-old client with psychosomatic stomach pain twice had a vision of herself dying alone:

Aya construed these visions as a sign that something was physically wrong with her, claiming: "These visions didn't come to me for nothing. They're a message that I should look for the right treatment. They mean that something is badly wrong with me."

In therapy, we focused on mindfulness exercises to learn to identify early signals of the kidney problems she suspected, so that in case some problem did arise she would recognize it in time. We reframed her visions as signals for her to take better care of herself through good nutrition, regular exercise, and vitamins. Only further imagery work helped her change the images she had. Talking and rational arguments did not do the job.

Active memory

In contrast to receptive imagery that just "pops up," active memory involves conscious and deliberate effort in constructing images – calling up images from memory or constructing new ones. Such memory is an inner drama that can involve the full spectrum of artistic expression, a sequence of fantasies produced by deliberate concentration on particular images. I often develop active memories for myself before going to sleep. I invent a story that I like, and then I can return to this story night after night, or daydream about it many times merely to enjoy creating it, or use it to escape reality when I face hard times. In this kind of memory, the person is an active creator of the imagery, rather than a mere passive receptor. See Chapter 1 for an example of active imagery when my daughter Efrat elicited Wonder Woman (Fitzsimons, Marston, & Ross, 1975–1979) to help her cope with pain. Battino (2007: 30) called this type of active memory a way in which the person can "speak to his or her body."

Concrete versus symbolic imagery

Efrat's use of Wonder Woman also exemplifies the term "realistic" or "concrete" imagery, which is the type of imagery often chosen actively by clients or therapists for the specific purpose of facilitating the ability to overcome difficulties, cope with challenges, or change distressing behaviors.

In child therapy, I often mobilize children's existing imagery from familiar movies, stories, or television to help them cope with distressing feelings or learn to change behaviors. For example, I might ask children to try to be as brave as Tarzan (Loter & Buck, 2001–2003) so as to cope with monsters hiding under the bed, or to be the hunter from Little Red Riding Hood who, instead of fleeing, stays and fights the big bad wolf to protect others (DeLisa & Flaxman, 2006), to help them face "scary" elevators or darkness. Likewise, I utilized the image of Mary Poppins relaxing and flying away with her umbrella to enjoy the wind's advantages (Walsh & Stevenson, 1997) in therapy with a boy suffering from a fear of strong winter winds (see Ari's case in Ronen, 2003b).

In contrast to these concrete, realistic, nonsymbolic images, symbolic imagery refers to creating meaning out of experience (Shorr, 1974). In symbolic imagery, some images have special significance, representing important messages for those who created or received them (e.g., Aya's spontaneous vision of dying). This type of imagery embodies a body/mind level of experience that links somatic, verbal, conscious, and unconscious memories. An example of symbolic imagery is the dark "soul bird" image created by Ayelet, my client with anorexia (see Chapter 1):

> Ayelet transformed the soul bird appearing in Snunit's (1985) internationally best-selling children's story into an ugly black bird – her symbolic vision of herself. The original soul bird, a good, pure creature, lives deep inside us and holds keys for opening and closing different drawers containing all our hidden inner emotions. While talking about herself as the black soul bird, Ayelet would break into tears from the pain that this symbolic image represented to her. (Ronen & Ayelet, 2001)

Often, the integration of symbolic and nonsymbolic imagery within the fabric of the therapeutic dialogue can be a major tool in facilitating change within clients.

Process imagery

Battino (2007) also referred to process imagery – the mechanics of how an image works or is usable in therapy. According to Battino, imagery is only employed rarely in the therapeutic process, as a one-shot picture that clients bring up occasionally. Alternatively, as advocated here in this book, imagery can be implemented in an ongoing fashion, offering a rich set of processes for working with and elaborating on clients' coping tendencies as they encounter various events and feelings. For example, old images that clients discussed earlier in treatment can undergo repetition and further elaboration relating to current material; images can also be modified or extended to envision permutations in different or future contexts. These comprise only some of the steps (processes) for manipulating images within therapy.

Guided imagery

One of the most frequent ways to work with images is guided imagery. In this therapeutic technique, facilitators employ descriptive language intended to benefit clients psychologically. It often involves several or all senses in the listener's mind, with the facilitator/therapist helping clients relax and inviting them to elicit images connected to a particular theme. The client then describes the internal images that spontaneously emerge, and the therapist invites the client to set up conversations between these images.

Battino (2007) defined guided imagery as any internal work that involves thoughts (uses the mind) and affects health positively. This can range from "thinking positive" to elaborately structured processes involving relaxation, meditation, and body postures (see Chapters 15 and 16). Simply put, guided imagery uses imagination, together with discussions, to promote mental and physical health.

The method can be self-directed, where individuals put themselves into a relaxed state and create their own images, or directed by others. When directed by others, individuals listen to therapist, video, or audiotape exercises in relaxation and imagery. Some therapists also apply guided imagery in group settings.

Guided imagery is a two-part process. The first component involves reaching a state of deep relaxation (see Chapter 9), and the second component is the imagery or visualization itself (see Chapter 10). Variations of guided imagery techniques are almost infinite. Some commonly used types include relaxation imagery, healing imagery, pain control imagery, and mental rehearsal. Some of these techniques are mentioned in detail in Chapters 13, 14, 15, and 16 as illustrations of imagery use for changing specific problems or acquiring specific skills.

One of the biggest benefits of using guided imagery as a therapeutic tool is its availability. Imagery can be introduced virtually anywhere, at any time. It is also an equal opportunity therapy. Although some initial training in the technique may be required, guided imagery is accessible to virtually everyone regardless of economic status, education, or geographical location.

Guided imagery also gives individuals a sense of empowerment or control. The technique is induced by a therapist who guides the client, but the resulting mental imagery is solely a product of the individual's imagination. Thus, clients who feel uncomfortable "opening up" in traditional therapist–client sessions may feel more at ease with self-directed therapy through guided imagery.

Pros and Cons of Working with Imagery

In line with the well-known saying "Don't rock the boat," when verbal therapy is sailing along at full speed and working well, there is no indication to search for alternative methods such as nonverbal, indirect, or creative therapies. In such cases, therapists may not select imagery as a treatment of choice. However, smooth sailing is often elusive. Even when clients are complying and therapy is proceeding, many obstacles may arise, whether regarding the client, the problem, the therapy process, or the therapist. When things are not proceeding well, it is a good starting point to see what imagery and metaphor therapy can offer to address such obstacles as in the following examples.

A Client-Related Obstacle

A client came to therapy after being fired from several jobs consecutively. Although his stated aim in therapy was to try to understand what was wrong with how he had functioned in his various lost jobs, any attempts on my part to verbally consider his possible behaviors were met with unwavering rejection and denial. However, he found he could identify with my suggested metaphor of a deaf person who "has very good intentions but simply couldn't hear what he was asked to do." I was able to ask him: "What do you think it was that your employers wanted from you that you never heard properly?" Perhaps because this metaphor made him feel less at fault, we began making headway in understanding his functioning.

A Problem-Related Obstacle

A client came to therapy feeling lonely, but also blaming others for her breakdown or lack of social relationships. Here I used imagery to ask her to stand, in her mind, in front of all her past friends, moving from one to the next, and telling each one what was wrong in their relationship. This imagery exercise helped her realize that at least some of the difficulties stemmed from within her, with respect to her social competencies.

A Therapy-Related Obstacle

Imagery may be warranted when therapist and client reach an impasse. At such a juncture, therapists might choose simply to use the metaphor of a dead-end street to demonstrate how both partners feel stuck and need to back up and change direction.

A Therapist-Related Obstacle

One client often told me I was wrong when I tried to repeat or clarify his statements. I had difficulty understanding what he meant. To increase my ability to help him, I asked him to imagine that I was climbing a ladder to get to where he was, but whenever I thought I was just about to reach him, I found myself falling down. So, I needed him to give me a hand and help pull me up to reach him. This image ("Can you please reach out and give me a hand?") became shorthand in therapy whenever I found it difficult to follow his verbal statements.

Imagery can be a very strong tool, which offers many advantages, but just as with other methods, it works only for those who comply with it, agree to participate in it, and enjoy it. For some people, imagery is something that comes naturally, and these individuals can spontaneously draw on images to help themselves cope, solve problems, and deal with difficulties. For others, imagery may in fact be uncomfortable and difficult to use, especially at first. Some individuals may not successfully elicit clear images at first, instead sensing vague feelings during guided imagery, for example. People who think of themselves as very logical, rational, and practical may shy away from using imagination, considering such ventures into imagery as beyond their ability, as "not their style," or even as uncontrolled or threatening.

Another group of people for whom imagery may not be an easy method initially are those who are naturally oversensitive to imagery, for whom certain images can be extremely evocative. For example, talking about his daughter's stomach virus during dinner might call to a father's mind a picture of the girl vomiting, which elicits such feelings of disgust that it ruins the father's appetite. For other people, these same words about the daughter's illness remain only words without translation into evocative pictures. When pictorial memory is so powerful that clients cannot talk about events without seeing pictures, as in cases of posttrauma, the overwhelming emotions may preclude effective therapeutic work unless the memory and difficult feelings are brought into therapy through gradual exposure. Furthermore, clients with certain problems (e.g., schizophrenia, psychosis) may require specific adaptations of imagery methods that meet their special needs (see Chapter 7). And, finally, it should be emphasized that imagery work may be dangerous in the sense that it is a powerful technique that very quickly brings up emotion (see the dangers outlined in Chapter 7).

However, even for people who do not exploit images naturally or for whom images carry intense emotional loadings, imagery can be trained. These individuals' brains and nervous system responses resemble those with more detailed imaginings. Everyone can imagine, and it is possible to teach anyone how to imagine by overcoming resistance or anxiety (Chapter 7). However, for imagery to create advantages rather than disadvantages, therapists must ascertain how each client's memory works, how the client elicits and responds to images, and how best to use those tendencies to facilitate imagery work.

A fitting metaphor for this need on the part of the therapist to continually maneuver the intensity, content, and pace of imagery depending on the client's characteristics and problems would be that of a driver. Good drivers adapt their driving to the environmental situation at hand. Those who drive too slowly and fear getting lost might pose a risk because this disrupts other cars' normal movement. Drivers who speed place themselves and others at risk. Those who ignore warning signs or road hazards may run into trouble. So, good drivers proceed carefully, speeding up when possible, slowing down and stopping when necessary. The same holds true for imagery. The therapist needs to know the extent to which metaphors and imagery should be applied with a specific client in a way that does not disturb but rather improves normal functioning.

The main issue facing therapists when making decisions about integrating imagery into therapy, therefore, should not be to question whether it is possible or not to use imagery in a particular client's therapy. Instead, therapists should ask how to use imagery with this specific client, in this specific situation, with this specific problem, to meet this specific goal. In other words, it is a matter of careful assessment about how to apply imagery rather than whether or not we should apply it.

Relating to the pros and cons for working with imagery, therapists must remember the power of imagery as a tool for change, perhaps due to the deep-seated unconscious level at which images connect to human dreams, fantasies, cultural icons, symbols, and spirituality. The added merit and fruitfulness of employing imagery may best be experienced when therapy needs to address emotions, feelings, and internal sensations, as well as when working through past traumatic events. For these goals in particular, it is often much easier to bring about changes using imagery than when using verbal therapy. The next chapter and others in this book elaborate in more detail about the major benefits of imagery in psychotherapy for bypassing verbal roadblocks to enable direct access to emotions, eliciting and working through memories, finding flexible solutions when problem solving, decreasing anxiety and stress, finding mind–body connections, facilitating a sense of power and control, searching for meaning, and fostering pleasure and positive thinking.

Summary

Lazarus (1977) asserted that every event that humans encounter is actually transformed into images and thoughts. Accordingly, everything we experience enters the mind and remains there. In time, those experiences influence our actions in various ways, of which we are not always aware. Inasmuch as whatever is going on in our minds relates to images, work with imagery can help the therapist enter previously unavailable places in the mind, release locked memory, and work with it – both to understand issues and to make changes in emotions.

In sum, several issues must be considered concerning the nature of imagery and the application of imagery training in therapy.

About the nature of imagery

- The process of imagery involves images (thoughts, words, pictures, numbers) and all the senses.
- Images are the prelanguage form of information deriving from the world around us.

- Images connect to an unconscious level of human dreams, fantasies, cultural icons, symbols, and spirituality.
- An image includes information derived from sensory input as well as past experiences.
- Everyone imagines – some concretely while others abstractly, some vividly while others loosely.
- Images can be receptive, popping up in the mind, or actively elicited by client or therapist.

About applying imagery training

- The imagery process is under one's own responsibility and full control.
- It is impossible to create an image that the person is not interested in creating.
- Images can focus on past, present, or future.
- Pictures have more meaning than words or sentences.
- Pictures transfer more meaning in less time.
- Images have idiosyncratic meanings, representing clients' reality, whether or not that reflects actual objective reality.

Practice: Guidelines for Increasing Therapists' Own Ability to Elicit Memories

Due to the inherent strength of imagery, it is essential for therapists first to practice eliciting their own memories before applying such exercises with clients.

- Every day before leaving home to go to work or to go shopping, sketch out your expected travel experience in your mind. Note the route, the other cars you might meet along the way, and traffic and weather conditions.
- Every night before sleeping, select one thing that happened to you that day and try to draw the whole picture of that event in your mind (a staff meeting, a lecture you gave, a conversation with a friend). Try to use as many senses as possible.
- After succeeding with the first two exercises, try to recall a memory from your past and draw it in your mind's eye as clearly as possible, paying attention to yourself, others who were around you, the place, and the atmosphere.
- Next, try daily to recall one nice memory from that day. See it play out as clearly as possible, as if you had recorded the event on a camcorder. Note how you felt at each stage of the memory.
- After practicing the above, start trying daily to recall one disturbing memory or thought from that day. Focus on it. Then make a new ending for the memory, and try to make this imaginary new story as

vivid as possible by focusing on little details such as smell, colors, touch. Over the next few days, while focusing on each day's memory, see if you can increase the ease with which you imagine a new good ending.

• Try to create a new good memory for your future. Try to focus on how you would like to see yourself in the near future – in a week, month, or year from now – and try to be aware of your thoughts and feelings when you experience this happy event.

After you are able to perform all these exercises smoothly, you will be ready to begin asking your clients to practice them. Try to practice at least one exercise per session with your client. Make sure that the client can actually bring up the image and that emotions appear along with the image, and assign this exercise again for the client to practice as homework. To increase and enlarge the positive experience, ask the client to complete the daily chart presented in Table 6.1.

Table 6.1 Chart for measuring ability to create images

	Day 1	Day 2	Day 3	Day 4	Day 5	Day 6	Day 7
Did I practice the use of imagery today? (yes/no)							
The extent to which it was difficult for me: 0------------------------10 (Slightly)　　　　(Extremely)							
The extent to which I enjoyed it: 0------------------------10 (Slightly)　　　　(Extremely)							

7

Using Imagery in Psychotherapy: How, Why, and What For?

This chapter expands on the specific importance of using imagery in psychotherapy. Lang (1977) claimed that the role of imagery in therapy poses a perplexing question for natural science behaviorists. Mainly, this question stems from the fact that images are private events available only to human introspection. However, imagery has been part of psychotherapy since its early days. Indeed, with the development and expansion of counseling methods, coaching, healing, and the new wave of mindfulness, there is a remarkable growth in applications of imagery methods (Hall *et al.*, 2006). There are many ways to utilize imagery exercises in therapy, and many therapies use imagery regularly, from psychoanalysis to coaching to healing.

The previous chapter discussed the pros and cons of working with imagery. Here I underscore the kinds of therapeutic orientations and client problems that can gain from imagery work, along with imagery's major benefits and unique contribution to the psychotherapy process and its caveats.

What Kinds of Therapies Can Integrate Imagery, and for Which Client Problems?

Most therapies integrate imagery into their routine work in one way or another. As part of psychoanalysis, imagery can help elicit dreams, associations, and insights. Singer (2006) presented psychoanalytical imagery therapy as part of free association processes used to tell clients' own stories. He also identified imagery as a way to convey transference and client fantasies.

The benefits of imagery in hypnotherapy are well detailed – for changing dissociative states and fostering integrative and "ego-strengthening" processes (Erickson & Rossi, 1980, 1981; Erickson, Rossi, & Rossi, 1976; Fromm, 1967).

The Positive Power of Imagery: Harnessing Client Imagination in CBT and Related Therapies,
First Edition. Tammie Ronen. © 2011 Tammie Ronen. Published 2011 by John Wiley & Sons, Ltd.

An important phase of hypnotherapy, as well as imagery, is induction. Induction is a phase where the client slowly enters a different phase of action, for example: slow down, take a deep breath, relax (Battino, 2007). In describing a typical induction in hypnosis to bring about ego strengthening, Pettletier (1979) recommended that hypnotherapists give an active suggestion in a suitable trance state that the client is like a mighty tree, which is tall, strong, firmly rooted, grounded, and made stronger by life's vicissitudes. Pettletier also reported that utilization of guided imagery during projective assessment, guiding respondents to take the viewpoint of selected images on cards while in a hypnotic state, led to richer responses on the Thematic Apperception Test (Bellak, 1954). Pettletier believed that greater subjective immersion in the image helped clients more fully take the perspective of the figures presented on the cards and thus "ascertain the abundance of . . . choices possible" (1979: 33).

Among the most well-known therapies applying imagery is Gestalt therapy (Perls, 1969), with its empty-chair technique utilized to express emotions, increase awareness, and clarify behaviors. Alternating between two chairs, clients are challenged to act out different parts of the self, personify both sides of intrapsychic conflict, or act out dialogue with an imagined person/thing in the other chair, or take the viewpoint of images in dreams to discover what they signify. Likewise, in psychodrama, Moreno (1972) designed a therapy where clients practice acting out drama with protagonists and supporting characters. Both therapeutic methods were designed to encourage expression, breaking down barriers of behavioral inhibition by role-playing and acting out situations and conflicts (Arbuthnott, Arbuthnott, & Thompson, 2006).

Most existing literature on imagery therapy pertains to healing or coaching. Imagery is commonly used to help clients overcome illness in general, improve their immune system, and find the right metaphors to cope with life stressors (Battino, 2007; Hall *et al.*, 2006); for example, imagining a battle inside the body can help cancer sufferers.

Art therapists also frequently employ imagery in their projective therapies, particularly with children. They draw on imagery to increase awareness and spiritual experience, work on body image and energies, and facilitate expression (Jones, 1994; McNiff, 1992).

As a cognitive-behavioral therapist, I mainly avail myself of imagery as part of CBT. Behavioral treatments apply imagery as preliminary training before *in vivo* skill practice, mainly to reduce fears and anxiety. For example, in systematic desensitization, clients rate their fears and are then led to imagine a series of increasingly anxiety-laden scenes while practicing relaxation and remaining with each scene until the anxiety subsides. Progressively, clients confront increasingly intense anxiety-arousing internal imagery until they are able to face exposure to these images for prolonged durations while staying relaxed (Singer, 2006; Wolpe, 1958). As a preliminary stage before *in vivo* exposure, clients vividly imagine what they fear and view themselves gradually nearing the feared place/object and eventually coping with it (Marks, 1969, 1978, 1987; Meyer, 1966). Marks *et al.* (2000) reported effective imagery therapy for clients with obsessive compulsive disorders.

In cognitive treatments, imagery has mainly been applied as a coping technique. Beck (1976) and Ellis (1973) applied imagery and imagination as part of cognitive methods linking thoughts to emotions and behaviors. Alford and Beck (1997) claimed that imagery activates rational processes, pinpointing its suitability for people with either rational thought deficits or overdependence on rationality. Thus, imagery can help in bringing people down to earth when they tend to "fly too high" and in daring people whose feet are too firmly "stuck on the ground" to take off into the air and change how they think, even when that leap feels precarious.

Imagery is a recommended technique for helping children overcome fears and anxieties, talk to themselves, and imagine themselves coping (Knell, 1993; Meichenbaum, 1979). Meichenbaum (1979, 1985) used imagery to help children cope with their fears and develop stress inoculation. As part of self-control training, Ronen (1997, 2003a, b) employed imagery to assist children in overcoming temptation, delaying gratification, gaining control over their actions, and coping with distress.

Freeman and Boyll (1992) used imagery, especially dreams, to apply cognitive restructuring and redefinition of clients' distorted thoughts. They asserted that clients cannot describe symptoms without describing accompanying images, whether visual, auditory, gustatory, or olfactory. Hence, images furnish a ready, accessible entry point for cognitive intervention. Images may supply an economy of words, but they provide directness of meaning and a vivid affective experience for the client.

The most common imagery applications in CBT are eliciting early memories, exposing traumatized clients to past trauma, learning about traumatic events, and overcoming current avoidant behavior (Foa, Keane, & Friedman, 2000; Foa & Rothbaum, 2001).

Imagery is enjoyed widely in constructivist therapy (Mahoney, 1991) and mindfulness therapy (Hayes, Follette, & Linehan, 2004; Hayes, Strosahl, & Wilson, 1999). Here clients explore themselves from inside, tune into their own needs and emotions, and increase awareness through relaxation, meditation, stream of consciousness, and other imaginal techniques (Hayes, Follette, & Linehan, 2004; Kabat-Zinn, 1990; Mahoney, 1991, 1995).

Positive psychologists use imagery and metaphors as effective tools to help clients become aware of their positivity, learn to capture happy moments, and increase joy (Fredrickson, 2009; Lyubomirsky, 2007). Fredrickson (2009) suggested a large range of imagery exercises to assist clients in developing the "10 positivity forms," including joy, gratitude, and happiness (see Chapter 3). Gilbert (2005: 18) described imagery as a way to "get double juice from half the fruit," Gilbert also suggested that using imagery exercises to anticipate unpleasant events can minimize their impact. He recommended working toward prospection to provide pleasure and prevent pain. Also, he offered exercises for gaining control, because people find it gratifying to exercise control and feel that they have influence, power, and an ability to make things happen.

As seen from this review of various imagery applications from different therapeutic orientations, imagery work appeals to diverse therapists and has been found to be effective in achieving multiple treatment objectives. This book aims to help therapists design their own imagery training, highlighting how to create personalized imagery customized to meet clients' specific needs at specific times with specific problems, rather than relying solely on preexisting or fixed imagery techniques.

Regardless of therapists' orientations or clients' characteristics, imagery may initially be daunting for the client, and require some special preparation.

Overcoming Resistance to or Anxiety about Imagery Work

Inasmuch as launching into imagery may be unknown territory for many clients, therapists should devote ample time initially to helping clients gradually learn how to create images and overcome early resistance. Imagery may be intimidating at first for anxious people or for those who are afraid of what their images or memories might evoke. Imagery may also especially be a challenge for some clients who rely primarily on verbal language and rationalization. Such clients characterize themselves as very organized and practical, and are accustomed to talking a lot, persuading others, arguing, and confronting any case they encounter. When I first try to bring imagery into play with such clients, they often tell me: "No, that's not for me. I don't have any imagination. I hate fantasy stories; I don't even like cartoons. Even when my daughter was young, I couldn't take her to see all those animated fantasy movies." Many people do not realize that everyone thinks on both verbal and nonverbal levels. Usually, when people are disturbed by an event and think repeatedly about it, they not only review the event's words but also simultaneously see pictures and visions concerning this event, and perhaps also experience additional aspects using the other senses.

Hence, I do not give up on using imagery with clients who shy away from images at first, due to the vast potential of imagery work specifically for those people whose eloquent and persuasive use of words often blocks their ability to deal with emotions and prevents them from achieving effective change. Knowing that even these clients can learn to apply imagery despite initial resistance, I uphold that imagery is worth trying and invite them to try to experience it together with me in the clinic.

The easiest way to teach people to use imagery exercises is by training them first to bring up some actual, specific, real memory after learning to relax (see Chapters 6 and 11):

> *Close your eyes and relax. Remember the last dinner you had with your family at home. Can you see yourself at the dinner table? Can you see how you're sitting? Can you see who is sitting beside you? Look at the table and note the plates. The colors, the kinds of plates and glasses. See what kinds of food you are having. Do you like the way it tastes? Can you see yourself eating? When you can, please open your eyes and return here.*

The client may respond by exclaiming: "But that wasn't imagery. That was reality. I can easily describe what happened over the weekend. It's just a memory."

I explain that imagery is everything we can elicit in our minds that is not actually present, whether images of actual events or of events we invent. Once clients succeed in memory-based exercises, they can proceed to images that are less real.

Thus, like any other therapeutic method, imagery works best when clients enjoy it, find it easy to apply, and feel enthusiastic about it. There is no reason to apply imagery with clients who refuse; the therapist then needs to find more appropriate methods. However, if therapists believe that imagery offers an important tool for specific clients who are unaccustomed to it, then therapists should take time to teach clients how to create images and become more open to this method and its benefits.

The Major Benefits of Imagery Use in Psychotherapy

Training in imagery may furnish numerous benefits to treat a wide range of client problems and disorders, particularly in reducing clients' maladaptive overt behavior and affects (Alford & Beck, 1997). Next I describe some of the major benefits of imagery in psychotherapy: detouring around verbal impasses to enable direct access to emotion, eliciting and working through memories, discovering flexible solutions for problems, reducing anxiety and stress, finding mind–body connections, searching for meaning, and promoting pleasure and positive thinking.

Bypassing verbal roadblocks to enable direct access to emotion

A prime reason for working with imagery is to sidestep barriers that impair direct access to emotion. Effective change in psychotherapy cannot be achieved without focusing on emotions and emotional change (Mahoney, 1991; Safran & Segal, 1990). Images offer a powerful strategy to detour around verbal roadblocks and get to the root of the matter (Lazarus, 1977). Some clients' overuse of rationality, logic, and concrete thought may block their ability to express emotions and look at internal feelings and sensations. For people who tend to overintellectualize, confusing everybody and themselves with verbiage, imagery could be the treatment of choice. Rather than focusing on explanations and interpretations of what happened, imagery enables clients simply to describe an event, see the real occurrence in their mind's eye, and thus directly access their emotions.

Some clients' emotional expression is blocked or stunted because they grew up in a family that does not customarily express emotion outwardly; others experienced negative responses from the environment while trying to express emotions and thereby learned to hide feelings from others and even from themselves. Problems in emotional expression can also result from fears, trauma, or skills deficits. Sometimes people get accustomed to talking about events that had a negative, aversive meaning for them without expressing emotion, or to blocking the

111

negative emotions that originally would arise in association with that distressing memory. For all those clients, imagery therapy offers a crucial means for eliciting emotion.

Even clients who do not use intellectualization or rationalization and who are capable of expressing emotion often find it difficult to bring up negative or unpleasant emotions. Spontaneous images focus on unpleasant emotions more easily than in verbal discussion. Images take people from their reality to another place and lower boundaries and barriers; therefore, clients can frequently allow themselves to dare to venture far beyond what they would in a regular verbal session. Using images, clients can reflect on fears, discover reasons behind an everyday upset, transfer knowledge on the emotional process itself, and even convey hope.

When emotions can be neither seen nor heard, it is very difficult to make a change in one's way of thinking or functioning (Ronen, 1997, 1998b). A simple imagery exercise demonstrates the importance of emotional color during verbal exchanges:

> *Imagine you hear a client telling you, in a very soft, monotonic voice without any changes in the tone or tempo, "It was terrible. I just stood there watching the car veer off the road, and people started screaming."*
>
> *Now listen to the same sentences, but this time, imagine that the client's voice is full of stressful emotion, loud, oscillating in tone, with a racing tempo. Can you feel the difference? Can you see how emotion changed the story?*

While using imagery, we speak the language of emotion rather than the language of words. The Jewish tale presented next illustrates the extent to which emotion can make a difference:

> An illiterate man asked his neighbor to read him a letter he received from his son. The neighbor read aloud in a very dry, angry voice: "Father, send me money. I need it immediately!" The father became infuriated with his son for making such rude, selfish demands and vowed not to send any funds. But that night he couldn't fall asleep, worrying that perhaps he had misunderstood his son. Next morning he went to another neighbor. When she read the same sentence in a very soft, pleading voice, the father cried: "Oh, my boy is in trouble. He is begging for help so respectfully that I must send money right away."

Usually, when a client talks and the therapist can view or feel what that client is describing, this signifies that the client is conveying emotion. In contrast, when therapists hear a difficult story and feel nothing, this may point to clients' problems in conveying what really happened to them and may indicate emotional blocking or numbness.

Images enable direct access to emotion because they are usually accompanied by emotions naturally, even before therapists ask for the emotion to appear. When observing clients as they begin to imagine, therapists can usually note nonverbal, bodily signs of emotion such as tears, laughter, rocking movements from side to side, or clenched fists. The pace, fluency, or tone of clients' speech may change (stuttering, slurring, yelling) as a sign of emotional flooding.

The following case illustration shows how the use of guided imagery about visiting her son's grave immediately helped this client access deep emotions that could not be accessed previously by prolonged talk therapy about her son's suicide.

Ricky had been divorced twice, had been abused as a child and as a wife, and had two living children and a son who had committed suicide four years earlier. She suffered from anxiety attacks and could not express emotions.

After much preparatory work, I asked Ricky to imagine she was in the graveyard, telling her dead son everything she wanted about her feelings during the last four years. She started weeping for the first time about her son, and cried that she no longer had a life: she was afraid of being in his old room, never slept a full night without waking up screaming, and checked on her daughter hourly to ensure she was still alive.

After she repeated variations of this emotionally intense graveside exercise twice in one week and then for several more weekly sessions, Ricky reported sleeping a whole night without nightmares for the first time in years. She also told me that, for the first time, she had entered her son's room, stayed there to look around, and opened his windows.

We will return to Ricky in Chapter 13, because her therapy contained plenty of imagery training and utilization in almost every session. At this point I want mainly to emphasize how imagery played an important role in overcoming the barrier Ricky built between herself and her emotions. Although she had attended many therapies before, only when she started imagining did her emotions burst outward, and that very access to emotions through imagery triggered the beginning of change.

We can explain this case according to the various trends within CBT (Chapter 2). In terms of behavioral therapy, imagery gradually exposed Ricky to her son's death and thus to experiencing her emotions, thereby reducing her nightmares and anxieties about something bad happening to her daughter.

In terms of cognitive therapy, Ricky used to think how terrible it was that her son had died, but she did not let herself cry or feel grief; therefore, she was not able to undergo the mourning process and developed fearful behavior. Once she visited the graveyard in her imagination, alone, she was able her to link her thought – that her child was dead – to her emotions – sadness and helplessness. Letting herself cry enabled her to unlock her emotions.

In constructivist terms, Ricky had to experience and explore her life again. By letting herself touch her emotions, she could reconstruct the meaning of her world in a new way, not by avoiding her son but by including him in her life as her dead child.

Finally, in line with positive psychology concepts, the expression of negative emotions is important for human wellbeing. It is not the negative emotion itself but rather the ability to express feelings that is important for mental health. In addition, it is important to maintain positive emotions at a ratio of three to one *vis-à-vis* negative emotions (Fredrickson, 1998, 2009). Before visiting the graveyard, Ricky blocked much of her emotional valence, expressing only negative emotions such as anxiety, fear for her daughter, and helplessness. But after visiting the graveyard through guided imagery and expressing her negative emotions toward her dead son, she could also immediately express positive emotions as well. These helped her find happiness again, despite the immense suffering she had seen in her life.

Whatever therapeutic approach we employ to interpret the use of imagery in this case, it is clear that Ricky needed to express her painful emotion. Expressing it through imagery was the first step toward starting to cope with those memories and find new meaning in life.

Utilizing imagery for eliciting and working through memories

Another major benefit of imagery is its effectiveness in working with memory. Often therapists find that memories trigger referral to therapy; people frequently feel preoccupied with and disturbed by what they recall from their past. Sometimes the distress stems directly from impinging perturbing memories ("I keep seeing this terrible wind whenever I close my eyes and I can't get rid of it") or from preoccupation with lost memories ("How can it be possible that I can't see my [deceased] husband's face? I feel I'm losing him. I don't remember how he used to look when he was happy"). Sometimes memories become problematic because they reflect on future plans or actions ("Whenever I think of taking the driving test again, I see myself failing like last time. Who needs that again?").

In many cases, especially when early trauma is involved, memories hinder progress in therapy. Clients are often missing details about the past or cannot remember events. Sometimes the difficulties relate to blocks, objections, or rejections of memory on the client's part.

Sometimes painful or frightening memories are so powerful that recollections of events recur intrusively, disrupting current functioning, as in posttraumatic stress disorder. Consensus exists that traumatic experience is difficult to overcome without using exposure therapy that confronts clients with the traumatic situation in order to deal with it in a new way. Imagery, then, offers a tool for unblocking barriers to memory and giving access to new, unfamiliar material that can help clients change. Many techniques were designed to elicit such memories and work with them in a comforting and encouraging atmosphere. Foa and Rothbaum (2001) used imagery for revival of earlier traumatic memories, encouraging clients to face and talk to past events (see Chapter 13 for detailed guidelines on working with trauma).

When clients know that their current problems are linked to distressing memories that prevent them from undertaking future action, this awareness can motivate them to utilize imagery to cope with their disturbing images. In contrast, when memories and realities start merging, clients' difficulties are usually more intractable, as in the following case illustration.

> A client of mine refused to go on vacation because she had a vivid dream that her plane crashed. She began relating to it as a memory, saying: "Remember I told you about that time the plane crashed and I was terrified? Can you explain to my husband that I can't fly with him, that I'm afraid?" When I attempted to differentiate between the dream and real memory, the two had become so intertwined that she did not really understand what I wanted. For her, the dream was as real as any event that actually occurred, and was thus preventing her from flying.

Even when it is clear that clients are talking about a dream and not a memory, therapists need to remember that human expectations, fantasies, and imagery are reflected in dreams and are part of memory, and therefore that dreams should be considered part of human life (see Chapter 6). Therapists should always remember, too, that it is the client who makes the images, and that whatever the client brings is his or her reality, no matter how we or others conceive the truth.

Imagery can help us remember any event, not only traumatic ones. As described above regarding initial resistance to imagery, memory-based exercises can target simple, routine events. Let's take the familiar case of looking for something missing: car keys, for example. We keep searching the entire house and rechecking to ensure that we've looked everywhere possible, and we get angrier and angrier when we cannot find those keys! Imagery might be the ultimate solution:

Sit down, close your eyes, and relax. Let all thoughts leave your mind. If any thoughts come in, don't fight them – just let them go as they came. Now see yourself in your house, when you returned home from your last drive. The keys are still in your hand, and you come in, rushing and knowing you have a lot to do. Note what you're wearing, where you're standing, the time of day. Look at what is going on in the house. Notice who is home and who is nearby. Look at the keys and see where you put them, before running on to your next task. As you see yourself putting the keys down, open your eyes.

Often, by putting away rational thinking and anger and going with the images, we can very clearly find what we are seeking. I often experience success at locating things or remembering the names of people or places I have forgotten by employing such imagery exercises as a way to unblock memory. In the same direction, the next section will illustrate imagery usage for enlarging solutions.

Employing imagery to find flexible solutions to problems

Arbuthnott, Arbuthnott, and Thompson (2006) maintained that the need to solve problems is usually the main issue in therapy and that it usually reaches an impasse at some point in verbal therapeutic work. When things get stuck and clients stop advancing toward their goals, imagery can come into play to help overcome the barriers.

Sometimes, one's deep involvement with a problem and deliberations about how best to handle it can disrupt one's ability to discover new, flexible, creative solutions. Images, which are clearer and more focused than words, can help change one's direction of thinking. They are also richer, because a single image can contain many cognitions and basic beliefs. Images combine stimuli and responses, reflect fears, and transfer knowledge on the emotional process itself. Thus, using images, clients can see another perspective for looking at an event that differs from their customary view.

The importance of flexibility and creativity when searching for new solutions can be seen in constructivism. Mahoney (1991, 1995) emphasized the need for clients to continually experience new activities and be open to fresh life events. The idea of using experiential techniques is also familiar in CBT. Ronen and Rosenbaum (1998) and Rosenbaum and Ronen (1998) claimed that experimentation and experiences involve more senses and emotions and therefore can often improve change processes more than verbal therapy.

A case illustration for problem-solving imagery is that of Daniela, age 20, who could not decide what major she should pursue at university.

> Daniela made excuses for why each study option was inadequate for building the future she wanted. Psychology studies would be extremely difficult, and if she weren't accepted to the master's program she would have no profession, so it would all be a waste of time and money. Education studies would be easier, but she wasn't really interested in becoming a teacher. She was good at art, but what could she possibly do with it?
>
> I asked Daniela to imagine walking down a very long corridor with many doors. She needed to enter each room, look at what she found inside, and see if it worked for her – looking at the advantages and disadvantages of being there. I asked her to enter doors she had not entertained before, like the door for literature studies and the doors for journalism, nursing, and communication. In each room, I asked her to imagine becoming a professional in that area, looking at herself, and imagining what life would be like for her in that profession. After several sessions, she decided that art therapy would combine her wish to be a therapist with the joy she experienced from art and creativity.

Thus, imagery expanded her ability to examine more alternatives and choices when facing her problem. Daniela found herself wishing to learn something

116

she had not considered before therapy, and felt comfortable with this choice.

Being open to new experiences and activities is important in life in general, but is of even more importance while working with fear and anxiety in therapy. New experiences provoking anxiety and avoidant behavior are a main difficulty in therapy (see Chapters 13 and 15). Using imagery enabled Daniela's problem-solving and reflected the difficulties as well as the solutions. Thus, it was easier to reach the proper solution after using imagery.

Finding mind–body connections

Much existing literature on imagery therapy relates to the connection between the mind and physical health. Scholars and therapists have emphasized the importance of imagery to promote relaxation, reduce stress, improve mood, control high blood pressure, alleviate pain, boost the immune system, and lower cholesterol and blood sugar levels. Alford and Beck (1997) claimed that using imagery in therapy serves to establish direct connections with bodily systems that are generally autonomic. Through guided imagery techniques, clients can learn to control functions normally controlled by the autonomic nervous system, such as heart rate, blood pressure, respiratory rate, and body temperature (Battino, 2007; Hall *et al.*, 2006).

In more generalized terms, evidence of mind–body connections has shown that changes in thoughts and emotions are followed by changes in bodily functions, health, and the immune system. Milton Erickson published several papers relating to the role of hypnosis in relation to clients' feelings, behaviors, and coping (Erickson & Rossi, 1980, 1981; Erickson, Rossi, & Rossi, 1976). His work served as the basis for many healers who draw on imagery as their main way of helping people cope with sickness, distress, and particularly cancer (Battino, 2007; Battino & South, 1999). Imagery can increase mind–body connections by helping clients first focus on internal bodily cues while feeling various feelings, such as anxiety, anger, or depression; then try to link those internal cues to their thoughts and emotions; and then to discover what those connections mean. For example, clients can identify stomach aches as a sign of increasing fear or clenched fists as a sign of impending angry outbursts (see Chapter 14).

Searching for meaning

People always look for meaning in life. Knowing that their life holds value or reason helps them cope better with stressful situations and difficult barriers they need to face (Frankl, 1984). A good way to find life's meaning is through imagery. Victor Frankl (1997) emphasized that people often neglect or fail to pay attention to what is really important in life or what their goals might be. In his writings, Frankl recommended imagery as a way to create meaning, search for goals, and cope with distress.

Shorr (1974) underscored the meaning-creating role of imagery. He emphasized several mutual tasks of clients and therapists: to assign meanings to images that are elicited, to bring images into play relating to the therapeutic process, to apply images for discovering new areas of awareness, and hopefully to employ images as vehicles for creating change.

Therapeutic techniques aim to foster change by helping clients explore the personal meanings that they attach to the self and the social system, and by helping them articulate, elaborate on, and reorganize their experiences and actions. In this process, metaphors, mindfulness, and imagery are the main tools (Neimeyer, 2009).

Memories and images can have "life-and-death" significance, meaning more than anything else in the client's existence. This was the case for a client I had who was dying from cancer.

> Sadly, doctors found a malignant tumor while she was pregnant and, despite the risk to herself, she refused treatment to avoid harming her baby. By the time she gave birth, her situation was irreversible. She knew she was going to die, but tried to live longer because she wanted to prepare a meaningful legacy for her baby daughter in the form of books, pictures, and letters. These images would eventually help the girl know her mother and how much she loved her. Although in great pain, she refused strong pain relief because she felt she needed to be sober enough to prepare all this.

Preparing memories for her daughter gave meaning to her life.

Fostering pleasure and positive thinking

Often we use imagery to cope with pain, stress, and anxiety, but imagery has advantages not only for decreasing difficulties but also for increasing pleasure, fun, joy, and positive thinking in the future (see Chapter 16). The following example illustrates how to increase pleasure and joy through imagery.

> I used to get very angry at the amount of time I wasted in traffic every day on my way to the university. By the time I arrived at campus, I would be tired and angry. Then I started imagining that I won the lottery (although I never bought a ticket) and spent the hour daydreaming about how I would surprise my family, buying each family member the thing he or she wanted most. This imagery helped the journey pass quickly and I arrived at the university smiling. Imagery became my best friend.

As we have seen, many reasons and advantages advocate working with imagery. However, one cannot avoid considering the difficulties and dangers that imagery can bring to therapy.

Dangers of Working with Imagery

I look at imagery as a therapeutic tool. As such, the same guidelines used for any therapy should be applied. First, therapists should always remember that imagery work is only one of many tools that can be selected during the therapeutic process. Like other tools, only if the therapist is a professional – an expert at therapy, at treating people, and in the kind of problem being treated – can imagery be applied safely to help bring about desired change. Admittedly, this technique has dangerous potential in the sense that it can very powerfully and very quickly elicit emotion. However, as when using any other technique or therapy, if therapists continually assess and reassess clients' responses to imagery work, ensuring that the tempo is right, then clients can cope with the images to which they are exposed. The process is safe and effective if therapists ensure that sessions end with positive emotions and that clients are not left in the middle of a crisis facing difficult emotions (see Chapter 10).

For an example, let's return to Ricky.

Ricky's graveside imagery unlocked intense emotions that had remained deep inside her over the previous four years. I could not let her experience "meeting" her dead son and then end the session and disappear when she needed support. Therefore, I followed her lead, watched her expression, and asked her how she felt and what she expected in the upcoming days, but that was not enough to ensure she was okay when we ended the session. I also gave her permission to call me whenever she wanted between sessions. I asked her to call me before going to sleep that night, and I saw her three days in a row that week.

Battino (2007) emphasized the importance of pacing clients in imagery therapy. He claimed that therapists should practice how to pace clients rather than push them toward a goal, suggesting the need to pace clients' breathing, body movements, and eyes. Therapists do not rush anywhere or expose clients to events with which they are not yet ready to cope. And while dealing with traumatic emotion, therapists slow down and work carefully. Thus, like hot-air balloon pilots, therapists need to learn to maneuver to the right height for that particular client's problem – which images to generate and when the client has had enough in a particular session.

Images aim to provide a way to release, unblock, practice, or train – a window to emotion. But imagery is a tool to use in therapy, subject to the same rules as any other tool. Thus, imagery can open the window to many possibilities, but therapists require systematic, careful training to teach clients how to use imagery for achieving their goals. So, just like any other method applied in therapy, with imagery the question is not whether or not we can use it, but how we can use it safely and optimally.

119

I would be remiss if I did not state that use of imagery with some populations may be considered dangerous without specialized training. Differences of opinion exist about the usefulness of imagery therapy for clients with severe mental illness who demonstrate poor reality testing or delusions, such as in schizophrenia or psychosis. When I was a young therapist working in an inpatient setting, I accepted the commonly held belief at the time that imagery was simply not an appropriate intervention method for such clients. Imagery was deemed apt only for clients with a very stable sense of reality, for "normative" people who merely needed to make some changes in their lives. It took me time to learn how mistaken I was. It wasn't until many years later, when I met a friend, Dr. Irene Oestrich from Denmark, that I revised my early misconceptions. Dr. Oestrich is a cognitive behavioral therapist who uses imagery in her work with severe mental illness. She does wonderful work with people who have schizophrenia (I. Oestrich, personal communication, September 23, 1996; April 15, 1997). I learned from her that we should ask ourselves not only whether or not we should work with imagery, and how we should work with it, but also who should work with it.

Care must certainly be taken when using imagery to treat a person who lacks contact with reality and who continually brings up fantasies as part of their everyday experience. Therapists should definitely not use imagery to join the client in a fantastical or psychotic "flight in the air" together. As this is not my area of expertise, I personally have not applied imagery techniques with such clients, but therapists who are expert in working with psychosis, like Dr. Oestrich, feel confident in using imagery with clients if it is applied appropriately and concretely.

For example, an important part of rehabilitation for clients with chronic mental illness involves training to rehearse and practice simple daily skills needed for life. This training necessitates a different use of imagery, such as asking clients to imagine going to the bank to withdraw cash, where and how they stand in line, how they request the money from the bank teller, and so forth. Imagery in this case simply comprises another method of role-play and practice to prepare such clients for the next step of *in vivo* practice: actually going to the bank. Therefore, therapists with appropriate training for working with populations having severe mental disorders may find imagery to be an extremely fruitful addition to their therapeutic repertoire.

In sum, regarding the dangers of imagery, here are some cautions to use as guidelines, considering the powerful nature of the imagery technique:

- Do not expose clients to events with which they cannot yet cope.
- Slow down when emotions are too traumatic.
- Do not use imagery to implement new information that was not part of the client's past before.
- Keep constant track of where the client is and what the right tempo is for that client.
- For clients with severe mental illness and poor reality testing, only use reality-based imagery, and only if the therapist has appropriate expertise.

Summary

Treatment models that incorporate imagery offer a holistic approach, planned to give perspective and greater meaning to many variables involved in therapy. Therapists can use imagery during all phases of therapy. At the outset, imagery can help establish initial rapport by enabling clients to represent their meaningful experiences symbolically. Evoking these images establishes rapport by entering into clients' unique frame of reference (Crampton, 1969). Likewise, imagery can aid in the phase of assessment, when making decisions concerning the goals of therapy. For example, Crampton suggested assessing clients' sense of self by asking them to imagine or draw a tree. I use imagery to pinpoint goals for change and construct the process of therapy (see the full description in the next chapters). Imagery also enhances processes such as seeking alternative behaviors, evaluating treatment outcomes, and maintaining change. Crampton stated that imagery actively involves clients in the therapeutic process because clients cannot talk about images as outsiders; clients must be an active part of therapy, talk "emotion," and sense thoughts, feelings, and behaviors more vividly. By giving an image a voice, drawing it, dialoguing with it, and transforming it in their imaginations, the image becomes compelling and meaningful to the client.

Imagery can be conducted in two central ways. It can be a therapy in and of itself, focusing on relaxation and imagery training for overcoming problems and facilitating change. Or, it can be integrated into traditional therapies, throughout the process of treatment, with images serving as stimuli for eliciting something new that can be discussed over the next sessions. In the latter way, imagery aims to help the therapist, client, and process of therapy stay on track and make the most out of the process.

Practice: Guidelines for Therapists and Clients to Foster Imagery in Therapy

I first demonstrate an exercise for therapists to retrieve an image from early childhood and then describe several additional exercises for therapists and clients.

Retrieve a childhood image (memory)

Sit comfortably, close your eyes, take a deep breath. Focus on what is going on inside you. Bring up a picture of yourself as a child coming back from kindergarten. Can you see yourself? Can you see where you are standing? Can you see who else is with you? Can you see yourself looking at others? Can you smell anything? Do you hear the voices around you? Can you hear music? Can you see the colors? Let the feeling you feel come deeper and deeper into you. Take a picture of it so that you will be able to save it...

In this very short exercise of not more than 2–3 minutes, you can elicit a picture that you have not recalled for a very long time. For some people a colorful picture comes to mind, whereas others smell forgotten, unique fragrances or hear music from days gone by.

When I practiced this exercise, the first memory that popped into my mind was of me at age 4, returning from kindergarten to my grandparents' home. My grandmother stood in the kitchen wearing a brightly colored apron, listening to classical music. I smelled the strong odor of eggplants cooking in tomato sauce. Seeing the picture in my mind evoked very strong emotions in me, of time spent with my grandparents and our special relationships. This glimpsed recollection also led me immediately to realize, for the first time, that maybe my early relationships with my grandparents are partly responsible for the significant relationship I am trying to develop today with my own baby grandchild. Thus, imagery can offer easy access not only to pictures, colors, sounds, and smells, but also to emotions and insights.

Increase awareness of your own imagination

During the next week, try to notice the existence of imagery in your life. When you wake up, try to notice if you dreamed anything. During the day, try to chart down if you had any vision or daydream of yourself doing anything. Write down if it happened, when, how often, and what the vision was.

Increase awareness of your clients' imagination

When listening to your clients, try to notice if they use the language of imagery when reporting about past, present, or future events. If so, what kind of words and language do they utilize?

Practice eliciting your own imagery

- *How many windows and doors do you have in your house? How many beds are there? Where are your books located?*
- *During the next week, every day before going to sleep, think of something you would like to happen in your life. It can be something very simple such as being able to bake a new kind of cake, practice a sport, or talk to a friend. After you pinpoint what you would like to see yourself doing, try to bring up a picture of yourself doing it. Note what you are able to see.*

Have your client practice the use of imagination

- *Ask your client to find one simple thing that s/he doesn't usually do, but would very much like to be able to do (e.g., say hello to a stranger in the street, ask a beautiful woman what time it is, write a letter to a friend, smile at someone at work to whom s/he does not usually speak).*
- *Ask the client to imagine himself/herself doing that and to write down the feeling that comes up while imagining.*
- *Practice the vision 5–7 times and repeat it until it feels natural.*

8

Using Metaphors in Therapy

Often when driving, even when their destination lies straight ahead, drivers take detours – because a side road is less crowded or nicer, or merely to learn a new, different route. The same goes for metaphors, which enable a detour because regular therapy is stuck, or simply to emphasize or clarify or liven things up.

Metaphors comprise a different way of intervening and could fill an entire separate book. However, metaphors resemble images in many ways, and sometimes it is difficult to draw the line between metaphors and images and to define which is which. While working with imagery, therapists often find themselves dealing with metaphors side by side with images. The simplest way to differentiate the two is by saying that we present metaphors and talk about them while remaining "outside" (e.g., a client metaphor: "I feel like a rag that my husband steps on"), whereas in imagery we "jump inside," becoming the image itself and acting as if we were there (e.g., therapist-generated imagery: "Could you please become the rag and explain what it feels like being down there while everyone steps on you?").

In this chapter, I will present a brief overview of working with metaphors, mainly to emphasize their unique nature and their differences from imagery. In the remainder of the book, I will relate to metaphors as part of imagery therapy.

What Are Metaphors?

A metaphor creates a resemblance or analogy between two different things. The word "metaphor" is derived from the Greek *meta*, meaning "over," "across," or "above," and *pherein*, meaning to carry from one place to another (Kopp & Craw, 1998). Holmes (2009) defined metaphors as "carrying over," like transference, and linking one thing with another. Holmes stated that metaphors are commonly used to make otherwise inaccessible feelings visible to others (e.g., "When I finally came home, I felt as hungry as a wolf").

The Positive Power of Imagery: Harnessing Client Imagination in CBT and Related Therapies, First Edition. Tammie Ronen. © 2011 Tammie Ronen. Published 2011 by John Wiley & Sons, Ltd.

Stott *et al.* (2010: 3) mentioned that metaphor literally means "a figure of speech in which an expression is used to refer to something that it does not literally denote in order to suggest a similarity."

> Metaphors are conceptual in nature; that is, they are not mere words used in a non-literal sense, but rather they are conceptual devices used for important cognitive jobs ... to create or constitute social, cultural, and psychological realities for us. (Kovecses, 2000: 17)

Metaphor is a distinct mode of cognition that may integrate two other distinct cognitive modalities: imaginal cognition and propositional/logical/syllogistic cognition (Kopp & Craw, 1998).

Traditionally, metaphors are defined as a figure of speech that implies comparison between two unlike entities (Stott *et al.*, 2010). This suggests that metaphors act as a bridge between a source domain, which is more concrete or more familiar, and a target domain, which is more abstract or less familiar. When extended into a brief coherent story, metaphors can deliver succinct, implicit messages, typically to convey abstract principles (Stott *et al.*, 2010).

Altogether, metaphors are viewed as a language, a form of communication that is expressive, creative, challenging, and powerful (Burns, 2007). Unlike other kinds of communication, metaphorical language requires active involvement, thus instigating an interactive process between clients and therapists. Metaphors use the language of emotion rather than that of cognition (Kovecses, 2000).

Kovecses differentiated between expressive emotion and descriptive emotion, suggesting that descriptive emotions are actually metaphors, for example: "I am boiling with rage." He suggested that metaphors mainly relate to emotions because people lack the skills to convey feelings. Utilization of metaphors enables people to conceptualize emotion and transfer its meaning to another culture. Thus, a metaphor can constitute a cultural model, describing emotion or transferring and reflecting meanings.

Metaphors and Emotions

In line with the view that metaphors are a language of emotion, they have been widely applied to depict and convey different affects. Kovecses (2000) suggested that each strong emotion has metaphors that are largely used in everyday language to convey its meaning, especially anger, fear, happiness, sadness, love, lust, pride, shame, and surprise. For example, anger is most commonly described as fluid ("I'm seething with rage"), as fire ("I am burning in anger," "I'm fuming"), or as a burden ("He carries his anger around") (Kovecses, 2000: 21). We relate metaphorically to fear as torture ("She was tormented by fear"), as illness ("He's sick with fright"), or as a struggle ("My fear grips me," "Fear dictated his action") (Kovecses, 2000: 23). Likewise, people commonly say they are "filled with sadness" or "feel a wave of sadness" and when happy they "are on cloud nine" or feel their "day became brighter." We relate to love and lust as hunger ("starved of love," "sex starved," or "brings out the beast in me") (Kovecses, 2000: 29). In general, we talk about emotions as "hot" or "cold." In a broad range of studies looking for common metaphors, Kovecses (2000) found similarities between different cultures in the popular metaphors they use to describe emotions.

The Role of Metaphors in Therapy

Metaphors can be mirrors reflecting inner images of self, life, and others (Kopp, 1995). As such, they can symbolize human beings and offer a potentially useful organizing principle for psychology, by rendering a large impact on change processes and facilitating the remaking of one's life stories. To return to Harry Potter's encounter with the Mirror of Erised (Rowling, 1997; see Chapter 3), the mirror reflects Harry's life. Raised without parents, he continually seeks them out but can only see them in the mirror – which reflects his inner world. If metaphors are mirrors, then metaphorical imagery can become a key that unlocks new possibilities for learning about clients' inner self and internal life, and for self-created "in-sight" and therapeutic change (Mahoney, 1991, 1995).

Regarding the uses of metaphor in therapy, three types of therapies should be differentiated. The first group of therapies, such as Jungian, Gestalt, or constructivist, shares a reliance on symbols and depends on metaphors as their natural, day-to-day language. The second group, such as behavioral or cognitive therapy, is much more cognitive and structured in nature, relying on metaphors for expressing specific ideas. Finally, the third group, including art therapy, metaphor therapy, or guided imagery, continually uses metaphors as its main tool or technique because these therapies are mainly nonverbal.

Metaphors as a natural language

Constructivism, exemplifying the first group, views the whole world and its inhabitants – including life, human beings, and therapy – as metaphors. Therefore, constructivist therapy cannot be conducted without this natural, day-to-day metaphorical language to demonstrate how clients form their selfhood and organize their world. Lackoff and Johnson (1980) stated that metaphors help people change because people are largely metaphorical in the way they think, what they do, and what they experience every day. In this view, metaphors do not reflect a specific problem, but rather symbolize human life in general. For example, Neimeyer (2009) stated that if clients are navigators who give therapists the map to navigate in their world, and if therapists are good listeners, they will use this map to learn how to navigate clients' lives and help clients find their own way. Similarly, to describe the human mind, Lazarus (1977) likened it to a computer having several cameras that continuously photograph and record a myriad of pictures – black and white, color, slides as well as motion pictures – that are mental images stored in various albums. On the other hand, Beck (e.g., Alford & Beck, 1997) turned against the metaphor of the human mind as a computer, emphasizing that humans are much more complicated, but still maintaining that metaphors can simplify understanding of clients.

Stott *et al.* (2010) suggested that within the constructivist, generative view of language, metaphors can go far beyond a merely interesting comparison between two distinct domains as mentioned above: the familiar, concrete source domain and the unfamiliar, abstract target domain. Metaphors can cross-fertilize knowledge and meaning for clients between these two domains, thus nurturing and cultivating change.

Metaphors to express specific ideas

The second group – of cognitive, structured therapies – emphasizes that people's conceptual systems play a central role in defining their everyday realities. Kopp (1995) asserted that in many ways people conceive their reality as a metaphor, which enables therapists to relate to that metaphor when trying to help them. Learning to identify clients' personal metaphors can give us a better idea about how they conceive and conceptualize their lives.

Stott *et al.* (2010) related to metaphors as a powerful companion to the main task of cognitive therapy: transforming meaning to further clients' goals and help their journey toward a more helpful, realistic, and adaptive view of the self and the world. In this type of metaphor usage, therapists may offer metaphors to try to describe how clients might be feeling, which can then be examined, dismissed, played with, or modified (Holmes, 2009). The basic element in working with metaphors and emotions is therapists' attempt to help clients find an apt metaphor to best depict troubling feelings. Client may generate their metaphors spontaneously, or therapists can pose "What was it like?" questions to guide them. Such questions include: What was it like to be the only child who wore tracksuits while everyone else wore jeans – like a fish out of water? What was it like to feel like Cinderella (Disney *et al.*, 1950) – a little girl who dreamed of becoming beautiful? Or how is it to become Alice in Wonderland (Disney *et al.*, 1951), go through a tiny door, and find a new whole world there – what would you expect to find while going through the door?

Stories and metaphors can be useful to help clients see themselves as they really are, to reflect back to them about their lives. I often use the following old Jewish tale while treating anxiety:

> Two Polish landowners sat in the local inn drinking wine, bragging, and arguing. Each one claimed that his bear was stronger than the other's. Being intoxicated, they didn't notice the fact that neither one owned a bear at all. They decided that at dawn their bears would fight each other in the forest clearing and that would determine whose was stronger. After settling this argument, each landowner jumped on his own horse and rode home. In the cold night, each man sobered up and suddenly realized he had no bear. Both reached the same conclusion: Each called on his Jewish servant and commanded him to wear bear fur, pretend he was a bear, and fight the other bear. The two Jews helplessly covered themselves with an enormous bearskin and approached the forest clearing. Terrified and shaking, knowing he was a fake,

each man was afraid he would die. The other bear looked so real – so menacing, big, and strong! As they approached each other, one Jew's fear of dying exceeded his fear of the landowner, and he started to mumble "Hear O Israel" (the ancient Jewish prayer said before death as an affirmation of faith in God). The other, "real" bear answered by continuing the prayer: "The Lord is Our God."

This metaphor emphasizes the idea that, actually, everyone is afraid. For everyone, their fear is real, even if what they fear may not objectively be a threat. Using this metaphor, therapists can ask clients to examine their own anxieties: Can you see that the thing you fear is actually just bear fur?

Unlike imagery work, where therapists help clients "become" the image they are describing, in metaphorical therapeutic work the client "stays outside" the picture. Therefore, working with metaphors does not entail working word by word, proposition by proposition, and testing each out against the current standards of evidence, but instead proceeds on a more holistic level whereby the adaptation of a new language game itself is used according to new standards (Russell, 1991).

Metaphors as therapy's routine or main tool

Metaphor is the source of novelty in language. Inviting clients to explore and transform spoken metaphors may be a source of novelty and change in psychotherapy (Kopp, 1995). A case illustration is metaphor work with an 11 year old who was preoccupied with a personal life story of getting lost. Whether Roy's story was reality or metaphor, he feared getting lost. In therapy, by relating to his story as reality, he gradually gained trust, confidence, and skills to reduce his fear.

Roy suffered from anxiety disorder. He wouldn't leave his mother, refused to attend school, and feared going to friends' houses. Roy explained that ever since he had got lost while visiting New York he feared it might happen again. His mother angrily denied it, but Roy stood firm in describing the incident and its aftermath.

Devising therapeutic work based on relating to him metaphorically as "the child who got lost," I asked Roy to practice getting lost in his hometown. Doing so, he gained confidence and skills, learning to ask for directions and remember landmarks. As homework, Roy charted his emotions, rating how stressful getting lost felt daily. Instead of helplessly saying "Oh, this is terrible" he learned to say "Oh, it's wonderful to find a new route home."

Getting lost became a metaphor to explain how he felt at school ("Could you get lost during the lesson?"), with friends ("Did you feel lost when the

(continued)

kids all laughed and you didn't know why?"), and at home ("Did you feel lost when your mother asked you why you didn't do your homework?").

For several weeks, he practiced finding new places around town, identifying "first-aid equipment" to cope with fear when "lost," and going alone to school and friends' homes. Gradually, he became more independent and confident, letting his mother out of his sight more and more, and enjoying these experiences.

In the last session, Roy was asked to draw a map and write a manual for children who get lost. He said he was no longer afraid of getting lost in New York. The mother, of course, replied that he was never lost in the first place...

I have no idea whether Roy really was lost in a foreign city, whether he was merely afraid of getting lost, or whether that identified fear represented his overall, generalized anxieties. Whatever really happened, his intractable metaphorical view of himself was indeed of a lost boy. Yet, this metaphor served as the key to unlocking his anxieties about many aspects of his life. By collaborating with his metaphor, therapy enabled him to reduce his fears and begin to function more normatively at school and at home. In line with Kopp and Craw's (1998) speculations, it may be hypothesized that Roy's process of shifting between his explored and transformed metaphorical imagery and his current life problems created the potential for new insights into the nature of his problem and new possibilities for constructive problem solving.

Another case illustration of metaphor work as a main tool in therapy can be seen in the treatment of Ari, a 6-year-old boy who feared thunderstorms, lightning, and wind. Therapy used metaphors of trees during storms to familiarize him with the good side of winter and overcome fears and anxiety (see details in Ronen, 2003b).

Ari was brought to therapy because he was afraid of winter and wind. Whenever the wind blew, Ari was "scared to death," refused to leave home, would not stay alone even in his own room, would watch the "poor miserable trees" out the window, and would frighten his younger sister by talking about how the wind would soon destroy their house and carry them away to their deaths.

Ari developed avoidance behaviors and refused to leave home (see the details in Chapter 17). To help him learn to look differently at the weather

(continued)

he feared so much, I introduced a tree metaphor, emphasizing the different shapes and qualities of trees each season. In spring, leaves are budding and new life starts; as summer comes, leaves continue to mature, providing a rich green canopy to protect us from the sun. When fall arrives, trees display a whole array of breathtaking colors. Winter provides opportunities to see trees' real structure; that is, their shape, branches, and surroundings (Ronen, 2003b: 99–104).

After describing the metaphor, Ari and I went outside to observe trees close up – to see what they look like, feel like, and do. Ari said happily: "Look, they're touching each other! Do you think they're friends? The wind makes them alive and move and meet each other so now they can touch each other." I asked Ari to draw the trees in the different seasons and to discuss which he liked best.

After working on cognitive restructuring, Ari started thinking differently, accepting that maybe wind was not that terrible, that there might even be some fun to winter and rain, and that maybe in the future he could learn to control his fears.

Metaphors along the therapy phases

Metaphors can promote therapeutic processes at all the different phases of therapy. First, metaphors are extremely useful as an aid in assessment processes. The metaphors that clients present of their lives, themselves, and the world around them offer an efficient assessment mechanism to assist therapists in learning more deeply and quickly about clients. Recall, for example, the child who drew himself as small on the inside but as a big figure from the outside, thus metaphorically relating to himself and to others' view of him (see Chapter 4). Second, during actual therapeutic work, metaphors can promote change by helping therapists learn more about where clients are, by reframing clients' viewpoints, or by transporting the therapist and client into the less tangible domains of life as a journey and as a story to be told (Carlsen, 1995). Finally, at termination or near the end of therapy, metaphors can be employed to evaluate the change that clients have experienced and to evaluate treatment outcomes.

Applications of metaphor in different therapeutic orientations

A long time ago people noticed that when things about the world or themselves were understood through different metaphors, a person's feelings about these things changed (Burns, 2007). Freud (1960[1923]) noted that thinking in pictures is closer to the unconscious than thinking in words. Thus, one might expect that images and metaphors would find a comfortable home in psychotherapy approaches that emphasize unconscious processes. Burns (2007) described stories and metaphors for healing purposes and showed how these can exemplify commonsense strategies, including vivid stories and metaphors, to help clients translate session material into behavioral change.

On the surface, CBT may perhaps seem unsuited to metaphors because it derives from logic and rationality, underscoring the cognitive formulations of beliefs, automatic thoughts, and schemata. However, the CBT approach employs metaphors widely to help clients understand and enhance skills for change. Stott *et al.* (2010) stated that the business of CBT is to transform meaning; therefore, metaphors offer one of the best ways of doing this, providing a conceptual bridge from a problematic interpretation to a fresh new perspective that can cast one's experience in a new light. The use of stories and metaphors in CBT enhances information-processing during sessions and thereafter. Alford and Beck (1997) related to metaphors as an explanatory device that therapists often use to explain and facilitate clients' understanding. The goal is to help transform therapeutic information into a form that is easy to remember, provides useful guidance, and can be applied at relevant moments in clients' lives (Otto, 2000).

Metaphors are of particular relevance for working with children in CBT. Allian and Lemieux (2007) described the use of metaphorical fables as part of their skills-acquisition program to help schoolchildren use problem-solving skills. Friedberg and McClure (2002) recommended metaphors and play as advantageous ways to raise curiosity and interest among children and to deepen their understanding in sessions.

Kopp and Craw (1998) claimed that using metaphors in CBT calls for therapists (i) to attend to their clients' metaphorical speech and select a metaphor to explore; (ii) to follow the interview protocol, asking a sequence of open-ended questions that allows clients to access their creative imagination and immerse themselves in sensory imagery as they explore, elaborate, and ultimately transform their metaphorical imagery; and (iii) to avoid interrupting their clients' inner work with comments, suggestions, interpretations, or even empathetic responses. Clients can employ metaphorical cognition to create connections (resemblances) between their chosen metaphor (formulated using primarily imaginal cognition) and their life problem (conceived primarily in terms of objective fact and logical/propositional cognition; Kopp & Craw, 1998).

As mentioned above, constructivist therapists naturally use the language of metaphors. Moreover, in constructivist treatments, specific metaphors introduced in different places in therapy may highlight or activate the process of therapy, offering "releasing" power to start working on specific difficulties (Neimeyer, 2009). Prime examples of specific metaphors in constructivist therapy are the popular metaphors of transitions and travel, which can speak to any client. On a journey, there are paths, mobility modes and aptitudes, pacing, pauses for obstacles, challenges, choices at crossroads, directions, and more (Mahoney,

1991). Mahoney suggested that these metaphors encourage clients to attribute the power of movement to themselves. As such, travel and transition metaphors lend themselves well to the inevitable separation process at the conclusion of treatment, where clients and therapists part ways and continue on separate paths.

With cognitive approaches to therapy undertaking an increasingly constructivist orientation, growing emphasis is now placed on clients' deep, tacit, or unconscious levels and on knowledge as represented in analogical and metaphorical ways. The use of metaphors was recommended as a promising therapeutic tool for accessing and changing such tacit or unconscious levels of cognitive representation (Gonçalves & Craine, 1990). Clients actively construct a cognitive representation of their own reality from their tacit knowledge representations, which are prelogical, immediate, global, and imaginistic. Further, these deep knowledge processes are represented in the form of metaphors and analogies that constitute the very essence of a person's ongoing construction of knowledge and reality. For constructivists, metaphorically constructed knowledge and reality contrast with an information-processing model of cognitive therapy characterized by surface, explicit, conscious processes such as self-talk, automatic thoughts, and problem-solving, which are represented in propositional or logical form (Gonçalves & Craine, 1990; Mahoney, 1991).

Over the years, a new type of therapy has developed – metaphor therapy. Metaphor therapy views metaphors as a mental process that differs distinctly from propositional or logical cognition. Metaphor therapy's cognitive model, however, posits that metaphorical cognition partakes in and may in fact integrate the relatively unconscious analogical processes of imaginal cognition and the relatively conscious logical processes of propositional cognition. The metaphor functions as a transformer through which words are translated into images (Kopp & Craw, 1998).

Both constructivist and metaphor therapy perspectives emphasize a theory of cognition and meaning that incorporates metaphorical, imaginal, and analogical processes along with verbal and logical cognitive forms. Similarly, both suggest that metaphor can play an important role in cognitive therapy.

In acceptance and commitment therapy, as well as in mindfulness therapy as a branch of CBT, metaphors are used frequently to elicit mindfulness and acceptance. Hayes, Strosahl, and Wilson (1999) asserted that metaphors are a good way to connect with clients and deepen understanding. They suggested that therapists develop new metaphors or exercises based on clients' history, personal struggles, and preferences.

The literature on positive psychology is peppered with a large range of metaphors for guiding clients toward focusing on their happiness and positivity. One example directs clients to look at themselves through the metaphor of a flower in springtime (Fredrickson, 2009). Flowers need sunshine and water and they turn toward the light. They also show great variety: some bloom only once, others blossom daily. So, how, as a flower, do we see our own life? What is our sunshine? Do we bloom at all? Would we like to bloom again? What do we need to reach blooming point?

Client- and Therapist-Generated Metaphors

There are many classifications of metaphors and proposed ways for metaphor work. The most common uses of metaphors follow Kopp's (1995) classification into client-generated and therapist-generated metaphors.

Client-generated metaphors

Clients generate their own metaphors, either spontaneously or with therapists' guidance. Therapists can exploit such metaphors to explore and transform clients' language in an attempt to deepen understanding of clients' belief systems, thus shifting clients' frequent language to emphasize or highlight important points in therapy. As Kopp (1995) proposed, like Alice traveling in Wonderland (Disney *et al.*, 1951), therapists' work with such metaphors is like going through the looking glass and journeying beyond the mirror's image, entering the domain of clients' creative imagination. Throughout therapy, client-generated metaphors emerge, such as the following:

- On receiving a low grade that would prevent her acceptance to university: "I had no air, I felt like I was drowning and going to die."
- On discovering her husband's romance with a friend: "I was living in a palace, enjoying what I had, and suddenly I felt the ceiling fall down on me."
- A 40-year-old man looking for life change: "All my life I've been blowing in the wind. I've reached a point where I want to decide where the wind will take me."

In all these examples, therapists can learn more about clients' emotions, thoughts, and meaning attributions by pinpointing and expanding on these metaphors: "Tell me what it was like for you to feel you've been blowing with the wind. What was going through your mind? What would you rather do?" or "What is the feeling of having the ceiling suddenly fall on you? Where do you feel the worst? What part of you is suffering? What are you telling yourself?"

Suggested steps for working with client-generated metaphors include:

- Listen to clients and pinpoint casual usage of metaphorical language.
- Invite clients to explore metaphorical images.
- Ask clients to experience and practice concentrating on the feelings and sensations elicited by metaphors. Help clients shift attention to each sense separately to feel it more fully.
- Invite clients to talk more about metaphors (a cognitive step) to better understand their meaning.
- Invite clients to transform metaphors by changing the metaphorical images or meanings. Offer the idea of extending the metaphor at hand or of adding another metaphor to help change its meaning.

The following two examples (from Ronen & Ayelet, 2001) illustrate how therapists can work with and expand client-generated metaphors.

> Ayelet said she was full of garbage and urgently needed to clean it up in order to live a normal life. Slowly, using metaphor sessions, I was able to enter Ayelet's world and help her "clean up the garbage" (see the details in Chapter 17). While imagining herself as a cleaning lady, we looked at all the things we were able to throw away, such as her obsessions, compulsions, fears, and anxieties. Ayelet was happy to notice the expanding metaphorical garbage can outside herself, and said she felt better when she was cleaner (Ronen & Ayelet, 2001: 171).
>
> Ayelet stated she had "some bad things" deep inside her. She often talked about "the big black hole of nothing," "falling down into the nothing," and "a big emptiness inside." I assured her that I could throw her a rope ladder into the hole and help her climb out. This trip was not easy. It involved tears, sobbing, and sorrow. At one point, I suggested that Ayelet replace the metaphors of emptiness and hole of nothing with the metaphor of gaps. She accepted this idea, demonstrating progress (Ronen & Ayelet, 2001: 174).

Therapist-generated metaphors

When therapists propose metaphors that they deem useful for clients and describe some details, such therapist-generated metaphors aim to enhance clients' understanding, feeling, or coping with issues currently addressed in therapy. The suggested metaphors offered by therapists must be tailored to clients' needs, style, and language if clients are expected to accept and expand on them further. Thus, it is completely up to clients to decide whether or not to accept invitations to join in with therapist-generated metaphors. The client may refuse to go with the idea, rejecting the metaphor, or may join in happily and expand on the proposed idea.

After presenting the metaphor and inviting the client to consider it, the next step comprises asking the client to fill in the details that are lacking. This request enables the therapist to determine whether the suggested metaphor suits the client and can be of benefit in therapy. When clients do collaborate, therapists can give interpretations or ask clients to consider how they would interpret metaphors, and then continue to pursue other metaphors later. However, when clients consistently cannot collaborate with metaphors and continually correct therapists, changing metaphors' meanings or arguing about accuracy, this means

133

either that therapists' understanding of clients was incorrect or that metaphor work may not be a method of choice for those specific clients, as in the following example.

I had a client who always corrected my metaphors and put my ideas into his own words. I always felt I'd missed something. I once told him I had a feeling that I'd set the dinner table and he kept coming to change the plates around. He answered that was because I never really understood him and the plates' setup wasn't what disturbed him. I asked what did disturb him, and he replied: "The way you put things." But I could never understand what was wrong. I tried to check: Was it the sequence or words I used, did I insult him, was it related to his needs to fix things, to maintain control, to ensure precision, to always get the upper hand? But whatever I said, he replied: "Kind of, but not exactly." I soon realized that no metaphor coming from me would suit him, and I gave up on using them with him.

Sometimes, a story can clarify things better, as a more distant metaphor with which the client can collaborate. The next illustration is from my days as a social work student.

I volunteered to work with a client in front of a peer supervision group on stories and metaphors in therapy. My client, age 36, was in a rehabilitation center after losing three fingers in a work accident. He feared that without two healthy hands he could not function "as a man"; therefore, he lost confidence, felt helpless and hopeless, and behaved as if trying to hide himself from the world. My supervisor told him a story, a metaphor: A farm had many chicks running around, but one was different – bigger and uglier. One day, as all the chicks flapped their wings and flew for a second or two, the ugly chick moved his wings too and found himself flying high up in the air. As he looked down, he realized that they were all chicks and he was actually a baby eagle. After completing this story, my supervisor looked at my client and asked him: And you, would you like to be a chicken or an eagle? My client straightened his back and answered assertively: Of course I would like to be an eagle!

He could easily collaborate with this metaphor, and for him it was a turning point for starting to change his life and beliefs.

134

Summary

The helping power of metaphors has long been known by poets, playwrights, and psychotherapists. Freud (1958) suggested that psychotherapists serve as a "midwife to the soul."

Like every other technique and methods, metaphors have pros and cons. Side by side with their benefits lie obstacles and limitations. One limitation can be if therapists "fall in love" with their metaphors, forgetting the client. Hayes, Strosahl, and Wilson (1999) asserted that therapists should be careful not to ramble on with metaphors and metaphor exercises without focusing on tailoring them to clients' stage and tempo. Alford and Beck (1997) also warned therapists not to go too far with metaphors because they are only metaphors – not reality. However, this warning rings true for every method used in therapy. Don't therapists always need to use tools, techniques, and methods critically, to determine their effects on clients?

In the rest of this book, I refer to metaphors as part of working with images, using similar strategies and approaches, turning them into imagination and trying to understand them, accept them, and change them.

Practice: Guidelines for Therapists Beginning Metaphor Work

- This week, try to listen to your clients and note every use of metaphors in their ongoing talk.
- After listening carefully for several days, see if each client's metaphors appear at characteristic times or under specific circumstances. What characterizes the metaphors' appearance: Difficulty conveying an idea? Feeling stressed? Desire to emphasize something?
- Try collaborating with the metaphor you heard by asking questions about it: What does it mean for you to be like. . .? How do you feel when you are like. . .? Is there any metaphor you can think of that you would want to use to replace this one?
- Try to suggest your own metaphor for the client. Note the client's response. Can s/he connect with your metaphor?

Part III

Preparing to Apply Therapy Through Imagery

9

Getting Ready to Start: Relaxation

The first two parts of this book presented the preliminary considerations for using imagery in therapy. Now it is time to jump into the water and learn to swim by starting therapy. This chapter presents the initial stage of using imagery, which comprises relaxation and meditation.

Preliminary Preparations

Imagine you want to go shopping. What preparations do you need to make? You need to decide what you would like to buy; bring your wallet with money or a credit card; think about where you can get what you want and select that shop; find out how to get there and its opening hours; and ensure that your car is nearby with the gas tank filled.

This is what we are going to do now. We are going to plan our use of imagery – our shopping trip. To get ready, we need information – the knowledge about where we want to go with imagery – and we need our car – the vehicle that will enable us to reach our destination. The first vehicle we would like to give our client is the ability to relax. A preliminary state of relaxation permits clients to begin the imagery work. Arranging the setting for the session is just like preparing our bag and wallet, and finding out the shop's hours and location. Only after those initial steps at home and on the way can we begin to start walking around the shopping mall, browsing, and then actually doing our shopping – or, in our case, can we begin to use instructions and start exploring imagery exercises as part of therapy.

Most imagery procedures are more effective if clients first achieve a state of general relaxation. This state makes it is easier for clients to close their eyes, concentrate, and avoid interference from external stimuli. Various techniques can improve this relaxed state. Just like the different cars people drive and their varying driving styles, many different roads can lead to relaxation. There is no

The Positive Power of Imagery: Harnessing Client Imagination in CBT and Related Therapies,
First Edition. Tammie Ronen. © 2011 Tammie Ronen. Published 2011 by John Wiley & Sons, Ltd.

one best way to achieve this state: Every person can find his or her own personal way to relax.

Some methods are performed alone, whereas others require the help of another person, often a trained professional. The therapist's voice often helps induce a relaxed state. Some techniques involve movement and activity, whereas other formal and passive relaxation exercises focus on stillness and are generally performed while sitting or lying quietly, involving a degree of withdrawal. For some, relaxation comes when visiting somewhere – like the beach – or when performing an activity – like singing. For others, sport activities can induce relaxation, reduce aggression, and improve self-control. Common relaxation techniques include yoga, tai chi, listening to music, massage, or meditation.

However, just as when shopping some purchases are harder to find and more time-consuming than others, it is important to remember that people definitely differ in their capacity to relax in order to form clear and vivid images. Not everyone can achieve this ability at the same pace or to the same extent. For those clients who spontaneously apply relaxation techniques in their day-to-day lives through sport or yoga sessions or while practicing meditation or other awareness-developing methods, beginning a therapy session with imagery will be easy. They can just "step into" the relaxation stage and then into imagery work.

In contrast, many new clients facing a problem feel extremely tense, suspicious, and pessimistic. They might find it difficult to start using the unfamiliar "language" of imagery, feeling out of control sharing nonverbal images about their suffering and problems, and even hesitating to close their eyes during initial practice. Hence, we need to give clients the most appropriate vehicles possible to achieve relaxation, tailored to their needs and tastes. Relaxation skills may be well adapted to various cultures and applicable worldwide, but individual differences still require therapists' consideration. Optimally, therapists should get to know clients before starting their first imagery session to determine which vehicles and tools may best help that particular client start imagining with the least trepidation and most benefit.

This chapter focuses on relaxation methods that have been applied, studied empirically, and found effective for helping clients relax. These include meditation and several forms of relaxation.

Meditation

Meditation is a good relaxation method originally taken from eastern cultures but currently applied as an integral part of many psychotherapeutic activities, especially in cognitive, constructivist, and mindfulness approaches. Segal, Williams, and Teasdale (2002) described meditation as a way to make one's relationships with thoughts more explicit, or to make one's thoughts the objects of awareness (see Chapters 2 and 7). They suggested that at the beginning of therapy, meditation helps clients "get friendly" with their thoughts and differentiate thoughts from facts. Segal, Williams, and Teasdale used the metaphor of a cinema, asking clients to view their thoughts as if they were on screen. As part of constructivist therapy, Mahoney (1991) used experiential meditation and imagery techniques to help clients focus attention and "look inside" themselves and at their lives.

Marlatt (1994: 176) depicted meditation as "bringing the mind back home through the practice of mindfulness," with the aim of viewing and accepting emotions rather than suppressing or indulging them. In the practice of meditation, the mind is trained to focus on present experience. The meditator focuses on an ongoing, repetitive, "here-and-now" experience such as breathing rhythm, mantra repetition, images, or emotions. Buddhists describe this open, present-oriented, nonjudgmental state of awareness as mindfulness (Marlatt, 1994). Likewise, Greenberg, Watson, and Lietaer (1998: 114) stated that meditation is one of the most transformative forms of invoking "the actual of which I am aware," constituting a whole process of learning to accept oneself as is, a process that invites clients to "take a tour" of their own body or to "enter oneself." Thus, meditation can be viewed as a whole way of looking at life.

In contrast, relaxation is just one step or specific technique used to reduce fear and gain a state of peacefulness.

Relaxation

Relaxation is largely applied to reduce recognizable signs of anxiety, although some people practice relaxation without experiencing anxiety (Fisher, 2009). Relaxation is any method, process, procedure, or activity that helps a person relax; attain a state of increased calmness; or otherwise reduce levels of anxiety, stress, or tension. Relaxation techniques are often employed as one element within a wider stress management program and can decrease muscle tension, lower blood pressure, and slow heart and breathing rates, among other health benefits.

Several motives exist for applying relaxation. First, relaxation increases clients' control over their bodies, emotions, and thoughts. Thus, by training clients in relaxation, therapists can help them gain a sense of control over themselves. For example, relaxation plays an important part in intervention packages fostering clients' self-awareness (Fisher, 2009; Mahoney, 1991; Moore & Watson, 1999; Segal, Williams, & Teasdale, 2002) or teaching aggressive clients to control their aggressive responses (Burke, 2007).

The second rationale for applying relaxation techniques posits that clients cannot be relaxed and tense at the same time; therefore, relaxation can serve as a preliminary stage for clients to achieve before facing anxiety, and imparting relaxation skills could help reduce anxiety and tension. In line with this incompatibility of relaxation and tension, Wolpe (1982) employed relaxation as part of desensitization procedures for treating anxiety, teaching clients relaxation before exposing them to feared stimuli. Through systematic desensitization, clients are gradually able to associate a relaxed state with the situation or stimulus that had previously been anxiety-provoking (MacLaren & Freeman, 2007). Training in relaxation can help clients learn a more appropriate, functional association and subsequent response to the distressing situation or experience.

Third, by engaging the mind in self-directed relaxation, automatic cognitive processes are disrupted (Burke, 2007). Relaxation thereby helps improve learning, by improving concentration, coping with fatigue, opening oneself up to new cognitions, and teaching oneself to focus inward and increase awareness. For example, relaxation techniques are applied for children in schools, for adults with learning difficulties, and for clients with test anxiety (Lindsay & Morrison, 2007; Ronen, 1997).

In this book, the application of relaxation tools will be motivated mainly by the goal of helping clients make the shift from their daily level of functioning to a state where they can concentrate on imagery. Thus, I view relaxation as an initial prerequisite for clients to accept the notion of imagery work and to focus awareness on the complexities of the products that imagination has to offer.

Effectiveness of relaxation applications in therapy

Relaxation has been integrated into many CBT therapies, particularly for reducing anxiety (Alford & Beck, 1997; Foa, Keane, & Friedman, 2000; Greenberg & Goldman, 2008). Based on outcomes of controlled CBT studies for disputing thoughts, Beck (1976, 1996) claimed that relaxation is not as successful a technique *per se* as cognitive restructuring. However, in their book on the integrative power of cognitive therapy, Alford and Beck (1997) nonetheless suggested that deep muscle relaxation be included as a means to help clients relax before therapy, especially while treating panic disorders. They also recommended its inclusion in exposure and cognitive restructuring techniques, in line with the treatment developed by Barlow *et al.* (1989). Clark *et al.* (1994) found relaxation as effective as cognitive therapy and self-exposure while treating 64 clients suffering from panic disorders.

Foa, Keane, and Friedman (2000) used relaxation effectively together with exposure techniques, asking clients to stay relaxed while bringing up traumatic memories. They also found it effective as a starting session for clients with post-traumatic stress disorder, inviting them to elicit a memory of themselves being calm, or as an introduction to induce hypnosis.

With anger disorders, Moore and Watson (1999) employed relaxation within their four-phase CBT approach for anger reduction. The first phase focused on enhancing personal awareness of the anger. The second phase comprised response disruption and relaxation, where clients practiced calming visualization, progressive muscle relaxation, mental distraction, and self-talk. The third phase focused on cognitive restructuring, and the fourth phase consisted of cognitive and behavioral skills enhancement.

In mindfulness therapy, a large range of relaxation strategies are available to help clients refocus attention to something calming and increase awareness of the body. Hayes, Follette, and Linehan (2004) suggested that training clients in multiple relaxation techniques facilitates treatment outcomes. With clients unaccustomed to relaxation, they recommended starting with deep breathing in the first session because it is easy to demonstrate and the majority of clients see immediate benefits. They recommended introducing full progressive muscle relaxation next (see below), followed by the addition of imagery and meditation techniques.

Types of Relaxation Techniques

Frequently used relaxation techniques include autogenic relaxation, visualization, and deep muscle relaxation.

Autogenic relaxation

Employing both visual imagery and body awareness, the goal of autogenic relaxation is stress reduction. "Autogenic" means something that comes from within. By repeating words or suggestions in the mind, one can relax and reduce muscle tension. It is helpful to imagine a peaceful place and then focus on controlling or relaxing one's breathing, slowing one's heart rate, or feeling different physical sensations such as relaxing limbs one by one.

The following sample instructions can help induce autogenic relaxation.

Sit comfortably and let your whole body relax. Take a deep breath. Let the air enter into you slowly, then hold it for a few seconds, and then let it go out. Feel your hands becoming heavier and heavier. Feel your legs pulling you down. Your torso is becoming heavy and warm. Empty your mind of thoughts, and if any thought comes in, just let it go. Just concentrate on yourself and feel how relaxed you can get.

Visualization

In this relaxation technique, one forms a mental image for taking a visual journey to a peaceful, calming place or situation. During visualization, one should try to use as many senses as possible, including smell, sight, sound, and touch. If imagining relaxing at the ocean, for instance, then one would imagine the smell of salt water, the sound of crashing waves, and the sun's warmth on the skin.

The following sample instructions can help induce visualization.

Close your eyes. Sit comfortably. Take a deep breath. Try to bring up a picture of a nice place. It can be a real place you actually visited, and would like to return. Or, it can be somewhere you heard of but have never been. Or, it can be somewhere you make up for yourself. Note the noises you hear around you. Note the smell, the colors. Feel all the emotions you like: relaxation, happiness, joy, satisfaction. Let these feelings wash over you, entering you more and more, and as you feel them all over, feel your breathing getting deeper and deeper, your muscles getting heavier and heavier, and your whole body feeling heavy and warm.

Deep muscle relaxation

Among the various types of relaxation, progressive relaxation – first suggested by Jacobson (1938) – is the most common, both in CBT and other interventions.

This method involves repeatedly tensing and then releasing a succession of muscle groups in sequence, across the whole body, to gradually release muscular tension (Fisher, 2009). Progressive muscle relaxation can reduce the physical symptoms of anxiety that clients often experience when confronted with anxiety-provoking stimuli or with reminders of past traumatic experiences. In this method, therapists teach clients to watch for early signs of anxiety, such as worrying thoughts or somatic symptoms (e.g., palpitations, abdominal discomfort, muscle tension), and to use these cues to immediately start the progressive muscle relaxation procedure.

This technique may be combined with or used separately from deep breathing exercises (Mason, 2007). In deep breathing, the therapist, like in all the other types of relaxation, uses age-appropriate language to provide clients with the rationale for breathing from the diaphragm in an effort to calm down when experiencing stress, thus helping reduce uncomfortable physical sensations.

Let me detail how I apply the progressive muscle relaxation technique. The phases, order, and instructions all derive from Jacobson (1938), with my addition of calming words throughout the process. By focusing on slowly tensing and then relaxing each muscle group, clients increase awareness of physical sensations and clarify differences between muscle tension and relaxation. We start by tensing and relaxing the hands and arms; then we move to the legs and feet; then to the torso, leaving the head for last. This progression moves from body parts most distant from the heart to those closest; only at the exercise's end do we get to what is closest for us. Probably, the reason for this sequence is that people experience fewer difficulties exercising arms and legs, whereas the central body – stomach, chest, head – may elicit more shame, avoidance, and rejection, so we would like people to feel more relaxed by the time they reach their more sensitive parts. I can't recall any client complaining that a toe on the left foot is ugly. However, many complain that they dislike their chest, bottom, stomach, or face. Therefore, this technique begins with those parts that elicit fewer self-esteem issues or health problems, which therefore may make the technique simpler to learn.

The instructions ask clients to tense and relax each muscle group twice before moving on to the next. Therapists should instruct clients to repeat the right side twice, then the left side twice, then both sides twice (right arm twice, left arm twice, both arms together twice) or merely twice for central, single body parts (stomach twice, back twice). It is always important to spend less time tensing than relaxing. Jacobson recommended tensing for 12 minutes and relaxing for 20, although I never found any studies documenting that length of time is important.

The following sample instructions present the progressive sequence, detailing the first body part (hands) and then giving general instructions for the remainder. Note that the first instruction, the deep breathing exercise, should be repeated at several intervals: at the beginning, after ending the upper extremities exercises, after ending the lower extremities exercises, and after the facial exercises at the end. Any time when clients find it difficult to stay calm, the breathing exercise can help them return to the state of relaxation.

Breathing

Take a deep breath through your nose, hold it inside for a few seconds, and let it go out slowly through your mouth. (Repeat.)

Hands

Put your right hand in front of you, make a fist, and tense up your fingers as much as you can. Now relax and let your hand fall down. Repeat it again: Put your right hand in front of you. . .

Now we will do this with the left hand. Put your left hand in front of you. . .. Again: Put your left hand in front of you. . ..

Let's repeat it with two hands together: Put both your hands in front of you. . . Repeat it again: Put both your hands in front of you. . .

Fingers

Now we will exercise our fingers. Stretch the fingers of your right hand, tense them up, and then relax. (Repeat it again, then move to the fingers on the left hand and repeat twice, then practice all fingers together twice.)

Arms

Bend your right arm at the elbow and tense all muscles from the shoulder to the fingers, then relax. (Repeat it, then practice the left arm twice, then practice both arms together twice.)

Breathing

Take a deep breath through your nose. . . (Repeat.)

Feet

Curl up the toes on your right foot, tensing them up as much as you can, and then relax. (Repeat it, then the left foot twice, then both feet together twice.)

Toes

Try to stretch the toes of your right foot, pointing them out and tensing them up, and then relax. (Repeat it, then the toes of the left foot twice, then all toes together twice.)

Legs #1

Lift your right leg up outstretched, tense it, and let it fall down and relax. (Repeat it, then the left leg twice, then both legs together twice.)

Legs #2

Bend your right knee, tense it, and then let it fall and relax. (Repeat it, then the left leg twice, then both legs together twice.)

Breathing

Take a deep breath through your nose... (Repeat.)

Abdomen

Contract the muscles in your stomach. Tense them up as if you were pushing them inside, and then relax, let them go out. (Repeat.)

Buttocks

Tense your buttocks. Feel yourself rising up in your seat, and then relax. (Repeat.)

Shoulders #1

Tense your shoulders and bring them closer to your head, then relax. (Repeat.)

Shoulders #2

Tense your shoulders by pushing them down, then relax. (Repeat.)

Head

Move your head down to the right side, roll it to the center, and then to the left. Then relax. (Repeat.)

Face

- *Tense your forehead, and relax. (Repeat.)*
- *Move your eyebrows up as if trying to reach the hairline, and relax. (Repeat.)*
- *Try to bring your eyebrows together, to touch each other, and relax. (Repeat.)*
- *Tense your nose like a little kid making a face, and relax. (Repeat.)*
- *Tense your mouth by stretching it like a smiling face, and relax. (Repeat.)*

Breathing

Take a deep breath through your nose... (Repeat.)

Throughout the exercise, the therapist should continually intersperse instructions to the client to enhance relaxation and awareness to the different body parts, such as:

- *Feel your —— getting heavy, pulling you down more and more.*
- *Feel your —— become warmer.*
- *Feel the blood flow in your ——.*
- *Feel the difference between tense and relaxed.*
- *Feel the difference between your right —— and your left ——.*

In addition, I recommend a few important rules for using this progressive muscle relaxation technique:

- When clients report pain in a certain body part, do not give instructions to work with this part.
- For some people, relaxation is difficult and takes time to assimilate. Divide learning into several sessions.
- Let clients practice with their eyes open if they have difficulty closing them.
- Most people find it easier to tense than relax. Have them practice letting their hand or foot fall down several times to help them understand what "falling down" means.
- Note signs of relaxation and ask clients to note them: slow breathing, no sweating, low heart rate.
- After clients undergo relaxation training, they require less time to achieve a relaxed state. At this point, give them cues like: "Take deep breaths and relax yourself."

With these relaxation techniques in their repertoire, therapists now know how to help clients relax in preparation for imagery work. They now hold the car keys and are ready to start driving. The next stage is arranging the setting for the imagery session (see Chapter 10).

Summary

Relaxation is a technique that can be applied separately to foster self-awareness, self-control, and stress reduction, but this book's emphasis is on relaxation as a preliminary stage of imagery training. Relaxation has become integral to many therapies: behavioral, cognitive, constructivist, mindfulness, acceptance, and imagery therapy.

Most of all, relaxation skills aim to regulate emotions (Follette & Rasmussen, 2004), sharing the objective of imagery therapy to help clients focus on emotions and sensations and bypass disruptions in thinking processes. Therefore, many of the exercises performed to help clients accept (in acceptance and commitment therapy), be aware of (in mindfulness therapy), or create a visual picture in their mind (in imagery therapy) first of all use relaxation exercises.

Practice: Guidelines for Therapist Self-Relaxation Exercises

Instructions for self-practice

- *Find a regular time during the day when you can set aside 20 minutes for practicing. Making a routine helps create new habits for daily relaxation practice.*
- *Find the optimal place for quiet alone time without interruptions.*
- *Arrange a technology-free environment: no telephone, radio, or television.*

- *Find a comfortable chair; sit comfortably. Many people prefer a partially reclining armchair.*
- *Closed eyes are recommended, but relaxation can be practiced with eyes open.*
- *If you like, play quiet background music or audio instructions for relaxation. You can type up the sample instructions I provided above and read them to yourself or, better still, make your own audio recording of these instructions.*

Selection of relaxation method

Choose the kind of relaxation that you believe will work best for you. Experiment with different methods – deep muscle relaxation, meditation, yoga, imagery, or any other.

Practice for 20 minutes daily
Complete the daily chart in Table 9.1.

Table 9.1   Chart for monitoring self-relaxation

	Day 1	Day 2	Day 3	Day 4	Day 5	Day 6	Day 7
Did I practice relaxation today? (yes/no)							
Did I succeed in relaxing? (yes/no)							
The extent to which I felt relaxed: 0-------------------------10 (Slightly) (Extremely)							
Was I less tense today? (yes/no)							

10

Basic Guidelines for Conducting Imagery Therapy: From Setting to Termination

This chapter presents basic guidelines that therapists need to prepare for conducting imagery therapy. Such exercises can stimulate clients to open up, express emotions, find flexible solutions, and so forth (see Chapter 7). However, it is important to remember that imagery can be helpful only if well integrated into the psychotherapy session and process, among other tools available within therapists' repertoire. As shown below, images generated in the session (or eventually brought to the session from home as clients learn to use this language of imagery) must be discussed and integrated into the therapeutic work.

The content of an imagery session with the client comprises several phases:

1. Preparing the therapist, setting, and client.
2. Pre-imagery exercises in eliciting images.
3. Pre-imagery practice of client relaxation, to set the stage for generating images.
4. Eliciting imagery and describing it.
5. Facilitating new coping skills through imagery by extending the image, working with it, and trying to change it.
6. Ending the imagery work phase within the session.
7. Follow-up to imagery work, including reflection, interpretation, and meaning-making.
8. Giving homework.

Preparation of Therapist, Setting, and Client

Before starting a session, therapists should take all necessary steps for conducting imagery within the upcoming session, including preparing clients for what will ensue and arranging the treatment setting optimally for imagery work.

The Positive Power of Imagery: Harnessing Client Imagination in CBT and Related Therapies,
First Edition. Tammie Ronen. © 2011 Tammie Ronen. Published 2011 by John Wiley & Sons, Ltd.

Therapist preparation

Therapists should plan each upcoming session's imagery work, tailoring it to clients' intellectual ability, age, and emotional readiness (Hall *et al.*, 2006). (See Chapter 11 for more on adaptations to children and Chapters 13–15 for specifics on imagery contents.) Time allotments require planning to ensure the availability of ample time not only for creating images but also for interpreting and discussing them after visualization. The phases of preliminary relaxation, image generation, and subsequent processing can dominate sessions (Hall *et al.*, 2006); therefore, imagery work should start at the beginning of sessions, to leave enough time for all the needed phases of work. If insufficient discussion time remains, clients may feel distressed rather than content with the session's outcomes.

Arranging the setting

Before starting, therapists should establish a treatment setting conducive to imagery training, including seating arrangements, lighting, and a quiet, intimate atmosphere with protection from outside interruptions. Seating should provide therapists with a good direct view of clients, to monitor body movements during relaxation, as well as facial expressions and physical signs of discomfort that would signal a need to end the current distressing imagery. A large, comfortable chair for the client is recommended. Although many people think relaxation is easier lying down, many clients feel uncomfortable supine. Dimmed lighting enables a more relaxing and intimate atmosphere. External distruptions during sessions should be eliminated (ringing phones, knocks on the door, or people entering).

A valuable tool to facilitate relaxation is an audiotape recorded by the therapist during the first relaxation exercises with the client, which provides opportunities to practice the therapist's instructions at home and gradually learn to relax faster. This can substantially lessen the time necessary for pre-imagery relaxation.

Client preparation

Clients coming to therapy generally do not expect to be asked to close their eyes and relax, or to engage in guided imagery (Hall *et al.*, 2006). Also, for clients with trust issues, closing their eyes can be difficult (Battino, 2007). Therefore, therapists should obtain clients' consent and cooperation by carefully explaining what to expect and by clarifying the goals of imagery work. It is important to explain how the process will work: its phases and stages, the kinds of instructions they will hear. Telling clients about the advantages of relaxation and imagery exercises is recommended. Therapists can give clients articles to read or a video to watch about relaxation or imagery training. A crucial preparatory element is ensuring that clients are certain no harm can befall them: They should be assured that they will be fully conscious at all times, the process will not hypnotize them, and they can stop whenever they wish.

Pre-Imagery Exercises in Eliciting Images

For some clients, using imagery is very strange and different from anything they have previously experienced. To reduce fears and increase motivation, practicing some preliminary relaxation and imagery exercises can give clients a first-hand experience of imagery training without actually entering into the practice itself.

Preliminary exercises based on suggestible thinking can be useful for preparing clients to experience "traveling" in their imagination. The following hand exercises can show clients how strong their thinking is.

Try to concentrate on my instructions. I will show you some exercises with your hands.

- *Sit comfortably and keep your hands in front of you. Focus on your hands. Feel them getting heavier and heavier, as if they are being pushed down. Slowly, watch them move lower (see Chapter 9).*
- *Put your two thumbs in front of you 10 cm apart. Look at them very carefully and notice how, very slowly, they are moving toward each other, as if they are trying to touch each other.*
- *Extend one hand in front of you. Feel your arm become as strong and hard as steel. Try to bend your arm at the elbow, using your other hand, and see how difficult it is (see Chapter 9).*
- *Put both hands in front of you and close your eyes. Imagine one hand is very heavy, as if tied to a weighty stone, and it descends further and further. The other hand is tied to a balloon and floats up in the air, becoming lighter and lighter. Open your eyes and look at the difference between the two hands.*
- *Put your hands in your lap. Feel as if your hands are falling asleep. Feel the end of the little finger becoming heavier and heavier. It is getting warmer and you feel it carrying you downward. Try to raise it and see how difficult it is.*

A similar exercise requires the therapist to prepare a piece of string and a ring in advance:

Thread the string through the ring and hold one end of the string in each hand. Tell the ring to move backward and forward, toward and away from your body.

Soon, if the client concentrates, the ring will begin swinging in the desired direction, seemingly without any volitional movement. The exercise can be repeated with the client telling the ring to swing right and left.

These are not magic tricks, but rather demonstrate the power of suggestion and help clients understand the possibilities inherent in imagery work. These exercises can show clients that the brain "commands" their hands to perform whatever is the object of their concentration, and soon they obey without even noticing. The point therapists can get across here is that if it is so easy to feel one's hand as heavy, one's fingers touching each other, one's hand flying upward balloon-like, then consider what could happen if clients practice concentration and awareness for longer periods.

Simple, small exercises are recommended next, asking clients to elicit neutral pictures or memories that do not involve difficult emotions, life goals, or problem areas.

- *Bring up the picture of yourself eating breakfast this morning (see Chapters 6 and 7). Can you see yourself? What are you wearing? Is there any food in front of you? Can you describe what you are drinking? Can you smell the coffee? Is it hot?*
- *Bring up the picture of yourself driving to work today. Note how much traffic there is. What cars are being driven next to you? How is the weather? What are you thinking about?*

Fresh memories of very recent events from earlier in the day, like talking with friends or watching television, are simple to generate without too much emotion or creativity.

After showing clients that they can elicit actual, real memories (e.g., "Could you bring up a picture of you talking with friends at work yesterday?"), therapists can also encourage receptive imagery – those images that just "pop" into the mind – through free associations (e.g., "When you say you passed a field with red flowers, can you see something in front of your eyes?" or "The wonderful vacation you had – is any picture appearing in your mind?").

Next, after learning to elicit present and past pictures of real events, clients can start generating fantasized memories, first neutral ones without intense emotions.

Imagine you are going to meet your employee, and you decided to reinforce him for his good work. Can you see yourself sitting at the head of the table, explaining how well he functioned? Can you see his face? Can you see the joy and surprise he feels?

Once therapists feel sure clients can elicit such pictures, they can start "flying" with images to view unreal and future events and thereby help clients begin changing and practicing the skills they need. For starters, very simple guided imagery exercises may help clients express emotion.

This time, you are going to meet an employee who angered you to express your dissatisfaction with his actions. You warned him before. Now is your chance to tell him how you feel and everything you think of him. Look at yourself: Where are you sitting? Where does he sit? What's there on the table? Listen to his voice – how loudly he talks, his tone. What do you want to tell him? Try to tell him that he made you feel angry and disappointed. Can you see yourself doing it?

In this type of fantasy exercise, clients no longer try to remember a real event that occurred (either past memory or passive memory that just pops into the mind), but rather imagine an unreal event. However, such fantasies are still reality based, referring to events that could possibly transpire under certain circumstances.

The following case illustration describes initial client resistance to imagery work when verbal therapy was ineffective, and the client preparation phase that I undertook to pave the way for Bilha to use imagery effectively.

Bilha, age 50, complained of perplexing, reoccurring nightmares where her mother accused Bilha of never really loving or caring about her. Bilha could not fathom why this nightmare appeared and no discussion revealed any insight, but she was not sleeping well at night. When I offered Bilha an imagery session, she laughed, saying she was a concrete, rational person without much imagination, and had never been one to use imagery. I persevered in suggesting some imagery practice, and she finally agreed.

Beginning with neutral, nonemotional current memory, I asked if she could close her eyes and describe her house to me. When she started describing it very dryly ("a three-bedroom apartment with a big kitchen and big living room"), I prompted her to see the living room in her mind's eye and to tell me the colors of the walls and furniture, her favorite seat there, and where the television was located. After a short time, when she provided some detail, I began challenging her to see images in her mind: "Can you see the painting on the wall? Can you describe what it depicts? Look in front of you – what color is it? Can you see it more clearly? You are facing it – what is there on the wall?"

After this process, Bilha became able to describe her living room more richly, in vivid colors. From her face, I could tell she was really seeing something in her mind, actually bringing up images, and I encouraged her: "Great, you are seeing something. Good. Let's continue..."

To shift to more dynamic, past imagery rather than static, present imagery, I asked her to tell me about the last program she watched on television in the present tense, as if she were sitting and watching it right now. After several attempts, she was able to relay the story "live." Bilha could now, for the first time, elicit a "real" picture in her memory from something she had actually seen. Suddenly aware of her active imagination, Bilha smiled and said this was a strange exercise that she had never done before.

We next embarked on several sessions of practicing "small, simple" images from everyday events. As homework, Bilha elicited memories of events that occurred each day, trying to see them as clearly as possible.

Only after these initial preparations of the therapist, setting, and client can training enter the next phases, where it is possible to engage in a completely different level of relaxation, fantasy, and imagery.

Pre-Imagery Practice of Client Relaxation, to Set the Stage for Generating Images

After completing the initial preparations, we are ready to start working with more difficult, emotion-provoking images, but relaxation is often a prerequisite phase within the imagery session. As described in Chapter 9, clients who do not use relaxation routinely may experience considerable apprehension when asked to sit comfortably, close their eyes, and relax, especially for those with a strong need for control. To help clients feel receptive to imagery work and open up to a greater breadth and depth of images, therapists should implement the relaxation exercises and practices outlined in the previous chapter. After clients undergo the preliminary preparation phase and know what they will experience, and have learned to practice relaxation, it is time to start working with imagery.

As an example, Ron, age 32, was offered a top position in a high-tech company but was afraid of accepting it, fearing he would not be a good manager. Beginning with instructions leading to induction (see Chapter 7), I tried to help Ron view himself leading employees and acquiring managerial skills. I started with induction to lead Ron to a less critical, more receptive mode of functioning; to train him to slowly drop all daily thoughts, tensions, and involvements behind; to move into another level of functioning, characterized by more acceptance and awareness of body and sensations; and to practice relaxation. We practiced relaxation as suggested in Chapter 9, and then I instructed Ron:

> Focus on your body, what you feel while sitting like that now, knowing that you can allow yourself to take the time for relaxation. Take a deep breath, and let yourself rest.

After brief training, Ron was able to relax and could continue.

Bringing up Images and Describing Them

When starting work with images, clients practice eliciting pictures and viewing them as vividly as possible, whether passive receptive images or even active images, therapist-generated or client-generated. In this core phase of the imagery session, clients must actively elaborate and describe the generated images, highlighting different aspects and expressing accompanying emotions. Clients elaborate and explain what they are visualizing in order to begin learning more about their own lives, problems, and situations, but do not yet interpret, extend, or change images, as they will in the next phase. For now, clients try to stay "inside" the image or "be with it" rather than "talk about it," as they will later. The following description of Bilha's therapy regarding her recurrent nightmares illustrates this phase of eliciting imagery and working with it.

After sufficient sessions of preliminary preparation and relaxation practice, I asked Bilha to see herself going to visit her mother – entering her mother's house, looking around, and viewing herself in the house. Gradually, over several sessions, Bilha became able to view herself talking with her mother on such "visits." At first, she would turn to me, saying: "You see, I can..." I told her not to speak with me but rather just try to "be there" and tell me what she saw.

In this phase, therapists need to follow several key instructions for helping clients elicit and work with their images. As detailed next, therapists should tailor suggestions to each client, employing open, flexible instructions and "soft" words, staying with the client's story, vocabulary, and pace, checking that the client has begun imagining, and encouraging clients to remain in the present tense, use multiple senses, and fill in details of the image. I will offer brief case illustrations to exemplify these instructions.

Tailor various suggestions to each client

Some people respond easily to sensation-oriented instructions ("Pay attention to your feelings"), whereas others respond better to direct muscle-oriented instructions ("Feel the tension in your hand and try to relax it"). Therapists should explore different options, watch clients for responses, and use terms that clients find more familiar and that seem more effective.

I instructed Ron: "Feel your body becoming heavier as you sit here. Feel your hands and legs pushing down. Try to empty your mind and just listen to the blowing of the wind; smell the flowers outside the room and focus on yourself."

Speak in the present tense

To create real, effective images, clients must see themselves as present in those pictures. Discussing images in the past or future tense disconnects clients, whereas the present tense maintains an active connection – a sense of really "being there" – in given images. Imagery exercises can be used both for "talking about" experienced images, pictures, or sensations (e.g., *Can you see the woman stepping toward you?*) and for "talking with" images; that is, sensing their actual presence and addressing them (e.g., *Can you tell the woman what you think about her?*) (McNiff, 1992). However, in either case, the present tense is used.

Ron was instructed: "Now I want you to try and see yourself entering the corporate conference room. Look around and see the room in front of your eyes. Note the furniture and how it is arranged."

Elicit as many senses as possible

The more senses involved, the more vivid the picture. This is because for different people different senses are stronger than others. Hence, involving as many senses as possible will ensure that every client can bring up his or her strongest ones. Therapists should therefore ask clients to try to "smell the odors around you; look at the surrounding colors; note the feeling or texture on your skin; listen to the voices; feel the taste on your tongue..."

Ron was instructed: "Listen to the noises around you in the conference room. Can you identify the voices you hear? Note your feelings while entering this room. Look at the colors of the furniture and the walls, focus on the pictures. Can you notice the sensation of your skin and the touch of your clothes? Can you smell anything? Maybe the smell of the coffee on the table?"

Use "soft" words

Instead of giving instructions that sound like urgent commands (e.g., "do," "see," or "go"), offer instructions that leave the client leeway to agree or disagree, to comply or refuse. Soft words may include "try to" or "could you" and so forth.

I asked Ron: "Can you see anyone else coming into the room? Is there anyone you know there? Are you familiar with the things on the table?"

Give open, flexible instructions

When therapists get to know clients well, specific instructions can be selected with the confidence that they are suitable for each client. However, at first therapists are unfamiliar with each client's needs, preferences, and life story; they cannot take it for granted that a specific picture will make the client happy or relaxed. For example, asking a client to elicit "a picture of the sea with white sand" could be counterproductive if that particular client hates the sea. Hence, unless clients have informed therapists beforehand about what the sea means to them, instead of specifics like "the sea" or "chirping birds," a safer option would be to offer

156

general instructions like "Think of a place that makes you feel good, relaxed" or "Note the pleasant sounds you hear." Open, flexible instructions can help each and every client generate whatever images they wish.

Thus, although therapists must give clear, specific instructions, care must be taken to avoid being too specific or intrusive with therapists' own imagery that is not clients' (Battino, 2007). By establishing a good balance between obscurity and specificity, clients can better activate their own memories. For example:

> I could not tell Bilha "Listen to your mother telling you not to worry," because I had no idea how her mother talks or whether such behavior would characterize her. Yet, I could tell Bilha "Listen to your mother; try to understand what she is telling you," expecting Bilha to put the words to her mother's voice.

Stay with the client's story and vocabulary

Although metaphors can be either client-generated or therapist-generated, therapists are usually the ones who generate images in therapy; yet, those images are generally designed in connection with clients' prior disclosures. Thus, to foster clients' continuation of images and filling in of details, therapists should start describing clients' "story" based on clients' previous revelations.

> Having revealed his anxiety about appearing before colleagues and employees, Ron was told: "You are sitting near the table and the person is going to introduce you as the new manager. Can you bring up the pictures of the faces of all those sitting around the table? What do they look like? What is on their minds? What are they saying?"

Attending to clients' natural language and utilizing words and verbs that are familiar to and favored by clients (i.e., staying with clients' vocabulary) will ensure a continued flow of imagery work, without abrupt interruptions due to unfamiliar or disconcerting contents.

> Knowing that Ron was a timid person who was unaccustomed to talking about his successes and abilities, I voiced that insecure vocabulary at first instead of asking him to imagine himself as immediately embraced by the employees. I inquired, "Can you hear someone asking: 'Why was he chosen for the job? What can he do better than us? How can he lead us?'"

Check that the client has started imagining

Therapists must carefully monitor whether clients can actually see what therapists are trying to elicit. Ask clients: "Do you see anything? Do you see where you are going?" In addition, watch clients to ensure that images are not overly difficult to produce or experience. Several cues can help therapists determine if in fact clients are now imagining:

- *Clients give small, specific details* (e.g., "I'm wearing a blue scarf that suits my eyes").
- *Clients begin talking to other people loudly as if seeing them, or start moving their eyes from place to place as if looking at someone there* (e.g., the client starts speaking as if to a good friend standing next to him: "Do you see? I really look good now").
- *The therapist starts visualizing* (e.g., the more a client described himself, I started seeing him in front of me. When I could see him, it meant he was really viewing himself and therefore could depict the picture very vividly to me).

Ensure that clients fill in details of the image

Clients need to feel ownership over created images – that those pictures are "theirs." Therefore, always involve clients in the process of developing images. For example, if therapists describe general pictures, clients should be asked to fill in some details: "Who else is with you in the picture? What are they telling you? How do their voices sound?"

> Ron was asked to fill in details about people in the boardroom: "What else are they saying? What are the other people thinking? What are they telling each other? What are their facial expressions? How do they feel about your appointment to the manager's job?"

Pace the client

When working with images, therapists must ensure that they pace clients – that clients are following the pace and continuing to elicit images. Therapists lead the process but should not intervene too much; clients must receive adequate time to look for images within themselves. Thus, therapists must find the optimum tempo and amount of interference, balancing between talking too much and remaining silent too long. For example, while using therapist-generated guided imagery, rapid instructions are important to lead clients along the road toward imagery without having time to stop and think, because the minute they stop, they come back to reality and interrupt their imaginary train of thought (Hall *et al.*, 2006). On the other hand, while working with a client-generated traumatic memory, the therapist should proceed very slowly to let the client focus, concentrate, and fill in details relating to the image.

An illustration of treating Jeff is a good example of pacing. Jeff, a very shy, unconfident 21 year old, came to therapy to learn how to conduct relationships with women. I told him:

"Close your eyes, take a deep breath, try to relax. If any thoughts come in, don't fight them; just let them pass away as they came. When you feel ready, please raise your hand so I know we can go on.

Great, you raised your hand, meaning you feel kind of relaxed. So, imagine you have a magic wand and can turn yourself into whomever you wish. Look how you're dressed as a sorcerer, look at your face, knowing you have a wand in your hand and can soon use it. When you can see yourself with a wand in your hand, please raise your hand up to show me. Thank you.

Great. You are now viewing yourself with a wand. Let's see if you can use this wand. Imagine you are raising the wand and quietly saying those magic words that turn you into what you would like to be. If you can view yourself raising the wand and saying those words, raise your hand so I know for sure you are with me. You are raising your hand halfway; if I understand you right, you can see yourself with a wand, but it is difficult to know you are going to say those words.

Take a deep breath, try to relax. Remember that there is nothing you can do with the wand that you won't be able to change back. You are not taking any risks. Just checking if you like yourself this new way before practicing it for real. Now, can you see yourself raising the wand and saying those magic words? When you can, raise your hand.

Great. You can see it. You are standing there with the wand, and already you start looking different. As you use the wand, you are turning yourself into a very handsome, confident, happy young man [as I knew he wanted to be]. Try to focus on yourself being confident. Look around you. Listen to the voices; look at the colors, the smells. Pay attention to the place where you are – the smell, your body, and the way it feels. Can you see yourself content? If you can – raise your hand. Wonderful, you can."

Next, after being able to elicit an image, fill in its details, and understand it, we can start elaborating on it and changing it to try to acquire the new skills that are needed.

Facilitating New Coping Skills Through Imagery

Once therapists understand how to prepare the session, start working with imagery, pace clients, and support clients' elicitation of images, they can begin to tailor the session content to clients' needs for different skills. The core of this book (Part IV) is devoted to this phase of the imagery work, where therapists help clients extend and work with various kinds of images to meet the session goals, such as past memory, receptive memory, active memory, fantasy, or guided imagery.

To demonstrate the shift from the phase of describing what happened in the image to the phase of working with the image, let's return to Bilha.

Finally, in one imagined conversation with her mother, Bilha suddenly broke into tears and shouted at her: "How can you blame me for not caring about you when I am always thinking of you?"

This emotional outburst later led Bilha to uncover her guilty feelings about her mother being left alone since Bilha's father had died. When Bilha finally expressed her feelings that she was not doing enough for her mother, her nightmares stopped. She was even able to tell her mother about the dream, and her mother told her: "You've always been like that. Expecting more from yourself than anyone else expects of you. Stop this nonsense and start enjoying your life. . ."

In this phase of extending and working with imagery, different methods of imagery training and different targeted goals or problems mean that the therapist needs to deliberate about different sets of instructions. Segal, Williams, and Teasdale (2002: 249) compared this deliberation process to a cat that attentively waits at the mousehole for signs of movement. If the mouse moves too slowly when it comes out, the cat might catch it. But if the mouse is agile, the cat will fail and the mouse will get away. Borrowing this metaphor but ignoring its aggressiveness, if therapists are sufficiently attentive and prepared, their instructions can be attuned to their clients' dynamics, thus meeting the clients exactly where they are.

Specific contents for extending and working with images to impart diverse skills to different clients are detailed in Chapters 13–17, including applying imagery to treat past traumatic events and to impart assessment and awareness skills, coping skills, positivity skills, and so on.

Ending the Imagery Work Phase
Within the Session

Therapists should attend to two main issues in terminating the imagery work within the sessions, regarding timing and regarding clients' emotional state.

Decide on the best time for the client to end the imagery work itself

Inasmuch as imagery is only a stimulus for eliciting change, the end of the imagery exercise is not the end of the session. Much of the therapy – interpretation, feedback, and extending forward – is conducted after ending the imagery exercise (see below).

Unless clients leave imagery exercises and stop visualizing on their own, therapists should decide on the best time to end the process, based on the following reasons. One reason to end the direct imagery work is to follow a client's tempo, maintaining slow progress without pushing on to a phase for which clients are not yet ready. For example, when eliciting memories with clients who are unfamiliar with this technique, it is better to try one or two pictures and then stop training until clients have practiced this skill at home.

Another reason for ending exercises is because the images depicted involve difficult emotions that therapists evaluate as overly distressing for the client at present. In such cases, therapists can steer imagery toward neutral pictures or positive emotions, or can end the images that would confront clients with negative ones. Importantly, therapists must ensure that clients end the exercise feeling powerful and calm. For example, at first Jeff and I remained with his image of looking at a woman smiling at him, but I did yet not lead him from there to face his difficulties talking with women, fear of rejection, or social skills deficiencies.

The third reason to end imagery exercises is success. Each time treatment progresses to more difficult assignments, clients might feel distress or fail. Therapists should end imagery work with a sense of success, and only next time begin the next difficult imagery.

> To help Ron end the imagery feeling successful, I asked him: "Can you also hear those who say: 'Great! Congratulations. We need you around here!' Can you see someone among them who looks very happy? Who is it?"

Once clients are ready, having already experienced success, to face difficult emotions during imagery, and provided that sufficient time remains in the session, therapists can initiate more difficult assignments, such as Ricky's imagined visit to her son's grave (see Chapter 7).

Ensure that the client separates plausibly from the image and reaches a calm emotional state

Ending imagery work is vital to successful imagery therapy. The crucial first step in terminating imagery is to help clients sum up, say goodbye, or imagine leaving the scene. This separation enables the client to return calmly to reality. The next step is to ensure that the client ends visualizing in a good emotional state. After working with difficult emotions during imagery, therapists must help clients end their images while experiencing a sense of coping, relaxation, or positivity. The imagery should never be terminated when clients are in the midst of experiencing distressing emotions.

For example, in one session Bilha elicited an image of arguing heatedly with her mother and thus expressed feelings that she was afraid to share with her mother in real life. To ensure sufficient time for her to calm down and discuss the imagery work, I used descriptions of her mother that Bilha had given previously and helped her end the meeting with her mother. I told her:

"Soon we will have to leave this meeting, but before we do I want you to stand near your mother. Could you come closer to her? Can you see your mother smiling at you? Can you hear her telling you that she loves you? Look at your mother's face – what do you see on it? How is she looking at you? What do you feel about her smile? Do you believe her? Can you tell her that you love her and never want to harm her? Can you hug her before leaving her?

"We are leaving now, but we will come to visit your mother next time."

Likewise, the next example illustrates the practice of a simple exercise for increasing happiness toward the end of the imagery work phase.

Before ending the session with Jeff, it was important for him to practice viewing himself as happy, focusing on the smile on his face while feeling happy, noting how he stands when happy, and trying to capture this moment of happiness, while telling himself: "I am happy now. I have a happy moment."

Segal, Williams, and Teasdale (2002) suggested that sessions should be ended with meditation and mindfulness exercises to help clients relax, connect thoughts with images, and leave imagery feeling calm. After practicing a calming exercise to foster clients' sense of coping, hope, and optimism, therapists also must allot adequate time for discussion.

Follow-up to Imagery Work: Reflection, Interpretation, and Meaning-Making

It is of great importance to talk about clients' imagery experiences. Battino (2007) emphasized the role of postimagery discussion to remind clients of the larger process and to review all the steps for future enhancement. Even more significant are emotional feedback, understanding, and interpretation. Therefore, therapists should always follow up after the imagery exercise by asking clients to reflect on the process of imagery that they experienced that day in the session, and by asking clients to interpret the images elicited and find personal meaning in them. Finally, it is important to relate to future sessions, asking clients how they would feel about repeating this exercise and how they would like the picture to change.

Reflection

The first major part of follow-up to the imagery work consists of self-reflection. To assist clients in performing reflective thought concerning the session's process of imagery work and the emotions they experienced, therapists may ask questions along the lines of the following:

- *How was it for you to elicit images?*
- *Do you think it was helpful for you?*
- *What did you feel? Was it joyful? Difficult? Stressful?*
- *What was difficult, what was easy?*
- *Did you like the process? Did you like* ———— *[meeting your mother again, being introduced as manager, meeting that girl at the bar]?*
- *Could you feel relaxed while imagining the scene?*
- *Would you like to continue practicing imagery?*

With Ron, I asked specifically:

> "How was it for you to see yourself being introduced to the other employees? How frightened did you feel? What did you think of yourself as a manager? What was good in that picture?"

With Jeff, I asked:

> "How was it for you to see yourself differently? Could you enjoy the thought that you look good?"

Overall questions about the process might include:

- What can you take out of this session?
- What emotions are you most impressed with?
- What is the most significant thing you remember from the exercise?
- Would you like to continue working with images in the future?

Interpretation and meaning-making

The second major part of follow-up to the imagery work comprises, first, clients' interpretation and understanding of the process:

- What do you think happened to you?
- What did you really see?
- What does it mean for you to do that?

Next, clients need to check what meaning they can attribute to the imagery elicited and the interpretations proposed:

- What does it mean for your future life?
- What can you do with this?
- How might it help you behave differently?
- What good can come out of it?
- How can you use it to help yourself in the future?

Specifically, for example, I asked Ron:

> "How do you think you will cope there as the new manager? Was the experience only frightening or also exciting and joyful?"

With Jeff, I could ask:

> "Could you believe you can look so good? Can you imagine yourself as a young man whom this woman wants to be with?"

Therapists must remember that imagery is a strong, powerful tool. Often, clients attribute clairvoyant meanings to the process itself of eliciting an image, as if by seeing this vision, it means that it will come true. We must carefully explore clients' meanings to see what impressions and beliefs go home with them after leaving the session.

Assigning Homework

Last, after summarizing the session, client homework in imagery is essential. Homework ensures that clients practice using imagery and foster their ability to enter more quickly and easily the relaxed, open state that is conducive to imagery work. Homework also maintains the gains made during the session's exercises, so that important images or meanings do not disappear over the course of the week between sessions. This preserves outcomes of previous sessions. Finally, homework should always involve a good experience that can cause joy and should never entail imagery of suffering or fear. The assignment should involve short, pleasant pictures or relaxation that the client is capable of bringing up and practicing alone until the next session.

For example, Bilha's homework could be:

> Until the next session, I want you to capture the way your mother looks at you, loving, smiling, and holding you gently. Try to remember her face as she is looking at you now, and during this next week, bring it up in your mind every day.

Jeff could practice every day:

> Imagine once a day that you are meeting a woman and tell her something each day. Listen to your voice and her reply. Or: Imagine you asked her out and she agreed.

Likewise, I assigned Ron homework tasks including practicing self-affirmation:

> - Try talking about your feelings, sitting there being introduced as the new manager.
> - Try to see those people who were very happy for you.
> - Tell yourself every day until the next session: "I know they chose me because I am good. I believe I can do it."

Regarding their content, homework assignments should never relate to tasks that clients had difficulties with in the session, or to difficult emotions. Instead, homework should help clients practice either something they have already succeeded in doing in the imagery session, or else new, positive exercises that might help them feel good. Thus, the content of the exercise should focus on the possibility that clients, despite all the problems they are experiencing, can increase their happiness. Positive psychologists suggest that happiness can be increased through daily exercising (Lyubomirsky, 2007).

Summary

The success of imagery sessions depends to a large extent on appropriate preparation of the therapist, setting and client; conducting pre-imagery exercises to ensure that clients can elicit images; guiding clients to carefully extend and deepen the experience of viewing an image; ending the exercise positively; following up with discussion, interpretation, reflection, and meaning-making; and assigning homework:

- Arrange the therapeutic setting.
- Be aware of clients' expectations.
- Use wording aimed at increasing motivation.
- Offer easy-to-follow suggestions.
- Gradually progress toward higher levels of ability to use imagery.
- Give clear instructions for termination.

For clients to start visualizing images, therapists need to help them by offering leading questions:

- Do you see a picture?
- Are you visualizing anything?
- Is anything going on in your mind now?
- Who else is in the picture?
- What are you doing? Saying? Feeling? Thinking?
- What are others doing? Saying? Thinking?
- What is happening?
- How did you get there?
- Can you make the picture clearer?
- Can you see yourself?
- Are you inside yourself?
- When do you first remember those pictures?
- What did you do, think, feel, then?

Practice: Guidelines for Summarizing Knowledge and Skills Needed for Conducting the Session

- Before you can start an imagery session, ensure that you have good rapport with the client.

- Gather enough information about the client to enable you to work with suit-able images. Gain sufficient familiarity with the client's vocabulary, history, and problems.
- Use preliminary exercises to ensure that the client can visualize.
- Pace the client's tempo and make sure that the client can elicit pictures, progress with instructions, and stay relaxed.
- Be aware of the client's body language in designing new exercises.
- Observe eye movements as a key to learning that the client is imagining as well as to learning what the client is experiencing.
- Make sure that you use all the guidelines described in this chapter.

11

Adapting Relaxation and Imagery to Children

Although relaxation and imagery training are often implemented in child ther-apy, contradictory findings have emerged regarding their long-term efficacy for children, particularly for those of younger ages. Furthermore, the majority of available research consists of clinical studies or small sample sizes without con-trol groups for comparison, which do not lend themselves to broad empirical conclusions. One rare, large-sample controlled study of children, for example, compared the effects of progressive muscle relaxation and imagination to two other conditions (non-tension-producing neutral stories and tension-inducing arithmetic problems) among 160 children aged 9–12 years (Lohaus & Klein-Hessling, 2003). Results showed clear short-term effects for both the relaxation and imagery techniques and the neutral stories. However, such empirical studies are not the norm, precluding sweeping statements about efficacy.

In general, applications of relaxation and imagery with children do not differ very significantly from applications with adults, although certain adaptations to children's abilities and interests are necessary, mainly regarding language, concrete tools, optimal duration, and content of the images. This chapter presents specific applications and adaptations to children of the guidelines for working with adults (Chapters 9 and 10), first regarding the prerequisite stage of relaxation and then regarding imagery work.

Applying Relaxation to Diverse Childhood Disorders

Relaxation is employed to treat a large range of childhood disorders. Fonagy *et al.* (2002) claimed that, in general, behavioral treatments for children's problems of anxiety, fears, Tourette's syndrome, and similar disorders seem to benefit from the application of relaxation. However, these researchers emphasized the need

The Positive Power of Imagery: Harnessing Client Imagination in CBT and Related Therapies,
First Edition. Tammie Ronen. © 2011 Tammie Ronen. Published 2011 by John Wiley & Sons, Ltd.

for lengthy training before children can successfully apply relaxation and succeed in reducing long-term symptoms.

Friedberg and McClure (2002) mainly described exposure methods for working with anxious children, emphasizing the role of relaxation as a foundation on which to build performance-based treatments. They suggested that children's tendency to avoid exposure to feared situations underscores the value of relaxation to calm them and boost confidence before starting exposure assignments. Friedberg and McClure recommended teaching children models of physiological arousal to facilitate relaxation and their understanding of their own anxiety.

In their work on evidence-based psychotherapy for children and adolescents, Kazdin and Weisz (2003) reported relaxation as an effective method to treat depressive children. They also found that relaxation techniques enhanced young people's ability to reduce problems such as tension, anxiety, and social anxiety.

Mason (2007) described the use of relaxation with abused children within stress-inoculation techniques, aiming to diminish physical symptoms of anxiety during confrontation by reminders of traumatic experiences. Mason suggested that relaxation can be useful to slow heart rate, lower blood pressure, slow blood flow to major muscles, reduce muscle tension and chronic pain, improve concentration, reduce anger and frustration, and boost confidence to handle problems. However, most of these are clinical reports and not outcome studies.

Relaxation has also been applied to antisocial behavior, targeting children's ability to increase control over the body. Burke (2007) claimed that teaching relaxation to antisocial children serves multiple purposes. First, inasmuch as relaxation is regarded as incompatible with tension, physical precursors of aggressive behavior (clenched fists, racing heart) may be reduced, thus lowering the likelihood of physical outbursts. Second, engaging the mind in self-directed relaxation efforts interrupts cognitive processes that might lead children to escalating hostile attributions and motivations for aggressive reactions. Likewise, Essau (2003) presented research supporting the efficacy of group training in relaxation skills (along with self-monitoring and self-statement skills) for children with conduct and oppositional defiant disorders.

Fonagy *et al.* (2002) reported contradictory outcomes for the efficacy of relaxation in the treatment of children with asthma. Some studies found that relaxation reduced attacks' duration and children's coping with attacks, whereas other studies suggested that relaxation in combination with self-statement techniques did not contribute significantly to these children.

Adapting Relaxation Techniques to Children's Needs and Abilities

The requirements of sitting down and concentrating on breathing and muscle tension are not easy tasks for children (Friedberg & McClure, 2002). Therefore, in applying relaxation techniques with children, the main challenge facing therapists is to select age-appropriate language, time duration, and imagery content, to make instructions concrete and understandable, especially with younger children.

For example, to help 7 year olds understand the rationale for deep breathing from the diaphragm (Mason, 2007; see Chapter 9), therapists might explain how breathing deeply through the belly can help the body slow down and relax so that they can feel better when they get scared or angry. Likewise, when training young children in progressive muscle relaxation (see Chapter 9), Friedberg and McClure (2002) recommended tensing and releasing only two or three muscle groups instead of progressing through the entire list, to simplify the exercise and reduce its duration. When asking children to tense and relax muscle groups in sequence, therapists can point to the right or left side and say: "Squeeze that hand really tightly, like you're squashing a cherry tomato!" or "Feel your hand as heavy as a very big rock." As for adults, children should practice skills in and out of the sessions to develop effective skill levels.

Therapists can design concrete instructions that are understandable for younger children to meet any therapeutic need: facilitating children's understanding of what a relaxed, calm state is ("Can you think of yourself being very happy? Nothing is bothering you, and even your brain, body, and muscles are happy"); verifying that children understand instructions ("Does your right hand feel the same as your left hand? Is there any difference? Does one feel more tense/achy/pressured than the other?"); or developing awareness of sensations ("Can you notice how warm your hand became? Do you like that feeling?").

Specific child-appropriate tools can also help children learn skills and monitor affects and progress. Videos of children relaxing can be screened as visual modeling (Friedberg & McClure, 2002). Children can learn to label and rate their feelings/behaviors using a numerical scale that describes a particular emotion's intensity or a behavior's frequency. Very young children can use a color-coded scale by identifying the color representing each end (e.g., red for very angry and white for not angry at all). By connecting such scales to specific situations, children can develop awareness of stressful circumstances and useful strategies for coping with them.

Three examples can illustrate some different adaptations for applying relaxation with children at various ages: 4-year-old Dianne's fear of a television character, 12-year-old Ronnie's stuttering, and 15-year-old Daniel's test anxiety.

Case I: Dianne's Television Phobia and Anxieties

Dianne, age 4, was so afraid of a certain television character that she developed an intense fear of television and of visiting friends' houses. I wanted to use gradual exposure with Dianne, but could not combine it with relaxation because 4 year olds cannot be trained to apply fully fledged relaxation. They cannot focus attention or sit for long periods; they move from one activity to another; they do not close their eyes; and their sense of time is limited, so they cannot delay gratification to achieve long-term benefit. Therefore, rather than using standard relaxation techniques, I sought stimuli that she associated with a relaxed, pleasurable state.

In reply to my questions about her likes, Dianne named a favorite storybook that her mother often read to her and a favorite candy bar. I brought both items to the next session and told her we were going to hear the story and eat candy. From time to time as I read and she ate, I turned to her and asked her if she was happy, and if her body and brain also felt happy.

Then I asked her permission to watch, just for a second, the television character that she feared (on a video that I had set up in advance), while she continued to hold the storybook and eat the candies (i.e., relax). She didn't want to comply at first, but after a short time "being happy" she was ready. As promised, I turned the video on and immediately off. Dianne then wanted to turn it on and off herself, which turned into a game. Gradually, she could tolerate watching the figure without anxiety.

I told her that she was very brave for throwing her fear away. I asked her was she happy now that she was no longer afraid of the television, and her answer was: "Yeaaaaaaaaaaaa!!!!"

Thus, when Dianne felt happy, she could tolerate exposure. This illustration demonstrates the importance of using substitutions that make young children feel relaxed, in view of the fact that the complete relaxation procedure advocated for adults is inapplicable. Elements such as stories, games, candies, and a figure they trust can replace the standard components of relaxation.

Case II: Ronnie's Stuttering

Older children who can already use relaxation nevertheless need adaptations. Ronnie, age 12, and I worked for several weeks in treatment to assess his stuttering patterns. According to Ronnie's self-recording and self-evaluation, he stuttered the most when at home with his father in the evenings, whereas his school-mates didn't even know he stuttered. Ronnie said that he became very tense and stuttered copiously when his father corrected him, demanded that he check his homework assignments, and tested Ronnie's knowledge. I decided to teach Ronnie relaxation and let him practice at home in the evenings before meeting with his father.

The relaxation procedure I implemented with Ronnie very much resembled what I described for adults (Chapter 9), with four main adaptations to his age:

1. I showed him a short video of a child practicing relaxation that I created with one of my previous clients (with parental permission).

2. The duration of relaxation was shorter than the adult recommendation of 20 minutes – too long for a 12-year-old to sit with eyes closed.
3. We focused on only three main muscle groups rather than the whole list – hands, feet, and breathing.
4. I gave him a considerable amount of verbal reinforcement.

The relaxation exercise began thus:

> *Please close your eyes and sit relaxed, as you saw in the video.*
> *Then we will start relaxing our hands.*
>
> *Could you please put your right hand in front of you, and try to make a fist like an angry child. As strong a fist as you can. Great, that's right. Now try to relax your hand. Let it fall down, with no control of the muscles. Good. Let's do it again. First tense it up, and then relax. Try to focus on the fist of your right hand and see how different it feels from your left hand. Feel the heat in your hand.*
>
> *Now let's move to the left hand and repeat the exercise. First we will tense it, and then after tensing, try to relax...*

We continued working on the fingers of each hand, then shifted to the feet and toes, and then moved on to breathing. Ronnie practiced daily at home using an audiotape of my voice giving him instructions exactly as we did in sessions. He was asked to practice relaxation as soon as he could after arriving home after school, and then again in the evening if he was able, before his father returned home. In addition to relaxation, Ronnie received training in self-control skills, learning that stuttering is a behavior that depends on him, and that, if he wished, he could change his way of thinking: Rather than feeling afraid and tensing up in his father's presence, he could practice relaxation and feel better and then could give up stuttering. He also charted his tense versus calm feelings while with his father, and gradually Ronnie reported that he felt more relaxed and found it easier to cope with his father's demands, and he was not stuttering as much as before.

Case III: Daniel's Test Anxiety

Therapy with 15-year-old Daniel practiced three main skill areas addressing test anxiety (see Chapter 15):

1. General learning skills at home included how to summarize material, how to decide when to study and for how long, how to make sense of material rather than learning it by rote, etc.
2. Skills for answering test questions included how to plan the time devoted to each question, how to decide on the sequence for answering, how to make educated guesses, how to check and recheck answers, etc.
3. Skills for reducing anxiety during the exam focused on practicing relaxation.

As an adolescent, Daniel could participate in regular relaxation sessions, but after learning to relax in sessions and successfully practicing relaxation daily at home, he remained embarrassed about applying these techniques in public, in class, during actual exams. I therefore gave Daniel instructions for cued relaxation, which I termed "secret relaxation" to appeal to his developmentally appropriate heightened sensitivity to peer ridicule. Daniel was asked to apply our secret relaxation whenever he noted his previously identified bodily signs of anxiety (feeling warm, wanting to vomit, or stomach aches). The secret procedure could be performed unnoticed by classmates.

Sit down and relax. With your hands down at your sides, tense up your right fist as hard as you can, and this time put all your tension and fear into your fist. Tense it up even harder, until you feel the pressure of your nails in your palm. Your fist is so tight you could crush anything inside. Now, let it relax, and feel the deep level of relaxation that you are used to feeling after practicing the whole process. Note how relaxed you are now. All your muscles are relaxed, and you feel good.

Remember: Whenever you tense up your right fist, it will be a signal to your whole body to enter that familiar state of relaxation, and soon you feel that your whole body is becoming heavier, warmer. You feel more and more relaxed.

At first Daniel had difficulty skipping the longer procedure and becoming relaxed only by stressing his fist, but after several exercises he reported some success. Eventually, utilizing this cued relaxation, Daniel could relax himself during exams, was not as anxious as before, and improved the outcomes of his studies.

Thus, despite arguments about the efficacy of relaxation *per se* and the paucity of controlled studies with children, clinical reports pinpoint the benefits of training children in relaxation, both in therapeutic settings and as homework assignments, and later on in natural settings.

Applying Imagery Techniques with Children

In contrast to adults, who must be taught how to use imagery in therapy and who often feel inhibited or reluctant to begin imagery work, children find imagery techniques much easier and more natural. This is because children use imagination spontaneously and widely during development – in their play and when establishing language and social connections. Imagining occurs first with toys and then as a way to develop self-talk.

When exaggerated in frequency or intensity, imagination can also be a symbol of distortion. For example, Attwood (2007) explained that imagination provides a natural way for children suffering from Asperger syndrome to escape reality. He claimed that such children develop complex and vivid imagery worlds, sometimes with make-believe friends, which are disconnected from real human contact. However, therapists can use these imaginary friends to talk to such children and help them gain control over their problems.

Inasmuch as imagination is generally more easily accessible in children, few adaptations to imagery work are necessary. Just as with adults, the main method for using imagery with children comprises imaginal exposure in sessions, which gradually exposes children to feared stimuli through images (Kazdin & Weisz, 2003). Imagery is frequently used to establish relaxation and calm in children, and to enable the practice of various skills for coping with fears or other difficulties. For example, mental imagery can be applied in addition to deep muscle relaxation as a secret calming method to use in public. Kazdin and Weisz mentioned imagery as a skill taught to children to address the tension and anxiety that often accompany depression. Zimmerman (1998) used imagery techniques with children to help impart self-regulation skills during learning. At each of the three self-regulation phases – forethought, performance, and self-reflection – imagery can assist children in forming mental pictures to facilitate planning, learning, monitoring, and evaluation processes.

Imagery has been applied for a range of childhood disorders, including impaired motor coordination or developmental coordination disorder (Wilson & Thomas, 2002). These children have difficulties internally representing the visuospatial coordinates of intended movements. Imagery was compared to other techniques designed specifically to train the forward modeling of purposive actions. The imagery protocol – delivered by an interactive CD-ROM – was shown to be as effective as perceptual-motor training in facilitating the development of motor skills in the referred children.

I next present a case illustration for applying imagery in child therapy, using drawings, metaphors, and imagery to treat a young child with a very traumatic past. Through imagery exercises, Lee, age 8, learned to control her past trauma, overcome her fears, and start developing emotional relationships with her adoptive parents. As a baby, Lee was abused by her biological parents, removed from home, and then adopted. Her adoptive parents brought her to therapy to help Lee accept them and learn to express emotions appropriately (see details in Ronen, 2003b). Although Lee had difficulty identifying and expressing feelings, she used imagination naturally at this age and therefore imagery seemed a treatment method of choice. Lee's initiation of the following conversation revealed her personal penchant for images:

> As Lee entered my room, she saw a painting of a lion and a rabbit. She commented: "That lion will eat the rabbit up completely, nothing will be left. I know it. That rabbit's going to die" (Ronen, 2003b: 130).
>
> I was able to use her natural imagery responses to continue talking about how the lion felt, what the rabbit thought, what she could do if she was the rabbit, and how children can learn to be afraid of lions and keep themselves safe.

Inasmuch as talking about her abuse was very painful for Lee, images and metaphors provided an effective way to discuss events from a distance. To help her understand more about her past and be able to accept her adopted parents as different from her biological abusive parents, for example, or to understand how she might act differently than her abusers if she had power and control over others, I could ask her:

> Let's think. If you were that lion, what do you think you would feel? Think? Do? What would you tell the rabbit?

Considering Lee's age-appropriate proclivity for images, I decided to use imagery techniques for many reasons. Imagination permits reaching out to many realities that are physically absent, as in playing both sides of a chess game in one's head. Lee's abuse transpired in the past, when she was still very young, and she demonstrated difficulty in remembering the details. However, her progress depended on her recall and expression of as many as possible of these fearful traumatic experiences.

At first, we used imagery to elicit her early memories, as a basis for trying to accept and understand the little Lee. We continued using creative imagination even as she progressed, because imagery not only emphasizes past events but also has healing power by pinpointing change. The following (Ronen, 2003b: 136) reveals how Lee could look at her past self and present self through images.

> I asked her to imagine two different Lees – the safe 8-year-old Lee and the young abused 5-year-old Lee – and then to draw them. At the beginning of treatment, "young Lee" (a black monster drawn with a large mouth and long arms) contrasted markedly from "big Lee," who was drawn very pale, thin, and vague. Later in treatment, when I asked her to draw both Lees again, the figures had changed. She drew "young Lee" much smaller and "older Lee" much bigger. When asked to portray "future Lee," she drew a large, brightly colored figure, but qualified it by saying she didn't exactly feel that way now but thought she would feel like it one day after finishing therapy.

Chapter 16 presents details and case illustrations on how to apply imagery with various childhood disorders.

Summary

Children, like adults, can learn how to use both relaxation and imagery. Although these techniques necessitate body–mind connections, control over behavior, and the ability to focus attention, children can learn to apply them if they receive age-appropriate instructions, language, time duration, and contents. Clear, short, understandable instructions; concrete and familiar language that connects implicitly to children's world of associations; concrete demonstrations and explanations; exercise duration and complexity tailored to children's time perception and cognitive stage; and provision of clear goals to achieve – all of these adaptations contribute to the success of imagery and metaphor applications with children. Just as with other techniques, the question is not whether relaxation, imagery, and metaphors can be applied to children, but rather how best to apply them effectively.

Practice: Guidelines for Adapting Relaxation and Imagery to Children and Young People

Adapting relaxation

With adolescents, therapists can usually apply relaxation procedures very similarly to their customary implementation for adults, without the need for major adaptations. However, when applying relaxation with children, some changes should be considered:

- Show children a video that visually presents the process of relaxation, helps them understand what they are expected to do, and reduces confusion and misunderstandings.
- Train children to tense and relax by first demonstrating the physical gestures yourself. Discuss the differences between tensing and relaxing. Give concrete and understandable instructions, especially with younger children.
- Remember that children get bored easily, and overly long relaxation durations can bring about the opposite outcomes – restlessness, impatience, and annoyance. Therefore, give short instructions at a faster pace. Brevity of instructions may also facilitate comprehension.
- Remember that children are not accustomed to sitting still for lengthy periods. Try to foster relaxation by initiating a fun exercise or a pleasant memory, rather than merely practicing relaxation.
- Create a pleasant atmosphere, a cueing stimulus, or a short exercise to prompt relaxation in children.
- Shorten relaxation by focusing on one to three muscle groups rather than the whole body sequence, and by emphasizing relaxation by cues rather than deep relaxation (as in the case of Daniel tensing only his fist).
- Remember to pepper the relaxation with many reinforcements to help children maintain attention and increase motivation for continued investment of effort.
- Talk about the relaxation after terminating the process. Try to understand children's experiences and their likes and dislikes of specific aspects.
- Ask children to rate both their ability to practice relaxation, and the extent to which they felt relaxed, on a scale of 1 to 10.

- Assign daily homework to maintain the skills that have been learned and avoid forgetting over the week between sessions.

Adapting imagery

- Inasmuch as most children can create a memory very easily, usually less time is needed to generate images, and instructions for working with images can be briefer and quicker.
- On the other hand, children usually cannot keep their eyes closed over time or persevere in working with imagery. Therefore, you can work with images as stimuli (i.e., elicit a picture), but be ready for children soon to open their eyes and leave the imagery, and then continue by talking about what children saw and what it meant, rather than continuing to be "in the image."
- Imagery work with children is often transferred into metaphors. In other words, you may start with imagery work and then, as soon as children elicit a memory, they may feel it is easier to open their eyes and continue talking about the imagery "from the outside," as a metaphor.
- With children, it is easier to talk about the images, role-play, and discuss them in the follow-up part of the session, not during the imagery exercise itself, which should be brief.

Part IV

Using Imagery while Assessing and Treating Clients

12

Using Imagery for Assessing Clients Throughout the Treatment Process

Holistic assessment processes from a CBT perspective, as mentioned in Chapter 2, occur throughout the therapeutic process, carefully identifying objectives, targeted behaviors, and appropriate methods of measurement, and concentrating on contemporary determinants of behavior rather than on early life events or a client's past. In line with the constructivist view of clients as responsible for their own lives, clients should be considered as active, equal partners in this assessment process, capable of assessing their own problems and needs in collaboration with therapists (Finn & Tbnsager, 1997; Horvath & Symonds, 1991; Raskin, 2002). In Chapters 2 and 14, there are also components regarding specific techniques for helping clients assess themselves, their life scenarios, and their problems.

In this chapter, I focus on the integration of imagery into the assessment process that occurs throughout the course of treatment, and accompany this discussion with guidelines and case illustrations. Imagery-based assessments can be used to meet various aims and targets at different phases of the therapeutic process.

Imagery Integration into Assessment

In trying to integrate imagery into CBT, Safran and Segal (1990) recognized that valid measurements are important for assessment, but emphasized the memories or images that emerge spontaneously when exploring interpersonal issues in an emotionally immediate way. Although memories may not always provide accurate, objective information, Safran and Segal recommended that therapists regard them as sources of significant information about client history, and especially about the meaning of elicited memories for that client.

The Positive Power of Imagery: Harnessing Client Imagination in CBT and Related Therapies,
First Edition. Tammie Ronen. © 2011 Tammie Ronen. Published 2011 by John Wiley & Sons, Ltd.

Danaher and Thoresen (1972) examined potential imagery-based assessment procedures with the intent of providing behavioral therapists with prognostic tools for determining the applicability of imagery intervention for specific clients. They recommended imagery as helpful in assessment, but were unable to present valid information about how it contributes to clients. Further studies are required to establish the validity of imagery-based tools for assessment purposes.

In constructivism, the use of imagery is a natural tool for the assessment process, and both metaphors and imagery are suggested as good ways to help clients unfold their reality, discover their needs, and self-assess their goals, strengths, and weaknesses (Neimeyer, 2009). Assessment is also recommended to gain familiarity with the client's personal story – the network of personal constructs or meanings through which clients anticipate the world (Neimeyer, 2009). By transferring stories to pictures, clients can focus more on emotion and thought than on explanations. Leaving behind the interpretation and focusing on events themselves are the main benefits of implementing imagery exercises. Neimeyer stated that constructivist therapists' goal is to understand not "why" people act in the first place but rather the direction in which their activity is likely to carry them. Mahoney (1991) claimed that simple, spontaneous imagery, fantasy, and meditation exercises can illuminate much about clients, especially refining therapists' understanding of clients' "felt experience" (Mahoney, 1991: 294). He recommended exercises such as fixed focus of attention or mindfulness, where clients shift attention to themselves and reveal more about what is meaningful for them.

Thus, using imagery for assessment aims to help therapists achieve four main goals.

Collect new information to gain better understanding of clients and their disorders and thus shape decision making at different phases of therapy

Images can provide a wide range of information, including data on clients' thoughts, feelings, and behaviors; clients' motivations and strengths; and the unique characteristics of the clients' problems. For example, when creating a behavioral profile (see Chapter 2), imagery can help both clients and therapists elucidate the answers to questions like: "How do you behave (think, feel) now, in the present, while facing the problems at hand?" Asking clients to imagine what they look like, to visualize their fearful behavioral reactions when confronting dreaded stimuli or their facial expressions while feeling "upset," can significantly clarify clients' reports. Likewise, when asking clients questions about the future, imagery can be extremely beneficial:

- *Can they imagine their lives without the problem (see how they look, think, feel, and behave) and pinpoint the differences between then and now, with the problem?*
- *Ask them to imagine their lives 10 years from now, when the problem is over. Can they see how happy and content they are?*

In identifying treatment needs, for example, imagery can help therapists determine whether clients are at the right stage to start working toward a specific goal for change and if the treatment process is headed in the right direction, or whether changes in technique or approach should be implemented (see Chapter 14). One of the advantages of imagery therapy is its empowerment of clients' self-assessment skills, by asking clients questions such as: "How do you explain this picture you are seeing? What do you think is happening to you? What is the reason? How do you assess your ability to change it?" This enables clients to become active partners in the whole process rather than passive recipients of assessment, thus highlighting the importance of assessing *with* clients instead of merely assessing clients.

Bypass verbal assessment's limitations

For example, as mentioned in Chapters 6 and 7, imagery detours around rationalization and permits clients to look at themselves and their disorders differently, not only in therapy but also in assessment. Hence, taking time out from talking to elicit a memory or an image, whether client-generated or therapist-generated, can furnish important new information that may color ongoing assessment differently. As a GPS aids our vehicle to arrive at its destination by various routes, so can various images and metaphors help therapists arrive at a more sound assessment of clients.

The following case example illustrates how imagery facilitated a more accurate assessment of a 12-year-old's social relationships than mere words.

In the first intake session, Joey complained of loneliness and sadness, but said he had many friends and everyone in class liked him. To bypass his vague verbal descriptions and interpretations and get a better understanding of the situation, I asked Joey to imagine: "You are in school, and you have a long break. Everyone goes out and plays football. What are you doing? Where are you standing? Who are you talking with?" Very soon, I realized that while everyone played outside, Joey remained in class, bored, because he did not like football.

I then asked him to imagine that the school day was over: "All the boys go home together. Where are you? Are you going with them?" He replied that he was the first to leave class and went home alone.

I next asked him to imagine a classmate's birthday party: "Where are you? What are you doing?" Joey replied that he did not go because he had nothing to do there. Thus, imagery-based assessment exercises clarified the gap between his verbal declaration of having many friends and the fact that he kept to himself and felt an outsider among other children at school.

Pinpoint specific areas where clients lack the skills necessary to facilitate more positive functioning

In line with positive psychology's focus on learning about clients' ability to express positive emotion, feel happy, and increase their future subjective wellbeing, imagery plays a major role in assessing how clients wish to see themselves and improve their wellbeing in the future (Lyubomirsky, 2007). Neimeyer (2009) accentuated the need to assess clients' emotional processes and how these processes cultivate clients' way of interacting in the world. Keyes (2002, 2006) pinpointed the need to assess clients' ability to flourish by expressing a large range of positive emotions together with a small range of mental problems. Assessment of positivity is very specific, evaluating clients' resources, strengths, and virtues so that therapists can pinpoint specific skills that clients need to acquire.

Assess clients' specific imagery- and metaphor-related abilities

This fourth aim of assessment uniquely characterizes imagery therapy, in which therapists use images and metaphors to determine clients' capacity to naturally elicit images/metaphors; learn this skill; deepen images through role-play or emotional expression; cope with the difficult, traumatic pictures they elicit; and perceive images/metaphors as an important part of their personal reality. This direction of assessment provides crucial information to guide therapists' implementation of imagery and metaphors at different phases of the therapeutic process.

Assessment in Different Treatment Phases

CBT advocates a nonstop, dynamic process of asking questions and conducting continual assessment that spans the entire course of treatment: beginning at referral, continuing throughout intervention, and culminating when treatment outcomes are evaluated and maintained. Overall, assessment is a way continually to learn more about clients, tapping therapists' impressions and reports from clients' environments (Kanfer & Schefft, 1988), and going beyond initial diagnostic labels that strictly compare clients' behavior to clinical criteria reflecting standardized norms. Thus, in each phase of intervention, the assessment and questioning processes differ in emphasis, in relation to the specific problem in the specific client at the specific stage (Ronen, 1993).

Pretreatment phase

At the earliest phase of therapy, assessment focuses on: (i) gathering diagnostic and prognostic information about the client and problem, especially the client's behaviors, thoughts, emotions (especially happiness), motivations, strengths, and expectations; and (ii) deliberating treatment plans – initial decisions about the

184

client's need and aptitude for treatment and about optimal settings and methods. These foci do not serve as the targets of assessment only in the initial phase; they receive continual assessment throughout the next phases as well.

According to Finn and Tbnsager (1997), in the pretreatment phase, assessment entails three steps: (i) data collection, often employing the administration of standardized tests; (ii) deductive unilateral interpretation of assessment data regarding clients' historical information; and (iii) developing recommendations for using assessment data and deductions in decision making about therapy. For example, collecting clients' predictions about treatment outcomes at the outset of therapy can provide unique insight into clients' beliefs about their strengths, motivations, and expectations, which may shape treatment-planning decisions. Mahoney (1991) stated that initial contact with clients affords global first impressions of clients' immediate needs.

Ongoing assessment phase

Unlike in the medical profession, where an initial, solid, reliable diagnosis (e.g., the kind, size, and stage of tumors) can crucially determine decisions about treatment (e.g., radiation, chemotherapy, none), in therapy assessment is ongoing. Therapy can proceed without a full initial assessment because treatment decisions are continually updated over the course of therapy, as client–therapist relationships develop, clients change, and new information emerges in each session. I liken this to my experience as a traveler: I cannot decide all the little details in advance and often find myself touring new sites spontaneously, staying in places longer or for a shorter time than planned, or doing things differently than expected. Part of the excitement and joy of journeys are the surprises produced by flexibly taking new routes and diversions.

During the body of treatment, assessment comprises constant checking and rechecking of information, asking questions about hypotheses and assumptions, and looking for changes indicating progress in clients' functioning.

Termination phase

As therapy winds down, evaluative assessment of treatment outcomes (Ronen, 1997) compares clients' current behavior to baseline levels, thus clarifying the treatment's efficacy and the extent of change exhibited by clients. This enables decision making regarding when therapy should end. Moreover, assessment at this phase targets self-help skills conducive to maintenance and generalization.

In general, assessment processes and phases with children do not differ dramatically from those of adults. However, additional considerations must factor into decisions about children's candidacy for therapy, relating to the disorder's developmental nature and to children's environments. In my book on cognitive developmental therapy with children (Ronen, 1997), I proposed guidelines for assessing children by focusing on the problem's characteristics as well as the child's characteristics (Mash & Terdal, 1988; Ronen, 1993, 1997). (Also see Chapter 5 for more details of developmental considerations.)

Targets for Conducting Assessment

As described above, assessment is a continuous process of inquiry that starts at the time of the referral, is ongoing throughout treatment, and only ends when treatment outcomes have been evaluated and maintained. I will now detail the specific targets for conducting assessment throughout the different phases of treatment, based on a positivistic CBT orientation and integrating imagery exercises.

Target 1: Assessing clients' problems

Whether at the initial stage of therapy or during ongoing assessment stages, imagery exercises can bridge gaps relating to missing information regarding clients' problems and their history and consequences (including valid diagnoses or reports by other professionals). Neimeyer (2009) suggested that therapists invite clients to examine themselves and their lives with an experiential focus and exercises in imagery and meditation.

To reduce stress and anxiety at the beginning of sessions focusing on problems' history and how clients view problems, therapists can ask clients to sit comfortably and then present some relaxation exercises (see Chapter 9). Then, therapists can ask clients to visualize an expert specialist image, which helps clients concentrate, organize their thoughts succinctly within time limitations, and concisely select and summarize the most crucial issues for presentation.

> *Imagine you are invited to meet with a specialist, a world-class expert in your area of suffering. You have only a short time with him, so you cannot really spend more than 15 minutes telling him about the problem.*
>
> *You are sitting in front of him. What are you telling him? What are the most important things you present to him? What things will help him diagnose you? You wrote a note before coming to him to help you remember the important things. Look at the note you wrote. What is written there? Have you missed anything?*

To further enhance clients' ability to look at themselves as if from the outside or from a distance, the same exercise can be repeated by asking clients to talk about themselves in the third person.

> *Imagine you are your own doctor and you are going to consult a specialist about your client's condition. What would you tell this specialist about your client?*

Third-person exercises ("Please describe your problem as if you were a stranger observing your problem") often permit a less emotional and more rational view of events, thereby complementing information provided by first-person exercises ("Please tell me about your problem"). The third-person and specialist viewpoints can change and enrich the information that the therapist receives.

Most exercises can be applied similarly with children, simply by adapting the situation to their lives. To obtain similar first-person information from children:

Pretend you are invited to meet the school counselor and need to tell her about your problems. You are sitting in front of her. What are you telling her?

To obtain third-person information:

Imagine you are listening to your best friend telling the teacher about your problem because your friend is worried about you. What does your friend say?

Another image-based assessment technique for collecting information helps clients focus on pictures rather than words in order to bypass verbal roadblocks:

I would like you to tell me the history of your problem through photographs in a photo album that outlines the stages of your problem's development. Look at the album. Can you see the first picture? It shows you just before the problem started. What was different? How do you look? How do you feel about this picture? Now go on to the next picture, just as the problem started – what has changed? What do you look like? How do you feel about it? What do you think about it? Look at the last picture – just before you came here. What is clear to you? What can you notice? What is it telling you? What do you feel about it?

As I have emphasized throughout this book in the context of imagery work, verbalization differs from emotional language.

Such image-based assessment techniques can be designed for numerous areas of interest. The decision about what to ask depends on therapists' deliberations concerning what is important to assess at that stage of assessment. If we need more information about vocational functioning, clients can be asked to elicit pictures of work meetings or conversations with colleagues to discover how clients behave and feel there. If more information about social activities is needed, we can "send" clients to an imaginary party and observe their behavior. If we need to know more about how clients think, we can ask them to imagine that they videotaped their thinking style and we are now watching the video together.

Target 2: Assessing clients' emotions, thoughts, and behaviors

To ascertain information about clients' thinking style, we can borrow an imagery exercise from literature or films with which the client may be familiar. For example, in a wonderful situation described by J. K. Rowling (2007) in her book (and film) *Harry Potter and the Deathly Hallows*, Albus Dumbledore, headmaster of Hogwarts School of Witchcraft and Wizardry, used his magic wand to extract a memory from his own mind. Then he and Harry together put their faces inside the retrieved memory and watched it unfold. Another time, Harry Potter "heaved on the desk and poured Snape's memories into the wide basin ... the memories swirled – white and strange … and Harry dived…" (Rowling, 2007: 532). We can use such methods as imagery exercises to assess our clients' thinking styles.

> *Imagine you are in Hogwarts, the school for wizards. You can take your magic wand just like Harry Potter and take the memory out. You can see it very clearly. What do you see? What does it look like? What is the story that is in front of you now?*
>
> *Imagine you can also take out all the thoughts and feelings you have about your memory and see them. Tell me what you see. What do you think about it? What do you feel?*

Another way of learning about thoughts is to ask clients to imagine that they can hear, read, or just "see" what other people are thinking about them.

> *Imagine you are using your magic wand now, to take a thought out of your wife's brain (or your mother's, or friend's). You extract the thought and dive into it. What do you see? What is their thought about?*

To provide considerably more information, therapists can apply a broader, image-based assessment technique, tapping clients' thoughts about different groups of people's thinking, in ascending order of familiarity.

> *Imagine you decided to walk to work. As you cross the street, you see several people whom you have never met before. They look at you as you stand together at the traffic signal and observe you. What do they think about your appearance? Your attitude? Your behavior? What can they know from simply crossing your path?*
>
> *As you continue, you realize that you are walking alongside your neighbor. You don't have a close relationship with this neighbor, but you do greet each other when you meet. What can this neighbor say differently about you, compared to those strangers who met you at the traffic light? What can the neighbor add to their opinion about your appearance? Your attitude? Your behavior?*
>
> *You now come across a distant friend, a friend of a friend. This person knows you; you have met on several occasions and even talked several times. What will this person say about you, in addition to what the others said? In what way can this person add information about you as a person – who you are, what you do, how you behave, maybe something about your nature?*
>
> *Next, as you get closer to work, you are very glad to see a good friend of yours. You really wish you had time to chat with this friend, but you need to get to work. What will this friend say about you? Your behavior? Character? Nature?*
>
> *And now you meet your best friend. There are some things that only this friend knows, only this friend can tell about you, and your nature. What will this friend say?*
>
> *Finally, you are alone. No one else is walking near you. Looking at yourself in the mirror as you face the entrance to work. What can you tell about yourself that no one else could know or say?*

In such an assessment exercise spanning concentric circles of figures in the client's environment, the therapist can obtain considerable information about the client's social situation, beliefs about how others relate to him or her, and conceptions and misconceptions. When I once assessed a young adolescent using this exercise, he told me that everyone who saw him in the street was afraid of him and thought he was aggressive because of his tall, strong build and walking style. However, only his family knew that he was actually a very shy young child and not at all violent. Younger children who may not have the verbal ability to describe these different perspectives can be asked to draw themselves as different people would see them.

In a similar way, imagery can elucidate clients' emotions. Using the wand extraction exercise, therapists can ask clients to remove not a thought but a feeling from the heart.

> *Can you look at the feeling and see what is it? Is this feeling familiar to you? Do you enjoy feeling it? Can you make this feeling grow more and more? Can you make this feeling become smaller and smaller?*

In assessing emotional variables, therapists should try to learn about changes in the emotions experienced by clients over time:

> *Imagine you would like to show us your emotional photo album. Let's look together at the album. What emotions do you see? Which one do you like the most? How do you feel seeing yourself feeling this way? Would you like to see yourself expressing this emotion again? What other emotions are there in the album? Is there any emotion you would like to take out of the album? Is there any emotion missing? If you could add pictures of emotions, which would you like to add?*

With young children, it is easier to use imagery and metaphors more concretely. Therefore, I often draw a circle and tell the child:

> *Imagine this is a circle of your emotions. Please color it in to show me which emotion you are feeling now [or which emotions you generally feel].*

Some children color very strong shades of black and red to express anger, stress, or sadness, in striking contrast to children who use light or bright pastels to express love, happiness, and joy.

If we know of a certain emotion that reflects our client's experience and wish to learn more about it, we can try to design an appropriate assessment exercise.

> *Imagine you are now in the Land of Sorrow. Everything around you is very sad. You have never been as sad as you are now in the Land of Sorrow. Look around you – what do you look like when you are in this land? What is your expression? How do you move? How do you feel? How do you like being there? What are you missing there? How familiar is this feeling to you? What part of you is filled with this emotion?*

Positive emotions deserve special mention, inasmuch as I view happiness as a crucial aim of therapy (see Chapters 3 and 16). To assess whether clients have positive emotions and can increase subjective wellbeing and happiness, therapists can ask clients to compare themselves now and earlier.

> *Look at yourself as you were at the beginning of therapy. Look at your face, your appearance, your clothes, your gestures. Look inside yourself at what you are sensing, feeling, thinking. How happy are you? How satisfied you are? What is there in your mind now? Now look at yourself now, after completing therapy. How happy and satisfied you are now? What are you feeling, sensing, and thinking?*

These are only a few examples of assessment techniques geared to learning more about the thoughts and emotions experienced by clients. Therapists can design different pictures or imagery exercises to assess each client at different phases of assessment.

We can learn similarly about behavior, by placing clients in a movie or on a theater stage.

> *Imagine you jump into the future and reach your 60th birthday celebration. Your family shows a video about your entire life's activities. Watch yourself. What are you doing? How do you behave? Is your behavior familiar to you? Do you like your behavior? Is there anything that surprises you? What? If you could change how you behaved "back then," what would you change?*

When contrasts emerge between clients' thoughts, emotions, and behaviors, or when trying to help clients understand the links between the three, a first step is to be able to assess them.

> *Imagine there are three of you standing here: One is your behavior. One is your thought. One is your emotion. Listen to what all three entities are saying to each other. What is your behavior figure telling everyone? What is your thought figure saying? What is your emotional figure saying? Do the three of them agree and comply with each other?*

Depending on the information we need to gather, we can focus on each component separately or combine the images to talk with each other and try to learn about the dynamics between the three.

Target 3: Assessing clients' motivations, strengths, and expectations

The prognosis of problems strongly depends not only on their severity and duration and on clients' perceptions, but also on clients' motivation for therapy and for change, and on clients' strengths and skills that fostered coping in the past. Everyone possesses strengths and resources, but not everyone is familiar with them. The role of assessment is also to help clients discover and learn about their own special capacities. Strengths might include an ability to persevere stubbornly without giving up, or a knowledge that others believe in them, or easy access to a support network.

The following exercises can serve as means for assessing clients' motivation at different phases of therapy:

- *You are starting a trek now, and you need to collect all your belongings to carry with you. You have to make sure you take all the motivation you can with you. Can you describe what you have taken with you? What are you lacking to make this trip successful? Would you like me to supply you with what you are lacking? What would you like me to give you?*
- *I am giving you a glass of motivation to drink, and you drink all of it. Do you feel different? What has changed? In what way?*

Therapists can apply a range of imagery exercises to collect information on clients' strengths and resources:

- *Imagine you are taking a written job interview. You need to write what your good characteristics are and in what areas you feel strong. What do you write?*
- *Imagine you need to recommend yourself for a certificate of honor. Here it is legitimate to brag and show off, without embarrassment. How do you explain why you deserve this honor?*
- *Imagine you need to take a tour inside your own body to look for your strengths and your abilities, and harvest them for eliciting change. What do you find? What can be of help to you?*
- *Imagine you need to start working on changing your situation, and you feel it is very difficult. You need help. Who can help you? Who can give you a hand? In what ways can you help yourself?*
- *Imagine you received lots of help to overcome your problems. Now it is time to send thank you notes to all those who helped you. Tell me who they are and why they deserve your thanks.*
- *Imagine there is a row of people standing here. Each of them is holding some skills and help for you. You walk from one to the other, receiving help from each of these people in your environment. Who is standing there? What are you taking from each one? Does it help? Is it enough?*

While some therapies differentiate assessment phases from treatment phases, I believe that assessment is an integral part of intervention, and that the process of change starts even when we focus on assessment. For example, when assessing clients' view of themselves and their motivations, we can already start helping them view themselves as they expect to be at the end of therapy, and can elicit their motivations to apply effort toward change and foster their beliefs in their ability to succeed.

Many people become so accustomed to their difficulties that they find it difficult even to imagine themselves without them. Hence, imagination can offer the best means for trying to develop a picture of oneself without the problem, in order to understand how the disorder has changed one's life. I strongly believe that in order for people to invest the necessary effort into achieving their desired change, they must be able to view a picture of themselves at the end of the process, after having finished working hard to change, imagining how they might enjoy being different. As I described in Chapter 1, if you don't have a dream, how can you expect your dream to become true? If clients are not able to elicit this picture, they will never make the change.

Such imagery exercises reflecting clients' predictions of treatment outcomes have an important quality of self-fulfilling prophecy, or, in professional terms, a self-efficacy assessment. Thus, assessment of oneself as changed is an important target:

- *Imagine your life without the problem: How would you like it to look? Who are the people who can help you fight the problem?*
- *Draw yourself in your imagination the way you look now. Draw yourself the way you would like to be at the end of therapy. What is different? What has changed?*
- *You are challenging a friend of yours to go to therapy, and in order to motivate him you tell him how successful your therapy was. Tell how much you have changed, what changes occurred in your life, and how happy you are now that you have ended therapy. What are you telling him?*

Just as women can endure great labor pains while giving birth, with the anticipation of a brand new baby as their expected outcome, so people can undergo many difficulties if they hold a picture of themselves as happy, improved, or changed afterwards. Therefore, in every therapy, therapists should help assess the client's picture of the final outcome – an image to work toward during the challenging periods of treatment, thus assisting the client in investing efforts during the process of change.

Target 4: Assessing treatment needs

Therapists can design a large range of imagery-based assessment exercises to learn about treatment needs. Using imagery, therapists should help clients assess what they expect from therapy and their desired setting and orientation. In parallel, imagery can help therapists assess their own understanding of how therapy should be conducted in terms of setting, modes, and techniques.

> *Let's imagine I have a magic wand that I use to impart to you the skills you lack for solving your/the client's problem. Try to focus on yourself/the client. You are now going to overcome/help the client overcome the problem. What helped you? What changes did the wand make? What helped you solve it all? In what way are you/is the client different now? What can you/the client do better?*

The following examples help therapists make treatment decisions by assessing clients' ability for self-help and coping:

- *Imagine you have to do this thing that you are afraid of – but suddenly you are not afraid any more. What helped you become able to do it finally? What did you do now that you were not able to do before? What changed your ability to cope? Who helped you?*

- *Imagine you have fallen into a big well and you cannot get out. You are sunk deep down under your problems, but I am throwing you a rope ladder. You are stepping out. What helped you step out? What was that rope made of?*

Even therapists who feel they do not know how to design therapy for a client can use imagery-based assessment to help themselves (see Chapter 18). Thus, therapists can help themselves find answers to deliberations about treatment needs through the following type of exercise:

> *Imagine you meet the client 10 years from now. You were not able to help the client overcome her problem, but she now tells you that she eventually found a skillful therapist who solved all her problems. Curious, you ask her: What did that therapist do? How did he treat you? What did he tell you? What worked for you? How did you solve your problems? What kind of therapy was it? What skills did you acquire? In what way are you different now?*

Target 5: Ongoing assessment of progress

Assessment, as mentioned before, spans the entire process of treatment, measuring change at different intervals across the course of therapy. A good way to assess progress during therapy is using ladder imagery in a variety of ways, to assess a wide range of variables. We can ask clients to imagine they are ascending a very long ladder (see Chapter 1). The first rung of the ladder, the lowest, reflects how they were when they first came to therapy – suffering from the problems they had, lacking skills, and feeling distressed. Through therapy, they climbed higher and higher. To help clients visualize the progress they have made thus far, the therapist can then ask the client:

> *Can you look at the rungs you have climbed and tell me what you see behind you? What is there far below? Can you see yourself, as you were when you first came here? Can you look and see where you are now? Can you tell me what has changed?*

The ladder image can also be extremely beneficial to help the therapist and the client assess the process of change thus far.

> *Can you tell me how difficult it was for you to climb the rungs? Can you tell me, looking at the ladder, if there were times you were afraid of falling down? Were there times when it was easier for you to climb? Describe each of those times.*

We can also use the ladder to evaluate the kinds of change the client has achieved up until now in therapy.

> *Tell me where you are standing now, on which rung. Can you look at yourself and explain to me what are you thinking now, on this rung? What are you feeling and how do you behave on this rung? Look down at the first rung and compare: What is different? Where do you feel better – here or down there? What does this change mean to you?*

Toward the end of therapy, the therapist can use the ladder to check with clients about the extent to which they have achieved their goals.

> *Look at where you are standing now, at the end of therapy. Do you feel good being on this rung, at the top? Is it comfortable for you? Are you happy with the ladder you have climbed? Do you think you can stay up there without falling down? Are you stable enough? Are you satisfied? Do you need to climb more?*

The ladder image can be implemented easily for assessment of progress in child therapy as well, sometimes calling for use of an actual physical ladder to help make the image more concrete for younger children. Children also respond well to ongoing assessments based on images produced through drawings. In a research and treatment project aiming to reduce aggression (Hamama & Ronen, 2009), we asked all the children in a small-group intervention to draw themselves twice: at the beginning of the first group session, when they were very aggressive, and then again at the end of the series of group meetings, relating to the change process they had experienced. We received a variety of drawings that illustrated the change through the children's eyes. For example, one child explained his picture: "Before the group I was a thunderstorm, rain, and lightning. After the group, I am sunshine with only a few clouds." Another child explained: "Before the group I was a lion; now I am only a little cat." We found that children are capable of assessing the change they experienced. Moreover, we found that by assessing and evaluating their own treatment outcomes, they also became committed to maintaining the changes they had achieved. As I mentioned before, drawings make metaphors or imagery more vivid for children.

Target 6: Evaluative assessment and maintenance at termination

Although assessment at this last phase can resemble previous phases, its particular focus is on assessing change, using various techniques such as the following:

- *Imagine yourself at the beginning of therapy: the way you behaved, felt, thought. Now imagine how you look, behave, think, and feel at the end of therapy. Look at the two figures and see what is different.*
- *Have the "new you" meet your "old you." Look carefully – do the two "yous" look the same? Do you speak the same? Do you think the same thoughts? Do you feel the same? What has changed?*
- *Can you see your "past you" talking to the "present you," reporting on the changes that have occurred? Listen to your "new you" explaining why it is better to be the way you are now, and why it was worthwhile changing. Do you think you can maintain the change?*

A most effective technique for assessing children at the end of therapy is to ask them to draw themselves the way they were before therapy and now, and then to compare the two figures. Another technique is to draw a map, which can be verbal for adults and concrete for children, including drawings of signs and landmarks along the route.

Imagine you are going on a tour. The tour started at the point you were before therapy. Pay attention to where you were then, what characterized you. Now, focus on the road you have traveled – the difficulties, changes, obstacles. Now, look and see where you are now. What has changed?

As can be seen in all of these examples, it is often difficult to draw a line between assessment and therapy. Good assessment also comprises the beginning of the change process, especially if therapists make sure to develop hope, optimism, and self-efficacy in their clients.

Summary

It is beyond the scope of this book to comprehensively present the role of assessment in therapy in general, but the principles that apply to assessment within any therapeutic orientation apply to imagery therapy as well. In this chapter, I have tried to propose some important aims and targets for using imagery to facilitate the efficacy of assessment.

The rule of thumb for imagery-based assessment throughout the course of therapy is that when therapists feel they lack direct access to the important, "hot" information they need regarding the client's history, problems, thoughts, emotions, behaviors, motivations, strengths and resources, expected outcomes, or happiness, then they should design images that best fit those purposes.

Practice: Guidelines for the Main Questions Directed at Each Assessment Target

Target 1: Assessing clients' problems

- How does the client present the problem's severity, history, and consequences, and the way the client copes with it?
- What prevented the client from overcoming the problem until now?
- How does the client view himself or herself without the problem?
- What can be better in the client's life without the problem?
- What do you know about this type of problem from the literature or from treating other clients?
- What information are you missing to make decisions about the needed therapy?
- How can you best find the missing information about the problem? (Literature? Asking the client? The client's family? Report from referrals?)

Target 2: Assessing clients' emotions, thoughts, and behaviors

- How does the client behave (think, feel) today, compared to previously and compared to his/her sociocultural environment?
- In what way does the client's behavior point to the client's feelings and thoughts?
- Is there a resemblance between the way the client thinks, the way the client feels, and the way the client behaves (see Chapter 7)?
- In what ways have the client's emotions changed over the years?
- What kinds of positive emotions does the client express and how do these reflect the client's strengths, resources, and virtues?
- What kinds of negative emotions does the client express? How do these emotions interfere with the client's ability to make desired changes?
- How does the client relate to the issue of enhancing happiness in life? Does the client have suggestions as to how he or she can increase happiness?
- Can you pinpoint the missing skills that prevent the client from being happier?
- How does the client assess his or her own positive and negative emotions and thoughts?

Target 3: Assessing clients' motivations, strengths, and expectations

- What kind of strengths and resources does the client have?
- How did the client overcome problems in the past?
- What kind of support does the client receive from the environment?
- What extent of motivation for change does the client exhibit?
- To what extent does the client believe in his or her ability to achieve change (self-efficacy)?
- What are the client's expected outcomes for therapy?

Target 4: Assessing treatment needs

- How can this client's referral be classified or explained using either accepted diagnostic criteria or concrete descriptions?
- How can you classify the client's goals for change? For example: needs to reduce behavior that is overexpressed (e.g., aggression), needs to generate behavior that is underexpressed (e.g., social skills), suffers from distress (e.g., fear, anxiety, trauma). In other words, what skills is the client lacking?
- What is the right setting for treatment? Individual therapy? Marital therapy? Family consultation? Group therapy?
- What is the optimal therapeutic setting in the client's eyes? Is there a gap between the client's preference and the therapist's recommendation?
- What are the optimal modes and techniques for intervention (e.g., verbal therapy, creative therapy, individual versus group or family therapy)?

Target 5: Ongoing assessment of progress

- How would you assess your working alliance (therapeutic relationship) at this point in time?
- What can you conclude from the first meetings about your future relationships with the client?
- What do you know about the client's compliance and motivation now, and how it is affecting the process of change?
- To what extent has the client progressed and achieved his/her goals over the course of treatment? What changes have already occurred?
- What can you learn from the way the client is progressing?
- How does the client assess the change process?
- After helping the client overcome or live with the referred problem, can you pinpoint other goals for change?

Target 6: Evaluative assessment and maintenance at termination

- What are your reasons for thinking about ending therapy?
- Does your intention to terminate coincide with the client's wishes?
- What changes have occurred in the client's behaviors, thoughts, and emotions?
- To what extent do you think the goals of therapy were achieved?
- What new skills did the client acquire?
- What does the client need to maintain achievements independently?
- Can you address issues of overlearning? Relapse prevention?
- Is the client happier?

13

Applying Imagery to Treat Past Events (Fears, Trauma, Posttrauma)

Naturally, therapists treat problems more than they treat happiness and joy. However, in line with the positive psychology orientation, I uphold the importance of focusing not only on difficulties but also on improving happiness and satisfaction. As mentioned in Chapter 3, Seligman and Csikszentmihalyi (2000: 5) described positive psychology as including three temporal aspects: "the value of subjective experiences ... in the past, the ability for flow in the present, and hope and optimism for the future." Following their view, the current part of this book, on therapy, is organized into past, present, and future. When clients bring their past to therapy, it mainly comprises their distressing experiences of fear, trauma, and posttrauma, which are the focus of the present chapter. Clients' ability to flow in the present relates to their awareness, skills, and social relationships, which are discussed in Chapters 14 and 15. Therapists' wish to enhance optimism and hope in the future is presented in Chapter 16.

Treating Distressing Past Events

The most common use of imagery in CBT relates to the treatment of fear and anxiety (for example, test anxiety, social and separation anxieties, phobias, panic attacks), trauma (such as crisis or change following divorce or death), and posttrauma (posttraumatic stress disorder – PTSD – following traumatic events such as accidents, terrorist attacks, and so on; see Chapter 7 regarding the treatment of traumatic memories). The definitions of fear and anxiety are often confounded, but in general fear refers to sudden calamity or danger when facing a concrete threat, whereas anxiety refers to a sense of emotional threat with no concrete threat (Beck, Emery, & Greenberg, 1985). Trauma refers to the feeling that a bad event occurred, necessitating new coping. Posttrauma refers to a complex, serious psychological condition that occurs as a result of experiencing a traumatic event (Foa, Keane, & Friedman, 2000).

The Positive Power of Imagery: Harnessing Client Imagination in CBT and Related Therapies,
First Edition. Tammie Ronen. © 2011 Tammie Ronen. Published 2011 by John Wiley & Sons, Ltd.

Therapists frequently select imagery as a means of exposing clients to traumatic events, helping clients recall memories, and trying to change distorted thoughts and emotions associated with those traumatic incidents. The common characteristic consequence of all these problems – fear, trauma, and posttrauma – is that clients have developed symptoms and avoidance behaviors that interfere with enjoying life in the present.

Beck, Emery, and Greenberg (1985), as well as Foa, Keane, and Friedman (2000), described PTSD as the most serious psychological condition occurring as a result of experiencing a traumatic event or its frightening elements. This condition includes avoidance of thoughts, memories, people, and places associated with the event, as well as emotional numbing and symptoms of elevated arousal. Foa, Keane, and Friedman described trauma and posttrauma as complex conditions that can be linked with significant morbidity, disability, and impairment of life functions.

According to White (2007), research indicates that service providers often find it difficult and stressful to treat survivors of trauma because of their resistance to change, their ways of relating to helpers and the work's emotionally demanding nature. Clients who experienced trauma and developed PTSD often have difficulty taking responsibility for their own lives (Palmer *et al.*, 2001). They may frequently exhibit self-destructive behaviors such as substance abuse in order to cope with their feelings (Beutler & Hill, 1992).

Foa, Hearst-Ikeda, and Perry (1995) presented a protocol for treating PTSD based on the assumption that many symptoms persist because clients do not adequately process the trauma. Treatment includes relaxation and imagery exercises, exposure, and cognitive therapy. Clients learn deep muscle relaxation and controlled breathing skills, and then undergo training in imaginal exposure – the use of imagery to bring up traumatic memories and describe them in the present tense as if they are happening again. Both the relaxation procedure and the imaginal reliving are audiotaped, and clients listen to the tapes as homework practice. Imagery is employed throughout the therapy via imaginal exposure, followed by further cognitive therapy designed to correct distorted beliefs. Chief targets include clients' beliefs about the world's unpredictability, uncontrollability, and dangerousness, as well as any extremely negative beliefs that clients hold about themselves. Therapists help clients identify these problematic beliefs, and homework addresses everyday negative thinking. Imagery is used again later to apply cognitive restructuring and to review the skills mastered by the clients in the program.

Foa and her colleagues implemented this protocol for various client disorders and reported positive results for survivors of physical or sexual assault (Foa *et al.*, 1999; Foa, Keane, & Friedman, 2000) and for grief symptoms (Shear *et al.*, 2001). Bryant's group also reported positive outcomes for the protocol in various groups, for example for acute stress disorders in firefighters who developed posttrauma (Bryant, 2000; McNally, Bryant, & Ehlers, 2003) and in survivors of industrial or motor vehicle accidents (Bryant *et al.*, 1998). Their results indicated that a combination of prolonged imaginal and *in vivo* exposure with cognitive therapy was more effective in preventing PTSD than was supportive counseling. CBT clients maintained most of their gains and did better than the supportive counseling group (Bryant *et al.*, 2003).

In a controlled study of 58 women with PTSD related to childhood abuse, participants showed significant improvement in affect regulation problems, interpersonal skills deficits, and PTSD symptoms following treatment that integrated CBT with imagery. Gains were maintained at three- and nine-month follow-ups. These outcomes suggested the value of establishing a strong therapeutic relationship and emotion regulation skills before exposure work among chronic PTSD populations (Cloitre *et al.*, 2002).

Thus, imagery is an essential component for solving problems related to traumatic events. Likewise, exposure is an essential feature for the treatment of PTSD. However, it is not always possible to apply exposure. There are two main ways for using exposure in imagery: one as a preliminary step before *in vivo* exposure, and the other when *in vivo* exposure is impossible. The next sections present scripts for both types of imagery applications to eliminate clients' PTSD.

Imaginal Exposure Followed by *In Vivo* Exposure

When clients are not yet willing to practice *in vivo* exposure, imagery can serve as a preliminary step. The case of Sara, who suffered from posttrauma and needed exposure to the feared situation to recover, illustrates such preliminary imaginal exposure for treating PTSD.

Sara, age 18, developed PTSD after being involved as a passenger in a car accident one rainy night a year earlier, when her boyfriend drove their car into two elderly pedestrians on a crosswalk. Sara had nightmares, mood swings, and anxiously avoided cars, her boyfriend, nighttime, and pleasurable events.

In early imagery work, Sara practiced relaxation and elicited simple positive memories like recalling breakfast and a nice meeting with a friend.

After three weeks, we started imaginal exposure, with Sara imagining herself getting into a car and sitting in the passenger seat next to the driver. She became tense and asked me to hold her hand. We then practiced relaxation again before continuing. Returning to the imagery of sitting in the car, I asked her to look at herself and focus on how she looked – her clothes, the expression on her face.

After two more sessions gradually approaching the accident through imagery, Sara was ready to "dive into deep water" by eliciting the memory of the accident. Using details she had disclosed, I asked her to imagine herself getting into the car that night – to see the rain and darkness, follow the road nearing the fateful intersection, listen to the song playing on the

(continued)

---

disc player, and see herself as the car approached the intersection while the traffic signal changed. I asked her what was going on, and she started shaking and shouting: "Oh no! Oh, no! We hit something! I can hear the car hitting something! There's so much noise. Shouting! Darkness! Rain! It seems like hell. Something very bad is happening." Trying to imagine the scene in more detail, Sara remembered the raindrops beating down on the car: "I'm so silly. Something bad is happening and I'm counting drops of rain." She felt she was someone else, outside herself: "a third person doing it." Describing her boyfriend as pale, she said: "I'm afraid to get out of the car. I don't want to see what happened. I don't want to know! Oh, God. What should I do?!" Then she added: "It's strange. Things are happening so fast, and then suddenly so slowly. I'm forcing him to get out. He doesn't want to. Someone is coming over, opening the front door on the driver's side. I'm going to vomit." Sara sounded ready to vomit and ran out to the bathroom. When she returned, she told me: "That was it. Next thing I remember was calling my father." Sara alternated from crying to shouting; tears dripped down her cheeks, and she kept repeating: "We didn't mean to. We didn't notice them. Oh, God."

I held her hand and tried to help her relax. She said it was the first time since the accident that she had faced these pictures again. Until now, she'd refused, and the images came to her at night.

After this imaginal exposure, we talked about the accident, her feelings, and the meaning of the event for her life. We also talked about the fact that it would always remain part of her life, but maybe she could keep it as her past and not as her present reality that followed her everywhere.

Over the next three days, Sara called me several times, asking me to help her use self-talk to reduce her fears and to check if it was normal to behave as she was.

After two more sessions of imagery exposure, Sara began driving lessons and her nightmares stopped. All her symptoms finally disappeared after gradual *in vivo* exposure to the accident site together with her father, where she tried to cope with her fears while actually in a car at the site and thinking about the accident.

Practice: guidelines

Some important guidelines can help in applying imaginal exposure as a basic training stage to enable clients to experience *in vivo* exposure later. First, because a major component of PTSD is avoidant behavior, therapists should be very careful in exposing clients, ensuring that steps are small, slow, and gradual and that clients are ready and strong enough for them. Too much exposure too fast, without adequate caution, might cause stronger avoidance. Also, longer-lasting avoidant behaviors make exposure training more difficult to begin. Moreover, these sessions elicit deep emotions in clients who have often been feeling numb; therefore, therapists should be ready for intense emotional experiences (several times I have found myself crying when I experienced my clients' suffering) and for the need to provide extra support and time in the hours and days after intense sessions.

The following specific guidelines can help therapists when applying imaginal exposure:

1. Because of the intensity and severity of posttrauma, verify that clients are able to relax and use imagery. If needed, devote more time to training (Chapters 9 and 10).
2. Before beginning actual imagery work, determine if someone in the client's life can support and help him/her in the days after exposure. This person should be someone with whom the client can share anxiety and stress.
3. Carefully schedule the imaginal exposure session to allot sufficient time for conducting the exercise and for staying longer with clients if necessary afterwards. Keep in close touch in the few days after the first exposure.
4. Plan the first imaginal exposure to be slow and gradual, making sure that the client is ready to face the memories.
5. Pay attention to changes that emerge when memories are elicited – in clients' tone, mood, and voice, frequently accompanied by crying.
6. Be ready and able to intervene if needed, sometimes by a touch or a soft, relaxing voice. Support and reinforce clients when necessary.
7. With stronger avoidance, carefully progress only slightly each time, without exposing clients to the whole event at once.
8. In every session, start the imagery exercise from those events to which clients have already been exposed and about which they already feel better. Each progressive step in exposure should be repeated several times; single exposure to each stimulus is insufficient.
9. Remember that ups and downs are expected and ensure that clients are not at risk by checking that no new symptoms are developing. However, strong emotions are to be expected.
10. Terminate each session with relaxation, ensuring that clients return to a calm emotional state. Try to connect clients to their strengths and virtues, sense of coping, positive events and emotions, or supportive people, in order to end sessions with hope and optimism.
11. Give homework assignments, including self-reinforcement for the courage to experience the traumatic incident, using positive self-talk. In the first stage of imaginal exposure, clients should not practice exposure alone at home without a therapist's guidance.
12. Don't expect imagery exercises alone to suffice. Each imaginal exercise should be followed by discussion, interpretation, self-talk, self-efficacy, and other CBT and supportive techniques to ensure that clients can use exercises and apply them *in vivo*.

13. Verify that therapy is progressing in the right direction: Check if clients stop avoiding stimuli associated with the trauma, if they begin doing new (or old) things, and if symptoms diminish.
14. Remember: Imaginal exposure is a powerful tool and usually has a strong impact on both clients and therapists.

Imaginal Exposure Instead of *In Vivo* Exposure

The main difference between imaginal exposure before exposure *in vivo* and imaginal exposure alone lies in the concern that the lack of actual *in vivo* practice may lead to regression. Therefore, when utilizing imaginal exposure alone, imagery therapy must be conducted differently to ensure that it will suffice to resolve the problem.

There are many benefits to practicing exposure *in vivo*. First, clients feel able to cope in real life, which surpasses the feeling they achieve while imagining. Often during imagery work, clients will ask: "Are you sure this really works in life?" Second, once clients are practicing *in vivo* exposure, their success serves as reinforcement, which facilitates further progress. During imaginal exposure alone, this reinforcement is unavailable, leaving doubts as to whether or not the problem has been resolved. Such doubts often remain for longer periods without *in vivo* exposure.

Combat trauma is a prime example of where *in vivo* exposure is not feasible. Veteran soldiers cannot return to battlefields; therefore, imaginal exposure must suffice. The following case illustration depicts Saul, a soldier who developed PTSD several years after witnessing his friends' deaths during war.

Saul, age 25, came to therapy feeling responsible for the death of his fellow soldiers – his friends – during a difficult battle because he couldn't call for help. Among other symptoms, he suffered from sleeplessness, headaches, and mood disturbances.

After learning many details, I asked Saul to imagine himself as a soldier in that battle. I used his previous descriptions but asked him to fill in the image's details, like the time of day, the way the place looked, his location among his friends, the weather, the smell of smoke rising up from the ground after bombing and shelling.

I asked him to view himself there, a soldier among soldiers, and describe what was going on around him in the present tense. When he did, I could tell he was viewing the scene because he moved his eyes, talked intermittently with silences, cried, and expressed intense emotions such as anger. His eyes were lowered most of the time, but he often raised them as if looking at something in the distance.

Using unorganized narrative and often incomplete sentences, Saul described how many soldiers were attacked and injured, and he was told to

(continued)

---

call for help using the communications equipment he carried on his back. However, when he tried to activate it, it wouldn't work. As he told me this, Saul began crying and repeating many times: "And I couldn't. I just couldn't."

I instructed him: "Focus on your hands, your fingers, and the equipment that's near you on the ground. Describe what's happening." At first, he talked about himself in the third person: "There's a soldier there. He can't move." I kept saying: "That soldier is you. Tell me what you are feeling. Tell me what you are doing." He said his hands were shaking and I told him: "You are there now. Speak in the present tense. Look at your hand. There is a battle. What do you see?"

As he described trying to activate his equipment, he was flooded with emotion: "My hands are shaking, and I can't steady them. I'm trying to activate the transceiver and I can't. There are whistles of bullets around. Terrible smell. I must get help. I can't get in touch with anyone. It's not working. Oh, help!" He repeated again and again: "It's not working. It's broken! What should I do? How can I get help? There's no one to help me!"

I asked him to focus on his shaking hands, his fingers, to describe the emotion. He used words like: "Disaster! Impossible! Helpless!"

He told me he could not activate the machine. He could not send for help.

As the battle ended and the rest of the corps returned to base, Saul checked the transceiver and it worked. He felt wracked with guilt, with a sudden knowledge that it was his fault his friends were dying because he had not got them assistance.

The next few nights following this imaginal exposure, Saul could not sleep and cried copiously. He called me several times, and once I initiated a call to check on him. In the next therapy sessions, we came back again and again to the equipment failure scenario. Each time we practiced this imagery exercise, it became easier for him to talk. We focused on his hands, his actions, his surroundings, his emotions, and his concern for his friends. Again and again, we checked his automatic internal thoughts during that time, verifying that he genuinely cared for his friends and wanted to help and rescue them.

After repeating this exercise several times, Saul told me that nobody ever blamed him; nobody even knew that he couldn't work the equipment, and he didn't know if any help was really available. But his job was to activate the machine and he was a good soldier, so he felt awful that he hadn't. He felt so bad that he never attended the corps reunion or, even more painful to him, his dead friends' memorial ceremonies on Memorial Day.

(continued)

The whole process lasted several weeks, with us returning to elicit different images from the war, and repeating work on the traumatic picture until Saul could cope better. After several weeks, when Saul was able to view the war images feeling sad but not crying or panicking, we ended the imagery session with him imagining two Sauls – the past soldier and the present university student – talking. I asked Soldier Saul to tell Student Saul how terrible his experience had been, and he did. Student Saul told Soldier Saul that it really was inconceivably terrible and that young people should enjoy life rather than fight, and that bad things happen in war, and that people sometimes feel helpless, but that what happened was not something he had planned or desired.

Due to the lack of *in vivo* exposure in Saul's case, I needed to repeat the exposure exercises and discourse between Soldier Saul and Student Saul, to ensure that he could deal calmly with this memory and not avoid it.

Next, as follow-up to the imagery work using reflection, interpretation, and meaning-making, we discussed life, beliefs, and responsibility. We worked on cognitive restructuring: Bad things happened, but he did not do them intentionally. He could not cope perfectly but he wanted to. He could not save his friends but he yearned to. (A detailed example of cognitive restructuring is presented later in this chapter.)

Saul had been in therapy for eight months when Memorial Day came round again and for the first time he participated in his fallen friends' ceremony at the military cemetery.

As seen in this example, there was no way for Saul to experience exposure *in vivo*. Therefore, I needed to ensure that imaginal exposure would be adequate to elicit and maintain change.

The principles of imaginal exposure in such cases are similar to those described above for use in imaginal exposure followed by exposure *in vivo*. However, when imaginal exposure cannot be followed by *in vivo* exposure, several adaptations are required to enhance change and prevent regression, as seen in the next section.

Practice: guidelines

In cases without *in vivo* exposure, all 14 of the steps are similar to the previous guidelines for imaginal exposure that does precede *in vivo* exposure. However, when *in vivo* exposure is lacking, additional exercises should be inserted before Step 11, as follows:

i. Due to the lack of subsequent *in vivo* exposure, repeat the imaginal exposure many times to ensure that change really does occur. Do not expect the first one or two exercises to suffice.

ii. Aim for clients not only to maintain but also to generalize their learning. This can be accomplished by overlearning, by repeating the imagined situation in several variations, or by designing different but similar exposure exercises (e.g., Saul can imagine standing on the battlefield in an upcoming war and losing his voice so that he cannot call for help).

iii. Once change begins, design homework assignments where clients imagine themselves practicing activities (e.g., Saul can imagine himself meeting his friends who did survive).

Imagery as a Way to Elicit Memories and Remember Forgotten Material

Posttrauma begets multiple symptoms. Fears, anxieties, and other symptoms decrease clients' subjective wellbeing (as in the case of Saul), and clients also exhibit avoidant behavior (as in the case of Sara). Both Saul and Sara suffered from impinging memories through nightmares and other PTSD symptoms, and their imaginal exposure focused on increasing their ability to withstand recurrent or intrusive memories.

However, sometimes clients with PTSD suffer from the absence of memories or false memories that cause distress, calling for imagery therapy to enhance clients' ability to recall and bring up memories. As a case illustration, we will return to Ricky, who first came to therapy for fears following her son's suicide (see Chapter 7). After dealing with that, Ricky asked to continue therapy. Because she suffered from multiple problems, we decided to tackle them one by one. The training session presented next related to her feelings of guilt regarding her father's death.

Ricky said that her father died "because of her," but could not add any relevant information other than the fact that she was sexually abused by her alcoholic father from age 11 to 13, when he died of liver problems. She had never told anyone about her abuse and had many guilt feelings as well as problems in intimate relationships.

I thought that Ricky's feelings of guilt related to three different issues: (i) her fear that her father died because of something she did; (ii) her feelings of relief at his death because he would no longer molest her; (iii) her feelings of guilt that she had agreed to accept him and his touch in a way that she should not have. I thought that I should treat her guilt feelings about being responsible for his death first, because this seemed to be the easiest of the three. The aim of the session presented below, therefore, was to help Ricky elicit forgotten details of her father's death by recalling the events of that entire day, to eliminate her feelings of culpability. Only later did I discover that Ricky felt responsible because he died the same night he

(continued)

---

had visited her room to try to have intercourse with her, but left suddenly because he felt ill.

I asked Ricky to participate in an imagery session recalling those memories. Already trained in relaxation, she could easily close her eyes and bring up images. She told me that she remembered waking up that morning to bedlam, so I asked her to try to remember: "You just woke up, you enter the living room. You hear voices. What's going on? Tell me what's happening in the room." Ricky started relating details about her confusion at first, when she saw her father lying supine, an ambulance outside the living room window, people wearing white running all around, and her mother crying. She described her confusion and fear, not understanding what was wrong.

I asked her what was going on in her mind, what thoughts she had, what feelings she had. She said: "It's because of me. I pushed him last night. It's my fault. I did something wrong to him." I asked her where this thought was coming from, how it was her fault. She replied: "He always told me that he felt good because I was there. He needed me. That he couldn't make it without me. So I probably didn't do enough..." This was important, but I decided we would deal with it later while treating her abuse, instead of disrupting the current flow of imagery about his death.

I asked her to try and listen to what the doctors told her mother at the hospital and whether anyone mentioned what was wrong with him. She replied: "They said all his systems crashed and his liver was completely destroyed by alcohol." I saw tears of sadness and mourning in her eyes, but I also knew she was relieved he could no longer visit her room.

I asked Ricky to listen to her mother and the doctors discussing his death. After repeating what she thought they'd said, Ricky could admit that he had been hospitalized before and that doctors had long warned her parents that he was putting himself at serious risk by drinking so much. To help Ricky accept that her father was responsible for his own death through alcoholism, and no one else, I asked her to imagine talking with the doctors, her mother, her siblings, and finally even her father. Each of the figures had to tell her why her father died, and each had to respond to her claim that she was responsible for his death. In the last imagery session, while she imagined talking with her dead father, she heard him saying: "I had many bad things in my life. You were the only good thing that happened to me. You gave me a reason to live longer." She was then confused and alternated between crying and laughing. I asked her to repeat each answer and see how much she agreed with it, until she was able to accept what they said.

I next asked Ricky to elicit a picture of young 13-year-old Ricky, to talk with older present-day Ricky. Today's Ricky told Young Ricky: "You

(*continued*)

cannot possibly be responsible. You are only a little girl. You should be busy playing with your friends and not coping with your family's problems. It was never your fault. You were the victim. You were not responsible."

After this dialogue, I asked Ricky to imagine standing in front of the mirror, looking at herself today, and telling herself that her father drank himself to death and it was no one else's fault. Ricky said those words to herself, and then after terminating that imagery exercise I asked her to repeat the words aloud to me. She turned to me and said loudly: "You know what? It really is true! It was never my fault! He died because of himself! He was responsible for his own death! If he cared about us, he wouldn't have drunk so much to begin with."

When asked about her feelings, she blurted out: "Children should not be blamed for their parents' behavior." I felt this was the beginning of the process of changing her misconceptions regarding her role in the abuse.

In several more sessions, we kept returning to the images of Ricky facing her father, herself in the mirror, the whole world, and telling them: "My father died because he drank too much. It's very sad." She reached the point where she could say that this sentence felt right, that she was not having any guilt feelings, and that she would never let her own children take responsibility for her behavior.

Thus, therapy with Ricky aimed to elicit memories in order to process problematic issues concerning those memories. She had developed negative automatic thoughts and emotions relating to these earlier events, and imagery work helped her elicit past memories and deal with the trauma those memories evoked.

Practice: guidelines

In applying imagery to elicit forgotten material, therapists should take several steps after checking that clients are ready for this treatment:

- Ask clients to describe past events in the present tense and to complete the details of events as vividly as possible.
- Focus on the main dilemmas that you believe are responsible for the trauma (e.g., difficulties recalling events, fear of being exposed to events, guilt relating to events), while reassuring clients that they are currently safe and protected.
- Try to tackle guilt feelings by exaggerating and externalizing the events' paradoxical tenets, to help clients realize that there should not be guilt feelings (see courtroom exercises below).
- Ask clients to create dialogue between two separate aspects of the self (e.g., current and past) or with figures involved in the situation, repeating variations until clients can accept what happened.

- Bring clients to the present and have them describe events again, after having undergone changes in thoughts and emotions.
- Ask clients to forgive themselves or others and accept how they behaved.
- Have clients describe a safe present environment.

Using Imagery for Cognitive Restructuring of Past Trauma

Many client disorders relate to basic, automatic, dysfunctional beliefs (Alford & Beck, 1997; Beck 1999a,b). Therefore, cognitive restructuring is an important CBT technique when helping clients establish new, more appropriate beliefs about themselves and the world. I next describe cognitive restructuring as applied via imagery training to another chapter in Ricky's therapy – treatment of her posttrauma from experiencing sexual abuse by her father.[1]

To treat Ricky's abuse posttrauma, we followed steps similar to those used for treating her father's death. Ricky practiced relaxation and described details so that I could lead her in imaginal exercises, and I reassured her that whenever images became overly stressful she could stop. I asked her to participate in imagery sessions recalling memories of herself as a young girl who was very confused and torn. On the one hand, she enjoyed her father's attention which she craved, and she deeply wanted to make him happy. On the other hand, she feared him and felt intense stress, confusion, and guilt when he approached her sexually. Although by this time Ricky was well experienced at relaxation and imagery, it was extremely hard for her to elicit pictures of herself during inappropriate sexual experiences with her father. Apparently, the mixture of guilt, shame, and anger confused her. She moved between anger at herself, anger at her mother, and, only later, anger at her father. I decided it was not necessary to describe the sexual events in detail; instead, I asked her to focus on her emotions, thoughts, and sensations in an attempt to clarify her feelings, let her express them, and help her identify and differentiate all those feelings.

In paradoxical imagery exercises repeated over several sessions, I asked Ricky to imagine she was in court, listening to the judge blame her for having sex with her father. This exercise aimed to increase cognitive dissonance regarding her emotions; help her stop blaming herself and start supporting, comforting, understanding, and accepting herself; and foster new meaning for the abuse experience rather than guilt. Indeed, the more she imagined hearing the judge accuse her of cooperating with her father's sexual demands, the easier it became for Ricky to say: "But how could I resist my father? Little girls should obey their fathers! I wanted to do what

(continued)

he wanted me to! I wanted to be a good girl!" Another time she said: "I didn't know it was wrong. He was smiling and happy!"

After beginning to learn to justify her behavior as that of a young girl caught in an impossible situation, we continued working on reconstructing her thoughts through other variations of imaginary dialogue. The main work centered on dialogue between the 11- or 12-year-old Ricky and the current Ricky, focusing on reassuring statements by the older woman, herself already a mother, telling the young girl: "It is the father's responsibility to make sure his children are protected and not vice versa." Ricky needed to hear herself repeatedly before she could begin believing that she was too young to make choices, that children need to obey their parents, that she did nothing wrong, and that the only blame was her father's.

In the last imagery session redressing this issue, Ricky faced her father and told him: "You know, I did enjoy it – not the sex, but the fact that you wanted me. I was your child. I wanted you to want me, but not in this way. I was naïve and abused. You were a bad father. I will never do what you did – I will always be a good mother to my children."

Another example of cognitive restructuring can be drawn from the story of 24-year-old Michele, who experienced survivor guilt after a fatal car accident while touring overseas.

Michele was driving with her boyfriend beside her, and a group of four friends drove behind them in another car. The roads were long, the landscape monotonous, the trip lasted many hours, and they hurried to their next stop. After a while, Michele and her boyfriend realized that the other car had dropped out of sight, and they stopped to wait. When the other car did not arrive, they drove back and found there had been an accident. The driver had probably fallen asleep while driving. All four of their friends had been thrown out of the car. The driver died, and the other passengers were injured but survived.

Immediately after this traumatic event, all these youngsters flew home. About four months later, Michele came to me, reporting nightmares, weight loss, and incessant crying. She was obsessed with guilty thoughts: She had stayed alive; she was the one who had suggested they take such a long route; she had driven too quickly and hadn't waited for them, and so on.

After three weeks of talking about the accident, I suggested imagery to reduce her guilt feelings. Following relaxation training and imaginal

(continued)

exercises, we started imagery sessions using Professor Dumbledore's magical thought-extraction exercise which I described in Chapter 12 (Newell & Heyman, 2005; Rowling, 2000). I asked Michele to imagine putting Dumbledore's wand next to her head and taking out a long, gray thought, which floated out of her mind like a thread. She told me the thoughts were: "You were irresponsible! You wanted to drive for too long a time! You drove too fast! You caused his death."

We then started tackling these thoughts, one by one, through Socratic questioning: "If you are irresponsible, why did the other driver have the accident and not you? If you drove too fast, why did he lose control of his car while you drove yours well? If you stayed awake and kept driving and he did not ask to stop and rest, why are you irresponsible and not him?" It was not easy for Michele to answer the questions, because she had become accustomed to blaming herself instead of him and because she felt bad blaming a dead person.

I then asked her to try to imagine her dead friend, the driver of the second car, coming alive and having a conversation with her while he drove: "What is he telling you?" She replied that he told her he was tired, it was a boring drive, it was too long, he needed a break. I then asked her if he had actually told her all of that or if she had just imagined it. She said he had never said any of that to anyone. "So, he is not the one who said that, but you think that was what he was wishing, right? Could you now turn to him and ask him what he wanted?"

With my instruction, Michele started talking with her dead friend, asking him what he felt like before the accident. I asked her: "What are you answering him when he says he is tired?" Immediately Michele replied: "Let's stop. It's irresponsible to drive when tired. Don't put yourself and others at risk!"

I turned to her and asked her if she believed that this is what she would have genuinely answered if he had complained of fatigue and she said she was absolutely sure she would have. In response, I posed the question: "Then whose responsibility is it for not expressing what was needed?"

I asked her to imagine talking with him again and telling him what she felt. She said: "I am so sorry you did not say anything. I feel so guilty! I wanted you to stay alive. I would have stopped if I knew."

Again, I posed the question: "So who is responsible for driving while tired?" She did not reply, and this time I asked her to hold a conversation between two parts of herself: the part that is very angry at him because he ruined their trip, died, and left them feeling guilty; and the part that felt guilty. She started talking as if she were these two parts and really expressed anger at him.

(continued)

> At last, she turned to me and said: "Well, I guess it is his fault, not mine. Maybe I should feel sad and grieving, and not guilty. I tried to be responsible. I even offered to drive but he refused. It is him, not me."

This case example demonstrates the importance of imagery therapy for the cognitive restructuring necessary to facilitate change processes. Thus, while using cognitive restructuring in imagery, therapists need first to let clients face – see, read, or confront – their misconceptions, then to help clients understand that the thoughts are not functional, and then to enable clients to find new, more functional, adaptive thoughts to replace the earlier ones. Arguing between the diverse thoughts, exaggerating one kind of thought, or increasing irrational thoughts to a ridiculous point can contribute to clients' ability to find new, more adequate thoughts (in Michele's case, sorrow and sadness rather than guilt and blame).

Practice: guidelines

Some important guidelines can help in applying imagery for cognitive restructuring:

- Before starting imagery sessions, be sure you are aware of clients' misconceptions or automatic thoughts.
- Design imaginal situations that offer clients opportunities to express all their misconceptions and allocate enough time for clients to fully express and confront all these misconstructions. Good methods include:
  - Put the client on trial so that all the distorted as well as rational thoughts can be voiced in court (judge vs. defendant or prosecutor vs. defence attorney).
  - Exaggerate situations so much that clients can see that their perceptions are unrealistic (e.g., tell Michele that he died because she was supposed to have seen in her mind's eye that the other driver was tired, or because she should have driven both cars simultaneously, or because she is a super-capable woman and he was only a man).
  - Divide clients into two figures or parts and instruct them to dialogue or argue with each other (child self vs. current self, victim vs. perpetrator).
  - Clients, not you, should be the ones to reflect on how wrong or distorted their thoughts are in order to change them effectively. You can use Socratic questioning to help confront clients with paradoxical thoughts and to reflect new, rational, mediated thoughts back to clients.
- Repeat these imaginal situations in multiple variations, until clients feel confident in their changed thought patterns.

213

- Try to reinforce clients' belief in the new, mediated thoughts that have developed using methods where clients:
  - practice taking the voice of these rational thoughts and persuading you of their validity;
  - tell you about the change by giving a lecture, presenting it, or explaining it;
  - perform homework assignments where they tell themselves or others about the change.
- Remember that imagery work must be followed up, as always, by discussion of the change, reflection on the reason for change, and examination of that change's meaning. Be sure that clients are confident about the longevity of the change before continuing to work on cognitive restructuring of other past events.

Summary

Imagery is a strong technique to be applied when treating past events, trauma, and posttrauma. Indeed, to work with these types of past problems, therapists cannot achieve effective outcomes without imagery. The focus of imagery training may differ in various sessions, including emotional expression (as suggested in Chapter 5) as well as imaginal expression, recalling memories, and cognitive reconstruction as suggested here. Therapists can use their own imaginations to lead clients where they need to go in order for change to occur, designing customized imagery to meet clients' particular needs.

However, it is important to remember that treating past events will neither begin nor end with imagery. It is only one technique or tool within an entire repertoire that enables the expression of emotion, exposure to traumatic past memories, or recollection of repressed ones, and work on changing thoughts and designing new beliefs. Discussion as well as additional CBT and supportive techniques should be an integral part of the process.

Practice: Guidelines for Choosing Between Options

Although the guidelines for all imaginal exercises regarding fear, trauma, and posttrauma are similar, I presented separate guidelines in this chapter for each option and integrated case studies for each. To determine the optimal type of imaginal exercise targeting past events, therapists should ask:

- What is the unique feature of this specific case, in addition to the symptoms the client presents and the fear and anxiety the client experiences?

- Does it relate to the traumatic memory itself, and to the development of avoidance of that memory, which prevents progress? If so, then the imaginal exercise should address gradual exposure, as suggested in the first two sets of guidelines in this chapter.
- Does the main feature relate to lack of memories, or to difficulties remembering? If so, then help the client elicit and recollect detailed descriptions of the image, attempting to imitate reality as much as possible.
- Does it relate to guilt, shame, or other negative thoughts? If so, then focus not on exposure but rather on the confrontation between different figures or sides, like the client's present versus their past or the confrontation of thoughts versus feelings.

Endnote

[1] As mentioned above, Ricky's complex therapy was lengthy (about two years) and combined CBT, imagery, and positive psychology to systematically address her multiple problems, one by one. After comprehensively treating her father's death, Ricky wanted to start treating her posttrauma stemming from her abuse. I persuaded her to postpone this treatment for several weeks, because I worried that such a lengthy focus on negative, distressing events would be overwhelming. First, for several weeks we worked on positive exercises to increase her happiness at work and with her daughter. During this time, I verified that she was really handling the previous issues (her father's death) and ensured that she could also find time to enjoy her family and work life. Only then did I agree to begin work on her traumatic two years of childhood abuse.

We decided to divide each session into two parts, one addressing her early abuse and one focusing on developing positive skills in her present life: talking with her daughter, taking time to promote and elicit positive emotions instead of dwelling only on her difficult sad past, developing social contacts, and engaging in fun leisure activities to enhance wellbeing and maintain the strength necessary to cope with the difficulties she was encountering in therapy and in her life.

14

Imparting Assessment and Awareness Skills for Changing Present Behavior

Skills are defined in Webster's dictionary (Merriam-Webster, 1965: 815) as: "The ability to use one's knowledge effectively and readily in execution or performance" or "a learned power of doing a thing competently." A skilled person is defined as someone who has undergone "training in a particular occupation, craft, or trade." During recent years, skills acquisition has become the main target of my therapeutic work. Although knowledge, awareness, and therapeutic relationships are all important components of change processes, without the necessary skills change will not occur. Just like riding a bicycle, one must want to ride, believe one can ride, know about riding, and have someone trustworthy to help, but only after actual training in how to sit still, hold the handlebars, and steer can one ride without falling. In line with traditional behavioral therapy, as well as in models emphasizing social information processing or self-control, skill acquisition constitutes the main feature of this present chapter.

Change is a matter of systematic skills acquisition. It is not an outcome of some kind of magical imagery work, nor of suddenly "discovering the truth." It is a process of acquiring skills. First, clients must become ready to see what lies in front of them in vivid imagination; they must reach a point at which they are motivated to uncover whatever "demons" are distressing them. Second, clients' new understanding, assimilation of knowledge, and gains in awareness are all important, but alone are not sufficient to enhance change. That is, therapists should not expect change to occur just because the client faced or confronted an imagery scene. We need to view imagery as a preliminary step toward helping clients open up to new avenues for change, but further real work on actual skills must be invested to actually achieve that change.

Imagery can expose clients to what they need to do, help them take their first steps toward change, increase their awareness and understanding, and offer

The Positive Power of Imagery: Harnessing Client Imagination in CBT and Related Therapies,
First Edition. Tammie Ronen. © 2011 Tammie Ronen. Published 2011 by John Wiley & Sons, Ltd.

them opportunities to practice skills. But after the imagery work clients must start applying acquired skills in real life. This therapeutic orientation coincides with my emphasis on continuously working systematically toward achieving goals while planning and mapping out the process of the therapy; while teaching, training, and applying specific relevant skills that are tailored to clients' needs and goals and are continually updated; and while assessing and evaluating treatment outcomes (see Chapter 2).

The most important role of imagery, therefore, is helping impart skills to clients to improve their functioning in the present. Clients usually come to therapy feeling helpless, distressed, and hopeless. Treatment that increases coping skills involves changing clients' way of thinking, feeling, and, as a result, behaving. Therefore, therapy should relate to the ability for self-assessment of all three of these realms of human functioning. This includes identifying internal cues, thoughts, emotions, and sensations, as well as behaviors.

This chapter will discuss four different contemporary skill areas that therapists may impart to clients: self-assessment, assessment of relationships, increasing awareness of internal stimuli, and changing automatic thoughts. Practical guidelines are presented for each of the four skill areas.

Imparting Skills for Self-Assessment

In Chapter 12, I detail how therapists can work with clients using imagery to assess the client, the problem, and the necessary therapy. Here I present examples of how imagery can be implemented to help clients assess their own situation and learn to monitor their own behavior.

One of the most important skills that therapists wish to impart to their clients is the ability to assess one's own problems, strengths, and resources. Self-assessment is considered a prerequisite basic skill for developing self-control (Kanfer & Schefft, 1988; Rosenbaum, 2000). Only after assessing one's own situation can one make decisions about deficient skills and then start working toward acquiring what one lacks. Self-assessment means observing one's own behavior, examining how that behavior is enacted, raising awareness about one's automatic thoughts that prevent the behavior from changing, and becoming sensitive to emotions and physical sensations that accompany those thoughts and behaviors.

However, self-assessment is not an easy task. Often, clients are so accustomed to the way they view themselves, to their well-established self-concepts and self-identity, that they cannot really see themselves as they are or learn about their behavior through more objective eyes.

Imagery here offers great benefit. Through imagery exercises such as trying to look at one's own behavior from the outside, from the perspective of another person, clients can examine themselves more objectively. Clients can be trained to apply self-assessment skills independently after practicing them first with therapists. The following case example illustrates how imagery assisted Helen to re-evaluate her physical appearance and demeanor in order to help her cope with insecurities in her prestigious workplace.

Helen was a beautiful, married, 36-year-old woman with two daughters, who worked in a very high position at a government ministry. She was very highly qualified, had quickly progressed to a managerial position, and was now being offered an even higher position. She was the only nonsecretarial female in the office, and she complained that the men at work all related to her as a "woman" rather than as a manager, often trying to flirt with her. As Helen's therapy sessions were held directly after her work day, I noticed that she always dressed provocatively – in a very short skirt, low-cut blouse, high heels, and glossy red lipstick.

After one important meeting where she felt put down and ignored, I asked Helen to imagine she was at the office, talking with her colleague. She described: "Well, he is looking straight into my eyes so I feel uneasy, and I look down and whisper." Seeing her blush as she relayed this, I continued: "Please, tell me exactly what you are telling him. Like you said, you are sitting on the table, and he is standing next to you, looking at your beautiful eyes; you are blushing. What are you saying?"

"Well, I am speaking in a very low voice, looking down, and telling him: 'Oh, this is stressful. What if we don't get the project?'"

I then asked her to become her colleague and elicit the image from his point of view: "You are standing near the table. You see this beautiful young manager sitting in front of you. You are not sure whether to look at this young woman's beautiful legs, or into her big blue big eyes. What is going on in your mind?"

She blushed and said: "I want to have sex with her..."

I asked her – taking his perspective: "What are you thinking of her?"

She replied: "She's too shy. She won't be able to cope with them tomorrow. I should protect her and help her."

Next, I asked her to become herself again and listen to what he just said about her: "How do you feel about it?"

She said she hated it because he was looking at her as a woman, not as a manager.

I asked her: "Can you understand his behavior? Can you do something with it?"

She blushed and told me: "Well, he is very good looking. Maybe I enjoyed him flirting with me."

I asked her: "Imagine you are another person looking at the two of you talking. What do you hear? What do you think of these two people?"

She thought for a moment and replied: "Well, maybe I deserve what he did to me, because listening to the way I talk, I really don't look or sound like a big-time manager. I don't leave the impression of someone who knows what she wants."

(continued)

> Using self-assessing imagery, Helen continued to uphold her feminist right to look beautiful and dress nicely, like a "beautiful sexy woman," but she also learned to assess the unintentional messages that she was transmitting to her colleagues – the impression of a weak, childish female rather than a confident, smart woman. She learned that if she wanted equal rights she needed to "broadcast" equal behavior and talk, be more assertive professionally, and be less provocative in her outward appearance and behavior.

Therapy with Helen was based on helping her assess her behavior by looking at what others saw when they were with her. She learned to assess her skills and presentation to others, and she examined the gaps between what she was and what she presented externally.

Diverse imagery uses can increase awareness about current functioning. Ayelet, my anorexic client (see Chapters 8 and 12), needed to work on developing her interpersonal confidence, because she had experienced no social relationships during most of her adolescence due to frequent hospitalizations. When she recovered, she was very lonely. At the age of 19, she had no friends and complained that nobody wanted to get close to her. As a way to help her develop confidence to start social relationships, I wanted her first to increase her awareness of the nonverbal language she expressed when meeting new people.

> In an imagery session, I asked Ayelet to imagine leaving her college campus (where she was studying to be a teacher) and seeing two young men at the bus stop standing and looking at her.
>
> Asked to describe her feelings, Ayelet responded that she was embarrassed and afraid she would not know how to carry on a conversation. Focusing attention on her appearance, she said that she was head down and had turned her back to them.
>
> I asked her to imagine she was one of these young men looking at her: "What is going on in your mind?" Ayelet answered as a man: "She wants me off her back. She doesn't want me to bother her."
>
> After a few more similar exercises, I asked Ayelet to reflect on these self-assessments and she admitted that she probably makes others run away. But it was not because she did not want them; it was because she was anxious.
>
> As homework, I instructed Ayelet to practice standing in front of the mirror every day and asking herself what signals she sent to others and how others read her signals. Next, I asked her to practice saying "Hi" to strangers at the supermarket, which was how she eventually met her husband...

Increasing self-assessment was very helpful for teaching Ayelet to understand that it was not "the others" who rejected her but rather she herself who was sending uninterested signals to others. Often, clients' misinterpretation of social cues prevents progress. Imagery enables clients to take one step back, look at themselves from the outside, and try to understand who they are, what they are doing, and how they seem. Often, clients glean a considerable amount of information from self-assessment, which can lead them to make changes while increasing awareness of their verbal and nonverbal behavior.

Practice: guidelines

Begin helping clients achieve self-assessment skills through imagery by asking them to imagine themselves doing whatever was troubling them. Ask clients to:

- Look at themselves doing that thing.
- Explain to others what they were doing.
- Try to experience being another person looking at themselves.
- (Finally, after the exercise) Describe what they are doing and how it looks to them now.
- Practice this imagery and similar variations frequently at home.

Imparting Skills for Assessment of Relationships

Just as clients can learn to assess their own behaviors, emotions, and thoughts (as seen above and in Chapter 12), so they can use imagery to assess relationships with others. Relationships are a vital part of human experience and figure importantly in any therapy and any attempt to achieve change. In individual therapy, relationship assessment can help clients learn about their relationships with the environment. Likewise, relationship assessment can be crucial in marital or family therapy to learn about how the couple or family members look at their relationships. In group therapy, group members can support and train together.

In this section, I focus on the value of and techniques for client assessment of relationships; such assessments are conducive to better understanding of one's support systems, social relationships, and social resources for coping with distress. (See Chapter 15 for an elaboration on acquiring social skills and social support to cope better with present life challenges.)

Studies have shown that social support reduces stress and strengthens coping ability (House, 1981). House (1981) distinguished formal from informal sources of social support. Informal sources include personal relationships in the workplace and home, such as friends, colleagues, and family members. Formal support sources generally include large bureaucratic systems that provide support services, such as schools and welfare agencies. In empirical scales used for assessing social support, respondents assess the support they can obtain. Similarly, imagery can be utilized to gain the same information, by asking clients:

> *Imagine your car just broke down, and you are in a hurry to get to work. Can you see yourself standing near the car? You are very frustrated, feel helpless, and know you need to be somewhere else right now. Look at yourself: What are you thinking? Feeling? Doing? Is there anyone you can call to ask for help? Who can you call? If you do call, how will this person respond? What will this person do? If this person cannot come to help, is there anyone else you can call? Who? What will happen?*

Therapists can use imagery to assess all the items that appear in scales measuring positive and negative affect (PANAS: Watson, Clark, & Tellegen, 1988) or social support (Cohen & Wills, 1985). Therapists can ask clients to imagine they are completing a scale measuring their positive and negative emotions: What emotion would you rate as most important for you? What positive emotion would you report you experienced today? In imagining they are completing a social support scale, therapists can ask: Who are the people you can rate as supporting you? Who would you like to support you?

Different images can be created to learn about relationships, support, trust, and mistrust.

> • *There is a secret you feel you must share with someone although it is important that it not yet become public. Look at yourself, feeling your need to share. Is there anyone you can trust to share your secret with? Who is this person? If you tell this person, what will s/he say? How will s/he react? How does it feel when you share it with this person?*
> • *Imagine that all your family, friends, and relatives are now standing in a row in front of you, waiting for you to share your secret with them. Look at them. Who will you never share your secret with? Who do you feel cannot be trusted?*

Many techniques may be employed to assess social support resources and interpersonal relationships. I will next give three examples, corresponding to the utilization of imagery to assess social functioning in three different settings: individual, group, and marital therapy.

Case 1: Relationship assessment in individual therapy

Let me return first to Ayelet, my anorexic client, for an individual case illustration, because her language was very metaphorical, and most of her therapy was conducted using metaphors and imagery. The following early imagery session was dedicated to uncovering the complex relationships between Ayelet and her parents:

Ayelet described how over the years her parents had not seemed to notice that she was losing weight and becoming anorexic. She felt that they ignored her repeated suicide attempts and practically disappeared throughout her course of hospitalizations. I conducted imagery sessions with Ayelet to elicit more about these mother–daughter and father–daughter relationships, as well as the parents' marital relationship.

I asked Ayelet to imagine she was an artist making a sculpture of her family: "Who do you sculpt first?" Immediately, Ayelet said she needed to start with her father, who was the most important figure to her, but not so in the family. There, in the family, he was completely ruled by her mother. She imagined sculpting him lying prone on the floor: "He's on the floor and she makes all the decisions."

She described her mother as "the school principal, the manager" and described her as a standing figure, with one foot on her father's back and her head facing right. When I asked why her mother's head was turned, Ayelet replied: "To avoid what she doesn't want to see. What you don't see doesn't exist." She added: "I need to sculpt her with her eyes closed." Ayelet always related to her mother as someone who refused to face reality.

She didn't sculpt her sisters, claiming they were not part of her life: "My little sister is too young to understand, and my older sister already left home and is living her own life; she's not involved at all."

Then, quickly, Ayelet exclaimed: "But I didn't put the most important figure in yet! I need to sculpt my dog." Throughout her sessions, Ayelet spoke often of her dog and this sculpture showed how much she considered him an integral part of her family.

At this point, Ayelet refused to put herself in the sculpture, claiming that she was not a real part of the family after being hospitalized for years. (Only later when we repeated this exercise could she insert herself.) As we ended the exercise, Ayelet told me that now, looking at her sculpture, maybe she should forgive her father for not being there for her all this time, because "he was very loyal to my mother, did what she wanted, and was torn between helping me and accepting her view that if you don't talk about things they don't exist. You know the second generation of the Holocaust? You hide the dirty laundry under the rug. You don't clean it in front of everyone."

After this session, I was able to invite Ayelet's parents to several family sessions, where we started working on creating new, trusting relationships in the family, now that Ayelet had returned home from the hospital.

Thus, this exercise aiming to assess her family relationships furnished both Ayelet and me with important feedback that enabled us to make decisions about how to continue working on her familial relationships.

Case 2: Relationship assessment in group therapy

A second case illustrating imagery usage to assess social relationships was part of a therapy group that I conducted voluntarily for mothers of at-risk children. Social welfare agencies referred all six mothers to individual therapy with a social worker because they were assessed as neglecting their children, yet they denied such behavior. One of the women, Eileen, was previously my own client in individual therapy, and, like her peers treated by other social workers, she was not progressing. For this reason, I decided that group therapy might offer a better route toward helping these women, and I volunteered to treat them with the aim of changing their relationships with their children and learning mothering skills.

In one group therapy session, I asked the mothers to imagine they were in a place they enjoyed and then asked them to imagine their child came in: "Look at your child. Note the child's appearance, the way the child is standing. On the ground near you, there is a rope. Take it in your hands and use this rope to tie yourself to your child. Try to focus on how you make the knot. Where do you tie it, what do you do with it? Look at yourself and your child. . ."

I didn't finish the sentence because Eileen shouted. She opened her eyes and looked at me, frightened. After hesitation, she said she had seen herself tying the rope around her child's neck and throwing him down the hill, and he was going to die. All the other mothers were shocked; they watched her without speaking.

I myself panicked for a second, thinking to myself: What possessed you to conduct this crazy exercise? What are you going to do with it now? But then, I quickly reminded myself that images are not reality and that whatever emerged were thoughts and emotions that those women felt, not something I caused them to feel. I thought that if Eileen had fantasies or thoughts of killing her child, it was something we must address and might be shared by other group members. We could cope with it through cognitive restructuring, redefinition, and support.

I took a deep breath and turned to her, saying: "Well, I guess you are very happy to open your eyes and see that it was not true. It is good to know your child is safe at school now. Isn't it?"

We started talking and Eileen confided: "I never wanted this son – he was an accident. But I never, ever really wanted to kill him! With all my other children, things were different. I never wanted to get rid of any of my

(continued)

---

children, but I do find it very difficult to handle him. I don't hate him, but do you all know what it means to be with a child who is always fighting? I just can't handle it any more . . . I can't even hug him . . ."

Eileen's homicidal image was one of the most shocking that I remember from using imagery with clients. However, looking back, I think that this imagery exercise triggered a real change in the group dynamics, and afterwards therapy progressed very quickly. Seeing herself killing her child was such a shock that it forced Eileen to admit for the first time that something with wrong with her relationship with her child and she became willing to accept help. Her confession helped the other women stop their denial too.

The key message I want to convey with this illustration is that negative, frightening images do not necessarily need to be the focus themselves. Rather, the therapist can use those images in therapy in a positive way that will build on clients' strengths and lead clients toward better understanding and coping. In the case above, I redefined the situation as not necessarily one of killing the child but rather of feeling helpless with him. Likewise, the powerful, vivid image evoked much identification in the other mothers, which I exploited to harness their motivation to accept and express their difficulties rather than denying them, thereby redefining the situation as an opportunity for growth. One of the most important therapeutic principles is to utilize every situation that arises and to regard it as something to work with, redefine, reconstruct, and shift toward clients' best interests.

Case 3: Relationship assessment in marital therapy

I can share with you that, following the above experience with the rope image, I became uneasy to use it again, although I had implemented it successfully many times before. I knew, logically, that I could never cause a client to view what they did not wish to view, but I also did not have control over any frightening direction they might choose for their imaginary wanderings. For example, I could guide them toward a beautiful blue sea, but they might go ahead and visualize drowning violently, if that was on their minds. Therefore, deciding that I needed a "corrective experience" using this rope metaphor to overcome my hesitation, I applied this exercise again, this time in marital therapy.

A young couple in marital therapy never stopped arguing. They had dated for two years before getting married at the age of 30. She desperately wanted to get married and he didn't, but he also didn't want to lose her, so he gave in, and they were wed.

(continued)

Like before, I asked each of them to imagine they were viewing themselves standing with a rope nearby. I asked them to visualize their spouse nearby and to take the rope and tie the spouse to them, without speaking.

I asked them to make sure they felt good about the way they tied themselves to the spouse: "If you don't feel comfortable, change your position until you feel good in it. You can move, turn, shift, or change the rope to get the best position for you."

As they opened their eyes, before I even asked them what they imagined, the husband laughed and told me: "It's so funny the different way she tied me and I tied her..." He continued: "She probably had me stand in front of her, face to face, and then tie the two of us together so close that I could hardly breathe, and I couldn't even look straight ahead because I would be stuck right in her face. I did it differently. I took my left arm, the one near my heart, put my left hand in her right hand, and tied them together very closely..." His wife interrupted: "Yes, but your right hand is free to go wherever you wish!"

In addition to serving as my "corrective experience," this rope exercise once again actualized its potential for assessing relationships. First, this couple really knew each other well, as evidenced by each of them accurately describing what the spouse would imagine. This is an important issue while treating couples. They may not agree with each other, but they do know each other well. Second, this imagery contributed a much clearer view to both the couple and to me about how each of them looks at their relationship and also where the differences lie.

Assessment of relationships is a key feature for client assessment and can include imagery where one looks at oneself participating together in an image with the partner; watches the relationship through one's own eyes and through the partner's eyes; finds metaphors like the rope image to describe relationships; or, as in the following example, views one's relationship through a third person's eyes.

In another session with the aforementioned couple, I asked them again to visualize themselves together. Then I asked each of them to bring their best friend into the picture: "Let the friend watch the two of you and look at how you two look together. The friend is noticing how you two are standing, walking, acting together. What can the friend say about you, as a couple?"

As with previous examples, introducing a third person into the situation and checking how this person views the relationship enables clients to look at their relationships from the outside and gain new perspective.

Practice: guidelines

To impart skills for improving relationships, clients first need awareness about relationships, which can be gleaned from viewing themselves in various situations. Ask clients to:

- Put themselves in a situation together with the partner with whom they wish to examine their relationship.
- Look at themselves through the relationship partner's eyes and note what can be seen from the partner's perspective.
- Look at both partners in the relationship (the client and the other figure) through the eyes of an outsider, from the perspective of a third person watching them.
- Describe the picture created from a metaphor symbolizing relationships – a rope to connect the partners, a family of animals, a sculpture.
- (For couples/families) Talk about similarities and differences in their images – to learn how each partner views the picture and how each thinks the other(s) see(s) the picture.

Imparting Skills to Increase Awareness of Internal Stimuli

Koons (2007) stated that awareness is directed toward the ongoing experience of thoughts, emotions, and sensations as an observer and with one's full attention. Awareness is very frequently practiced through meditation and mindfulness. According to Jon Kabat-Zinn (1990), mindfulness means paying attention in a particular way: intentionally, in the present moment, and non-judgmentally. By accepting current conditions or aspects of themselves that rarely change overnight – like being depressed, anxious, obese, or a single parent – clients can begin to tolerate the pace and pain of change. Additionally, some circumstances, such as the fact of a history of abuse, will never change (Koons, 2007). Linehan (1993a,b) claimed that people suffer because they are unable or refuse to accept pain, they refuse to accept what they have, and they resist reality.

Meditation and mindfulness aim at developing awareness, but a host of other techniques share this aim. Whether using one method or another, clients who succeed in developing awareness can let go of ruminative thinking and accept their emotions. Developing awareness is therefore a crucial component for helping clients improve their subjective wellbeing.

When coping in the present with various disorders, an important skill is clients' ability to tune into their own bodily sensations. Some clients are oversensitive to the different internal feelings and sensations that they experience, and thereby misinterpret those signals as overly important. The anxiety thus provoked in such clients may be symptomatic of a range of disorders such as hypochondria, free-floating anxiety, or panic attacks. Other clients are practically oblivious to their internal stimuli and cannot successfully differentiate when body signals should be noticed as warning signs. For example, pain may warn of medical problems or external dangers, whereas sensations of muscle relaxation and smiling may signal wellbeing in people who have difficulty acknowledging happy moments. Likewise, flushed cheeks, racing heartbeat, and clenched fists may warn of an imminent angry outburst. Imparting skills to increase differentiated awareness of these internal stimuli can enhance coping with various current disorders.

To help clients deal with undifferentiated anxiety and pain, Segal, Williams, and Teasdale (2002) suggested a combination of imagery techniques with mindfulness to increase awareness. They claimed that clients can cope with pain and anxiety after practicing exercises that focus awareness on the body location that hurts most and then on those sensations. Greenberg and Goldman (2008) employed guided meditation and imagery to attune to bodily tension areas and free associate to those areas, thus helping clients physically meet their anxiety and experience what emerged.

An example of this method can be illustrated by the case of Hannah.

Hannah, age 36, suffered from generalized anxiety. She came to therapy complaining of various pains, especially stomach aches. Although thorough medical examinations revealed no pathological findings, Hannah continued to fear that she had a severe, untreated medical disorder.

I thought that Hannah was overinterpreting every little change in her body – sensations that other people would interpret as normal – as something wrong. Therefore, we established the therapeutic goal of helping her gain more differentiated awareness of her internal sensations.

First, we targeted the goal of increasing awareness, with an expected secondary gain of reducing her anxiety. She learned relaxation and then focused on identifying her internal cues. I asked her to go through the various parts of her body while trying to focus on the feeling in each part and while continuously maintaining her relaxed position.

After she was able to focus on her muscles, body heat, relaxation, and blood flow in each body part, I asked her to note whether or not she was experiencing any distress, pain, or stress at that moment. At first, she had great difficulty saying she was feeling good, even though she was relaxed. Instead, she would reply: "I feel nothing." I started asking her to realize that feeling good is a lot and not nothing, but she could not acknowledge a positive feeling. Slowly, as we repeated such imagery, she reached a point where she could say "I am not in pain now." Only later was she able to say: "I feel okay now."

(continued)

> I asked her to try to differentiate the sensations of muscle tension and relaxation. She reported feeling tense most of the time, and the feeling of relaxation was unfamiliar.
>
> As homework, I instructed Hannah to practice relaxation every day, focus on the few minutes she felt good, attune to that good feeling, and rate the extent to which she was able to sense good sensations in various parts of her body.

Thus, Hannah learned skills for identifying internal cues, focusing attention on her body, and rating different frequencies and intensities of feelings and sensations. These are all crucial components in learning to control behavior.

Another example illustrating the usage of imagery to help increase awareness of internal stimuli focuses on a different type of case – a client who was undersensitive to his internal cues and therefore missed important warning signs that could help him control undesirable behavior. In this treatment of an aggressive man, therapy aimed to help him identify internal cues predicting impending dangerously aggressive outbursts.

> Bob, age 38, entered anger management treatment by court order after hitting his wife. I trained him in identifying preliminary cues that could hint to him that his anger was on the rise and that he should be careful. To assist him to identify such internal stimuli, we practiced many imagery exercises where Bob viewed himself becoming angry in various situations. In each situation, I stopped him and asked him: "Now, imagine that you have a mirror in front of you and you are looking at yourself. What do you see now while you're angry?"
>
> After several exercises, Bob could state that when he looked at himself just before exploding there were telltale signs: "Well, I can see that I am standing very tensely. Actually, my fists are clenched very tightly, like they're getting ready...I think my heart rate is faster...I feel a headache. Something is going on in my head. It's as if I am about to explode..."
>
> After several times practicing this exercise, I assigned him homework: to practice standing in front of an actual mirror every time he thought he was getting angry and to observe himself, especially his face and fists.

An important part of controlling an undesired behavior is the ability to identify the warning signals that predict its occurrence. Therefore, imagining how one looks, looking at oneself in the mirror, and learning how emotions influence behaviors are key features in trying to control those behaviors. Our research and treatment teams very frequently use such exercises in our project to reduce aggression for children and adolescents (Ronen & Rosenbaum, 2010). To adapt these exercises to children, we often help children choose actual traffic signs or invent their own (Stop!, Danger Ahead, Caution: Fists Means Anger Is Coming) to remind themselves of the links between internal sensations and the risk of upcoming undesired behaviors. These tools were shown to be effective in reducing aggression according to the reports of therapists, parents, teachers, and the youngsters themselves.

As in the other realms of skill acquisition, after practicing skills for increased awareness of internal stimuli, clients can be trained to apply imagery exercises where they imagine looking at themselves as if they were other people, and assessing their own behavior from the outside, as if looking at someone else. These exercises can be especially fruitful each time clients feel unsure about how they are behaving.

In addition, some imagery exercises are unique to this domain of enhancing sensitivity to internal sensations. For example, clients can be asked to visualize themselves becoming minuscule entities taking a virtual tour inside their own body, traveling to whatever body location is of relevant interest. This way, clients can enter a specific part of the body, looking at it from the inside. Many other imagery exercises can specifically help clients differentiate important from routine physical symptoms and learn to identify anxiety, pain, anger, or other sensations and emotions in a timely fashion (see guidelines below for more ideas). The main benefit of imagery in these techniques is that in addition to enabling relaxation and focused attention, therapists can take clients into their own bodies and thereby offer a powerful tool for helping clients gain a sense of understanding about what is happening inside them. I have found that clients who practice these skills in therapy can use them later effectively at home.

Skills for increasing sensitivity to internal stimuli comprise an important component of many therapeutic orientations. In CBT, it is considered a vital element for empowering clients in general; it plays a key role in mindfulness training to teach clients to become more aware of their own sensations and emotions; and it also is a basic element in self-control training to learn to identify internal warning signals that can caution clients about impending automatic behavior. The components most common to all these methods consist of helping clients focus attention, listen to changes in the body, assess those sensations, and try to change behavior regarding the interpretation or manifestation of those internal stimuli.

Practice: guidelines

To increase awareness of internal stimuli, you should start by asking clients to practice exercises:

- Use relaxation that offers a considerable focus on different parts of the body.
- In addition to general relaxation, ask clients to focus attention on internal stimuli such as muscle tension, blood pressure, heartbeat, body heat, or perspiration.

- When you identify a problem with a specific part of the body, stay there and focus relaxation and imagery on what is going on at that spot.
- Design imagery exercises to help clients gain greater sensitivity to internal stimuli, both physical and emotional sensations, including:
  - Becoming a miniature camera or submarine and entering the body to examine specific parts from inside (e.g., sites of pain).
  - Becoming one's own heart or eyes and looking at how emotions are expressed or sensed.
  - Becoming one's own fist when angry and describing what happens.
  - Visualizing a science researcher who can look at one's body and describe what is going on in that body from a third-person perspective.
- After clients understand what they feel, ask them to practice listening to that part of the body daily for several weeks as homework and to practice learning to be more aware of their internal cues and what they signal.

Imparting Skills for Changing Automatic Thoughts

One of the basic components of CBT involves skills for identifying clients' negative automatic thoughts and then for redefining those thoughts by reconstructing them into more functional ones. Although this CBT method is often applied, therapists frequently face challenges when trying to give clients the skills to "see" their negative automatic thoughts. Clients who are accustomed to automatically seeing reality in a certain way may feel convinced that theirs is the one and only truth and may resist any attempts to modify those thought patterns, often justifying and rationalizing their way of thinking. Here again, imagery techniques can bypass clients' rationalizations of their automatic thoughts, helping clients effectively gain the skills to identify such thoughts, which can elicit quick, strong outcomes.

An example can be taken from Dalia, an abusive mother of four.

Dalia's social welfare agency hoped to help her cease her abusive behavior in order to retain custody of her children. She was being considered as a possible candidate for group therapy conducted at the agency, which would impart mothering skills and offer support. However, to qualify for participation in this group, Dalia needed first to accept responsibility for her abusive behavior; therefore, she was referred to me for individual therapy first, to help her reach acceptance of herself as an abuser.

Dalia used to justify her behavior with statements like: "You don't know my son. If you were there, you would hit him too." "The bible says that he who spares the rod hates his son." "There is no other way to get him

(continued)

to understand." To work toward the goal of helping Dalia change her automatic thought that hitting offered the only solution, I asked her to close her eyes, relax, and imagine herself at home, sitting in the living room:

"You can see your house around you – familiar objects, familiar voices, familiar smells. Now imagine that, through some miracle, you went back many years to the time you were a child. You are no longer you, the mother. Instead, you have become yourself as a child. Look at yourself as a child, notice what year it is and see how old you are, feel what really bothered you as a child. Try to focus and see what you look like as a child, what you are wearing, what you are thinking to yourself. You can see your mother coming toward you and you know she is angry. What are you thinking? Why is she angry at you? What happened?"

Dalia said very quietly: "I came home very late from school and my mother is very angry."

I asked her to attune to her internal feelings: "Your mother is angry at you. Can you see her anger? Are you happy that your mother is angry at you? Do you like her to be angry?"

Dalia stammered in a strange, low, quiet voice with a mixture of pleading and crying: " I . . . I didn't do anything . . . I just . . . I just came back late. I didn't mean. . ."

I told her: "Can you hear your mother telling you: 'You're a bad girl! You're always late! You don't care that I'm worried about you! You don't mind what I feel! You are just a selfish bad girl!' "

Dalia started crying and said: "But . . . I didn't mean to . . . I just wanted to be with my friends. She never understands. I want . . . I don't want to be bad . . . I just . . . All the kids are going together, and I didn't want them to go without me . . . " She started crying more loudly.

I asked her: "Can you, the child, tell your mother that, not me?"

Dalia tried: "Mom, I don't mean to . . . I never mean to . . . I don't want you to be angry. . ."

I then asked Dalia to return to the present day and try to imagine listening to her child saying that. She replied that it was very easy to hear him because that was what he always said. I asked her if her child's words sounded similar to what she told her own mother. Dalia said that she was trying to listen to her son and was being more patient, but still the situation made her feel angry.

I asked her if she could tell her son: "I believe you didn't mean to come home late. I want you to enjoy being with friends. But I can't worry all the time." Dalia repeated those words, and I asked her if they sounded sincere. She said they did.

(continued)

Next I instructed Dalia to try an exercise at least once a day during the next week: "Every time you get angry and start thinking how terribly your son is acting, please bring up the image of yourself as a child, telling your mother your misbehavior wasn't on purpose; it was wrong, but not intentional."

Dalia said she would try. During the next week, she practiced imagining that she was her son and trying to explain that she had no bad intentions, no desire to make her mother angry.

With some clients, verbal discussion about automatic negative thoughts may be sufficient, but once such thoughts are thoroughly rooted in behavior, they are extremely resistant to change. Imagery furnishes a way of bypassing this resistance using several different types of techniques. For example, using imagery, clients can be exposed to their automatic thoughts through the eyes of a third person ("Can you listen to yourself explaining to me why you need to hit him?"). Also, therapists can simply let clients talk with their own thoughts, debating or arguing with themselves, and thereby learning to identify automatic thoughts more easily and change them into mediated ones. Finally, a good method to use is to take the situation to the extreme, as in a courtroom scenario. As I mentioned, clients develop staunch beliefs in their negative thoughts, and these thoughts sound very true to them. Taking situations to the extreme – driving to the future, 120 years from now; being sentenced in court and getting an extreme punishment; being laughed at by the whole neighborhood – can be powerful enough to enable a change in those automatic thoughts.

Practice: guidelines

A large range of exercises can increase clients' awareness of their automatic thoughts in order to replace them:

- After relaxation, generate a picture in which clients can see themselves in the situation where automatic thoughts ordinarily arise.
- Let clients express the automatic thought.
- Let clients become someone else who hears that thought and responds to it.
- Let clients play the "two chair" exercise, in which the negative thoughts argue with the positive ones, while clients shift places.
- Have clients be interviewed by others, requiring clients to express automatic thoughts to others.
- When change is difficult, create an extreme situation by exaggeration: Place clients in court, in prison, or being sentenced to death because of their behavior.

233

- Generate a situation in which clients can accept and repeat positive thoughts, trying to check if those words sound true to them.
- Assign homework to practice positive functional thoughts.

Summary

The present chapter aimed at giving clients the most important skills of increasing awareness of internal stimuli. As suggested in constructivism and mindfulness, awareness of internal cues is not a skill that is routinely pursued. Usually, we ask people to become more sensitive to others, not to themselves. By learning to be sensitive to ourselves, we can cope better and conduct a happier, healthier way of life.

Practice: General Guidelines

Throughout this chapter, I have provided separate guidelines for practicing each of the skill areas discussed. Here I just want to add several concluding guidelines:

- Before practicing specific skills, note what the client lacks, what the client needs, and what skills need to be imparted.
- Sometimes the problem is not skill deficits but rather difficulties in expressing or presenting these skills.
- Often, clients lack all of the aforementioned skills: general self-assessment, assessing relationships, developing awareness of internal stimuli, and awareness of automatic thoughts. However, you cannot impart all of these simultaneously. Focus on one skill at a time, and only after ascertaining clients' ability to apply it do you move on to train another one.

15

Imparting Skills to Improve Present Coping

This chapter focuses on ways to incorporate imagery into therapy in order to foster clients' acquisition of the skills necessary for coping with current problems, challenges, and fears. Some imagery applications here resemble previous techniques such as exposure or mindfulness. However, the specific application of imagery techniques to the treatment of current fears and anxieties differs in several ways from the techniques presented earlier for the treatment of traumatic past events and posttrauma (Chapter 13). Trauma and posttrauma are difficult, harmful problems that cause much distress; therefore, imagery therapy must be conducted at length, gradually, and under therapists' full supervision and responsibility to carefully regulate clients' difficulty and pain levels.

In contrast, all clients always experience some fears, anxiety, and stress daily in their natural environments – at work, at home, and with friends (Marks, 1978, 1987; Stewart & Chambless, 2009) – without necessarily undergoing serious breaches in functioning. Thus, to enhance quality of life and wellbeing, clients can benefit substantially from brief treatments that give them the appropriate skills they lack, and these new skills can be applied independently in their various environments according to need. Therefore, therapy targeting current coping focuses on exercises and the practice of specific skills, targeting specific feared events or challenging situations.

In this chapter, I detail a series of skills that can be divided into two general domains: coping with performance and test anxiety, and coping with social relationships. This is not to say that only these issues are treatable through imagery. Rather, inasmuch as it is impossible to cover all the possible problem areas that affect clients' current functioning, this chapter presents a sample of such problems to exemplify various usages of imagery intervention. These examples can and should, of course, be transferred and generalized to a broader range of issues as met by therapists in their day-to-day work.

The Positive Power of Imagery: Harnessing Client Imagination in CBT and Related Therapies,
First Edition. Tammie Ronen. © 2011 Tammie Ronen. Published 2011 by John Wiley & Sons, Ltd.

Skills for Coping with Performance and Test Anxiety

Many of the disorders necessitating clients' development of coping skills are anxiety-related. Anxiety disorders encompass a large range of fears, anxieties, phobias, and avoidance disorders that harm clients (Himle, 2007) and that are associated with substantial impairments in overall health and wellbeing, family functioning, social functioning, and vocational outcomes (Mogotsi, Kaminer, & Stein, 2000). CBT demonstrated positive results with long-term effectiveness for the treatment of various kinds of anxiety disorders such as phobias (Marks, 1987) and panic disorder (Stuart, Treat, & Wade, 2000; Wade, Treat & Stuart, 1998). Many anxiety-provoking disturbances relate to clients' fears about expected performance in various domains, such as academic tests and work interviews.

People who report test anxiety experience diverse anxiety reactions and negative emotions during learning, but their main complaint is the gap they perceive between their ability to achieve good outcomes and their real outcomes, which are impaired by their thoughts, emotional processes, or self-efficacy processes. Performance anxiety is a similar phenomenon that occurs regarding upcoming events, such as preparing a presentation to give at a work meeting, preparing a lecture in front of a live audience, or acting in a play. The materials needed to be memorized for each of these events as well as the performer's sense of competence can be considerably impaired by high levels of anxiety.

Test anxiety and performance anxiety generally derive from two areas of difficulty: successfully preparing for the test/performance and successfully executing the test/performance. CBT applies several techniques for coping with such anxieties, based on methods that address the preparation phase, especially skills for preparing learning materials: how to summarize materials, how to plan the amount of time needed, how to memorize material, how to differentiate between what is and is not important to learn. Beyond these techniques helping clients organize studying processes and materials to prepare better, skills for the execution phase are also involved. Execution skills focus on maintaining concentration, reducing anxiety, and improving recall during the test/performance itself through a variety of methods, such as learning strategies for completing questionnaires or for performing in front of a live audience.

Preparation Phase: Learning and Memorizing Materials through Visualization

Coping with test and performance anxiety first and foremost requires an ability to relax. Part of the reason people feel so pressured during performance is because of impinging cognitions about how important and fateful the test, lecture, or interview will be for their lives. To bypass these thoughts and reduce tension, clients can practice relaxation as suggested in previous chapters (meditation, deep muscle relaxation) before practicing specific methods for anxiety reduction. Once clients have undergone training in relaxation techniques, they can start practicing imagery for both preparing and performing the material and for reducing anxiety.

In the first phase – preparing performance materials – clients need to use vivid visualization to elicit pictures of the study materials and to recall, plan, and assess relevant materials (see Chapters 6 and 10). To help clients try to remember more of the materials they need to learn, as well as to reduce forgetfulness and memory "blackouts," visualizing how materials are written and organized on the page can help. Toward this end, materials should be prepared in a visualizable way, dividing written material into subsections and employing different shapes, colors, and locations on the page. People who undergo training in this technique can often sit in an exam and see the written page in their mind's eye, focusing on the text's colors, contours, and structure on the page. These visual clues in the elicited image facilitate performers' recall of studied material.

The case of Shira, a 24-year-old undergraduate psychology student, illustrates how this imagery technique can be applied.

Shira described herself as extremely stressed while taking tests: She would always forget everything she'd learned and therefore did not receive the grades she expected.

As a pre-imagery stage, I asked Shira to take chapters from books, or sections from her notebooks, and prepare visualizable summaries of those materials. That is, she needed to utilize different colors to emphasize different topics; highlight important definitions that she needed to remember in different geometrical shapes; and write up the material using columns, rows, boxes, and so on. All in all, she had to prepare each page as if it were a picture.

In the first stage of imagery work in the clinic, to help her memorize the material with the help of visual clues, I instructed her to read over all the highlighted material and then pass it to me and close her eyes and relax. Next, to enhance her recall of the material she had just read, I asked her to elicit as similar a picture as possible to the natural conditions in which she usually studied; that is, imagining herself sitting at her desk or on her sofa at home, and reading the material on the first piece of paper.

I asked: "Can you tell me what is written there?" She thought for a moment and then started telling me sporadically about information that appeared on that page. I stopped her and said: "Wait a second. Don't tell me about it. Read it to me. You can see the page now. There is a green circle on the top left corner. What is written there?"

After practicing, Shira could elicit the picture of the written page and was asked to continue practicing at home.

Thus, imagery as pictorial memory offers a good method to prepare clients for memory recall during performance, but it must go hand in hand with advanced preparation, highlighting, and marking of the learning materials. Therapists should also remember that not all performance anxieties relate to forgetting. The suggested method can be of help only after the therapist ensures that the client possesses the needed performance skills. The following section discusses skills related to the execution phase of performance.

Practice: guidelines

Imagery can help clients in the preparation phase of treatment for test or performance anxieties:

- Teach deep muscle relaxation first, so that clients can focus only on breathing techniques or practice cue relaxation (Chapter 9).
- Instruct clients to prepare learning materials in a visualizable way, incorporating many colors, shapes, and contours to create a pictorial page.
- Train clients to read the prepared page first and then start the imagery session.
- At the initial stage of imagery training, ask clients to try to memorize the material by imagining sitting at home in the familiar room where they ordinarily study, holding the page they have prepared in front of them, and trying to memorize small parts from it. Lead the client to see what is in the lower right-hand corner, what is written in blue, what is highlighted in a box, etc.
- As the client progresses, you can move in two directions:
  - Ask the client to memorize more material.
  - Ask the client to imagine more stressful performance situations and then practice memorizing material within those scenarios, as shown next.

Execution Phase: Alternative Positive Images, Gradual Exposure, Humor, and Role Reversal

Preparation skills must be combined with execution skills; that is, the client must not only prepare materials and practice recall, but also must know how to practice relaxation, how to study for examinations (e.g., differentiating important from trivial information, summarization skills, etc.), how and when to select various strategies for answering multiple-choice test questions, how to maintain eye contact and project one's voice during public speaking, and so on. For example, in the above case of Shira, preparatory work was followed by a second, execution stage of imagery work.

> I asked Shira to imagine she was sitting in the examination room at the university, feeling very stressed by the test but practicing relaxation through breathing, as she had learned in therapy. While she imagined herself in this stressful situation, she then was asked to try to elicit the images of the
>
> *(continued)*

written pages again, to help her cope with the memory recall task during the stress of the exam. After learning the key features of visualization and relaxation and also practicing the material's recall under stressful simulation conditions, Shira found herself able to cope much more easily with real exams and started improving her grades significantly.

To cope with fears that arise during the test/performance itself, in addition to relaxation exercises, several methods based on imagery can help clients. Three methods are described next. One method is to learn how to create a calm, funny image that can easily be elicited during the stressful performance situation to promote relaxation. The second is gradual exposure to the feared situation. A third method is to reduce the impact of the feared event or authoritative figure by using humor and role reversal in one's imagination, thus enhancing one's sense of control and confidence.

Eliciting Positive Images During Stressful Performance Situations

When clients consider a testing situation to be frightening or overwhelming, a pleasant or amusing image can be practiced until nearly automatic and then can be elicited during the stressful situation. This serves both to relax and to desensitize the client by helping put the stressful event together with a pleasant event (thus changing the conditioning, as in desensitization; see Chapter 6).

The case of 32-year-old Joseph illustrates the elicitation of pleasant imagery to cope with a stressful job interview process.

Joseph was an intelligent and capable young man looking for a job in high-tech project management. In job interviews, he always made a very good impression and felt successful. But when he needed to complete the typical computerized test as part of the job interview process, he always felt that he was not at his best because he was too anxious. One technique he found effective was turning the exam into something nonfrightening.

I asked Joseph to imagine he was sitting at home at his computer, and while playing on the internet he came across one of those silly tests that promise you a free cruise around the world if you succeed on it. I asked him to see himself looking at the test, knowing that the chances to win were low, but why not try it? "Besides a half hour of your time, you have

(continued)

nothing to lose. So, you sit there smiling and complete the test. As you do it, you are very happy, fantasizing that you might win the cruise. Note the smile on your face, your relaxed feeling, and your readiness to complete this test, which is actually very easy."

As we terminated the imagery, I asked Joseph to try to rehearse this memory every day at home. After he could view himself completing this cruise test successfully while maintaining a very good feeling, I asked him to try to elicit this memory the next time he was interviewed for a job. Joseph came back after his next work interview, telling me that it was very funny because he was so busy focusing on that cruise that he almost forgot he was not going to win a cruise but to find work.

Practice: guidelines

In the execution phase of treatment, using imagery can help clients elicit positive images under stress:

- Generate a pleasant image based on your knowledge of the client and in collaboration with him/her, using client feedback about the extent to which suggested images arouse positive emotions and stimulate interest.
- Once a pleasant picture has been created, ask the client to focus on it and on the positive emotion it elicits, and to practice eliciting the picture repeatedly.
- After the pleasant state can be induced almost automatically through elicitation of the positive image, ask clients to elicit the stressful picture and imagine being in that stressful situation.
- Next, have clients imagine themselves in the stressful situation. As stress increases, have them try to elicit the alternative calm, positive picture.
- After several practice attempts, clients should feel better during the imagined performance scenario.
- It is important for the client to practice the pleasant situation regularly, as homework.

Implementing Gradual Exposure to the Feared Situation

One of the main techniques suggested for coping with anxiety disorders is exposure therapy, which involves focusing one's attention on the phobic stimulus, then coming into close contact with that stimulus as quickly as possible, and then remaining in place until the fear subsides (Himle, 2007). While treating trauma and posttrauma, these exercises are part of a broader treatment intervention (see Chapter 13). Here, while dealing with current fears and anxiety, they comprise the main core of treatment. Several studies demonstrated the utility of exposure therapies (Koch, Spates, & Himle, 2004; Marks, 1978, 1987). We can use gradual exposure through imagination as a method to help clients cope with performance anxiety, as shown in the following example.

Edith was a young Israeli lecturer planning to attend an international scientific conference for the first time in her career. She felt very happy and honored at the idea of presenting her work in England, but was also frightened about the need to lecture in a foreign language in front of senior colleagues.

Edith felt very confident when lecturing for students in her mother tongue at her home university. Therefore, in therapy I asked her first to imagine that she was lecturing to her regular students in her regular university classroom. As she did so, she said she felt relaxed, so I asked her to imagine that she was lecturing her regular students as usual, except that the lecture had been moved to a large auditorium at a different local university. Edith remained relaxed while imagining this picture, so I next told her that the lecture had moved to England, where the upcoming international conference would be conducted, but still she was lecturing her own students in her mother tongue. Edith said she was a little excited but not nervous at all.

Next, I invited several British students to join the imagined lecture. Edith reported that her excitement increased, but she continued to feel relaxed.

I therefore asked her to imagine that she was at the conference. I asked her to see the lecture room, her computerized presentation projected onto the white screen at the front of the room, all the seated people waiting for her to begin speaking, and herself standing behind the podium with her notes in front of her, trying to give a lecture in a foreign language. After she elicited this picture, I asked her to imagine that the audience members were the conference participants. Edith immediately reported feeling tension, so I asked her to shift the picture and imagine that the audience members were her own students but still she was lecturing in English. Edith reported that her anxiety reduced and she felt calm again, so I repeated asking her to imagine that now she was giving a lecture in English to the conference participants. After repeating this scene several times, Edith reported feeling excited but not anxious at the prospect of her upcoming lecture.

Thus, therapy employed imagery to expose Edith gradually to the anxiety-provoking scene, while practicing relaxation and coping skills.

Practice: guidelines

To practice gradual exposure, you first need to identify the least stressful situation for the client and start imagination from there:

- Help clients practice relaxation and feel calm.
- Ask clients to imagine the first, least stressful situation while continuing to feel calm.
- As clients progress to increasingly stressful situations, verify each time that they are still calm. If not, return to the prior situation, where clients were calm.
- The goal is for clients to be able to imagine the most stressful situation and yet remain calm.
- Use various exercises to help clients imagine the most stressful situation possible, and then imagine changing it into a less stressful situation.

Using Humor and Role Reversal to Gain Control and Confidence

Another kind of image that clients find helpful is envisioning anxiety-provoking events or persons in a humorous or inverted way. The purpose of such exercises is either to turn a frightening situation or event into something amusing, or else to turn an authoritative figure into a funny, harmless one that is under the client's control, in order to stop feeling stressed. This imagery method minimizes the imagined effect of the test/performance and maximizes the imagined ability of the client.

The power and effect of a feared figure (examiner, play director, boss, lecturer) can be reduced by using imagination to change who the figure is, what situation the figure is in, or how the figure looks. For example, clients may view authoritative figures in funny situations like brushing teeth, wearing pyjamas, or shopping for shorts and taking off their pants. To help clients gain a sense of control and confidence, they can also be led to imagine role reversal: themselves interviewing and then failing the interviewer, directing and reprimanding the director, or firing the boss.

Practice: guidelines

In the execution phase of treatment, using humorous and role-reversal imagery can help clients gain control and confidence:

- Try to understand the situation that clients fear and then design an image that is very similar but ends differently, humorously. For example, rather than the feared process of competing for a job, give the client an image of competing for something funny that will not raise anxiety – for example, becoming the

King of White Teeth or becoming the ugliest person in the world, the one with the curliest hair, or the funniest.

- Regarding a feared person, change how the figure looks, adding humorous elements like wearing a clown's suit, putting on an avocado facial mask, or jumping on a trampoline while holding a basket of fruit. These elements change the conditioning of the specific person with a fearful feeling and enable new conditioning of the figure to a funny picture, thus increasing amusement and reducing anxiety.

- To add humor to an anxiety-arousing situation, change the surroundings – such as taking a test while naked or while lying in bed, giving a lecture while accompanied by background singers, and so forth.

- For practicing role reversal, ask clients to imagine becoming the teacher or manager and testing the candidate.

- For all these humorous and role-reversal situations, clients need to be trained repeatedly to practice retaining a good feeling while simulating the anxiety-arousing situation, in the session and as homework.

Skills for Improving Social Relationships

Among the most frequent skills for which clients need training are basic social skills. As human beings living in society, we need social support to cope with stress, and we need social relationships to prevent loneliness, feel self-confident, share responsibility for raising children, and so on. Many disorders such as anxiety, aggression, depression, loneliness, and more relate to problems in establishing contacts and maintaining adequate relationships.

Discussion of social competencies can fill an entire book, but here I will focus on some of the social skills necessary for coping with current interpersonal problems and challenges. Social skills encompass the main means for gaining social support – a major resource that people require to improve their lives. The availability of social support can moderate or buffer the negative impact of stress on the individual (Natvig, Alebrektsen, & Qvarnstrom, 2003; Winefield, Winefield, & Tiggemann, 1992). The moderating influence of social support manifests itself in individuals' less threatening evaluations of stressful situations, increased perceived effectiveness of their resources for coping with those situations, and better direct solutions for the problems they face.

Social support influences people by providing acceptance, belonging, stability, and recognition of self-worth (Cohen & Wills, 1985; House, 1981). As mentioned in Chapter 3, social support increases people's level of wellbeing, leading to a healthier lifestyle, both physically and mentally (Keyes, 2006; Keyes *et al.*, 2008). Supported individuals think more actively and openly, feel a greater sense of control over their lives, cope better with stressful situations, and set life goals (Diener *et al.*, 1999; Keyes & Ryff, 2000; Veenhoven, 1991).

The problem starts when one wants to achieve support but does not possess the skills necessary to achieve it. Many clients who come to therapy presenting problems related to social relationships actually exhibit a whole range of missing skills.

Such skills begin with how to decide who can be one's friend and continue with techniques for initiating and then maintaining relationships, expressing emotions, being assertive, and more (Gambrill & Richey, 1988).

Social skills can be defined as a complex set of skills that facilitate successful interactions while making appropriate discriminations; that is, deciding what would be the most effective response and using verbal and nonverbal behaviors that facilitate interaction (LeCroy, 2007). The conceptualization of social skills as training suggests that problem behaviors can be viewed as remediable deficits in a response repertoire (King & Kirschenbaum, 1992; LeCroy, 2002). This perspective focuses on building prosocial responses as opposed to eliminating excessive antisocial responses.

Gambrill (2006: 431) listed a number of social skills that clients should be taught through social skills training: dealing with passive and aggressive behavior; establishing first contacts; interpersonal problem-solving and conflict resolution; disagreeing with others; responding assertively to refuse others' demands; speaking more; listening more; and so forth. I next present several examples of skills that clients can learn and practice to improve various aspects of their social interactions, focusing on skills for the initiation of social contacts and assertiveness skills.

Practice: guidelines

As guidelines for imparting social skills, I extended several steps described by LeCroy (2007: 293) for effective social skills training:

- Present the social skill being taught, and explain its importance.
- Discuss the social skill and give examples for its usage.
- Present a problem situation and ask clients to practice ways to deal with it.
- Model skills not used by clients to enlarge clients' repertoire.
- Help clients assess outcomes of using each specific skill.
- Ask clients to think of additional applicable techniques for the current situation.
- Have the client rehearse the skill; provide coaching if necessary.
- Ask clients to assess their performance.
- Give feedback to clients regarding performance.

Skills for Initiating Social Contacts

Many clients find ways to maintain relationships once they already have them but do not feel confident enough to begin new relationships and do not know how to decide on appropriate partners for such relationships. Therefore, clients should learn techniques for meeting people and getting to know them. These social skills are very difficult to train without *in vivo* exposure; however, many clients resist practicing in real social situations, thereby highlighting the benefit of imagery as a preliminary rehearsal method.

An example can be taken from Ayelet, my client with anorexia (see Chapters 12 and 14).

> Hospitalized most of her adolescence, Ayelet had not participated in social activities and had developed social fears (Ronen & Ayelet, 2001). I asked her to imagine that she was calling friends from her school days and practicing talking with them. After several practice sessions, Ayelet actually called some schoolmates.
>
> Another technique was practicing imaginary exposure to situations where she acted sociably to strangers. One at a time, she would elicit pictures of going out to shops, the library, markets, and other public locations where she would meet strangers her own age. I instructed her to imagine smiling toward them and saying hello to them.
>
> After being able to imagine such encounters, she shifted to *in vivo* exposure by actually going downtown and saying hello to old friends she met on the street. Gradually, she even dared to invite an old friend to visit her.

Another example for imagery use to help a client feel good, raise confidence, and start relationships is the case of Bar.

> Bar, age 26, came to therapy complaining that he never dated a woman without becoming fearful (see Chapter 10). He was asked to imagine himself going out to the local pub and seeing a girl there. First he had to imagine someone who was not really attractive, on whom he could merely practice his skills.
>
> I asked him to look at her: "What is the first thing you say to her?"
>
> After a brief silence, Bar answered: "Well, I have no idea. What can one say? I don't know her."
>
> I asked: "Can you see her? Actually, when you are near her, you can see that she is not a beauty queen, but she doesn't look bad. What is your goal?"
>
> Bar said: "I guess just to try to talk with her."
>
> I said: "OK, she's smiling. What can you say to her?"
>
> Bar said: "Hi, I'm Bar."
>
> I replied: "Great. Look at her. She smiles back and says, 'Hi, I'm Sofie.' What else can you ask her? Remember, it's just small talk, nothing serious."
>
> Bar then said: "Do you live nearby?"
>
> I asked him: "What is her answer?"
>
> He said: "Actually no. This is my first time here. I came with friends."
>
> *(continued)*

245

As the imagined conversation continued, Bar felt more and more relaxed and started role-playing her role as well as his, stating that it was easy to talk with her.

Afterwards, I asked Bar to pinpoint sentences or comments that he used in this conversation that he thought would be good to remember for future conversations. As homework, I instructed him to imagine every day where he would invite a woman to a drink, a dance, or a conversation.

After two weeks of practicing, I asked Bar to try an *in vivo* exercise. He came back reporting on his experience: He had talked with one girl, in whom he wasn't interested at all, but did not feel anxious.

In subsequent imagery sessions, Bar dared to talk more, moving the conversation to other topics. Then, after another session, he told me that he went to a pub and although it was not what he was supposed to do, he tried to talk with a very attractive girl. Surprisingly enough, she seemed to enjoy it and even gave him her telephone number – but he had not called her yet.

Here, as described in Chapter 13, social skills training focused on imaginal exposure as rehearsal prior to *in vivo* exposure. In Bar's case, he was exposed first to choosing girls who were not really important to him, which was less anxiety-provoking, until he gradually could choose someone he valued. While rehearsing and practicing social conversation skills in imaginary situations, Bar learned which questions to avoid, how to come across as interesting, how to continue conversations after a lull. Once he felt confident in these newly learned skills, it was easier to actually practice them in natural social environments.

Practice: guidelines

The following guidelines help clients practice skills for improving social contacts:

- Select a goal that clients are interested in achieving and have them describe it.
- Create a situation in imagery where clients can practice the necessary skills for achieving that goal.
- Have clients practice those skills first, in a place (or with people) where clients feel confident.
- Highlight clients' positive interactions and emphasize what went wrong in social conversations to identify inappropriate behaviors.
- Have clients identify positive behaviors and repeat them with different environments, people, and situations.
- Create homework assignments to continue practicing skills using imagery.
- Ask clients to start practicing the learned skills *in vivo*, gradually moving from less to more anxiety-provoking situations.

Assertiveness Skills (Learning to Say No)

Assertiveness encompasses a set of skills that can help individuals maneuver more efficiently and less stressfully within human relationships. Assertive communication can reduce the stress experienced during interpersonal conflict and help avoid a sense of overload in the face of excessive requests from family, friends, and coworkers. Assertiveness means finding a middle ground between aggression and passivity that does not disrespect others, yet does help the individual protect and guard personal interests and boundaries (Gambrill & Richey, 1988; LeCroy, 2002).

One assertiveness skill that many people find hard to activate is refusing a request from a friend, family, or colleague. People are taught from an early age to value behaviors such as helping others, showing empathy, and giving support. Thus, many people feel that refusing to help is a selfish act, and they often find themselves doing things they don't want to do, just because they want to be considered nice people or feel guilty if they say no.

A case in point is that of Tali.

Tali, age 36, a married mother of two, moved with her family to a new apartment and the couple's best friends became their neighbors. The relationship between the two families started very well. The children became friends and spent hours together, and both families enjoyed it. But slowly, Tali started feeling more and more exploited by her friend.

At first, she was annoyed to discover that the friend used Tali's spare key to enter her apartment during the day while Tali was at work, without knocking on the door. Then, one day Tali returned from work and found that the meat she had planned to cook that night was missing; her neighbor had taken it without asking to prepare for her family. The last straw came when the housekeeper cooked a week's worth of meatballs for Tali's children, but the neighbor took most of them while Tali was at work and told her that they were delicious.

At this point, Tali came to me saying that she needed to put an end to this "sharing," but she was afraid it would also end their friendship. Tali said that she knew she needed to stop things but just didn't know how.

I decided to apply imagery therapy and use exaggeration methods to enhance Tali's assertiveness skills. I asked her to imagine she was coming home from work, tired and hungry and wanting to rest, but when she opened the refrigerator it was completely empty, with a note from her friend saying, "Thank you. I didn't feel well enough to go shopping, so I took everything I needed from you." I added: "Consequently, you can't even make yourself a sandwich, and your dream of resting dissipates into thin air; you need to immediately go shopping for food." I asked Tali to

(continued)

---

describe her feelings, her fatigue, and her thoughts, and, as expected, she was getting angrier than before.

I continued, telling her that as she come home carrying all the groceries, she opened the drawer to put her purse away and there, where she kept her extra money, was another note: "I took your money. I thought I needed it more than you do." This time, Tali really became furious and said: "Well, that isn't just an image! She's not far from doing that to me again! I can't stand it any longer!"

I told her to notice the quiet around her home: "Where is everybody?" She walked around the apartment trying to see where her children and husband were, and she found another note saying: "I think your family will enjoy being with me more, so I took your kids and your husband." Now Tali became enraged: "Enough is enough! I must put an end to it!"

As we neared the end of the session, to help her practice different verbal and nonverbal styles of assertiveness, I introduced another exercise. I asked her to imagine she had to walk past a row of 10 people she knew, each of whom was stretching a hand out toward her, asking her for something. She needed to practice saying no and looking for the best way to refuse.

As we terminated the session, Tali said that she knew she would now start saying no, that she understood that it was necessary, and that she even thought she knew how to do it. But she was afraid her friends would feel very bad and stop being her friends. It took many sessions, but finally Tali confronted her neighbor.

People continually do things because they feel they "should." Albert Ellis (1973) called this "shouldism" or "mustrubation." Nietzsche said that people do things because they think they only need to do it now, this one time; however, if people imagine they need to keep doing the things they don't really like to do for the next 100 years, they will probably stop doing them right now (Yalom, 1992). For example, I asked Tali to imagine that this was not only this time she was being exploited; she would be exploited 100 more times unless she learned assertiveness.

The "Nietzsche" technique is illustrated next in the case of Edna and her sister.

Edna, age 45, was married and had three children and a successful job. Edna used to complain in therapy that her mother hovered over her younger sister (age 35), spoiled her, and never let her be independent, although the sister was a married mother of three and a successful musician. However, when the mother died, Edna found herself in her mother's shoes, taking care of her little sister.

(continued)

Edna worked more hours than her sister and was very busy, but her sister would call her several times a week, complaining she felt ill and needed medication, or needed help in the house, and Edna, who felt bad about her sister, would drive 30 minutes to her sister's house, only to find that she was actually fine.

Edna was very angry but could not express her anger with her sister, nor could she stop helping her. So, she found herself in a position where she was angry at her sister, angry at the need to do things for her sister, and angry that she was not able to say no.

In one imagery session, I asked Edna to imagine herself getting a phone call from her sister, who asked her to come and make a cup of tea for her because she was feeling bad and didn't feel like making it for herself. Edna practiced refusing, and I continued the scene acting the part of her sister. Acting the part of her sister, I told Edna what a bad sister she was, how I didn't have anyone to take care of me, and how she would be sorry when I died. Edna relented and agreed to help me.

At that point, using an exaggeration technique, I told her that now she would have to keep her promise to come and prepare tea for me (her sister) 100 times – three times a day, every day. This time Edna got really angry and said she would never do that, not any more, it was wrong for me to ask it of her, and it was not fair.

I turned to her and said: "If you are sure you shouldn't go 100 times to prepare tea, why should you do it this time? Why can't you say no to begin with and get it over with?"

Edna had to practice this exercise – of saying no to her sister's request for 100 bouts of help – repeatedly over a period of three weeks. Only then was she "brave" enough actually to confront her sister and assertively set limits on her sister's demands.

As described in the previous chapter, imagery can be used to help people assess themselves as they act with others in the present. As they become more self-aware, clients can learn to change their passive behaviors. Chapter 14 presented ways to increase such awareness; however, these techniques were insufficient for clients like Gail and Edna, who required not only increased self-awareness but also explicit training in assertiveness skills, through practice of techniques for saying no. The techniques of exaggerating events and outcomes, bringing them to an extreme, are very useful in these cases for helping clients dare to stand up for themselves and find balance in their lives.

Practice: guidelines

Skills for assertive training help clients practice how to say no, how to refuse a request, how to express feelings to others, and how to make decisions about what is really right for them, not what they should do because others want them to.

- To teach clients to think of themselves, not only of others, help them take a different perspective. This can be facilitated in two ways:
  - Help clients take the position of a third person looking at the event from the side and seeing what others can see in the situation.
  - Exaggerate the (i) situational demands or (ii) outcomes or (iii) timing, until clients come to a point where they feel it is "too much" or "enough is enough."
- To exaggerate demands (item i above), take clients' problems to an extreme by having clients imagine more and more problems accumulating, whether they involve the inability to say no to others' requests, giving away belongings, or agreeing to things that the client actually does not like or want to do.
- Design situations that are so extreme that clients eventually say: "No more!" In practicing assertiveness, it is important for clients, not therapists, to put an end to the exploitation or exaggerated demands of others.
- Exaggerate outcomes (item ii above), describing clients as lacking all their belongings because they have all been taken away, or else sentencing clients to death or trial because they said no. Again, it should be clients' decision, not therapists', when to stop acting passively like before.
- To exaggerate timing (item iii above), go 100 years ahead to a time that is not real, when it is easier to imagine performing difficult acts.
- Have clients practice different means for saying no until they accumulate a repertoire of assertive behaviors. Ask clients to imagine many people and practice ways to say no to each.
- Homework assignments help clients practice assertiveness skills in day-to-day life.

Summary

Some of the main components responsible for the human facility to flow and increase subjective wellbeing in the present are the ability to reduce fears and anxieties on the one hand and the capacity to enhance social relationships and support on the other. As mentioned in Chapter 3 on positive psychology, negative and positive emotions comprise different mechanisms. Decreasing negative emotions can help improve coping, but does not necessarily increase positive emotions. Fostering positive emotions can assist in gaining support, self-confidence, and happiness, but does not necessarily diminish negative emotions. Both abilities – to decrease negative events and to increase positive ones – together enable human beings to make the most out of life. The present chapter proposed several examples of how both can be achieved via the use of imagery.

16

Imparting Skills for Developing a Positive View of the Future

As mentioned in Chapter 3, positive psychology was described by Seligman and Csikszentmihalyi (2000) as relating to subjective experiences in the past, present, and future. Relating to the past, I have presented techniques to apply imagery for overcoming, coping, and dealing with past trauma and posttrauma as a way to improve subjective wellbeing. Relating to the present, positive psychology has addressed issues such as flow and happiness, and in the previous two chapters, I mainly focused on imagery techniques to impart skills for increasing awareness and coping in the present.

The last component is the future. Positive psychology views the future as relating to hope and optimism (Seligman & Csikszentmihalyi, 2000), which are the focus of the imagery work proposed in this chapter. As a positive therapist from a CBT orientation, I strive to go beyond problem-solving and also empower clients and increase their happiness, subjective wellbeing, and life satisfaction. Therefore, clients' future functioning should be an important part of therapy.

A large range of literature addresses the topics of hope and optimism. Victor Frankl (1984) stated that happiness must happen, and the same holds for success. He suggested that people must let it happen. He also emphasized that there are always choices to make.

In this chapter, I focus on how to help facilitate positive thinking, optimism, and hope in the future. I propose several exercises to teach clients how to enhance more positivity and introduce more happiness into their lives.

Snyder *et al.* (1996) described hope as two separable components: agency and pathways. Agency reflects one's determination that goals can be achieved. Pathways refer to one's beliefs that successful plans can be generated to reach one's goals. Snyder *et al.* devised a scale measuring agency by asking for people's self-assessed ability to pursue their goal, and measuring pathway, by asking about people's belief that they can achieve their goal and be happy with this achievement. Snyder *et al.* found that goal expectancies, perceived control, self-esteem, positive emotions, coping, and achievements were positively linked with hope.

The Positive Power of Imagery: Harnessing Client Imagination in CBT and Related Therapies,
First Edition. Tammie Ronen. © 2011 Tammie Ronen. Published 2011 by John Wiley & Sons, Ltd.

Optimism was defined as a

> mood or attitude associated with an expectation about the social or material future –
> one which the evaluator regards as socially desirable, to his or her advantage, or for
> his or her pleasure. (Tiger, 1979: 18)

An important implication of this definition is that there can be no single or objective optimism, at least as characterized by its content, because it depends on individuals' subjective perceptions of what is desirable. Optimism is predicated on evaluation – on given affects and emotions, as it were (Peterson, 2000). Contemporary approaches usually treat optimism as a cognitive characteristic – a goal, an expectation, or a causal attribution – which is sensible so long as we remember that the belief in question concerns future occurrences about which individuals have strong feelings (Peterson, 2000).

Magaletta and Oliver (1999) studied hope and optimism among 204 adults. They found that hope and self-efficacy predicted levels of optimism. Peterson (2000) claimed that optimism is an inherent aspect of human nature. He viewed optimism as an individual trait and showed that it can be a highly beneficial psychological characteristic linked to good mood, perseverance, achievement, and physical health. Optimism was also linked to positive mood and good morale; to perseverance and effective problem-solving; to academic, athletic, military, occupational, and political success; to popularity; to good health; and even to long life and freedom from trauma. Pessimism, in contrast, foreshadows depression, passivity, failure, social estrangement, morbidity, and mortality (Magaletta & Oliver, 1999; Peterson, 2000; Snyder *et al.*, 1996).

In a special issue of the *American Psychologist*, Seligman and Csikszentmihalyi (2000) predicted that this new century will see both a science and a profession of positive psychology emerge, which will come to understand and build the factors that allow individuals, communities, and societies to flourish. At the individual level, they highlighted positive individual traits such as the capacity for love and vocation, courage, interpersonal skill, esthetic sensibility, perseverance, forgiveness, originality, future mindedness, spirituality, high talent, wisdom, hope, and optimism. At the group level, the factors expected to flourish comprise civic virtues and the institutions that move individuals toward better citizenship, such as responsibility, nurturance, altruism, civility, moderation, tolerance, and work.

Seligman and Csikszentmihalyi (2000) claimed that psychology is not merely a branch of medicine concerned with illness or health; it is much larger. In their view, mental health practitioners and scientists need to make a switch in how they regard research and therapy. Treatment, therefore, should not only fix what is broken; it should nurture what is best. In this quest for what is best, positive psychology does not rely on wishful thinking, faith, self-deception, or fads; it tries to adapt what is best in the scientific method to the unique problems that human behavior presents to those who wish to understand it in all its complexity. However, after many years of working exclusively on personal weaknesses and on damaged brains, science today is poorly equipped to prevent illness effectively. Psychologists need now to call for massive research on human strengths and virtues. Practitioners need to recognize that much of the best work they already do in the consulting room is to amplify clients' strengths rather than repair their weaknesses.

As Lyumbomirsky (2007) and Fredrickson (2009) suggested, one can facilitate and enhance happiness and positivity in the future. I echo Seligman and Csikszentmihalyi's (2000) imploring as the main rationale for the present chapter: focusing on the future while wishing to impart positive forces to clients. In this sense, therapy should be about work, education, insight, love, growth, and play. And imagery allows these strengths and resources to emerge.

Fredrickson (2009) suggested imagery exercises to elicit the ten forms of positive experience that can make an affirmative difference in people's lives: joy, gratitude, serenity, interest, hope, pride, amusement, inspiration, awe, and love. She stated that all people have the power to turn positivity on and off for themselves. For example, to imagine serenity, Fredrickson suggested that clients can visualize that their surroundings are safe and familiar, and that things are going well. Or, as an imagery exercise for gratitude, she suggested that clients can imagine that they have just realized that someone has gone out of their way to do something good for them, and then therapists can ask clients how they feel in this situation.

In light of this positivity rationale, I will present several exercises and case studies to help apply imagery techniques to improve clients' functioning in the future, as well as to increase hope and optimism regarding what lies ahead.

Planning the Future

I believe that a major aim of therapy is to help clients gain optimistic and hopeful attitudes conducive to planning a bright future and seeing the positive that it holds in store, rather than merely fearing problems that might lie ahead. I view this aim as integral to treatment of all clients, regardless of the original cause of their referrals. Several techniques may help clients plan the future. They often combine games, metaphors, and imagery.

While supervising parents, I often find that they feel more confident and stronger in dealing with their child's present challenges when they gain an optimistic view of the future. For children with a good prognosis, I frequently ask parents to draw their child (either on paper or as an imagery exercise) as they view the child now, in the present, having difficulties, worrying them, and annoying them. Then I ask them to close their eyes and imagine their child 20 years from now, as an adult.

Look at your child all grown up. Look at how your child looks. At the way he or she stands, smiles, talks, acts. Look at your child's thoughts. Look at your child's behavior. What is your child doing? Thinking? Feeling? Focusing on the changes your child has experienced, what can you tell yourself? Are you satisfied? Are you happy? Are you content?

During this exercise, parents frequently tell me "In 20 years, my son will be great" or "My daughter can cope with her future; she is smart." When I hear such positive attitudes, it is easy to tell those parents that their current problem is not a fear that their child is at risk or a concern that the child's functioning today might harm his or her future, but rather that the problem they face is in handling the child now, in the present. Looking at the future and knowing that a good picture is forecast offers much comfort to parents and enables them to "put things into proportion" and deal differently with their children's present disturbances.

In contrast, when parents are very pessimistic about their child's future, we can look together at that dark picture and try to discover some positivity nonetheless, as a way to enlarge alternative solutions and problem-solving skills.

The following technique, of planning a drive on the road, can help adult and child clients alike to think about the future while considering possible obstacles and resources that might be available to them. Once clients anticipate the future in more detail, they can prepare to deal with it more confidently.

Imagine you are a driver on the highway. There are many cars around you, and some of them are really driving like crazy. If you want to return home safely, what do you need to do? Where do you look? What or who can help you? What kind of warning signals can help you? Can you prepare your own warning signals?

Preparing warning signals for navigating future experiences may give clients a sense of confidence and feelings of control. Children especially respond to the notion of preparing road signs for themselves. For example, a schoolgirl may prepare for Wednesdays, when she is liable to fidget in class and talk out of turn, by mentally drawing a cautionary sign to herself: "Beware! Homeroom Teacher Has the Day Off! Don't Get into Trouble!" Or a teenage boy trying to avoid the path that has repeatedly led him to trouble with other aggressive boys may design warning signs like: "No Entry to Fights" or "Keep Away from Tom – Danger of Explosion Ahead."

Adults, too, enjoy the process of discovering warning signs. For example, parents of adolescent children can imagine signals to remind themselves: "Back off! That face means it's not the right time to speak with him" or "Bad move! Leave her alone for an hour." One aggressive husband I treated was able to imagine warning signals to help him curb his urge to lash out at his wife: "She is on the telephone again. Leave the room before it makes you angry!" or "Beware wife's tasteless food. Just shut your mouth before saying something you'll regret!"

In a workshop I attended with Bob Neimeyer in the 1990s, he employed constructivist therapy techniques, asking people to write a chapter for a book about their lives. I find this technique very useful for learning how clients view themselves in the past, present, and future, especially when I want to enhance change in the future and ask clients to see how they believe they can be different. I often avail myself of this technique, sometimes in writing or drawing, but mostly I enjoy asking my clients to elicit their life's book in their imaginations during session.

Imagine you are writing a book about your life now. You are about to end the book. You have finished writing everything about the past and the present. You now merely need to add another chapter – about your future. What are you going to write about? What do you imagine your future will hold? Where will it take you?

The same imagery technique can be implemented using other media, such as film, instead of written narrative:

You are preparing a movie about your future. Describe yourself: Note how you look in the future, what are you doing, what you are feeling, what is going on in your mind. How does the future look to you? How much do you like what you are doing and who you are?

Practice: guidelines

The practice aimed at developing optimism and positivity in the future includes:

- Ask your clients to think of several positive goals they would like to achieve in the future.
- Ask your clients to think of the future as a tour they will take. On that journey, ask the clients:
  - Can you plan the drive?
  - Can you plan the stops?
  - Are there any warning signals you can put on the roadside to help you be careful?
  - Can you locate some danger spots that may disturb you, and try to detour around them?
  - Are there new skills you would like to gain?
- Close your eyes and imagine yourself 10 years from now. How happy are you with what you see?

Facilitating Positive Emotions and Sensations

As mentioned before, once clients can get in touch with their good feelings, learn to express positive emotion, find their happiness, and develop optimism, they find it easier to cope with problems and improve subjective wellbeing. Hope for the future is something that urges people to create change in their lives. The following case illustrates how therapists can help clients develop positivity toward the future.

Michael, age 30, was divorced from his first high school sweetheart after she had an affair with his good friend. They had no children. By the time he came to me, he had accepted the divorce and was no longer angry at his ex-wife. However, Michael seemed very pessimistic about love and was unable to start new relationships for fear of getting hurt again. He claimed he lacked happiness, joy, and optimism about the future.

Therapy aimed at helping him gain positivity. We practiced the "Land I Wish" exercise in a similar way to that described in Chapter 9 to induce visualization. I asked Michael to close his eyes and take a trip: "The land you wish is a place where you feel happy. It can be a place you have been to before and would like to return to; it can be a place you heard about but never visited; it can be a place you make for yourself. Put yourself in the land you wish and look around. Note the smells, colors, climate, time of day, sounds. Note how you look when you are in the land you wish – the smile on your face, your good feelings, your good sensations, the way you stand when you feel all the good things you wish to feel. Pay attention to the kind of feeling you want to feel – it can be confident, trusting, relaxed, joyous, happy, calm, successful. Let those feelings come to you more and more until you are very happy with what you sense, what you feel, what is there inside you – once you feel all those things. When you are sure that you feel all the things you would like to, look at yourself and the way you look. In a few seconds, you will open your eyes – without sorrow to be letting go of this land. You know that the land you wish remains within you, and you can take it with you. You can return there whenever you like..."

This exercise reminded Michael of positive emotions lying dormant inside him, and could help him in developing future optimism.

Next session, I asked Michael to put himself into a past situation that made him happy. He mentioned getting together with two of his old friends, watching football together, drinking beer, and laughing. I asked him to imagine inviting his friends to come over to his house to watch the game, and focusing on his feelings and trying to increase them. I also invited him to bring his friends into the Land I Wish.

Next session he told me he'd met his old friends, commenting that he hadn't laughed like that for a very long time.

As a next step, I asked Michael to return to the Land I Wish once again, but this time to imagine a new situation in which he had felt happy or good – in a different place, with different people. It was important for him to see that opportunities for happiness in his life were not limited to one place

(continued)

with those two friends. I wanted to help him generalize his first positive experience in a long while to other relationships and situations.

For the next month, I asked him to practice viewing these scenes each day and to bring to each session another image of himself being happy, specifically targeting situations relating to himself, other people, and other places.

As happens many times, once clients allow themselves to begin viewing themselves as happy, telling themselves how happy they are, and letting themselves accept those feelings, then the natural situations, people, and places in their normal environment gradually become perceived as making them feel more and more happy. This way of thinking resets the mind to be oriented toward the positive, and, once it begins, we can recognize that we feel happy just hearing a song on the radio. I have applied the Land I Wish exercise to many clients and they always seem to enjoy practicing it. They often even surprise me by finding new and creative ways to become happier.

Whereas the Land I Wish exercise primarily addresses finding happiness around and outside ourselves, other imagery exercises can help us find happiness inside ourselves. The following case exemplifies imagery to foster a client's view of her own body as containing places that made her happy.

Sheila was a happily married, 54-year-old mother of two grown daughters. She came to therapy after undergoing surgery to remove a malignant melanoma tumor. Her prognosis was good; she needed no further treatments after surgery, only regular skin checkups. However, she was unable to become optimistic, demonstrated many fears, and thought that her cancer derived from her stressful life.

In collaboration with Sheila, we defined the aim of therapy as trying to help her feel happy with herself, become more relaxed, learn to reduce her long working hours, plan her time better, and stop running all the time. I hoped to show Sheila that she could be happy while resting or at home with her family.

I asked Sheila to focus inward on her bodily sensations, to learn to find happiness inside, instead of continually running after it on the outside. This choice was especially warranted in Sheila's case because of her traumatic recent experience with her body; cancer inevitably arouses feelings of betrayal by the body and anxiety about further physical illness lurking inside.

In the imagery session, Sheila was asked to imagine that she became as small as a match and entered her own body. While touring it, she was asked

(continued)

257

to see how different places felt and then to find where she felt best: "See what part of your body makes you feel content and relaxed. As you find it, stay there and look at it from inside. Note where this place is located. See how you feel there, what it means for you to be there. Notice what kind of feeling you have there. Let this feeling fill you more and more before you open your eyes to return here."

Sheila said that she found herself staying in her heart, which was full of good emotions toward many people. I asked her to stay in her heart and pinpoint her various emotions toward others and relay them to me. She did.

I also suggested that she try to see if she could find some good emotions for herself as well. It was easy to see Sheila as a loving person who cared for others, but she clearly found it very difficult to talk positively and affectionately about herself. At last, she said that she had found a warm place where there was acceptance and caring for herself. I asked her to describe those caring feelings – how big they were, what color they were, what shape they had.

As homework, she practiced touring her body daily, finding a nice place to be in, focusing on the positive emotion there, and writing down what she felt toward herself, as a way to keep records and return to these experiences later on.

Sheila was also asked to imagine that she had a happymeter and to measure her happiness when she was alone, at least twice a day, at different times. Until now her happiness had always stemmed from outside activities with others, and she was afraid of being alone and did not know what to do with herself. Using the happymeter, she gradually discovered that she could find some happy moments within herself even when she was at home on her own.

Finally, Sheila reported that she had allowed herself to take a long time relaxing in the bath. She had watched a silly television series and enjoyed it, and she could also just lie down with her eyes closed, thinking of nothing.

Therapy with Sheila aimed to help her find happiness within herself, not only outside herself. Focusing on a happy place that causes us happiness, as well as focusing on our inner selves and finding which parts and emotions can lead to happiness, are important skills that can benefit everyone and thereby enrich life satisfaction.

Practice: guidelines

To facilitate happiness in everyday life, ask clients to:

- Take five minutes per day to focus on happy time – moments with their environment or within themselves.

- Focus on things that cause happiness – situations, places, or body parts. Then ask clients to try to find what characterizes these things, and to work toward increasing these feelings by repeating the exercise daily.
- Use self-talk to tell themselves how happy they are. "Talking happy" increases happiness.
- Measure their happiness. Writing down that one is happy increases one's sense of happiness.

Increasing Happy Relationships

One of the main elements conducive to increasing happiness is social support or social relationships. For many clients, happiness is something they find hard to achieve when they are alone and feel lonely. Treatment for eliciting happiness is therefore often related to enhancing skills for creating meaningful relationships.

Dana, a single woman age 42, was a devoted and proficient bank employee, in a high position. Although she had a few girlfriends, she felt lonely because they all had families and she found herself sitting alone at home. In collaboration with Dana, we defined the aim of her therapy as developing an optimistic view of the future.

We started utilizing an imagery technique of jumping to the future (similar to those in Chapter 3). However, whenever we tried to jump ahead by 2, 4, or 6 years, Dana would not cooperate. We had to jump ahead to an extreme – 100 years from now – when she would be 142 years old and as she said: "Actually, I no longer exist at that time."

I asked her to imagine that I was taking her on a trip 100 years in the future, and to view herself then: "Look at yourself there, in the nonexistent future. You are a nice-looking woman, and you live in a place you love to live in. Look at your house, at how it looks; go around the house entering the different rooms. Notice how you decorated each room, how it looks and what it contains. Note how satisfied you are with what you see. Pay attention to the colors, the smells, the furniture. Tell me what you see." Dana described her house as brightly colored and very modern, with lots of light and straight lines.

I asked her to look carefully and see if she could see anyone inside the house. She answered that she saw two children coming back from school. I asked if there was any partner there and she said: "No partner, only children." Dana described her children and seemed to be very happy.

We gradually moved from 100-year images to 80-year ones, then 60, then 40, 20, 10, and finally 2 years from the present. When she eventually opened her eyes from that near-future image, she started laughing and

(continued)

---

telling me that she had visualized her secret dream, which up till now she had never believed could come true: children.

Dana had always wanted children but was not sure she could have them. Viewing the visual picture of her future with children became an impetus to start taking concrete steps toward having a baby. Slowly, we started checking possibilities, and eventually, after many months, Dana decided to try artificial insemination. She experienced infertility but rallied and persevered until giving birth to beautiful healthy twins 19 months after we first worked on the imagery.

When she brought her twins to show me how wonderful they were, I asked her if she had found the happiness she had envisioned for her future. She said no; she had found out how mistaken she was. She was not just happy, she was the happiest person in the whole world.

Without a picture of future positive relationships, it is often too difficult for people to make changes. The most important issue here will then be to create a positive interpersonal picture of the future. Possessing such a picture enables clients to believe that it can come true.

People who express positive emotion toward others also report that it facilitates their own happiness. Jonathan, for example, learned to express positive feelings toward others and thereby improve his own sense of wellbeing.

Jonathan, age 69, had retired three years earlier and spent most of his time at home. His children lived abroad. He complained that life was unsatisfying; he was not as active as he used to be, his wife was busy cooking and cleaning each day, and he was bored. He enjoyed working in his garden and he loved reading, but those were not enough for him. Jonathan was very critical toward everything and everyone. I thought it was important to teach Jonathan to find positivity within himself and become more optimistic regarding himself and his environment. In therapy, I asked him to try and put on rose-tinted glasses instead of the gloomy black ones he said he was wearing, but he refused and said that was a game for naïve people, not for him.

We began imagery. Jonathan had told me that every morning he took the dog out and walked it, buying fresh bread and milk. Then in the evening he walked the dog again. I asked him now to elicit these everyday images of himself leaving home and describe to me everyone he met on his way. Jonathan said that he would usually see several people, who generally would say "hi," and he would answer with a short "hi" also. I asked him

(continued)

to imagine meeting many people while walking the dog, and assigned him the task of expressing one short positive emotion (such as interest, awe, or gratitude) to everyone he met. At first he refused, saying it was nonsense. I agreed that he should only say simple little things that felt right to him.

He had a coughing fit when he first tried to tell a neighbor he said he was meeting: "Hi, you look very active this morning." I asked him if it felt too embarrassing, and he replied very dryly: "It's okay." The exercise was too much for him at that point.

So, we practiced this imagery along several steps. First, I instructed him merely to imagine seeing people on his walk with the dog and just saying "hi" with a smile. Next, I asked him to meet people and relate to their appearance: You look happy; you have a nice shirt; you have a charming dog. Finally, I asked him to express graciousness or gratitude toward people he met in his imagery. For example, while buying bread he could say to someone: "It seems you are in a rush. Would you like to go ahead of me?" Or to the baker: "It looks so fresh and warm. Thank you."

At first, Jonathan was very angry at me, telling me that the whole exercise was a silly childish game. I apologized for making him feel that way and asked his permission to continue just a little bit more each time. Being polite, he agreed. Eventually, I asked him to try practicing these new interpersonal skills *in vivo* as well. After several weeks of practicing in the session and *in vivo*, it became easier for him. As we practiced expressing graciousness in imagery, he was able to say: "Your garden is blooming so nicely. What kind of flower is this?" and also: "You clean the entrance to your house every morning. It is so nice walking here."

Then, as it became easier for him to express positive comments, he started smiling more and told me that when he actually walked the dog at home, people around him were talking to him more, and he found the walk to be much more pleasant. We continued addressing Jonathan's interpersonal encounters in many domains, one by one through imagery, until he began to feel a sense of community, belonging, and connections that felt meaningful and gave more purpose to his day.

There is a saying that when we are aware of something in ourselves, we can very quickly see it all around us. So, pregnant women very quickly identify other pregnant women; when we buy a certain model of car, suddenly all the roads seem full of the same model of car; when we suffer from a specific sickness, we very quickly realize that many others suffer from the same. Along the same lines, when we start smiling and thinking positively, we start discovering more and more positivity around us. Thus, the way to increase relationship positivity lies in the ability to find positivity within ourselves and others. Not only do we begin to identify positivity more, but also people tend to respond to gratitude with gratitude. As Fredrickson (1998) suggested, these interactions are a good way to increase happiness and positivity.

For increasing positivity and improving relationships with both ourselves and others, we can look inside ourselves, find the positive wishes, hidden thoughts, and positive emotions, and attempt to enlarge, externalize, and realize them – expressing them and following their lead to create positivity.

Practice: guidelines

The following guidelines can help therapists promote clients' positive relationships:

- Wishes and dreams cannot come true unless clients can see a picture of them coming true. Help your clients elicit a picture of themselves as maintaining happy relationships in their ideal future before starting work toward achieving that.
- For many people, happy relationships are something that they do not believe is under their control. Help your clients believe in their ability to influence happiness.
- When clients have difficulty creating a happy future picture of themselves within relationships, have them jump to a time when they can no longer reject the image because it is so obviously impossible.
- Only then, after the picture starts changing, help clients move the image closer and closer to the near future.

Summary

People feel happy when they are satisfied with life, feel they have others' support, can spend time with the people they like, possess hope and optimism, and hold a positive view of the future. To work toward a better future, clients should learn to plan and think ahead, openly exploring various life roads and viewing themselves as successfully navigating them. In the meantime, expressing positive emotion, both inward and outward, toward others, can facilitate happiness now. Fredrickson (1998, 2009) suggested that expressing gratitude and other positive emotions toward others helps increase happiness through reciprocal prosocial contact that begets a deeper sense of belonging.

A good way to end this chapter is to advise clients to design imagery exercises based on their belief systems. For example:

> *Imagine that you are looking inside your body. Enter your conscience, and see what is there for you to read, see, or hear about yourself, and your relationships with other people. Pay attention to what your conscience advises you to do, say, or think; which way you should go. See if that advice means doing what is best for you and others. Do you have the skills to do what you are advised to do, and do you feel like doing it? See how wonderful you feel when you follow what you believe is the best for you.*

17

Imparting Skills to Help
Children Change: Further
Guidelines and Case Illustrations

The main core of this book advocates imagery for treating clients in general, mainly referring to adults. Adolescents can be treated very similarly to adults. Chapter 5 describes developmental considerations while treating children, and Chapter 11 focuses on guidelines for applying relaxation and imagery with children. This chapter concentrates on specific adaptation of imagery therapy to children's needs and abilities, dealing here with specific guidelines and case illustrations to clarify applications of skills-directed imagery therapy at different developmental stages.

Major goals in child therapy comprise enabling children to grow up healthy and well adjusted within their family, peer group, and academic environment. To give children the necessary skills to improve their functioning in all these domains, intervention techniques must focus squarely on skills acquisition. With children, emphasis must be placed on assessment to determine which skills children perform and execute competently, which skills children lack, how the deficient skills influence the children's behavior, which skills children need to resolve existing problems and develop more optimally, and how best to design children's training to impart the needed skills through teaching and practice.

Good therapy with children should also take developmental components into consideration, as described in Chapter 5. For example, Lazarus (1977) suggested specific steps for imagery with children. Among them, he recommended learning about the child's admired figures from television or real life and then guiding the child to use those superheroes, for example, to fight whatever fears or anxieties arise during the imagery exercise. Thus, usage of imagery with children should follow some important rules shared by treatments for adults, but also should follow some specific guidelines for children based on cognitive, emotional, and social developmental components. Next, I present some of these general and child-specific guidelines.

The Positive Power of Imagery: Harnessing Client Imagination in CBT and Related Therapies, First Edition. Tammie Ronen. © 2011 Tammie Ronen. Published 2011 by John Wiley & Sons, Ltd.

Practice: guidelines resembling those for adults

- Establish a relaxed atmosphere and help children attain relaxation.
- Carefully apply imagery as suggested in previous chapters.
- Take precautions to ensure that children reach a good emotional state by the end of the therapy session.
- Assign homework assignments to train, practice, and foster generalization in newly acquired skills.
- Do not expect one imagery exercise or session to render change, but rather be ready to repeat skills training using the same and different variations.

Practice: guidelines relating to children's unique developmental characteristics

- Young children can only participate in brief imagery exercises, although older children can remain within imagery for longer processes.
- With young children, utilize imagery as a stimulus for the session's work, whereas older children can employ images as part of the session itself.
- Inasmuch as imagery constitutes only a stimulus for young children, continue working on the picture you elicit through drawings, playing, and role-play. Older children can remain with the images.
- Direct imagery exercises with young children to provoke the issue that you want to discuss later, whereas with older children direct imagery toward changing automatic thoughts, eliciting emotions, and training in skills.

To demonstrate the unique nature of imagery applications with children of varying ages, I next present several brief vignettes relating to various disorders.

Treating Young Children

The first two case illustrations present the treatment of young children at age 6 years. Children this age are still in a stage of concrete thinking and can focus only for a short time on imagery. Therapy, therefore, should be short, concrete, and connected to their day-to-day lives. The case of Ben, a young child with selective mutism, is presented in detail in Ronen (2003b: 80–97).

Ben was referred to therapy four months before entering the first grade in school. Ben had never talked to anyone other than his parents and 4-year-old sister. At kindergarten, he never spoke with the teacher or other children. Ben's parents said that he had started talking as a baby, but soon enough, he began to get along by pointing at things and not talking. In the presence of others, he would whisper in his parents' ears, but no one else

(continued)

---

ever heard his voice. They were worried how he would get along in school and therefore came to me for therapy.

It was clear that Ben (unlike his parents) did not want to give up his mutism and was unmotivated for therapy. He would not talk to me, of course, so therapy had to focus either on me talking to him or on his writing and drawing. Therefore, the combination of metaphors, drawing, and imagery was the treatment of choice.

As therapy began, I used imagery as a stimulus to increase Ben's motivation to collaborate with me (see Ronen, 2003b: 86–90). I invited him to draw the way he felt, and he labeled his drawing "a big mess." I asked him to close his eyes and imagine that he was that mess. He closed his eyes and then quickly opened them again. Seeing that it was difficult for him to keep his eyes closed, I asked whether he could show me what he saw in his imagination. Acting out this mess to me, he lay down on the floor, moved from side to side, rolled over, and then jumped around. I thanked him for showing me what he saw in his imagination, and I added that, if he wanted, my job would be to help him get rid of this mess. He agreed. I asked him if he had any idea how we could do so, and he nodded.

In a subsequent session, I showed Ben the picture he'd drawn of the mess and I gave him a ball of yarn as a metaphor for that mess. I asked if he could show me how that mess felt, using the ball of yarn. He first unraveled all the wool and then knotted it all back up. I offered to work together with him to untangle the big mess into one single long strand of wool. He started trying to untangle it but tore the yarn. I told him that the task would not be easy and would require time and patience, but I had these, if he did. I suggested that whenever he would tire of the work of untangling the mess, either we would take a break or else I would take his place. Ben agreed, and based on these initial images we designed a treatment contract that we both signed.

Because Ben did not talk, the combination of drawing, metaphors, and imagery could be suitable for helping him change. My main aim was to follow constructivist therapy and convey the idea that I could understand him, and let him present his own meanings for situations, while at the same time trying to help him be his own architect and change the picture from a mess to a coping young child. However, it is not easy for young children to close their eyes and keep imagining for long time; therefore, the imagery work needs to be brief, with eyes open, and non-anxiety-provoking. Ben's selective mutism – which results from anxiety on the one hand and the need to control others on the other hand – was another indication for using imagery only as a stimulus, for a very short time. Thus, at first I merely asked Ben to imagine himself as the mess he had drawn. But most of the early part of therapy then focused effectively on this brief image – with Ben drawing this mess, role-playing the mess, being the mess he saw in his imagination, and playing metaphorically with the mess as yarn to be untied or knotted. The combination of imagery as a stimulus with drawing, writing, and role-playing is very easy to apply with children and can often bring effective results, as in Ben's case. He was happy to collaborate with me as long as I did not force him to talk, and willingly entered into a therapeutic contract.

Another example is that of Ari, a young, very thin, small boy in first grade who came to therapy because of anxiety. The treatment of choice for Ari was also a combination of play, metaphors, and imagery (see the whole case in Ronen, 2003b: 104–119).

As presented in Chapter 8, Ari was afraid of winter and wind. In addition to working with the tree metaphor, through a gradual exposure exercise in the safe environment of my clinic, I placed a large fan in front of us and suggested that we both would move like the trees in his imagination. I asked him to give me instructions in how to act out his imagery with him. When we acted as trees moving and being pushed in a storm, Ari seemed to be at war with the wind, fighting it, trying to stay put, and attempting to keep his hair from blowing around. Then, frustrated from the fight, he fell on the floor and began to cry and complain of pain. Suddenly he looked up at me enjoying the wind and his expression changed: He began to laugh. He stood up as a tree and slowly swayed his arms like branches, saying, "Oh, wonderful. All summer long I had to stay still. It's so good to move" (Ronen, 2003b: 115). I then asked Ari to close his eyes and try to see himself again as a tree in the winter, and to see how happy the tree was that it could get water and move.

In another session, we watched part of Walt Disney's *Mary Poppins* video (Walsh & Stevenson, 1997), and I asked Ari to express his feelings during rainy or windy scenes. I also asked him to notice what Mary Poppins felt in the wind, especially how much she enjoyed being carried away by the wind.

As homework during the week, Ari had to collect leaves from the ground and examine their colors, and he was instructed to examine trees and tell his parents how happy he thought the trees were. Gradually, Ari was able to say that he didn't like winter but thought the flowers and trees were happy in wintertime.

I brought him an Indian rain stick and then in an imagery session, I asked him to imagine he was the Indian chief, dancing the rain dance because the trees needed rain. After Ari imagined himself dancing, we practiced this dance with the stick in the clinic. Ari took the stick home and later was very excited when he danced and it started raining. He thought he'd caused the rain to come, and, rather than being frightened, he opened the window and looked out. That was the beginning of the change in his anxieties.

Therapy with Ari focused on exposure therapy. However, due to his age and avoidant behavior, therapy involved exposure through imagery, metaphors, and drawing. I was thereby able to redefine his anxiety and change the way he constructed his beliefs, so that fear and anxiety changed into joy and fun, deriving from the new meaning attributed to his fears.

In Ari's case, once again imagery was very efficient in creating a meaningful picture that helped this young child gain a vivid impression of his problem. It also served as a stimulus for various creative techniques that elicited his curiosity and interest. In light of 6 year olds' difficulties in focusing attention, closing their eyes, and maintaining images for long periods, imagery with young children should be short, quick, and simply play a stimulus role. Both when imagining the trees and when imagining the rain dance, the imagery exercises were followed by *in vivo* role play.

I did find imagery to offer the best technique for helping both Ben and Ari change, but I had to work with the imagery over a long period, elaborating on it repeatedly with role-playing, acting, talking, and drawing, in order for the children to persevere in therapy, collaborate, and really change their emotions and behaviors. In sum, for younger children, imagery can be an effective stimulus if used in conjunction with imagery work in role-play, metaphors, or just play.

Treating Children in Middle Childhood

In middle childhood, therapists can start working with imagery in a way that more resembles imagery work with adults; nevertheless, therapy must still undergo adaptations to children's ages and cognitive stages. Examples can be taken from the stories of Dan, Guy, and David, who were age 11–12 years. In this stage, cognitively, operational thinking is already viable. Children this age can already use abstract concepts and focus attention for longer periods. It is easier to apply relaxation and the full process of the imagery session with them.

Dan was referred to me for unexplained psychosomatic stomach aches, nausea, and the urge to vomit (see Ronen, 2003b: 144–158 for details).

Dan, age 11, had been in and out of hospitals for over a year, undergoing numerous aversive medical examinations that eventually ruled out medical etiology for his symptoms. The doctors finally recommended trying to determine if anxieties or fears could account for his somatic pain.

Therapy aimed to help Dan differentiate between worrisome and normal bodily sensations, and to help him accept and live with his pain. To increase Dan's differentiated awareness of his internal stimuli, we began imagery exercises for "getting acquainted with the pain" instead of avoiding and

(continued)

fearing it. For example, applying mindfulness exercises, I invited Dan to close his eyes and get to know his pain (Ronen, 2003b: 152). I asked him to look at the pain, see how it looked, how big it was, in what colors it was painted. When he told me he could vividly see the pain in front of him, I asked him to describe it to me.

In another imagery exercise, I asked Dan to imagine himself as a very small figure the size of a match, and to enter his body to take a tour and look for the pain. As he searched for the pain, I asked Dan to travel around and see what he saw and felt from inside. During these repeated internal excursions, each time Dan reached two locations in his body he insisted on stopping the exercise immediately – his throat (too hot and crowded, a feeling he was going to vomit) and his stomach (a whole big, dark mess that he hated and couldn't find his way out of). In light of Dan's motivation and enjoyment during the imagery, I sought to prevent his feelings of failure about his desire to stop the exercise when he reached his throat or stomach: I redefined his request to stop as reflecting his dislike for his pain and as a positive first sign that he didn't like being in there and therefore we could eventually get rid of the pain.

After he relaxed, Dan gave me permission to help him get closer to the pain again through another metaphorical exercise that we audio-recorded. I asked him to close his eyes, take a deep breath, release all tension, and feel his body parts becoming heavy. Then I instructed him to see if he felt pain. Dan pointed at his stomach and told me he felt great pain that day and had not even gone to school that morning. In response to my specific guiding questions, Dan located the pain's exact location in the stomach, described its shape as a small, concentrated ball, and said it was too heavy to move. I asked him to very slowly try to move this heavy ball around inside him, and after some initial difficulty he said it was moving very slowly. When asked, Dan described the ball of pain as a deep purple that he hated. He added that he liked green, so I asked him to imagine rivers of green flowing from his brain to color his purple ball, and he slowly could see it becoming green. Next, we started working to move the ball toward the direction of his hand, push it into his fist, and hold it tightly so that it would not disappear. This imagery exercise lasted the whole session.

At the end, Dan said that he only felt pain in his hand muscles. As homework, Dan practiced listening to the audiotaped exercise daily to learn about that day's pain (size, location, shape, color, etc.) and to try to decrease the pain by moving it into his palm. At first, he could not decrease the pain significantly when alone at home (constantly rating his pain on a scale of 0 to 10), but after three weeks of practice, he was able to gain significant relief that enabled him to attend school and function regularly.

Therapy with Dan combined mindfulness therapy, constructivism, and exposure to help him become more aware of his internal stimuli, change the meaning of his pain, and reduce fears through exposure to the pain and relaxation.

As can be seen, at the age of 11, longer imagery sessions can already be conducted, not only using images as stimuli but also working with them in detail to start changing misconceptions and feelings. This method resembles working with adults, although therapists must carefully monitor children to ensure that exercises are not too long, that children can link imagery to reality, and that children can understand the meaning of the exercise.

Other examples of working with imagery in middle childhood are the cases of Guy and David, both aggressive children. Details of Guy's treatment are presented in Ronen (2003b: 180–197).

Guy, age 12, exhibited long-term behavior problems at school. During the intake session, he was very cynical and negated everything his parents said about him, denying any culpability for his aggressive actions. After working with his environment (teachers and parents) to eliminate negative reinforcements and foster positive reinforcements for Guy, I began treating him individually.

To learn more about Guy's behavior and how he got involved in all those fights, I asked him to keep a daily record that would help him identify the links between events that occurred outside therapy and his own ensuing thoughts, emotions, and behaviors. His homework assignment was to select one event each day, noting his thoughts at the time, what kinds of emotions they aroused, and how he acted.

At first, he found this assignment to be overly difficult to perform at home alone, so we practiced it as an imagery exercise in the session. I asked him to close his eyes and try seeing himself playing at school with friends – to look around at the other kids and see them. When I asked him to focus more on how his peers were looking at him, Guy suddenly yelled angrily that one boy was laughing at him again and said: "I'll show him!" When Guy opened his eyes, I asked him to detail how this boy in class who "usually mocked him" looked, what he did, and how he behaved. From this description and others, it became apparent that Guy was impulsively interpreting others' behavior (e.g., the boy's laughter) as personally and negatively directed toward him.

I worked with Guy for the rest of the session to encourage him to consider other alternatives that might explain his image of that boy's smiling facial expression. After much work, Guy was able to offer some possible neutral explanations like "he might just be happy" or "maybe he just heard a joke," instead of automatically assuming that the smile was a derisive one directed at him.

With Guy, therapy combined traditional CBT aiming to redefine his behavior and reconstruct his thinking, skill acquisition to overcome aggression, and finding new meanings in alternative behavior. Imagery here offered a good method for assessing Guy's thought patterns and emotional reactivity, to learn what was underlying his explosive behavior. Clearly, Guy was easily able to imagine a scene that insulted and agitated him, and in the imagery session he reacted to it similarly to his real-life reactions.

Another example of aggressive behavior can be seen in the case of 12-year-old David, whose mother brought him to my clinic because of his undisciplined behavior (Ronen, 2004):

David's mother worried that his aggressive behavior at school (physical fights, teasing, mistreatment of peers; disruptiveness, rudeness, antagonism toward teachers in class; frequent restlessness during class that "drove the teacher crazy"; refusal to complete homework; and truancy and tardiness to school) would result in his transfer to a special education setting. Treatment of David followed the self-control model developed by Ronen and Rosenbaum (2001) as applied for aggressiveness. This intervention helped David accept responsibility for his own behavior, work on cognitive restructuring, and link his behaviors to his thoughts and emotions. As part of this model, the imagery exercises that I describe next focused on increasing David's awareness of his internal sensations and emotions.

Through mindfulness exercises, David learned to get acquainted with his anger and then to identify preliminary physical signs that preceded his aggressive behavior. In an imagery exercise, he was asked to imagine himself getting very angry at his friend and then to focus on his internal sensations, paying close attention to the location in his body where he felt the anger, what exactly he was feeling there, how big the anger was, what shape and color it had, and so forth: "Imagine you are in the middle of fighting with your friend. You get very angry at him and you want to hit him like you always do. Stop for a minute and try to focus on your internal feelings. Where do you feel the anger?" David stated that he felt it in his stomach. "Try to focus on your stomach. What do you feel there, inside?" David stated, "It's very hot." I asked him to imagine the shape of the anger. David described a big, hot, red circle of anger hiding inside himself. We then worked to alter the size and intensity of this feeling.

After learning to get acquainted with his anger, we continued with exercises to identify the first preliminary sensations pointing to an upcoming eruption of anger. David was able to state that he was getting warm and red and feeling uneasy in his stomach.

The next step was using imagery to develop self-control: "Imagine you already feel angry and are just about to hit your friend, but you see the

(continued)

school principal in front of you, and you know she will punish you if you hit your friend. Look at yourself and see what you are about to do." David replied that he would walk away because he didn't want to get punished. I repeated the same exercise but this time asked him to imagine: "This time, just as you are about to hit him, you see me coming toward you, holding the remote-controlled car you wanted to buy. You know I will give it to you if you don't hit him. What do you do?"

David said that he would not hit his friend. After achieving this imagined restraint, he received as homework an imagery exercise to practice daily as a way to help him stop hitting. Every time David got angry during that week, he had to imagine that he was about to receive the toy he wanted. By the end of the week, David stated that he had not been involved in any fights that week at all. We then started using imagery to develop other skills for improving his behavior.

As can be seen, David experienced traditional CBT aiming to change the links between his thoughts, emotions, and behaviors, combined with constructivism and mindfulness.

Thus, in both cases of middle childhood, we could start working differently with imagination. Not only was it easier for these older children to practice relaxation, close their eyes, and stay in this position for longer periods, but they also could elicit images and start working with them. Thus, at this stage, imagery can be extremely beneficial for children to practice skills and train in new behavior patterns.

Treating Adolescents

The older the child is, the closer therapy can resemble that of adults. The following two cases illustrate how during adolescence, youngsters can already be treated very similarly to adults. In adolescence, therapists can start attacking misconceptions as well as changing thoughts and emotions, not only behavior. The case of Jacob was presented in detail in Ronen (2003b: 202–221).

Jacob, age 17, suffered from mild depression. For several years before coming to me, he tried psychodynamic therapy and medications prescribed by a psychiatrist, but did not feel significant improvement. One of the main problems I tackled with him through therapy was the fact that Jacob did not believe that he would be able to change or that the future could be different for him.

(continued)

I asked Jacob to imagine that our clinic room contained a large ladder (see Chapter 12; Ronen, 2003b: 211). I told him that an imaginary sign appeared on the bottom rung, reading: "sorrow, fear, depression, and hopelessness," representing where he was now. I asked him to imagine wherever he thought he would like to be at the end of treatment and to tell me what would be written on the top rung, if nothing stood in his way of changing himself in whatever direction he wished. His imaginary sign on the top rung read: "happy, satisfied, feeling good with myself and others."

We had to work together for a long while in order for him to complete the other rungs. Eventually he labeled the rungs in ascending order as: (i) being able to perform ordinary tasks like reading, writing, and talking with people; (ii) being able to concentrate on his studies; (iii) improving his grades; (iv) enjoying being with people; (v) feeling hopeful, happy, worthy, and competent; (vi) liking his own behavior and himself; and (vii) feeling happy and content with himself and others.

I then asked him to return to the highest rung and to imagine himself 100 years in the future as a very happy person. I asked: "What do you look like? How do you behave? What do you feel?" Jacob laughed at the notion of his elderly self, but he cooperated and described himself being happy at age 117. However, it was still impossible for him to view himself as a happy person in the present.

In the next session, Jacob repeated a metaphor that he often used, referring to himself as feeling like he was drowning. We used this as a metaphor for him sinking in the mud. In an imagery exercise, I asked Jacob to look around while sinking and see what and who were around him. He described a number of people surrounding him and trying to save him from sinking, but to no avail. He described himself as sinking deeper downward into the dark, heavy, stinking, airless mud. When I asked him if there was anything good about it, Jacob replied: "You know, I don't need to fight. I can just be there, because if I try to get out, I only sink deeper. It's a strange feeling just to be there, I don't need to do anything. I can rest. Well, if I don't die, if it's not the end, if it doesn't get into my mouth and nose, maybe I will even enjoy it" (Ronen, 2003b: 218).

Later, when Jacob discussed the meaning of being in the mud for him, using another metaphor of knocking his head against a wall, I noticed that both metaphors placed him in jeopardy but also set up ways for him to be rescued. In this new metaphor, Jacob stood banging his head against a wall until he hurt and bled, but suddenly it became pleasant and he started feeling relaxed. He explained that perhaps he relaxed because he believed suddenly that someone might save him – me, his therapist.

(*continued*)

I asked how I could help him, and he suggested that I throw him a thick, long rope for him to grab and try to pull himself out. He couldn't tell me what that rope might be, but I ended that session by telling him that I would be happy to throw him a rope if he would only decide what was in that rope that could help him get out.

As can be seen from this case illustration, imagery can serve adolescents just as it can adults. A whole session was devoted to eliciting a picture, working with it, imparting skills, changing thoughts, and constructing new ways of coping.

The same trend is reflected in the treatment of 18-year-old Ayelet, my anorexic client whom I described in earlier chapters (Ronen & Ayelet, 2001).

As mentioned in Chapter 8, Ayelet described herself metaphorically as "full of garbage," saying that she urgently needed to clean all this up in order to live a normal life.

In one imagery session, I asked Ayelet to let me enter her world of garbage. First, I asked her to imagine that she was working for the city as a garbage collector or cleaner. I joined her, helping her look at all the things she was ready to discard, like her obsessions, compulsions, fears, and anxieties. Ayelet was glad to see the expanding garbage can and remarked that she felt better when she was cleaner (Ronen & Ayelet, 2001).

Ayelet repeatedly stated that she had "some bad things" deep inside her and that she would never recover if we did not deal with them. She often talked about "the big black hole of nothing," "falling down into the nothing," and "a big emptiness inside." At this stage in the treatment, I asked her to lead me into her big hole. I wanted to learn, together with her, how this "hole of nothingness and emptiness" looked. I assured her that I could throw her a rope ladder into the hole and help her climb out.

This trip was not easy. It involved tears, sobbing, and sorrow. Ayelet thought that the "real issue" to be treated related to her dark hole. I thought that the real issue was that she did not like herself, and could not accept how she looked or behaved. I believed that by finding significance in her life, and filling the big hole with self-esteem and self-love, she would stop feeling empty. I suggested that she replace the metaphors of emptiness and the hole of nothing with the metaphor of gaps. She accepted this idea, demonstrating progress. We defined our next target as helping her accept herself similarly to the way in which others related to her.

As illustrated here, therapy with these two adolescents – Jacob and Ayelet – very much resembled therapy with adults, in the sense that imagery could be freely utilized to design a picture that could help clients confront misconceptions, change automatic thoughts, exercise new skills, and so forth. One of imagery's benefits is its ability to take clients with us wherever we need for the purpose of successful treatment; hence, imagery can go far beyond traditional verbal therapy with children and adolescents, as well as with adults.

Summary

This chapter focuses on the unique nature of imagery therapy when applied with children, depending on their ages and developmental stages. As mentioned before, the general notions and methods for creating images with children and adolescents resemble those used with adults. However, especially for young children, attention should be focused on adapting treatment techniques, language, and applications to children's developmental needs, shortening time, focusing mainly on exposure, and using art therapy. In middle childhood, therapy can last longer and children can already focus on verbalizing their emotions, so verbal therapy can be applied as well when directed to real, concrete topics. With adolescents, as with adults, therapists can start linking thoughts, emotions, and behaviors and can direct therapy to cause–effect links, increasing sensitivity to internal stimuli and adolescents' meaning-making processes.

Practice: Guidelines for Imparting Skills to Children

- Focus on children's developmental stage to design the length of imagery work, main goals, and means for helping children change.
- Pinpoint your main goals for children's skills acquisition, such as redefining behavior, reconstructing thought processes, stopping avoidant behavior, reducing fears, increasing confidence.
- Find the best means to achieve these goals: imagery, drawing, metaphors, talking.
- Help children generalize what they have just learned.
- Enable practice, both in sessions and as homework assignments.

Part V

Notes and Conclusions for Imagery Therapists

18

Helping Therapists Help Themselves

After presenting the theoretical background, explanations, guidelines, and case illustrations for imagery applications with adults and children, I would like to add a short chapter relating to ourselves – the therapists.

Therapy is a challenging profession. It necessitates many skills for helping others, but we often end the day feeling tired, sad, or depleted of resources. Therapists frequently carry their clients' experiences with them, sometimes finding it difficult to "close the door behind them" and move on to their personal lives and activities. Mahoney (1991: 357) explained that "one cannot participate in a therapeutic role and bear witness to the narratives of many human lives without being profoundly influenced in the process." He also stated that therapists are changed by their work and suffer from the paradox of wrestling "hope from hell: because of what we are being asked to do as therapists while listening to clients and trying to help them" (Mahoney, 2003: 196).

Yes, being a therapist is challenging and sometimes takes the most out of us. Although most therapists report that the profession has helped them become better people, enrich their lives, and live up to stimulating challenges, psychotherapy remains a very difficult and complex process for both therapists and clients (Mahoney, 2003). Looking at the process, we can note that therapists sometimes change as much as clients do.

Mahoney (1991) asserted that research tends to attribute a great deal of the variance in clients' change processes to therapist variables. He noted that the "person" of the therapist is at least eight times more influential than his or her theoretical orientation. He emphasized that just like their clients, therapists continually change in complex ways that they often did not anticipate. However, despite such solid endorsements, the impact of therapist variables on client outcomes remains controversial. For example, studies are just as likely to show a positive relation between therapy-seeking therapists and client outcomes as they are to show no relation between the two (Bikes, Norcross, & Schatz, 2009; Norcross, 2005); hence, evidence is insufficient for a strong

The Positive Power of Imagery: Harnessing Client Imagination in CBT and Related Therapies, First Edition. Tammie Ronen. © 2011 Tammie Ronen. Published 2011 by John Wiley & Sons, Ltd.

claim of the importance to clients of therapists' involvement in their own therapy.

Taking care of oneself is important not only for improving therapy with clients, but also for therapists' own wellbeing (Bikes, Norcross, & Schatz, 2009). The average, well-functioning therapist suffers from most of the same problems as any other human being – anxiety, depression, health problems, and so forth (Mahoney, 2003). In light of this humanness as well as the belief that improved self-understanding in the therapist can lead to more effective professionalism, much research has examined the importance of therapists' personal therapy. Studies conducted over the past four decades show that psychotherapists consider personal therapy an indispensable element in improving therapeutic work as well as their own wellbeing (Mahoney, 1991, 2003; Norcross, Strausser-Kirtland, & Missar, 1988; Stevanovic & Rupert, 2004) and ongoing professional development (Norcross, 2005).

Bikes, Norcross, and Schatz's (2009) large-scale therapist survey showed that 84% of their sample reported participating in personal therapy at least once. Male therapists tended to seek therapy for training purposes and career concerns, whereas female therapists tended to seek therapy for family-of-origin conflicts. Bikes, Norcross, and Schatz proposed that participating in therapy heightened therapists' appreciation of interpersonal relationships and their clients' vulnerability. Also, they suggested that the vast majority of psychotherapists undergoing personal therapy experienced considerable improvement on all three outcome dimensions: behavioural–symptomatic, cognitive–insight, and emotion–relief.

In addition to seeking therapy, therapists can help themselves through self-therapy, and imagery provides one of the best ways to achieve this self-help mode. Therapists can help themselves using imagery to solve varied difficulties encountered in their therapeutic work, or on the personal level to leave behind difficult sessions, gather their strengths, and point their resources toward the future. I next present several examples of how therapists can make use of imagery for self-help skills such as self-supervision, trying to leave things behind, focusing on their own positive abilities as a therapist, planning future therapeutic processes, and general skills for helping themselves.

Skills for Self-Supervision

I would like to suggest a multiple-step exercise that therapists can use to supervise themselves in their role of therapist. This three-step self-supervision exercise utilizes videotaping imagery for the purpose of assessing the therapist–client interaction and learning to identify any problems that might be contributing to therapists' difficulties with clients. The first step allows you to practice looking at the therapeutic situation from the third-person viewpoint (Chapter 12), but does not yet incorporate video imagery.

Please close your eyes, relax, let your body feel heavy and warm. Note what your body signals to you, and try to let go of thoughts, worries, and difficulties.

Think of the client with whom you had difficulties and imagine you are in a session with this client.

Try to focus on the client. See how the client sits, how the client looks, how the client speaks, how the client relates to you. See if there are any more nonverbal variables that you didn't note before.

Look at yourself and focus on your nonverbal language: where and how you sit, the way you are dressed, the way you look.

Look at the two of you from the side. Focus on the dynamics between you and the client. How do you two look? How far apart are you from the client? What can others who watch the two of you together say about your relationship?

Listen to the conversation: the way you talk to each other, the tone of your voices, the music of the conversation. Look at the gestures of both of you. What can you learn from this?

Notice how satisfied you are with the way the conversation is proceeding. What is there that feels right? What is missing? What needs to change?

Looking at yourself from the third-person perspective can help you learn about yourself and your client and attend to variables that you previously missed. After performing this initial exercise, you can move to the next step of deepening your assessment through the eyes of a video recording.

Imagine you are watching yourself with your client on a video screen. Take the remote control and try to mute the words but not the voices. It is a magic remote control – you can hear the tempo of the talk, the music, the pace of the voices, without hearing the words. What can you say about the two of you? How do you look and sound? What does this mean to you?

As you continue watching the video carefully, mute the sound completely. Now you can hear nothing. You can just look at the nonverbal language. What do you see? What does it tell you? What do you notice that you didn't before?

As you feel you understand the interaction better, select "pause" and stop your movement; look at the still picture. What has changed now? What can you tell about yourself? Your client? Do you have any new insight?

Often, by blocking out one component of our observation (such as sound or movement), we can focus more on the other components and gain new insights about our clients, ourselves, and the dynamics of the conversation. Now you can move to the third step of imagery, where you try to change the interaction.

Remember that you have a magic remote control that you can use to make changes. You can change your location in the picture – you can sit closer or further away from the client. You can change the nonverbal language – your gestures or the tempo, music, or tone of the conversation, or its content.

Try playing with the remote control and making different changes until the situation looks optimal to you. Keep changing and adjusting various aspects until you are satisfied. What do you see when you have finished all your adjustments? Do you think that the changes you made can facilitate any change in the client?

Self-supervision through imagery thus encompasses not only looking at ourselves and our clients from the outside to gain better understanding, but also learning to use that imagery to experiment with different directions for change, and to correct and supervise ourselves as to what should be changed and how. After practicing and mastering this type of self-help, we can then reflect better on the following:

What did we learn? What happened? What was wrong? How can we improve? Is it better for us now? Are we happier?

When using this exercise to supervise myself during impasses or difficulties with clients, I often felt surprised at what I learned through the video imagery. For example, I once "watched" a session in which I had felt stuck and wasn't sure how to continue. As I imagined myself and my client in the video, I realized that I looked very bored. Usually I am very attentive to my clients. This time, therapy seemed to be stuck and the client repeatedly told the same story over and over again, in a slow tempo, in a quiet, distant voice. Whatever I suggested, he refused and said that it would not help. He seemed to want to complain, but was not really motivated to take any action to create change. When I imagined looking at myself in the video, I saw that I seemed very distant, bored, with eyes glazed over, checking the wall clock every few minutes. If someone else were to "watch me," it would be clear that I wanted the session to end. If it was clear to me, it probably conveyed some unpleasant feelings to my client. If I didn't seem to be involved, interested, and motivated, it was most likely difficult for him to feel involved. Thus, I could not expect him to take any further step for making a crucial change if I was unmotivated to help him increase his motivation. I imagined "changing" my position with the remote control, sat closer to him, changed my tone, and became more challenging, and as I did it, in my imagination he seemed to become more engaged, changing his nonverbal behavior in turn. This is a two-person interaction; therefore, change in one person elicits change in the other.

Practice: guidelines

To implement self-supervision:

- Gain some distance from yourself as a therapist by imagining that:
  - You are sitting next to a video player, television screen, or movie as suggested above.
  - You are coming to supervision and presenting your case to your supervisor.
- Try to focus on looking at both yourself and the client. Note your thoughts, emotions, and behaviors as well as the client's and then note the interaction between the two of you.

- As you gain understanding about what is going on, try to change various aspects until you are satisfied with the new situation.
- When you feel satisfied, try to reflect on the necessary change and how you are going to apply it *in vivo*.

Skills for Learning to "Get Rid" of Difficult Things and Continue Toward the Future

Looking at the past, learning from it, and making changes in light of past learning are all important skills for every therapist. However, sometimes we also need to learn to leave things behind and look ahead. This is, in time, an important skill that might help us care for our own wellbeing, meaning that we sometimes need to discard and forget events and people, even if only temporarily, and move forward. We do care for our clients, but we cannot carry them with us all the time. Neither can we always blame ourselves for mistakes that we made. We need to forgive ourselves and forget – but also to learn from the experience and improve.

The same way we help our clients enter the "Land I Wish" (Chapter 16) to help them gain positivity and feel happy, we as therapists can enter the "Land of I'm Sorry," to aid us in leaving things behind.

Imagine you are going to the Land of I'm Sorry. It may be a real place you visited have before; somewhere you have heard of but have never seen; or an imaginary place that you make up for yourself. The Land of I'm Sorry houses all your past actions, thoughts, and feelings – ones you experienced in life in general and ones you encountered in therapy in particular. Every client you have treated in your lifetime lives on in the Land of I'm Sorry in rooms that symbolize your process of therapy with that client.

You enter the first room, where you saw your first client. You were still young, didn't feel expert, and had lots of hesitations and doubts. Your time is limited, so you can only visit this room very quickly. It is full of souvenirs. Sentences you said, sentences your client said, images, pictures, reports. You need to hurry, so you can only take one small souvenir out with you in the large sack you carry on your back. See what you are taking with you and move to the next room.

This next room is divided up among all the clients you treated when you had already been working for a year. You had more experience and felt better as a therapist in some senses, but you also had more questions and pockets of insecurity. There are many stories, clients, and images in this room. Look around and take one small souvenir with you as a memory. You need to go on to the third room.

As you progress, you see more and more rooms. Each room holds a year of working, a year of stories. Successes, failures, frustrations, joys. In each room, take one memory to put in your sack and keep going. The sack on your back is getting heavier and bigger. Now you are entering the last room – the present day. Things here are very vivid. You have just experienced them.

As you leave the last room, you see a very big well. You stand next to it and have two options: Either you can keep carrying all the souvenirs with you or else you can throw them all down the well and start collecting a new sack. You hesitate. It's hard to get rid of the past; you enjoy carrying things on with you. But sometimes you need to learn to leave the past in order to look ahead at the future and focus on what is waiting for you. You turn your back, and as you are about to leave the Land of I'm Sorry, you feel sorry – that you were there in the past and made mistakes. You need now to forget things from the past that interfere with your ability to continue working in the present, and only remember those that help you "learn the lesson." You now have to move on to the future. But you know that you are moving now to the Land of Hope. Therefore, you do discard the sack and with easy, quick steps you start progressing toward the future. . .

Therapists must develop their professional identity, which is an outcome of the past, present, and future. We need to learn from our past experiences and make changes where necessary; focus on the present for developing skills to address clients' needs; and look forward to an optimistic and hopeful future. Thus, therapists must both remember and forget – otherwise our past experiences become too heavy a burden. This exercise helps us practice techniques for leaving behind what we no longer need to carry and for enabling us to focus on the important issues we would like to carry into the future.

Practice: guidelines

You can employ imagery to help you take actions directed at helping you forget things from the past that interfere with your ability to continue working in the present:

- The imagery exercise should establish a situation that enables you to leave things behind, grow out of difficult experiences, learn from them, and move on to the future. Such images may include:
  - The Land of I'm Sorry.
  - A house-cleaning image where you throw things away to make room for new possessions, or to get ready to move to a new house.
  - Deleting files from your computer hard drive because it is too full and has no room for new data.
- Remember always to leave open an option for keeping things that are hard to discard, but try to keep them at a distance. For example, store items on a flash drive instead of in the regular memory of the computer; store items in the closet instead of displayed in the room.
- Always give yourself the option of progressing to the future when the exercise ends – never stay in the past.

Skills for Focusing on Your Own Positive Abilities as a Therapist

Sometimes we feel burned out or distressed because a difficult session or experience makes us forget all the good things we have achieved. Imagery exercises with reminders of strengths and resources or with different self-reinforcements can rejuvenate us and permit us a better perspective on our work and professionalism.

When we see things from where we are, our perspective is different than if we see them from a distance. A good way to receive a more realistic and positive picture is to be at a distance from the event. Different exercises can foster a better perspective on our role as a therapist. One is to go far above ourselves, up into the air.

Imagine you are taking a flight high up in a hot-air balloon. The higher you get, the more you feel the wide open air, the beautiful sky. You feel free and happy. You are free of all earthly rules; they cannot affect you up here. Look at yourself now, when you are happy and contented. Notice your body, your mind, your heart. There is this thing with your client that has been disturbing you and causing you distress lately. Look at it from where you are at now. Look from up here and see how small you seem, how distant you are. Look at you down there and see what a small human you are in this big world. Look and feel the air, the wind, the sky.

See yourself in the world – to what extent do you really think you can cause change in this client's life? Look at your client while floating up here and see him in his natural world. There are people surrounding him, talking with him, relating to him. Look at your position in relation to the client. Can you notice that he has more in life than you? That as much as you try to help and sometimes do, you cannot really damage the client? Can you believe from up here that it is the client's responsibility for change, not yours? That you did your best for the client? That the client can cope and get along in the future?

Another way to gain perspective as a therapist is to jump into the future.

Look at yourself 80 years from now. You are old and wise. You look back at your life, knowing that you have done a lot. You tried to do the best you could for the best interests of your clients. You know that you helped many of them. There were a few it was not possible for you to help. Sometimes it annoyed you.

From this future, 80 years from now, look back at this client you feel bad with today. See how much it really seems to be your fault, how many mistakes you have made. Who do you think could really make the change? Could you be blamed for not helping her? Bring your client into the picture. She is also older. What does the client look like? What does the client tell you? Listen carefully – can it be that in spite of your bad feelings you did help her? What does the client say about her behavior 80 years earlier? How does the client refer to the therapy experience with you? Did she take anything from therapy?

Another option for gaining perspective due to feelings of inadequacy or guilt about your actions as a therapist is to use both a magnifying glass and a shrinking glass.

Look at your mistakes as a therapist with a magnifying glass. Look how enormously enlarged they are by the magnification. They are really big! Now that you see them so large, how terrible are those mistakes? What is the worst thing you think you have done?

Now turn the glass over and look from the other side, which shrinks and contracts those mistakes until they become smaller and smaller. What can you say about your mistakes now? How terrible are they?

We often underappreciate our successes and overappreciate our failures. To boost positivity, we should take these same magnifying and shrinking glasses and view our successes through them, too.

Self-reinforcement and accepting your strengths and virtues are very important for your functioning and wellbeing in this challenging and sometimes discouraging profession, but they are not easy to accomplish. If you feel comfortable completing a chart on a daily basis, you can emphasize the positive just by marking down one good thing you did as a therapist each day and thus reinforcing yourself. If this is too difficult, then you can use imagination.

One good method for helping us accept ourselves using imagery for reinforcement is the following.

Imagine a long line of all your clients standing outside your home, leading all the way from your front door out onto the street. They are all waiting for you to leave your house, and each of them wants to tell you something. Each of them needs to share with you one sentence about what you meant for him or her, what therapy was like with you, and how they feel about you. You are quite tense, not feeling completely comfortable about hearing them, fearing they might criticize you, but deep down inside you believe that you have done more good than bad.

Open the door and go outside. Come up close to the first person in line and stand there. This client is telling you something. What do you hear? What is s/he telling you? How do you feel hearing what s/he has to say? Move to the next client. More things are being said. You smile. You start relaxing. You realize that your clients have many good things to tell you. What are they saying? How do you feel about what you hear? What does it mean for you?

We can take this image a step further, to enhance reinforcement.

Imagine that you are receiving a national prize for all the years you have been a therapist, at a big, crowded ceremony. Look at yourself, at how you look, at how you feel. Notice what is going on in your mind. They call your name. Now they are reading what is written on the certificate you are getting. What is written there? What do they say?

You are very excited and you need to thank them. You are going to talk about what it means to be a therapist. What are you saying? What do you tell them?

Practice: guidelines

To focus on your positive qualities as a therapist:

* Relating to your abilities with a specific client:
  – Try to recall one positive picture from every session with your client, where you experienced success or happiness.

284

- Try to elicit a picture of yourself every day experiencing a positive emotion related to your experience in the session.
- Regarding your professional abilities in general, imagine someone else reinforcing you; it can be clients, friends, or supervisors.
- Mark down one good thing you did as a therapist each day and thus reinforce yourself.
- Imagine writing a letter about yourself, recommending yourself for the job of therapist.
- Pay attention to what others or you say about yourself and then:
  - Check within yourself: How do you feel about what was said about you? How comfortable are you with it?
  - Check: How true does it feel to you?
  - If it feels true, repeat it to yourself several times.
- Try to focus only on good things and, for a while, avoid criticism.

Skills for Planning Future Therapeutic Processes

The search for evidence-based practice, as well as the desire to achieve effective outcomes, necessitates better planning and designing of the treatment process. The reliability of assessment and diagnosis as well as the process of making decisions related to our clients is a source of deliberation, hesitation, and sometimes even stress for therapists. This stress occurs especially because change is not a linear process, and therapists must cope with ups and downs. The next exercise aims to help therapists design the treatment process for a specific client.

Imagine you are getting ready for a trip out in the countryside. You prepare your clothes, your maps, your car. You devise the general plan for the trip, although you are not sure how long it will take, what you will face during the trip, or how long you will stay in each place. You also know that you might face some obstacles that will necessitate changing your original plans.

Look at yourself and see what you feel like, going into the unknown. Are you feeling excited about facing new surprises and challenges? How excited are you? Are you also a little anxious about what is lying out there for you? Consider to what extent you believe you possess the tools and capabilities to face these problems.

Now, tell yourself that you are ready and that you have whatever skills you need to face any surprises.

Think of your new client. Look at the therapy you are going to start with this client as a trip. Can you clarify to yourself the point from which you embark on this trip? Where are you standing now? What are the advantages, strengths, support systems, and positive sides of this client? Can you see the client's problems? How severe are they? What obstacles are standing before the two of you? What could prevent the change toward which you are striving?

Now, looking at your tour plans, could you make a decision about where you would like to end the trip? What is the final destination? What should the last session include? What changes should have occurred by then? What should the client look like at the end? What should be different in the client's thoughts, emotions, and behaviors?

Now try to draw the route leading from here, your starting point, to this last stop on the trip. Can you see the problems that you as a therapist might face along the way? Can you chart the places where you think you might get stuck? Where you will face difficulties? What kind of difficulties do you expect?

Can you pinpoint tools you will need to cope better with situations of impasse? Is there any change you can make along the way to decrease difficulties and increase successes? Are there any preparations that might help you?

Our imaginative potential can become useful to us as therapists for grasping the details of clients' narratives, for occasionally identifying their false beliefs or self-defeating schemata or scripts, and also for helping patients overcome problems. Singer (2006) stated that therapists should always be on their guard. In my view, being on our guard means not only ensuring that we are doing the right things with our clients throughout the therapy process, but also taking good care of ourselves and improving our own subjective wellbeing and happiness.

Practice: guidelines

Facing obstacles and preparing for the process ahead can make therapists' future work with a new client easier. Think of a client with whom you have difficulties and try to focus on what you can learn from that experience for your future:

- As you continue to treat this client in the future, what will you do differently? Think about the client's thoughts, emotions, and behaviors, as well as the kind of relationship you would like to have with this client.
- Try to pinpoint your goals as well as the client's goals – what should the end of therapy look like?
- Try to map out the route leading to that ending, including any expected obstacles such as regression or anger on the client's part.
- Think about what you can do when facing those obstacles.
- Think of techniques that usually help you cope with other clients and situations – getting supervision, using self-talk, clarifying things with the client.
- Imagine that you are using those techniques – do they cause any change?
- Chart what was helpful for you and try to use it next time.

General Skills for Helping Yourself

In line with my view that good therapists help their clients and also care for themselves (Mahoney, 1991), I espouse positive psychology as the main theoretical orientation that focuses on methods and techniques for improving subjective wellbeing. Based on the positive psychology orientation and CBT, I believe that enhancing positive thinking, optimism, and hope in our personal lives will also have an impact on our positive orientation with our clients.

Most of the exercises that I described above relate to therapeutic work with clients. However, imagery can and should also be applied as exercises directed at ourselves as human beings, not necessarily as professionals. Such exercises can help us give ourselves positive reinforcements, imagine a great future, learn to relax and meditate, or simply enjoy happiness and gratitude.

In the first part of the book, I suggest exercises for facilitating feelings of happiness that are unrelated to specific problems or clients (e.g., Chapter 3). Therapists can adapt those exercises to themselves instead of to clients, thus practicing various techniques to increase positivity and happiness.

Practice: guidelines

The following general guidelines offer therapists self-help in gaining positivity and happiness:

- Imagery exercises should not necessarily relate to your clients. They can connect to your professional work, but also may be linked with the general positivity in your life, whether regarding past, future, or present.
- Regarding the past:
    - Every day elicit a memory of yourself having fun and enjoying some event or activity.
    - Every day elicit a memory of you trusting yourself, feeling confident and secure.
- Regarding the future:
    - Every week imagine a picture of yourself being happy in the future. Focus on your face and try to see how you look when happy.
    - Imagine your face in the future when you accomplish something that is important for you. Try to see what you succeed in.
    - View yourself in the future, expressing a positive emotion to someone. What emotion did you express and how it was for you?
- The most difficult exercises are to express flow and happiness in the present; therefore, they will be the last to practice. Such exercises can foster strengths and virtues, expression of positive emotion, and flourishing.
- To find your own strengths and virtues:
    - During the first week, find two minutes to look at yourself in the mirror and tell yourself why you like what you see.
    - On every day of the second week, write down one strength or virtue that you find in yourself.
- To express positive emotions:
    - On every day of the first week, write down at least one positive emotion you sensed during the day.
    - On every day of the second week, write down one positive emotion you expressed toward someone else that day.
    - Tell yourself every day when you notice you are happy, even if the feeling stemmed from a very small event.

- To enhance flourishing:
  - During this week, close your eyes, look at your day as if it were a movie (see Chapter 3), and ask yourself: What is going right for me today?
  - During this week, close your eyes, look at your day on the cinema screen, and ask yourself: What made me happy today?
  - During this week, look at your day on the cinema screen, and ask yourself: What was positive in my day that I might take with me and repeat tomorrow?

Summary

Psychotherapy is a demanding, difficult profession that necessitates therapists' constant sensitivity to their clients, clients' problems, and themselves as therapists. Often, being attuned to ourselves as human beings helps us maintain our separateness from clients and ensures that we can stay sane while undergoing incessant, stressful exposure to clients' difficulties.

Imagery can be a good tool not only for helping our "therapist selves" solve problems that arise in therapy by taking a different perspective for looking at our clients and interactions, but also for helping our "personal selves" by facilitating happy, positive, and flourishing thoughts, emotions, and behaviors.

19

Summary: Limitations, Dangers, and Future Directions

Imagery is part of the human journey. Symbols, pictures, and images feeding from our other senses are all a vivid part of human life. As humans, we have memories, we think, we plan, and we fantasize. We are always on a ride, always traveling from somewhere and to somewhere, and images play a role in all those travels. Images accompany us whether we are trying to reach back to places we have been in the past, or we are taking the freedom to drive fast and flow in the present, or we are dreaming and fantasizing about the future. Everything we think of – that is not present in front of us – is imagery, whether it is a thought, a picture, or a recall of touch or odor. So, imagery plays an integral part in our everyday lives, during our waking minutes as well as in our daydreams and nighttime dreams, whether or not we are aware of it.

Imagery is an integral part of all therapy, as well. When clients come to therapy fearing they will fail a test, be rejected when proposing marriage to their beloved, never find their ideal job, or flounder directionless in the future – these self-images of standing alone failing are what causes the underlying fear. When clients lack social skills, it is the pictures of themselves not knowing how to conduct relationships with others or of being lonely without friends that cause distress. As Beck (1967, 1976, 1996) suggested, the event itself is not what causes problems but rather how one interprets that event. Interpretation is profoundly influenced by the inner pictures one imagines about coping or not coping with the event. We can therefore state unequivocally that the problems humans experience derive from their imagery.

Now, if we accept that imagery is a natural part of human life and an integral part of human distress that brings clients to therapy, can we also accurately state that a key to clients' problem resolution derives from imagery as well? I believe that we can.

As I have proposed in this book, I uphold that people cannot cope with their difficulties or resolve their problems unless they possess a positive image of themselves coping, or, in other words, unless they believe that at the end of the road

The Positive Power of Imagery: Harnessing Client Imagination in CBT and Related Therapies,
First Edition. Tammie Ronen. © 2011 Tammie Ronen. Published 2011 by John Wiley & Sons, Ltd.

they will reach their target. Call this self-efficacy if you will, based on CBT or positive thinking. Labeling aside, I propose that these internal images are crucial for progress toward goals. I therefore start each therapy asking clients to view themselves as they wish to be when therapy terminates. This is certainly imagery work, and it relies on a goal-specific, positivistic orientation toward the client and the therapeutic work.

Thus, I believe that human distress derives from negative self-images – viewing oneself failing, helpless, alone, and hopeless. I believe that therapy terminates not when all of a client's behaviors have changed, but when clients can adopt a positive image of themselves coping successfully and being happy regardless of the challenges ahead.

So, how do I see the role of imagery in therapy?

All therapists use imagery in therapy, the question is to what extent. Some very rational therapists talk about memory, automatic thoughts, and positive thoughts as cognitive mechanisms and relate these to reality without using the positive power of the images themselves. Other therapists use images only seldom, for specific purposes, such as to rehearse or practice a particular skill before actually performing it *in vivo,* or to prepare for a future assignment. These therapists jump right into images but use them as pictorial thoughts with which the client needs to work.

A third group of therapists considers images to be a major part of the human experience, and this book focuses mainly on this third way of integrating imagery into mental health treatments. These therapists actually train in imagery work, emphasizing the preliminary preparation for such work, including relaxation exercises, and they employ images as focal points for treatment, encouraging clients to practice talking about images, deepening pictures, and looking for solutions in imagery. These therapists' comprehensive process of helping clients get in touch with their imagery – this predominant language for human experience – enables clients to grasp that they possess control over their images and can eventually learn imagery-rooted self-help techniques to serve them after terminating therapy.

There are many ways to address imagery in therapy. Overall, three different kinds of imagery techniques have been presented in this book:

1. *Imagery-based behavioral and cognitive techniques.* These techniques are common in CBT, but are specifically applied here using imagery. The most frequent are exposure, desensitization, redefinition, and cognitive restructuring.
2. *Fixed therapist-generated imagery.* These are images that I have often employed successfully with various clients and recommend to you for direct application as is in similar situations. Such fixed, ready images include using a rope to pull clients out of their distress (holes, mud), watching oneself on video, flying 100 years into the future, visiting the Land I Wish, the Land of Sorrow, or the Land of I'm Sorry, convening court, establishing dialogue between past and present aspects of self, and so on.

3. *Customized therapist-generated imagery.* These are images developed specifically for use with particular clients, based on their own client-generated metaphors or imagery, and adapted to each individual client according to his or her problem and to characteristics such as age. Examples of such customized images that I have presented in this book include cleaning up Ayelet's garbage with her (Chapter 8), throwing a ladder to Jacob in his mudhole (Chapter 17), and using Ben's "big mess" as a stimulus for role-playing, the yarn metaphor, and drawing (Chapter 17). In all of these examples, clients elicited their own metaphors or imagery, and I utilized these to help instigate changes in their view of themselves/problems and to promote their search for solutions. Here is where the sensitivity and creativity of therapists must come into play – first sensitive listening, to hear the client-generated images and metaphors and to explore their meaning for the specific client, and then creative thinking to personalize verbal and nonverbal methods for effectively elaborating on and working through those personal images in collaboration with the client.

There is no doubt that imagery can be an important tool at therapists' disposal for a range of purposes at different phases of therapeutic process – for assessment, treatment, and evaluation. Using imagery for assessment procures information about clients, the world in which they live, how they conceive of and conceptualize their lives, and how their problems manifest themselves. Imagery therapy can be of great importance in facilitating change in therapy at all levels – cognitive, affective, and behavioral. Images during therapy can emphasize important components, highlight special events or behaviors, and facilitate shared communication between therapists and clients. As treatment progresses, imagery can substantially contribute to clients' evaluation of their change and to predictions of their expected trajectory of changes in the future.

Limitations: Is Imagery Therapy Evidence Based?

As much as I enjoy applying imagery therapy and writing about it, I cannot ignore its limitations and disadvantages – some of which I delineated in Chapters 4, 6, and 7 in relation to imagery, therapists' role, and types of disorder. The main limitation I see relates to the difficulty in proving imagery therapy's efficacy in terms of evidence-based practice. Due to this tool's very diversity and versatility, especially regarding customized, therapist-generated imagery, it is almost impossible empirically to pinpoint its exact contribution at various stages of therapy. Moreover, if images and metaphors are considered part of internal life, can they be accurately assessed? Can we really measure the full meaning these pictures hold for individuals? Victor Frankl (1984) stated that the meaning of life differs from person to person and from moment to moment, thus defying attempts at defining images in any generally acceptable way.

Nevertheless, modern society searches for evidence-based intervention, and rightfully so. At the start of this new millennium, the mental health professions face shortages of resources on the one hand, and the need to help distressed individuals to quickly ameliorate unwanted behaviors and develop improved adjustment on the other. With the wide and complex variety of techniques, theories, research studies, and professional disciplines involved in helping human beings change, policy-makers and individual therapists require clear information to make optimal, effective choices.

Today, the decision of whether to apply a specific technique or not relies crucially on the quality and amount of evidence-based knowledge available about its treatment outcomes. Do we have enough valuable outcome studies on the efficacy of imagery therapy? Do we have sufficient evidence about its advantages and disadvantages? Can we adequately control different treatment variables to determine precisely how imagery affects clients? There is no clear answer to these questions. Many research studies have been conducted, but most have relied on clinical accounts rather than controlled studies. Numerous illustrations of clinical changes following the use of imagery in therapy nonetheless do not readily allow us to draw robust empirical conclusions.

Even those empirical studies that have been conducted often encountered methodological problems. For example, Marks *et al.*'s (2000) controlled trial used functional magnetic resonance imaging to assess mental imagery for problems such as obsessive-compulsive disorder. However, their conclusions were limited by their small sample and the small change documented for the guided imagery exposure group.

Nevertheless, during recent years, a growing number of studies have investigated the efficacy of imagery in therapy (Bikes, Norcross, & Schatz, 2009; Bryant, Guthrie, & Moulds, 2001; Clark *et al.*, 1994; Foa, Keane, & Friedman, 2000; Marks *et al.*, 2000). Most empirical outcomes on the use of imagery in therapy derive from treating fears, anxiety, and trauma (Clark *et al.*, 1994; Foa, Keane, & Friedman, 2000; Marks *et al.*, 2000) or from medicine and nursing, relating to health behaviors (e.g., Hall *et al.*, 2006). In the latter domain, some impressive reviews have supported the efficacy of guided imagery for helping clients cope better, mainly during recovery after surgery or serious illness, in reducing stress and infectious illness, and in management of chronic pain. Heinschel (2002) presented some research on imagery's efficacy for treating anxiety, alleviating pain, reducing hospital stays following medical intervention, and improving immune functions such as blood cortisol levels. Arbuthnot, Arbuthnot, and Rossiter (2001) also provided an impressive review of imagery's efficacy in medical settings for recovering from illness or surgery and for reducing stress.

In terms of controlled studies, Kolcaba and Fox (1999) measured the effectiveness of customized guided imagery for increasing comfort in 53 women with early-stage breast cancer, randomly assigned to an experimental group (26) or control group (27). They reported that guided imagery patients improved significantly more than controls in three domains: bodily pain, vitality, and mental health. Likewise, Mannix *et al.* (2002) reported that guided imagery patients improved significantly more than controls in managing chronic, tension-type headaches. Foa and Rothbaum (2001) and Foa, Keane, and Friedman (2000) did provide outcome data regarding the efficacy of their imagery treatment of posttrauma. However, in most of these studies, imagery was part of a larger protocol within an intervention package, precluding clear differentiation of the imagery component's unique contribution to the package's effectiveness.

Decades ago, Lang (1977) stated that despite the apparent importance of imagery therapy, objective data on its specific effects were limited. Lang explained that we cannot routinely determine how well clients will respond to an "as if" set before we proceed to treatment. Thirty years later, when writing his book on imagery in psychotherapy, Singer (2006) stated that although he and others have been working with imagery for 60 years, there is no manual that enables a replication of this technique or comparison studies as for cognitive and interpersonal therapies. Not much has changed in this regard since 2006. Although many reports have been published, very few controlled studies have been conducted that could prove the method's efficacy. Although many research studies and applications have been attempted, the answers today are no clearer.

Despite all of these caveats regarding the efficacy of imagery therapy, reports of clinical experiences abound. My professional and personal experiences lead me to believe wholeheartedly in the efficacy of this as yet unproven method. However, it is up to you readers to experiment with this versatile tool, and hopefully some of you will embark on the controlled studies necessary to finally verify the efficacy of imagery therapy – which so many therapists already accept based on their own encounters with the tool.

Let me finish this section with a recent anecdote about practice that is not necessarily evidence based. While writing this book, I experienced new, severe pains in my back and neck. After hearing that my only recourse was risky surgery, I sought other medical opinions from experts. Several doctors claimed that surgery would be my only hope for a return to routine functioning and relief of my pain and suffering. For several months, I was in so much pain that I couldn't sit down to work on the computer, I couldn't drive, I had difficulty sleeping at night, I couldn't carry things, and eventually I experienced numbness in my hand to the extent that I couldn't pick up or hold anything with that hand.

Still hesitant to undergo an operation, I found a chiropractor who treated me. At first I was frightened because I did not understand what he was doing, what would come next, and whether my increased pain after treatment sessions was something I needed to experience as part of the recovery process or was a sign of deterioration. I have been seeing this chiropractor now for three months, and throughout, I know that I have given him a hard time. I always feel better when I can control a situation, so whenever I go to him, I am quite insistent that he explain what he is doing at every step of the way. I want to know how long each treatment phase is going to last, what I am meant to feel, how it will affect me, and what the expected outcomes are. He could not always explain why he did what he did, but he tried his best to describe what he was going to do next to prepare me, and he kept reminding me how I felt this week in comparison with last week, identifying together with me what changes had occurred immediately after the last treatment and then a day or two later, to learn together what was helpful for me. Gradually, I improved and could return to all my activities, with complete pain relief. I got my life back and regained control through the use of chiropractic therapy, which is certainly not evidence based. However, I personally have the evidence: I was in pain, and now I am not.

Psychotherapy is often like that. We sometimes have proof but no reports of clinical changes. At other times we have clinical reports but no empirical proof of change. My ultimate answer to the question of the efficacy of imagery therapy will therefore be that we cannot always measure it, but we try to make sure that we help our clients improve their quality of life. And if we can relate to imagery techniques and find them a meaningful addition to our repertoire of therapeutic tools, then we should confidently integrate them into our everyday work.

Therapists and empiricists alike would want to be able not only to recommend imagery as an evidence-based effective therapy in general, but also to pinpoint the specific mechanisms and types of imagery techniques that are most effective for different clients with different problems and personal characteristics. Unfortunately, such specific details on the way imagery works are currently unavailable. One of the reasons is that therapists rarely use imagery alone in therapeutic intervention; usually, imagery comprises only one part of a larger process. Therefore, determining the efficacy of specific uses of imagery is very difficult.

Are There Dangers in Applying Imagery Therapy?

As I discussed in Chapters 6 and 7, another important question that prospective imagery therapists ask concerns the possible dangers involved in using imagery in therapy due to this tool's powerful impact. Hall *et al.* (2006) claimed that there is no evidence that guided imagery can in any way damage clients. They asserted that large numbers of reports have shown negative outcomes for imagery experiences, where clients complained about increased distress. However, in those reports, follow-up evaluations found that in the long run, the experience appeared to be one of growth.

These findings indicate that sometimes in therapy gaps emerge between clients' immediate response and long-term effects, implying that what appears to be risky at one moment usually turns out to be beneficial later on (like my postchiropractor pain increases, which ultimately led to healing). Hall *et al.* concluded that images are usually drawn from clients' own experiences; therefore, clients are the ones controlling the process in some way. When clients elicit difficult pictures, they may feel distress, but as they cope with these pictures, they feel much better.

I propose that another way of answering this question is to say yes, the use of imagery is dangerous, just as in any other therapy – when it is not applied by professionals. Thus, the question of therapist expertise poses a major limitation for this therapeutic method, as for any other method.

First and foremost, we need to look at imagery as a form of therapy. The same rules applying for all other therapies apply here, too. Therapists must be expert in what therapy is, how to design therapy to best fit clients' needs, and the problem at hand. Therapists must monitor changes and make sure to pace, lead, and adjust therapy to particular clients' needs. When therapists are not responsible and expert, any kind of therapy conducted by them can be dangerous.

We might therefore conclude that the question is not whether or not imagery therapy should be applied with clients, but rather what is the best way to apply imagery therapy considering outcome data, available clinical reports, the problem's nature, and the adaptation of imagery language to that of clients and therapists.

Last Words

In Chapter 4, I asked you to imagine that you have already read this book, writing:

> Imagine that you, a therapist, have just finished reading my book. You have learned how to apply imagery therapy with clients. You are now eager to start applying it, and you decide to start by using an exercise you have read here that aims to obtain better information about your client's social relationships. Now, let's see: What exercise are you going to design for your client?

Now, you really have finished reading this book. Does the reading change anything in the way you think you can apply therapy in the future? Did it add anything to your previous knowledge? Is there anything you will do better?

From my experience, I discovered that the best learning fits our previous knowledge and integrates naturally into it, without contradicting it. I do hope that this book has opened up some new directions for travel for you as a therapist, showing you some new stops you can enjoy along this profession's challenging journey, helping you develop some novel, positive expectations for future professional and personal adventures, and fostering your confidence about your current therapeutic applications.

As I have written throughout this book, therapy is a journey of human change that is profuse with new routes, detours, barriers, and successes. The process of human change is never ending, but we therapists can accompany our clients along their path for some time, guiding them, teaching them, and helping them. When we encounter the inevitable challenges and pitfalls of working with clients, a vision of ourselves as good therapists, with the belief that we can be of help, will help us travel smoothly down that road and make the journey meaningful for clients.

I do not know of a better way to end this book than to quote my dear friend whom I miss so much, the late Michael Mahoney. I felt his presence with me while writing this book. He once wrote a poem to one of his clients, and he read it to me and my husband afterwards, before it was printed in the book he edited with Robert Neimeyer, *Constructivism in Psychotherapy* (Neimeyer &

Mahoney, 1995: 396). This excerpt is from his poem entitled "The Pilgrim in Process":

> ...It's a season of transition and you're on the move again
> On a path toward something you cannot disown
> Searching for your being in the labyrinths of heart
> And sensing all the while you're not alone.

I certainly wish you great travels wherever imagery leads you. And I sincerely hope you will feel that you are not alone, because this book can serve as one of your trusted travel guides, helping you open new windows to see the beautiful landscapes of possibility and to find your own way along the paths you travel.

References

Achenbach, T.M. (1985) *Assessment and Taxonomy of Child and Adolescent Psychopathology*, Beverly Hills, CA: Sage.

Achterberg, J., Dossey, B., & Kolkmeier, L. (1994) *Rituals of Healing: Using Imagery for Health and Wellness*, New York: Bantam Books.

Alford, B.A. & Beck, A.T. (1997) *The Integrative Power of Cognitive Therapy*, New York: Guilford.

Allian, G.B. & Lemieux, C.A. (2007) The use of metaphorical fables with children. In T. Ronen & A. Freeman (eds.), *Cognitive Behavior Therapy in Clinical Social Work Practice*, New York: Springer, pp. 213–235.

Amabile, T.M. (1996) *Creativity in Context*, Boulder, CO: Westview Press.

Amabile, T.M. (1998) How to kill creativity, *Harvard Business Review*, 76(5), 76–87.

American Psychiatric Association (1994) *Diagnostic and Statistical Manual of Mental Disorders*, 4th edn, Washington, DC: Author.

Andersen, H.C. (2004) *Fairy Tales* (ed. J. Wullschlager), New York: Viking.

Antonucci, T.C. & Akiyama, H. (1994) Convoys of attachment and social relations in children, adolescents, and adults. In F. Nestmann & K. Hurrelmann (eds.), *Social Networks and Social Support in Childhood and Adolescence*, New York: Walter de Gruyter, pp. 37–52.

Arbuthnott, K.D., Arbuthnott, D.W., & Rossiter, L. (2001) Guided imagery and memory: Implications or psychotherapies, *Journal of Counselling Psychology*, 48(2), 123–132.

Arbuthnott, K.D., Arbuthnott, D.W., & Thompson, V.A. (2006) *The Mind in Therapy*, Mahwah, NJ: Erlbaum.

Assagioli, R. (1965) *Psychosynthesis: A Manual of Principles and Techniques*, London: Turnstone.

Attwood, T. (2007) Asperger's disorder: Exploring the schizoid spectrum, in A. Freeman & M.A. Reinecke (eds.), *Personality Disorders in Childhood and Adolescence*, Hoboken, NJ: John Wiley & Sons, Inc., pp. 299–340.

Bandura, A. (1969) *Principles of Behavior Modification*, New York: Holt, Rinehart, and Winston.

The Positive Power of Imagery: Harnessing Client Imagination in CBT and Related Therapies, First Edition. Tammie Ronen. © 2011 Tammie Ronen. Published 2011 by John Wiley & Sons, Ltd.

Bandura, A. (1977) Self-efficacy: Toward a unifying theory of behavioral change, *Psychological Review*, 84, 191–215.

Bandura, A. (1997) *Self-Efficacy: The Exercise of Control*, New York: W. H. Freeman.

Bandura, A., Caprara, G.V., Barbaranelli, C., & Pastorelli, C. (2001) Sociocognitive self-regulatory mechanisms governing transgressive behavior, *Journal of Personality and Social Behavior*, 80, 125–135.

Barkley, R.A. (1997) Behavioral inhibition sustained, attention, and executive functions: Constructing a unifying theory of ADHD, *Psychological Bulletin*, 121, 65–94.

Barlow, D.H., Craske, M.G., Cerny, J.A., & Klosko, J.S. (1989) Behavioral treatment of panic disorder, *Behavior Therapy*, 20, 261–282.

Barrios, B.A. & Hartman, D.P. (1988) Fears and anxieties. In E.J. Mash & L.G. Terdal (eds.), *Behavioral Assessment of Childhood Disorders*, 2nd edn, New York: Guilford, pp. 196–262.

Barron, F. (1988) Putting creativity to work. In R. Sternberg (ed.), *The Nature of Creativity*, Cambridge: Cambridge University Press, pp. 76–98.

Battino, R. (2007) *Guided Imagery: Psychotherapy and Healing through the Mind–Body Connection*, Carmarthen: Crown House.

Battino, R. & South, T.L. (1999) *Ericksonian Approaches: A Comprehensive Manual*, Carmarthen: Crown House.

Baumeister, R.F. (1999) *The Self in Social Psychology*, Philadelphia: Taylor & Francis.

Baumeister, R. & Boden, J. (1998) Aggression and the self: High self-esteem, low self-control, and ego threat. In R. Geen & E. Donnerstein (eds.), *Human Aggression*, San Diego: Academic Press, pp. 111–138.

Beck, A.T. (1967) *Depression: Clinical, Experimental, and Theoretical Aspects*, New York: Harper & Row. [Republished as Beck, A.T. (1972) *Depression: Causes and Treatment*, Philadelphia: University of Pennsylvania Press.]

Beck, A.T. (1976) *Cognitive Therapy and the Emotional Disorders*, New York: Meridian.

Beck, A.T. (1996) Beyond belief: A theory of modes, personality, and psychopathology. In P.M. Salkovskis (ed.), *Frontiers of Cognitive Therapy*, New York: Guilford, pp. 1–25.

Beck, A.T. (1999a) Cognitive aspects of personality disorders and their relation to syndromal disorders: A psychoevolutionary approach. In C.R. Cloninger (ed.), *Personality and Psychopathology*, Washington, DC: American Psychiatric Press, pp. 411–429.

Beck, A.T. (1999b) *Prisoners of Hate: The Cognitive Basis of Anger, Hostility, and Violence*, New York: HarperCollins.

Beck, A.T. (2010) Foreword. In R. Stott, W. Mansell, P. Salkovskis, A. Lavender, & S. Cartwright-Hatton (eds.), *Oxford Guide to Metaphors in CBT: Building Cognitive Bridges*, Oxford: Oxford University Press, pp. vii–viii.

Beck, A.T., Emery, G., & Greenberg, R.L. (1985) *Anxiety Disorders and Phobias*, New York: Basic Books.

Beck, A.T., Freeman, A., & Davis, D.D. (2003) *Cognitive Therapy of Personality Disorders*, New York: Guilford.

Beck, A.T. & Ward, C.H. (1961) Dreams of depressed patients: Characteristic themes in manifest content, *Archives of General Psychiatry*, 5, 462–467.

Bellak, L. (1954) *Thematic Apperception Test*, New York: Grune & Stratton.

Ben Shahar, T. (2007) *Happier*, New York: McGraw-Hill.

Beutler, L.E. & Hill, C.E. (1992) Process and outcome research in the treatment of adult victims of childhood sexual abuse: Methodological issues, *Journal of Consulting and Clinical Psychology*, 60, 204–212.

References

Bikes, D.H., Norcross, J.C., & Schatz, D.M. (2009) Process and outcomes of psychotherapists' personal therapy: Replication and extension 20 years later, *Psychotherapy: Theory, Research, Practice, Training*, 46, 19–31.

Biswas-Diener, R. & Dean, B. (2007) *Positive Psychology Coaching: Putting the Science of Happiness to Work for Your Clients*, Hoboken, NJ: John Wiley & Sons, Inc.

Bogart, G. (1991) The use of meditation in psychotherapy: A review of the literature, *American Journal of Psychotherapy*, 45, 383–413.

Bradburn, N.M. (1969) *The Structure of Psychological Well-being*, Chicago: Aldine.

Brigham, T.A., Hopper, A.J., Shaw, B.F., & Emery, G. (1979) *Cognitive Therapy of Depression*, New York: Guilford.

Brown, G.K., Newman, C.F., Charlesworth, S.E., Crits-Christoph, P., & Beck, A.T. (2004) An open clinical trial of cognitive therapy for borderline personality disorder, *Journal of Personality Disorders*, 18(3), 257–271.

Bryant, R.A. (2000) Cognitive behavior therapy of violence-related posttraumatic stress disorder, *Aggression and Violent Behavior*, 5, 79–97.

Bryant, R.A., Guthrie, R.M., & Moulds, M.L. (2001) Hypnotizability in acute stress disorder, *American Journal of Psychiatry*, 158, 600–604.

Bryant, R.A., Harvey, A.G., Dang, S.T., Sackville, T., & Basten, C. (1998) Treatment of acute stress disorder: A comparison of cognitive-behavioral therapy and supportive counseling, *Journal of Consulting and Clinical Psychology*, 66, 862–866.

Bryant, R.A., Moulds, M.L., Guthrie, R.M., & Nixon, R.D.V. (2003) Treating acute stress disorder following mild traumatic brain injury, *American Journal of Psychiatry*, 160, 585–587.

Burke, J.D. (2007) Antisocial personality disorder. In A. Freeman & M.A. Reinecke (eds.), *Personality Disorders in Childhood and Adolescence*, Hoboken, NJ: John Wiley & Sons, Inc., pp. 429–494.

Burns, G.W. (2007) *Healing with Stories*, Hoboken, NJ: John Wiley & Sons, Inc.

Butler, A.C., Chapman, J.E., Forman, E.M., & Beck, A.T. (2006) The empirical status of cognitive behavioural therapy: A review of meta analysis, *Clinical Psychology Review*, 26, 17–31.

Carlsen, M.B. (1995) Meaning-making and creative aging. In R.A. Neimeyer & M.J. Mahoney (eds.), *Constructivism in Psychotherapy*, Washington, DC: American Psychological Association, pp. 127–153.

Carr, A. (2004) *Positive Psychology: The Science of Happiness and Human Strength*, New York: Brunner-Routledge.

Carrigan, A. (2007) Developmental factors for consideration in assessment and treatment. In T. Ronen & A. Freeman (eds.), *Cognitive Behavior Therapy in Clinical Social Work Practice*, New York: Springer, pp. 89–106.

Casasola, M. & Cohen, L. (2000) Infants' association of linguistic labels with causal actions, *Developmental Psychology*, 36, 115–168.

Case, R. (1991) Stages in the development of the young child's first sense of self, *Developmental Review*, 11, 210–230.

Case, R. (1992) *The Mind's Staircase: Exploring the Conceptual Underpinnings of Children's Thought and Knowledge*, Hillsdale, NJ: Erlbaum.

Clark, D.M. (ed.) (2004) *Intrusive Thoughts in Clinical Disorders*, New York: Guilford.

Clark, D.M. & Beck, A.T. (1999) *Scientific Foundations of Cognitive Theory and Therapy of Depression*, New York: John Wiley & Sons, Inc.

References

Clark, D.M., Salkovskis, P.M., Hackmann, A., Middleton, M., Anastasiades, P., & Gelder, M. (1994) A comparison of cognitive therapy, applied relaxation and imipramine in the treatment of panic disorder, *British Journal of Psychiatry*, 164, 759–769.

Cloitre, M., Koenen, K.C., Cohen, L.R., & Han, H. (2002) Skills training in affective and interpersonal regulation followed by exposure: A phase-based treatment for PTSD related to childhood abuse, *Journal of Consulting and Clinical*, 70(5), 1067–1074.

Cohen, G. (2000) *American Academy of Pediatrics Guide to Your Child's Sleep: Birth through Adolescence*, New York: Villard Books.

Cohen, S. & Wills, T.A. (1985) Stress, social support and the buffering hypothesis, *Psychological Bulletin*, 98, 310–357.

Cole, M. & Wertsch, J.V. (2005) *Beyond the Individual-Social Antimony in Discussions of Piaget and Vygotsky*, retrieved from http://www.massey.ac.nz.

Copeland, A.P. (1982) Individual difference factors in children's self-management: Toward individualized treatment. In P. Karoly & F.H. Kanfer (eds.), *Self-Management and Behavior Change: From Theory to Practice*, New York: Pergamon, pp. 207–239.

Crampton, M. (1969) The use of mental imagery in psychosynthesis, *Journal of Humanistic Psychology*, 9, 139–153.

Crick, N.R. & Dodge, K.A. (1994) A review and reformulation of social information processing mechanisms in children's social adjustment, *Psychological Bulletin*, 115, 74–101.

Csikszentmihalyi, M. (1966) *Creativity: Flow and the Psychology of Discovery and Invention*, New York: HarperCollins.

Csikszentmihalyi, M. (2000) Creativity: An overview. In A. Kazdin (ed.), *Encyclopedia of Psychology*, Washington, DC & New York: American Psychological Association and Oxford University Press, pp. 442–444.

Csikszentmihalyi, M. (2002) *Flow: The Classic Work on How to Achieve Happiness*, 2nd edn, London: Rider.

Cull, J. & Bondi, M. (2001) Biology/psychology of consciousness: A circular perspective, *Constructivism*, 6, 23–29.

Dalai Lama & Cutler, H.C. (1998) *The Art of Happiness*, London: Hodder & Stoughton.

Danaher, B.G. & Thoresen C.E. (1972) Imagery assessment by self-report and behavioral measures, *Behaviour Research and Therapy*, 10(2), 131–138.

Davies, D. (1999) *Child Development: A Practitioner's Guide*, New York: Guilford.

DeLisa, P. & Flaxman, A. (2006) *Little Red Riding Hood: The Classic Grimm's Fairy Tale*, Herndon, VA: Bell Pond Books.

Demetriou, A., Shayer, M., & Efklides, A. (eds.) (1993) *Neo-Piagetian Theories of Cognitive Development*, New York: Routledge.

Diener, E., Suh, M., Lucas, E., & Smith, H. (1999) Subjective well-being: Three decades of progress, *Psychological Bulletin*, 125(2): 276–302.

Disney, W. (Producer), Geronimi, C., Jackson, W., & Luske, H. (Directors) (1951) *Alice in Wonderland* [motion picture], Hollywood, CA: Disney Studios.

Disney, W. (Producer), Geronimi, C., Luske, H., & Jackson, W. (Directors) (1950) *Cinderella* [motion picture], Hollywood, CA: Disney Studios.

Dodge, K.A. & Pettit, G.S. (2003) A biopsychosocial model of the development of chronic conduct problems in adolescence, *Developmental Psychology*, 39, 1–41.

Dodge, K.A., Pettit, G.S., McClaskey, C.L., & Brown, M. (1986) Social competence in children, *Monographs of the Society for Research in Child Development*, 51(2, Serial No. 213).

References

Dodge, K.A. & Price, J.M. (1994) On the relation between social information processing and socially competent behavior in early school age children, *Child Development*, 65, 1385–1398.

Doyle, M.C. (1984) Enhancing dream pleasure with the Senoi strategy, *Journal of Clinical Psychology*, 40, 467–474.

Duckworth, A.L., Steen, T.A., & Seligman, M.E.P. (2005) Positive psychology in clinical practice, *Annual Review of Clinical Psychology*, 1, 629–651.

Durlak, J.A., Fuhrman, T., & Lampman, C. (1991) Effectiveness of cognitive-behavior therapy for maladaptive children: A meta-analysis, *Psychological Bulletin*, 110, 204–214.

Ellis, A. (1973) *Humanistic Psychotherapy: The Rational–Emotive Approach*, New York: McGraw-Hill.

Erickson, N.H. & Rossi, E.L. (1980) *The Collected Papers of Milton H. Erickson on Hypnosis: Vol. 11. Hypnotic Alteration of Sensory, Perceptual and Psychophysiological Processes*, New York: Irvington.

Erickson, N.H. & Rossi, E.L. (1981) *Experiencing Hypnosis: Therapeutic Approaches to Altered States*, New York: Irvington.

Erickson, N.H., Rossi, E.L., & Rossi, S.I. (1976) *Hypnotic Realities*, New York: Irvington.

Essau, C.A. (2003) *Conduct and Oppositional Defiant Disorders*, Mahwah, NJ: Erlbaum.

Feldman, D.H. (1988) Creativity: Dreams, insights, and transformations. In R. Sternberg (ed.), *The Nature of Creativity*, Cambridge: Cambridge University Press, pp. 271–297.

Finn, S.E. & Tbnsager, M.E. (1997) Information-gathering and therapeutic models of assessment: Complementary paradigms, *Psychological Assessment*, 9(4), 374–385.

Fisher, P. (2009) Applied relaxation, *Common Language for Psychotherapy (CLP) Procedures*, retrieved from http://www.commonlanguagepsychotherapy.org.

Fitzsimons, C., Marston, W.M., & Ross, S.R. (Producers) (1975–1979) *Wonder Woman* [TV series], New York: American Broadcasting Company and Columbia Broadcasting System.

Foa, E.B., Ehlers, A., Clark, D.M., Tolin, D.F., & Orsillo, S.M. (1999) The posttraumatic cognitions inventory (PTCI): Development and validation, *Psychological Assessment*, 11, 303–314.

Foa, E.B., Hearst-Ikeda, D., & Perry, K.J. (1995) Evaluation of a brief cognitive-behavioral program for the prevention of chronic PTSD in recent assault victims, *Journal of Consulting and Clinical Psychology*, 63, 948–955.

Foa, E.B., Keane, T.M., & Friedman, M.J. (2000) *Effective Treatments for PTSD*, New York: Guilford.

Foa, E.B. & Rothbaum, B.O. (2001) *Treating the Trauma of Rape: Cognitive-Behavioral Therapy for PTSD*, New York: Guilford. (Original work published 1997.)

Follette, V.M. & Rasmussen, H. (2004) Acceptance, mindfulness and trauma. In S.C. Hayes, V.M. Follette, & M.M. Linehan (eds.), *Mindfulness and Acceptance: Expanding the Cognitive Behavioral Tradition*, New York: Guilford, pp. 192–208.

Fonagy, P., Target, M., Cottrell, D., Phillipa, J., & Kurtz, Z. (2002) *What Works for Whom? A Critical Review of Treatments for Children and Adolescents*, New York: Guilford.

Forehand, R. & Weirson, M. (1993) The role of developmental factors in planning behavioral intervention for children: Disruptive behavior as an example, *Behavior Therapy*, 24, 117–141.

Frankl, V.E. (1984) *Man's Search for Meaning*, New York: Simon & Schuster.

Frankl, V.E. (1997) *Viktor Frankl, Recollections: An Autobiography*, New York: Insight Books (Plenum Press).

Fredrickson, B.L. (1998) What good are positive emotions? *Review of General Psychology*, 2, 300–319.

Fredrickson, B.L. (2009) *Positivity*, New York: Crown.

Fredrickson B.L. & Losada, M.F. (2005) Positive affect and the complex dynamics of human flourishing, *American Psychology*, 60, 678–686.

Freeman, A. & Boyll, S. (1992) The use of dreams and the dream metaphor in cognitive behavior therapy, *Psychotherapy in Private Practice*, 10(1–2), 173–192.

Freud, S. (1958) *The Dynamics of Transference*, London: Hogarth Press.

Freud, S. (1960) *The Ego and the Id* (trans. J. Riviere, ed. J. Starchey), New York: W. W. Norton. (Original work published 1923.)

Friedberg, R.D. & McClure, J.M. (2002) *Clinical Practice of Cognitive Therapy with Children and Adolescents*, New York: Guilford.

Fromm, E. (1967) Dissociative and integrative processes in hypnoanalysis, *American Journal of Clinical Hypnosis*, 10, 174–177.

Gable, S. L. & Haidt, J. (2005) What (and why) is positive psychology? *Review of General Psychology*, 9, 103–110.

Galton, E. (1883) *Inquiries into Human Faculty and Its Development*, London: Dent.

Gambrill, E. (2006) *Social Work Practice: A Critical Thinker's Guide*, New York: Oxford University Press.

Gambrill, E. (2007) Critical thinking, evidence-based practice and cognitive behavior therapy. In T. Ronen & A. Freeman (eds.), *Cognitive Behavior Therapy in Clinical Social Work Practice*, New York: Springer, pp. 67–87.

Gambrill, E. & Richey, C. (1988) *Taking Charge of Your Social Life*, Berkeley, CA: Behavioral Options.

Germer, C.K (2005) Mindfulness: What is it? What does it matter? In C.K. Germer, R.D. Siegel, & T.R. Fulton (eds.), *Mindfulness and Psychotherapy*, New York: Guilford, pp. 3–27.

Gilbert, D. (2005) *Stumbling on Happiness*, New York: Vintage Books.

Gonçalves, O.F. & Craine, M.H. (1990) The use of metaphors in cognitive therapy, *Journal of Cognitive Psychotherapy*, 4, 135–149.

Graham, P. (1994) Prevention. In M. Rutter, E. Taylor, & L. Hersov (eds.), *Child and Adolescent Psychiatry: Modern Approaches*, 3rd edn, Oxford: Blackwell, pp. 815–828.

Grave, J. & Blissett, J. (2004) Is cognitive behavior therapy developmentally appropriate for young children? Review of the Evidence, *Clinical Psychology Review*, 24, 399–420.

Greenberg, L.S. & Goldman, N. (2008) *Emotion-Focused Couples Therapy: The Dynamics of Emotion, Love and Power*, Washington, DC: American Psychological Association.

Greenberg, L.S. & Safran, J.D. (1989) Emotion in psychotherapy, *American Psychologist*, 44, 19–29.

Greenberg, L.S., Watson, J.C., & Lietaer, G. (1998) *Handbook of Experiential Psychotherapy*, New York: Guilford.

Grimm, J. & Grimm, W. (1932) *Selected Folktales/Ausgewählte märchen: A Dual-Language Book* (ed. & trans. S. Appelbaum), New York: Dover.

Guidano, V.F. (1995) A constructivist outline of human knowing processes. In M. J. Mahoney (ed.), *Cognitive and Constructive Psychotherapies: Theory, Research, and Practice*, New York: Springer, pp. 89–102.

Guilford, J.P. (1950) Creativity, *American Psychologist*, 5, 444–454.

References

Guilford, J.P. (1967) *The Nature of Human Intelligence*, New York: McGraw-Hill.

Halford, G.S. (1993) *Children's Understanding: The Development of Mental Models*, Hillsdale, NJ: Erlbaum.

Hall, E., Hall, C., Stradling, P., & Young, D. (2006) *Guided Imagery: Creative Interventions in Counseling and Psychotherapy*, London: Sage.

Hamama, L. & Ronen, T. (2009) Drawing as a self report measurement, *Child and Family Social Work*, 14, 60–102.

Hamama, L., Ronen, T., & Rahav, G. (2008) Self-control, self-efficacy, role overload and stress responses among siblings of children with cancer, *Health & Social Work*, 33, 121–132.

Harrington, R., Whitaker, J., Shoebridge, P., & Campbell, F. (1998) Systematic review of efficacy of cognitive behavior therapies in childhood and adolescent depressive disorder, *British Medical Journal*, 316, 1559–1563.

Harter, S. (1983) Developmental perspectives on the self-system. In P.H. Mussen (series ed.) & E.M. Hetherington (vol. ed.), *Handbook of Child Psychology: Vol. 4. Socialization, Personality, and Social Development*, New York: John Wiley & Sons, Inc., pp. 275–386.

Hayes, S.C., Follette, V.M., & Linehan, M.M. (2004) *Mindfulness and Acceptance: Expanding the Cognitive Behavioral Tradition*, New York: Guilford.

Hayes, S.C., Strosahl, K.D., & Wilson, K.G. (1999) *Acceptance and Commitment Therapy: An Experiential Approach to Behaviour Change*, New York: Guilford.

Heinschel, J.A. (2002) A descriptive study of the interactive guided imagery experience, *Journal of Holistic Nursing*, 20(4): 325–346.

Herbert, H. (2002) The human life cycle: Adolescence. In M. Davies (ed.), *The Blackwell Companion to Social Work*, Oxford: Blackwell, pp. 355–364.

Himle, J.A. (2007) Cognitive behaviour therapy for anxiety disorders. In T. Ronen & A. Freeman (eds.), *Cognitive Behaviour Therapy in Clinical Social Work Practice*, New York: Springer, pp. 375–399.

Holmes, J. (2009) Metaphors, *Common Language for Psychotherapy (CLP) Procedures*, retrieved from http://www.commonlanguagepsychotherapy.org.

Horvath, A.O. & Symonds, D.B. (1991) Relation between working alliance and outcome in psychotherapy: A meta-analysis, *Journal of Counseling Psychology*, 38(2), 139–149.

House, J.S. (1981) *Work Stress and Social Support*, Reading, MA: Addison-Wesley.

Hughes, J. (1993) Behavior therapy. In T.R. Kratochwill & R.J. Morris (eds.), *Handbook of Psychotherapy with Children and Adolescents*, Boston, MA: Allyn & Bacon, pp. 181–220.

Hume, D. (1912) *An Inquiry Concerning Human Nature*, Chicago, IL: Open Court.

Hurwich, C. (1992) Late-life potential, panel discussion presented at the annual meeting of the American Society on Aging, San Diego, CA.

Isen, A.M., Daubman, K.A., & Nowicki, G.P. (1987) Positive affect facilitates creative problem solving, *Journal of Personality and Social Psychology*, 52, 1122–1131.

Jacobson, E. (1938) *Progressive Relaxation*, Chicago, IL: University of Chicago Press.

Jones, D. (1994) *Innovative Therapy*, Buckingham: Open University Press.

Joseph, S., & Linley, P.A. (2006) *Positive Therapy*, London: Routledge.

Joyce, J. (1980) *Finnegan's Wake*, London: Faber and Faber.

Jung, C.G. (1958) *Psyche and Symbols* (ed. V. de Laszlo), New York: Doubleday.

Kabat-Zinn, J. (1990) *Full Catastrophe Living*, New York: Dell.

References

Kabat-Zinn, J. (1994) *Wherever You Go, There You Are: Mindfulness Meditation in Everyday Life*, New York: Hyperion.

Kabat-Zinn, J. (2005) *Coming to Our Senses: Healing Ourselves and the World through Mindfulness*, New York: Piatkus.

Kanfer, F.H. & Schefft, B.K. (1988) *Guiding the Process of Therapeutic Change*, Champaign, IL: Research Press.

Kazdin, A.E. (1988) *Child Psychotherapy: Development and Identifying Effective Treatments*, New York: Pergamon Press.

Kazdin, A.E. (1993) Psychotherapy for children and adolescents: Current progress and future directions, *American Psychologist*, 48, 644–656.

Kazdin, A.E. (2000) *Psychotherapy for Children and Adolescents: Directions for Research and Practice*, New York: Oxford University Press.

Kazdin, A.E. (2005) *Parent Management Training: Treatment for Oppositional, Aggressive, and Antisocial Behavior in Children and Adolescents*, New York: Oxford University Press.

Kazdin, A.E. & Weisz, J.R. (eds.) (2003) *Evidence-Based Psychotherapies for Children and Adolescents*, New York: Guilford.

Kelly, G.A. (1955) *The Psychology of Personal Constructs*, New York: Norton.

Kelly, G.A. (1969) The language of hypothesis. In B. Mahrer (ed.), *Clinical Psychology and Personality*, New York: John Wiley & Sons, Inc., pp. 147–162.

Kendall, P.C. (1993) Cognitive-behavioral therapies with youth: Guiding theory, current status, and emerging developments, *Journal of Consulting and Clinical Psychology*, 61, 235–247.

Kendall, P.C. (2006) *Child and Adolescence Therapy: Cognitive Behavioral Procedures*, 3rd edn, New York: Guilford.

Kendall, P.C. & Braswell, L. (1993) *Cognitive Behavioral Therapy for Impulsive Children*, 2nd edn, New York: Guilford.

Kendall, P.C., Hudson, J.L., Gosch, E., Flannery-Schroeder, E., & Suveg, C. (2008) Cognitive-behavioral therapy for anxiety disordered youth: A randomized clinical trial evaluating child and family modalities, *Journal of Consulting and Clinical Psychology*, 76, 282–297.

Kenneth, D.J., Worth, N.C., & Forbes, C.A. (2009) The contribution of Rosenbaum's model of self-control and transtheoretical model to the understanding of exercise behaviour, *Psychology of Sport and Exercise*, 10, 602–608.

Keyes, C.L. (2002) The mental health continuum: From languishing to flourishing in life, *Journal of Health and Social Behavior*, 43, 207–222.

Keyes, C.L. (2006) Subjective well-being in mental health and human development research worldwide: An introduction, *Social Indicators Research*, 77, 1–10.

Keyes, C.L. & Haidt, J. (eds.) (2002) *Flourishing: Positive Psychology and the Life Well-Lived*, Washington, DC: American Psychological Association.

Keyes, C.L. & Ryff, C.D. (2000) Subjective change and mental health: A self-concept theory, *Social Psychology Quarterly*, 63, 264–279.

Keyes, C.L., Wissing, M., Potgieter, J.P., Temane, M., Kruger, A., & van Rooy, S. (2008) Evaluation of the mental health continuum–short form (MHC–SF) in Setswana-speaking South Africans, *Clinical Psychology and Psychotherapy*, 15, 181–192.

Kincheloe, J.L. (2005) *Critical Constructivism Primer*, New York: Peter Lang.

King, C.A. & Kirschenbaum, D.S. (1992) *Helping Young Children Develop Social Skills*, Pacific Grove, CA: Brooks/Cole.

Knell, S.M. (1993) *Cognitive Behavioral Play Therapy*, Northvale, NJ: Jason Aronson.

References

Koch, E.L., Spates, C.R., & Himle, J.A. (2004) Comparison of behavioral and cognitive-behavioral one-session exposure treatments for small animal phobias, *Behaviour Research and Therapy*, 42, 1483–1504.

Kolcaba, K. & Fox, C. (1999) The effects of guided imagery on comfort of women with early stage breast cancer undergoing radiation therapy, *Oncology Nursing Forum*, 26(1), 67–72.

Koons, C.R. (2007) The use of mindfulness intervention in cognitive behaviour therapy. In T. Ronen & A. Freeman (eds.), *Cognitive Behaviour Therapy in Clinical Social Work Practice*, New York: Springer, pp. 167–186.

Kopp, R.R. (1995) *Metaphor Therapy: Using Client-Generated Metaphors in Psychotherapy*, New York: Brunner/Mazel.

Kopp, R.R. & Craw, M.J. (1998) Metaphoric language, metaphoric cognition, and cognitive therapy, *Psychotherapy*, 35(3), 306–311.

Kovecses, Z. (2000) *Metaphor and Emotion*, Cambridge: Cambridge University Press.

Lackoff, G. & Johnson, M. (1980) *Metaphors We Live By*, Chicago, IL: University of Chicago Press.

Lang, P. (1977) Imagery in therapy: An information processing analysis of fear, *Behavior Therapy*, 8, 862–886.

Langley, R. & Jones, R. (1988) A computational model of scientific insight. In R. Stenberg (ed.), *The Nature of Creativity*, Cambridge: Cambridge University Press, pp. 177–201.

Layard, R. (2005) *Happiness*, London: Penguin.

Lazarus, A. (1977) *In the Mind's Eye: The Power of Imagery for Personal Enrichment*, New York: Guilford.

LeClerc, G. (1992) Late-life potential, panel discussion presented at the annual meeting of the American Society on Aging, San Diego, CA.

LeCroy, C.W. (2002) Child therapy and social skills. In A.R. Roberts & G.J. Greene (eds.), *Social Work Desk Reference*, New York: Oxford University Press, pp. 406–412.

LeCroy, C.W. (2007) Problem solving skills and social skills training in groups for children. In T. Ronen & A. Freeman (eds.), *Cognitive Behaviour Therapy in Clinical Social Work Practice*, New York: Springer, pp. 285–300.

Levitt, E.E. (1963) Psychotherapy with children: A further evaluation, *Behavior Research and Therapy*, 60, 326–329.

Lindsay, W.R. & Morrison, F.M. (2007) The effects of behavioural relaxation on cognitive performance in adults with severe intellectual disabilities, *Journal of Intellectual Disability Research*, 40, 285–290.

Linehan, M.M. (1993a) *Cognitive-Behavioral Treatment of Borderline Personality Disorder*, New York: Guilford.

Linehan, M.M. (1993b) *Skills Training Manual for Treating Borderline Personality Disorder*, New York: Guilford.

Lohaus, A. & Klein-Hessling, J. (2003) Relaxation in children: Effects of extended and intensified training, *Psychology and Health*, 18, 237–249.

Lopez, S.J. (2008) *Positive Psychology: Exploring the Best in People*, Vols 1–4, Westport, CT: Praeger.

Loter, S. (Producer) & Buck, C. (Director) (2001–2003) *The Legend of Tarzan* [TV series]. Hollywood, CA: Walt Disney.

Ludwig, A. (1995) *The Price of Greatness*, New York: Guilford.

References

Ludwig, A. (2002) *King of the Mountain: The Nature of Political Leadership*, Lexington, KT: University Press of Kentucky.

Luria, A.R. (1961) *The Role of Speech in the Regulation of Normal Behaviors*, New York: Liverwright.

Lyubomirsky, S. (2007) *The How of Happiness*, London: Sphere.

MacLaren, C. & Freeman, A. (2007) Cognitive behaviour therapy model and techniques. In T. Ronen & A. Freeman (eds.), *Cognitive Behavior Therapy in Clinical Social Work Practice*, New York: Springer, pp. 25–44.

Magaletta, P.R. & Oliver, J.M. (1999) The hope construct, will, and ways: Their relations with self-efficacy, optimism, and general well-being, *Journal of Clinical Psychology*, 55, 539–551.

Magyar-Moe, J.L. (2009) *Therapist's Guide to Positive Psychological Interventions*, New York: Elsevier Academic Press.

Mahoney, M.J. (1991) *Human Change Processes: The Scientific Foundations of Psychotherapy*, New York: Basic Books.

Mahoney, M.J. (1993) Introduction to special section: Theoretical developments in the cognitive psychotherapies, *Journal of Consulting and Clinical Psychology*, 61, 187–193.

Mahoney, M.J. (1995) Continuing evolution of the cognitive sciences and psychotherapies. In R.A. Neimeyer & M.J. Mahoney (eds.), *Constructivism in Psychotherapy*, Washington, DC: American Psychological Association, pp. 39–67.

Mahoney, M.J. (1999) *Constructive Psychotherapy: Exploring Principles and Practical Exercises*, New York: Guilford.

Mahoney, M.J. (2003) *Constructive Psychotherapy: A Practical Guide*, New York: Guilford.

Mannix, L.K., Chandurkar, R.S., Rybicki, L.A., Tusek, D.L., & Solomon, G.D. (2002) Effect of guided imagery on quality of life for patients with chronic tension-type headache, *Headache: Journal of Head and Face Pain*, 39, 326–334.

Markova, D. (1996) *Open Mind*, Berkeley, CA: Conari Press.

Marks, I. (1969) *Fears and Phobias*, New York: Academic Press.

Marks, I. (1978) *Living with Fear*, New York: McGraw-Hill.

Marks, I. (1987) *Fears, Phobias and Rituals*, New York: Oxford University Press.

Marks, I.M., O'Dwyer, A.M., Meehan, O., McGuire, P., Greisht, J., & Baer, L. (2000) Subjective imagery in obsessive-compulsive disorder before and after exposure therapy: Pilot randomised controlled trial, *British Journal of Psychiatry*, 176, 387–391.

Marlatt, G.A. (1994) Addiction and acceptance. In S.C. Hayes, N.S. Jacobson, V.M. Follette, & M.J. Dougher (eds.), *Acceptance and Change: Content and Context in Psychotherapy*, Reno, NY: Context Press, pp. 175–197.

Mash, E. & Terdal, L.G. (1988) Behavioral assessment of child and family disturbance. In E.J. Mash & L.G. Terdal (eds.), *Behavioral Assessment of Childhood Disorders*, 2nd edn, New York: Guilford, pp. 3–65.

Mason, R. (2007) Working with abused children and adolescents. In T. Ronen & A. Freeman (eds.), *Cognitive Behavior Therapy in Clinical Social Work Practice*, New York: Springer, pp. 235–260.

May, R. (1975) *The Courage to Create*, New York: Norton.

McGinnis, E. & Goldstein, A. (1997) *Skillstreaming the Elementary School Child*, Champaign, IL: Research Press.

McKellar, P. (1957) *Imagination and Thinking*, London: Cohen & West.

References

McNally, N.R., Bryant, R.A., & Ehlers, A. (2003) Does early psychological intervention promote recovery from posttraumatic stress? *Psychological Science in the Public Interest*, Nov. 4, 45–79.

McNiff, S. (1992) *Art as Medicine: Creating Therapy of the Imagination*, London: Butler & Tranner.

Meichenbaum, D.H. (1979) Teaching children self-control. In B. Lahey & A. Kazdin (eds.), *Advances in Clinical Child Psychology*, Vol. 2, New York: Plenum, pp. 1–30.

Meichenbaum, D.H. (1985) *Stress Inoculation Training*, New York: Pergamon.

Merriam-Webster, G.C. (1965) *Webster's Seventh New Collegiate Dictionary*, Springfield, MA: Author.

Meyer, V. (1966) Modifications of expectations in case with obsessional rituals, *Behaviour Research and Therapy*, 4, 273–280.

Mischel, W. (1973) Toward a cognitive social learning reconceptualization of personality, *Psychological Review*, 80, 252–283.

Mogotsi, M., Kaminer, D., & Stein, D.J. (2000) Quality of life in the anxiety disorders, *Harvard Review of Psychiatry*, 8, 273–282.

Moore, E.K. & Watson, J.C. (1999) *Expressing Emotion: Myths, Realities and Therapeutic Strategies*, New York: Guilford.

Moreno, J.L. (1972) *Psychodrama*, New York: Beacon House.

Natvig, G.K., Albrektsen, G., & Qvarnstrom, U. (2003) Methods of teaching and class participation in relation to perceived social support and stress: Modifiable factors for improving health and wellbeing among students, *Educational Psychology*, 23, 261–274.

Neimeyer, R.A. (1995) Constructivist psychotherapies: Features, foundations, and future directions. In R.A. Neimeyer & M.J. Mahoney (eds.), *Constructivism in Psychotherapy*, Washington, DC: American Psychological Association, pp. 11–38.

Neimeyer, R.A. (2009) *Constructivist Psychotherapy*, Hove: Routledge/Taylor & Francis.

Neimeyer, R.A. & Mahoney, J.M. (1995) *Constructivism in Psychotherapy*, Washington, DC: American Psychological Association.

Neimeyer, R.A. & Raskin, J. (eds) (2000) *Constructions of Disorder: Meaning-making Frameworks for Psychotherapy*, Washington, DC: American Psychological Association.

Newell, M. (Director) & Heyman, D. (Producer) (2005) *Harry Potter and the Goblet of Fire* [motion picture], Hollywood, CA: Heyday Films.

Niven, D. (2000) *Happy People: What Scientists Have Learned and How You Can Use It*, New York: HarperCollins.

Norcross, J.C. (2005) The psychotherapists' own psychotherapy: Educating and developing psychologists, *American Psychologist*, 60, 840–850.

Norcross, J.C., Strausser-Kirtland, D., & Missar, C.D. (1988) The processes and outcomes of psychotherapists' personal treatment experiences, *Psychotherapy*, 25, 36–43.

Oller, D., Cobo-Lewis, A., & Eilers, R. (1998) Phonological translation in bilingual and monolingual children, *Applied Psycholinguistics*, 19, 259–278.

Otto, W. (2000) Stories and metaphors in cognitive-behavior therapy, *Cognitive and Behavioral Practice*, 7, 166–172.

Palmer, S.E., Brown, R.A., Rae-Grant, N.I., & Loughlin, M.J. (2001) Survivors of childhood abuse: Their reported experienced with professional help, *Social Work: Journal of the National Association of Social Workers*, 46, 136–145.

Paul, G.L. (1967) Outcome research in psychotherapy, *Journal of Consulting Psychology*, 31, 109–118.

References

Paul, R.J. (1993) *Critical Thinking: What Every Person Needs to Survive in a Rapidly Changing World*, 3rd edn, Sonoma, CA: Foundation for Critical Thinking.

Pavlov, I.P. (1927) *Conditioning Reflexes* (trans. G.V. Anrep), New York: Liveright.

Perls, F.S. (1969) *Gestalt Therapy Verbatim*, Moab, UT: Real People Press.

Peterson, C. (2000) The future of optimism, *American Psychologist*, 55(1), 44–55.

Pettletier, A.M. (1979) Three uses of guided imagery in hypnosis, *American Journal of Clinical Hypnosis*, 22, 32–36.

Piaget, J. (1969) *The Child's Conception of Time* (trans. A. J. Pomerans), London: Routledge.

Piaget, J. (1977) *The Development of Thought: Equilibrium of Cognitive Structures*, New York: Viking.

Pink, D.H. (2005) *A Whole New Mind: Moving from the Information Age into the Conceptual Age*, New York: Riverhead.

Powell, M.B. & Oei, T.P.S. (1991) Cognitive processes underlying the behavior change in cognitive behaviour therapy with childhood disorders: A review of experimental evidence, *Behavioural Psychotherapy*, 19, 247–265.

Power, M. & Dalgleish, T. (1997) *Cognition and Emotion: From Order to Disorder*, Hove and New York: Taylor & Francis.

Raskin, J.D. (2002) Constructivism in psychology: Personal construct psychology, radical constructivism, and social constructionism. In J.D. Raskin & S.K. Bridges (eds.), *Studies in Meaning: Exploring Constructivist Psychology*, New York: Pace University Press, pp. 1–25.

Raviv, A., Keinan, G., Abazon, Y., & Raviv, A. (1990) Moving as a stressful life event for adolescents, *Journal of Community Psychology*, 18, 130–140.

Richardson, A. (1969) *Mental Imagery*, London: Routledge & Kegan Paul.

Riordan, R. (2009) *Percy Jackson and the Last Olympian*, New York: Puffin.

Rode, S., Salkovskis, P.M., & Jack, T. (2001) An experimental study of attention, labelling and memory in people suffering from chronic pain, *Pain*, 94(2), 193–203.

Rodgers, R. & Hammerstein II, O. (1949) *South Pacific* [Broadway musical], New York: Majestic Theatre.

Ronen, T. (1993) Decision making about children's therapy, *Child Psychiatry and Human Development*, 23, 259–272.

Ronen, T. (1997) *Cognitive Developmental Therapy with Children*, Chichester: John Wiley & Sons, Ltd.

Ronen, T. (1998a) Direct clinical work with children. In K. Cigno & D. Bourn (eds.), *Cognitive-Behavioural Social Work in Practice*, Aldershot: Ashgate/Arena, pp. 39–59.

Ronen, T. (1998b) Linking developmental and emotional elements into child and family cognitive-behavioural therapy. In P. Graham (ed.), *Cognitive-Behaviour Therapy for Children and Families*, Cambridge: Cambridge Press, pp. 1–17.

Ronen, T. (2003a) Client self-assessment of therapy process in the treatment of anorexia, *Journal of Constructivist Psychology*, 16, 49–74.

Ronen, T. (2003b) *Cognitive Constructivist Psychotherapy with Children and Adolescents*, New York: Kluwer/Plenum.

Ronen, T. (2004) Imparting self-control skills to decrease aggressive behavior in a 12-year-old boy: A case study, *Journal of Social Work*, 4, 269–288.

Ronen, T. (2006) Cognitive behavior therapy with children: Skills directed therapy (Invited paper), *Hellenic Journal of Psychology*, 3, 1–22.

Ronen, T. (2007) CBT with children and adolescents. In T. Ronen & A. Freeman (eds.), *Cognitive Behavior Therapy in Clinical Social Work Practice*, New York: Springer, pp. 189–211.

Ronen, T. (2008) Cognitive-behavioural therapy. In M. Davies (ed.), *The Blackwell Companion to Social Work*, 3rd edn, Oxford: Blackwell, pp. 193–203.

Ronen, T. & Ayelet (2001) *In and Out of Anorexia: The Story of the Client, the Therapist and the Process of Recovery*, London: Jessica Kingsley.

Ronen, T. & Dweik, A. (2009) The relationship between subjective well-being, self-control, and aggression among adolescents, *Violence*, 2, 41–70 (Hebrew).

Ronen, T. & Rosenbaum, M. (1998) Beyond verbal instruction in cognitive behavioural supervision, *Cognitive & Behavioural Practice*, 3, 3-19.

Ronen, T. & Rosenbaum, M. (2001) Helping children to help themselves: A case study of enuresis and nail biting, *Research on Social Work Practice*, 11, 338–356.

Ronen, T. & Rosenbaum, M. (2010) Developing learned resourcefulness in adolescents to help them reduce their aggressive behavior: Preliminary findings, *Research on Social Work Practice*, 20, 410–426.

Ronen, T. & Seeman, A. (2007) Subjective well-being of adolescents in boarding schools under threat of war, *Journal of Traumatic Stress*, 20, 1053–1062.

Ronen, T., Wozner, Y., & Rahav, G. (1992) Cognitive intervention in enuresis, *Child and Family Behavior Therapy*, 14(2), 1–14.

Rosenbaum, M. (1990) The role of learned resourcefulness in self-control of health behavior. In M. Rosenbaum (ed.), *Learned Resourcefulness: On Coping Skills, Self-Control and Adaptive Behavior*, New York: Springer, pp. 3–30.

Rosenbaum, M. (1998a) Learned resourcefulness, stress, and self-regulation. In S. Fisher & J. Reason (eds.), *Handbook of Life Stress, Cognition and Health*, Chichester: John Wiley & Sons, Ltd, pp. 483–496.

Rosenbaum, M. (1998b) Opening versus closing strategies in controlling one's responses to experience. In M. Kofta, G. Weary, & G. Sedek (eds.), *Personal Control in Action: Cognitive and Motivational Mechanisms*, New York: Plenum, pp. 61–84.

Rosenbaum, M. (2000) The self-regulation of experience: Openness and construction. In P. Dewe, A.M. Leiter, & T. Cox (eds.), *Coping and Health and Organizations*, London: Taylor & Francis, pp. 51–67.

Rosenbaum, M. & Ronen, T. (1998) Clinical supervision from the standpoint of cognitive-behavior therapy, *Psychotherapy*, 35, 220–229.

Rosner, R. (1997) Cognitive therapy, constructivism, and dreams: A critical review, *Journal of Constructivist Psychology*, 10(3), 249–273.

Rosner, R.I., Lyddon, W.J., & Freeman, A. (eds.) (2004) *Cognitive Therapy and Dreams*, New York: Springer.

Rothenberg, A. (1988) *The Creative Process in Psychotherapy*, New York: W.W. Norton.

Rowling, J.K. (1997) *Harry Potter and the Philosopher's Stone*, London: Bloomsbury.

Rowling, J.K. (2000) *Harry Potter and the Goblet of Fire*, London: Bloomsbury.

Rowling, J.K. (2007) *Harry Potter and the Deathly Hallows*, London: Bloomsbury.

Russell, A. (1991) Culture and the categorization of emotions, *Psychological Bulletin*, 110(3), 426–450.

Ryff, C.D. (1989) Happiness is everything, or is it? Explorations on the meaning of psychological well being, *Journal of Personality and Social Psychology*, 57(6), 1069–1081.

Ryff, C.D. & Keyes, C.L.M. (1995) The structure of psychological well being revisited, *Personality & Social Psychology*, 69(4), 717–729.

References

Safran, J.D. & Segal, Z.V. (1990) *Interpersonal Process in Cognitive Therapy*, New York: Basic Books.

Sahler, O.J.Z. & McAnarney, E.R. (1981) *The Child from Three to Eighteen*, London: Mosby.

Salkovskis, P.M. (ed.) (1996a) *Frontiers of Cognitive Therapy*, New York: Guilford.

Salkovskis, P.M. (ed.) (1996b) *Trends in Cognitive Therapy and Behavioral Therapies*, New York: John Wiley & Sons, Inc.

Salkovskis, P.M. (1999) Understanding and treating obsessive-compulsive disorder, *Behaviour Research and Therapy*, 37, 29–52.

Salkovskis, P.M. (2008) Cognitive behaviour therapy: Contradicting the poison of stigma and prejudice. In D.C.K. Lam (eds.), Cognitive *Behaviour Therapy: A Practical Guide to Helping People Take Control*, Hove: Routledge, pp. x–xv.

Salkovskis, P.M., Clark, D.M., Hackmann, A., Wells, A., & Gelder, M.G. (1999) An experimental investigation of the role of safety-seeking behaviors in the maintenance of panic disorder with agoraphobia, *Behavior Research & Therapy*, 37(6), 559–574.

Samoilov, A. & Goldfried, M. (2000) Role of emotion in cognitive-behavior therapy, *Clinical Psychology: Science and Practice*, 7(4), 373–385.

Sarason, B.R., Sarason, I.G., & Pierce, G.R. (1990) *Social Support: An Interactional View*, New York: John Wiley & Sons, Inc.

Schaefer, C. (1999) *Innovative Psychotherapy Techniques in Child and Adolescent Therapy*, 2nd edn, New York: John Wiley & Sons, Inc.

Schaffer, H.R. (1990) *Making Decisions about Children: Psychology Questions and Answers*, Oxford: Basil Blackwell.

Segal, Z.V., Williams, J.M.G., & Teasdale, J.D. (2002) *Mindfulness-Based Cognitive Therapy for Depression: A New Approach to Preventing Relapses*, New York: Guilford.

Seligman, M.E.P. (1999) The president's address, *American Psychologist*, 54, 559–562.

Seligman, M.E.P. (2002) *Authentic Happiness*, New York: Free Press.

Seligman, M.E.P. & Csikszentmihalyi, M. (2000) Positive psychology: An introduction, *American Psychologist*, 55, 5–14.

Seligman, M.E.P, Rashid, T., & Parks, A.C. (2006) Positive psychotherapy, *American Psychology*, 61, 774–788.

Seligman, M.E.P., Steen, T.A., Park, N., & Peterson, C. (2005) Positive psychology progress: Empirical validation of interventions, *American Psychologist*, 60, 410–421.

Shear, M.K., Frank, E., Foa, E., Cherry, C., Charles, C., Reynolds, C.F., Vanderbilt, J., & Masters, S. (2001) Traumatic grief treatment: A pilot study, *American Journal of Psychiatry*, 158, 1506–1508.

Sheldon, B. (1987) Implementing findings from social work effectiveness research, *British Journal of Social Work*, 17, 573–586.

Sheldon, K.M. & King, L. (2001) Why positive psychology is necessary, *American Psychologist*, 56, 216–217.

Shirk, S.R. & Russell, R.L. (1996) *Change Process in Child Psychotherapy*, New York: Guilford.

Shmotkin, D. & Lomranz, J. (1998) Subjective well-being among holocaust survivors: An examination of overlooked differentiations, *Journal of Personality and Social Psychology*, 75, 141–155.

Shorr, J. (1974) *Psychotherapy through Imagery*, New York: Intercontinental Medical Book.

Singer, J.L. (2006) *Imagery in Psychotherapy*, Washington, DC: American Psychological Association.

Skinner, B.F. (1938) *The Behavior of Organism*, New York: Appleton-Century-Crofts.

References

Snunit, M. (1985) *The Soul Bird*, Givatayim, Israel: Massada.

Snyder, C.R., Sympson, S.C., Ybasco, F.C., Borders, T.F., Babyak, M.A., & Higgins, R.L. (1996) Development and validation of the state hope scale, *Journal of Personality and Social Psychology*, 70, 321–335.

Southam-Gerow, M.A. & Kendall, P.C. (2000) Cognitive-behavior therapy with youth: Advances, challenges and future directions, *Clinical Psychology and Psychotherapy*, 7, 343–366.

Stevanovic, C.P. & Rupert, P.A. (2004) Career sustaining behaviors, satisfactions, and stresses of professional psychologists, *Psychotherapy*, 41, 301–309.

Stewart, R.E. & Chambless, D.L. (2009) Cognitive-behavioral therapy for adult anxiety disorders in clinical practice: A meta-analysis of effectiveness studies, *Journal of Consulting and Clinical Psychology*, 77(4), 595–606.

Stott, R., Mansell, W., Salkovskis, P., Lavender, A., & Cartwright-Hatton, S. (2010) *Oxford Guide to Metaphors in CBT: Building Cognitive Bridges*, Oxford: Oxford University Press.

Stuart, G.L., Treat, T.A., & Wade, W.A. (2000) Effectiveness of an empirically based treatment for panic disorder delivered in a service clinic setting: 1-year follow-up, *Journal of Consulting and Clinical Psychology*, 68, 506–512.

Swell, K.W. (1996) Constructional risk factors for post-traumatic stress response after a mass murder, *Journal of Constructivist Psychology*, 9, 97–107.

Teasdale, J.D. (1993) Emotion and two kinds of meaning: Cognitive therapy and applied cognitive science, *Behaviour Research and Therapy*, 31, 339–354.

Terwogt, M.M. & Olthof, T. (1989) Awareness and self-regulation of emotion in young children. In C. Saarni & P.L. Harris (eds.), *Children's Understanding of Emotion*, New York: Cambridge University Press, pp. 209–237.

Thelen, E. (1993) Self-organization in developmental processes: Can systems approach work? In M.H. Johnson (ed.), *Brain Development and Cognition*, Cambridge, MA: Blackwell, pp. 555–592.

Thompson, R.A. (1989) Causal attributions and children's emotional understanding. In C. Saarni & P.L. Harris (eds.), *Children's Understanding of Emotion*, New York: Cambridge University Press, pp. 117–150.

Thyer, B. & Kazi, M.A.F. (eds.) (2004) *International Perspectives on Evidence-based Practice in Social Work*, Birmingham: Venture Press.

Tiger, L. (1979) *Optimism: The Biology of Hope*, New York: Simon & Schuster.

Torrance, E.P. (1974) *Torrance Tests of Creative Thinking*, Princeton, NJ: Personnel Press.

Vasta, R., Haith, M.M., & Miller, S.A. (1995) *Child Development*, 2nd edn, New York: John Wiley & Sons, Inc.

Veenhoven, R. (1991) Question on happiness: Classical topics, modern answers, blind spots. In F. Strack, M. Argyle, & N. Schwarz (eds.), *Subjective Well-being: An Interdisciplinary Perspective*, Oxford: Pergamon, pp. 7–26.

Vygotsky, L. (1962) *Thought and Language*, New York: John Wiley & Sons, Inc.

Wade, W.A., Treat, T.A., & Stuart, G.L. (1998) Transporting an empirically supported treatment for panic disorder to a service clinic setting: A benchmarking strategy, *Journal of Consulting and Clinical Psychology*, 66, 231–239.

Waldman, I.D. (1996) Aggressive boys' hostile perceptual and response biases: The role of attention and impulsivity, *Child Development*, 67, 1015–1033.

Wallas, G. & Smith, R. (1926) *Art of Thought*, New York: Harcourt Brace.

References

Walsh, B. (Producer) & Stevenson, R. (Director) (1997) *Mary Poppins* [video film] Holly-wood, CA: Walt Disney.

Ward, T. (2003) Creativity. In L. Nagel (ed.), *Encyclopedia of Cognition*, New York: Macmillan, http://www.newworldencyclopedia.org/entry/Creativity.

Watson, D., Clark, L.A., & Tellegen, A. (1988) Development and validation of brief measures of positive and negative affect: The PANAS scales, *Journal of Personality and Social Psychology*, 54, 1063–1070.

Webster-Stratton, C. (1993) Strategies for helping early school-aged children with oppositional defiant and conduct disorders: The importance of home–school partnerships, *School Psychology Review*, 22, 437–457.

Webster-Stratton, C. (1994) *Trouble Families – Problem Children. Working with Parents: A Collaborative Process*, Chichester: John Wiley & Sons, Ltd.

Weisberg, R.W. (1993) *Creativity: Beyond the Myth of Genius*, New York: Freeman.

Weisz, J.R., Southam-Gerow, M.A., Gordis, E.B., Connor-Smith, J.K., Chu, B.C., Langer, D.A., McLeod, B.D., Jensen-Doss, A., Updegraff, A., & Weiss, B. (2009) Cognitive–behavioral therapy versus usual clinical care for youth depression: An initial test of transportability to community clinics and clinicians, *Journal of Consulting and Clinical Psychology*, 77(3), 383–396.

Wells, A. (2000) *Emotional Disorders and Metacognition: Innovative Cognitive Therapy*, Chichester: John Wiley & Sons, Ltd.

White, B. (2007) Working with adult survivors of sexual and physical abuse. In T. Ronen & A. Freeman (eds.), *Cognitive Behavior Therapy in Clinical Social Work Practice*, New York: Springer, pp. 467–489.

Wikipedia (2009a, March) *Creativity*, retrieved from http://en.wikipedia.org/wiki/Creativity.

Wikipedia (2009b, March) *Linus Pauling*, retrieved from http://en.wikipedia.org/wiki/Linus Pauling.

Wilson, P.H. & Thomas, P.R. (2002) Motor imagery training ameliorates motor clumsiness in children, *Journal of Child Neurology*, 17, 491–498.

Winefield, J.R., Winefield, A.H., & Tiggemann, M. (1992) Social support and psychological well-being in young adults: The multi-dimensional support scale, *Journal of Personality Assessment*, 58, 198–210.

Winnicott, D.W. (1971) *Playing and Reality*, London: Routledge.

Wolpe, J. (1958) *Psychotherapy by Reciprocal Inhibition*, Stanford, CA: University Press.

Wolpe, J. (1982) *The Practice of Behavior Therapy*, 3rd edn, New York: Pergamon.

Wright, B.A. & Lopez, S.J. (2002) Widening the diagnostic focus: A case for including human strengths and environmental resources. In C.R. Snyder & S.J. Lopez (eds.), *The Handbook of Positive Psychology*, New York: Oxford University Press, pp. 26–44.

Yalom, I.D. (1992) *When Nietzsche Wept*, New York: Basic Books.

Yanai, Y. (1971) *A Voice Says Call*, Tel-Aviv: Alef (Hebrew).

Zimmerman, B.J. (1998) Developing self-fulfilling cycles of academic regulation: An analysis of exemplary instructional models. In D.H. Schunck & B.J. Zimmerman (eds.), *Self-Regulated Learning: From Teaching to Self-Reflective Practice*, New York: Guilford, pp. 1–19.

Zohar, D. & Marshall, I. (2000) *Spiritual Intelligence: The Ultimate Intelligence*, London: Bloomsbury.

Index

Abraham, Dr Yair 5, 6
abuse 175–6, 210–11, 215, 231–3
active memory 98
adolescents
  CBT techniques 80
  image therapy with 271–4
  relaxation techniques 170, 177
  SDT model reducing aggression 33–4
  self-control skills 8, 46–7
  use of ladder metaphor with 7–8
age as a mediator in child therapy 79–80
aggressive behavior, overcoming 269–71
Alford, B.A. 34, 109, 117, 130, 135, 142
Allian, G.B. 130
anger
  and assertiveness 247–9
  and automatic thoughts 231–3
  metaphors for 124
  for past abuse 210
  physical signs of, identifying 270
  relaxation reducing 142
  warning signs to manage 229–30, 254
anorexic client 9, 41, 99, 220, 222–4, 245,
  273
antisocial behavior, relaxation for 170
anxiety disorders
  in children 76, 127–8, 170, 171–2
  efficacy of CBT for 31, 108, 199
  exposure therapy for 240–2
  increasing awareness to reduce 227–8
  using metaphors to treat 126–7
  see also test anxiety

Assagioli, R. 91
assertiveness skills 247–50
assessment and awareness skills 217–18
  changing automatic thoughts 231–4
  internal stimuli, increasing awareness of
    227–31
  relationship assessment 221–7
  self-assessment 218–21
  therapist guidelines 234
assessment in CBT 25–7
  in different treatment phases 184–5
  integration of imagery into 181–4
  targets for conducting 186–95
    guidelines for main questions
      195–7
Attwood, T. 174
autogenic relaxation 143
automatic thoughts 19
  helping clients change 77, 231–4
  self-control training 20, 33
avoidant behaviors 202–3
awareness
  attentional focus, SDT model 33
  of automatic thoughts 231–3
  of internal stimuli 227–31
  and mindfulness 23–4

Bandura, A. 18
Barlow, D.H. 142
Barron, F. 65
Battino, R. 96, 98, 99, 100, 119, 163
bear story 126–7

The Positive Power of Imagery: Harnessing Client Imagination in CBT and Related Therapies,
First Edition. Tammie Ronen. © 2011 Tammie Ronen. Published 2011 by John Wiley & Sons, Ltd.

Beck, A.T. 18–19, 31, 34, 96, 109, 117
  on metaphors 125–6, 130, 135
  posttraumatic stress disorder 199–200
  on relaxation 142
behavioral therapy 15
  Bandura's work 17–18
  integration with cognitive therapy 18–20
  traditional 17
Ben-Shahar, T. 59
Bikes, D.H. 278
Biswas-Diener, R. 43, 47
Bogart, G. 24
borderline personality disorder 31
Boyll, S. 109
Brown, G.K. 31
Burke, J.D. 170
Burns, G.W. 130

car accidents, case studies 201–2, 211–13
Carlsen, M.B. 64, 68
children 169
  childhood abuse 175–6, 210–11, 215
  childhood disorders
    applying relaxation to 169–70
    characteristics of 75–6
  childhood image/memory, retrieving 121–2
  developmental CBT with 73
    applying 77–8
    developmental components 78–85
    differences from adult CBT 76–7
    therapist guidelines 85–7
    guidelines and case studies 263–4
    children in middle childhood 267–71
    treating adolescents 271–4
    treating young children 264–7
  imagery techniques with 174–6, 178
  metaphors aiding therapy with 127–9
  relaxation techniques, adapting for 170–4, 177–8
  unique developmental nature 73–5
Clark, D.M. 142
client preparation 150
cognitive-behavioral therapy (CBT)
  basic view underlying 15–17
  constructivism 21–2
  guidelines for developing client's profile 34–5
  integration with behavioral therapies 18–20

  major tenets and processes 24–5
  assessment in CBT 25–7
  efficacy of intervention 30–2
  relationship with client 29
  rules for supervising therapists 29–30
  techniques 28–9
  therapeutic process and setting 27–8
  mindfulness 22–4
  self-control models 20
  skills-directed therapy 32–4
  traditional behavioral therapy 17
    transition to an approach integrating cognitive therapy 17–18
  see also developmental CBT with children
cognitive development 78–9
cognitive mediation 19–20
cognitive restructuring
  of past traumatic events 210–14
  skills-directed therapy (SDT) 32–3
Cohen, G. 59
concrete versus symbolic imagery 98–9
conditioning 17
constructivism 21–2
  use of metaphors 130–1
convergent thinking 58
coping in the present 235
  assertiveness skills 247–50
  improving social relationships 243–4
  initiating social contacts 244–6
  performance and test anxiety 236
    execution phase 238–43
    preparation phase 236–8
  summary 250
coping skills, facilitating new through imagery 159–60
Crampton, M. 121
Craw, M.J. 130
creativity 10–12
  characteristics of creative people 65–6
  definitions of 55–6, 57–9
  and emotion 60–1
  guidelines for activating 72
  and intelligence/creative genius 62–3
  promoting creative action 63–4
  techniques to facilitate therapist 70–1
  within therapy 56–7, 66–9
    noncreative imagery 69–70
Csikszentmihalyi, Mihalyi 38, 59, 63, 65, 71, 199, 251

Dalai Lama 42
Dalgleish, T. 82–3
Danaher, B.G. 182
dangers of imagery therapy 119–20, 294–5
Daubman, K.A. 60
Davies, D. 85
Dean, B. 43, 47
deep muscle relaxation 143–7
depression
  in adolescents 271–2
  Beck's work on 19
  and creativity 60
  efficacy of CBT for 31
  use of positive thinking 39–40
desensitization 69–70, 108, 141
developmental CBT with children 73
  applying 77–8
  childhood disorders 75–6
  developmental components 78
    age 79–80
    cognitive components 78–9
    emotional development 82–4
    family 84–5
    gender 80–1
    information processing 81–2
    language acquisition 82
    social development 84
  differences from CBT with adults 76–7
  therapist guidelines 85–7
  unique nature of children 73–5
divergent thinking 58
Dodge, K.A. 81
Doyle, M.C. 96
dreams 96, 97
Durlak, J.A. 76

efficacy of CBT intervention 30–2
Ellis, Albert 18–19, 109, 248
Emery, G. 200
emotional development 82–4
emotions
  assessment of 187–90, 196
  and constructivism 22
  constructivist therapy for exploring 50
  facilitating positive 255–9
  and metaphors 124–5
  using imagery to access 111–14
Erickson, Milton 117
Essau, C.A. 170
evidence-based practice 291–4

exposure therapy
  for anxiety in children 170
  gradual exposure 240–2
  imagery exposure followed by *in vivo* 201–4
  through imagery alone 204–7
externalizing problems, childhood disorders 75

familial components, child CBT 84–5
fear 199
  of getting lost 127–8
  gradual exposure to 240–2
  of television character 171–2
  of wind 128–9, 266–7
Feldman, D.H. 62
Finn, S.E. 185
Foa, E.B. 31, 114, 142, 200, 293
Follette, V.M. 23, 24, 142
Fonagy, P. 169–70
forgetting past events, skills for therapists 281–2
Fox, C. 292
Frankl, V. 117, 251, 291
Fredrickson, B.L. 39, 41–2, 45–6, 109, 253, 262
Freeman, A. 109
Freud, S. 129–30, 135
Friedberg, R.D. 130, 170, 171
Friedman, M.J. 142, 200, 293
Fuhrman, T. 76
the future
  developing positive view of 251–3
  helping clients plan for 253–5
  jumping to the future, imagery technique 259–60
future therapy, skills for planning 285–6

Gable, S.L. 41
Gambrill, E. 30, 244
gender as a mediator in child therapy 80–1
genetics, creativity and intelligence 62–3
genius view of creativity 62
Gestalt therapy 108
Gilbert, D. 43, 49, 109
Goldman, N. 22, 228
gratitude, expressing 52–3, 253, 261
Grave, J. 76
Greenberg, L.S. 22, 141, 200, 228

group therapy, relationship assessment
224–5
guided imagery 99–100, 108, 117
  for accessing emotions 113–14, 152
  efficacy of 292–3
Guilford, J.P. 58
guilt feelings
  following fatal road accident 210–13
  and parental abuse 207–9

Haidt, J. 41
Hall, E. 96, 294
happiness
  exercises for increasing 49
  five "hows" for happiness exercises 47–9
  increasing happy relationships 259–62
  metaphor about 37
  and positive psychology 42–4
  self-help skills for therapists 286–7
happy people, characteristics of 43–4
Harry Potter books/films 50, 96, 97, 125,
  187–8
Hayes, S.C. 23, 24, 131, 135, 142
Hearst-Ikeda, D. 200
Heinschel, J.A. 292
Holmes, J. 123
homework assignments 165–6
hope, definitions of 251–2
House, J.S. 221
How of Happiness, The (Lyubomirsky) 49
Hume, D. 92
humor, use of 242–3
Hurwich, C. 65
hypnotherapy 107–8, 117

imagery 11–12, 91, 95–6, 103–4
  historical uses of 94–5
  integration into assessment 181–4
  kinds of imagery 96–100
  major concepts 91–3
  and memory 93–4
  pros and cons of working with 100–3
  techniques for use with children 174–6
  therapist guidelines for increasing 103–5
imagery in psychotherapy 107
  basic guidelines 149
    assigning homework 165–6
    bringing up images and describing
      them 154–9
    ending imagery work phase 160–2

facilitating new coping skills through
  imagery 159–60
followup to imagery work 163–4
pre-imagery exercises in eliciting
  images 151–3
pre-imagery practice of client
  relaxation 153–4
preparation of therapist, setting, and
  client 149–50
therapist guidelines 166–7
client problems applied to 109–10
dangers of working with 119–20
guidelines for fostering 121–2
major benefits of 111–18
overcoming resistance to 110–11
role of 290–1
types of therapies that use 107–8
imagery to treat past events 199
  cognitive restructuring of past trauma
    210–14
  eliciting memories and forgotten
    material 207–10
  imaginal exposure followed by *in vivo*
    exposure 201–4
  imaginal exposure instead of *in vivo*
    exposure 204–7
  options, guidelines for choosing between
    214–15
  treating PTSD 199–201
induction in hypnosis 108
information processing models 81–2
internalizing problems, childhood
  disorders 74–5
interpretation, follow-up 164
in vivo exposure
  imaginal exposure instead of
    204–7
  imaginal exposure prior to 108,
    201–4
  interpersonal skills 261
  social skills training 244–6
irrational thinking 18–19
Isen, A.M. 60

Jacobson, E. 143–4
job interviews, coping with 239–40
Johnson, M. 125
Joseph, S. 38
Joyce, J. 28
Jung, C.G. 94

Index

Kabat-Zinn, J. 23, 24, 227
Kanfer, F.H. 29–30
Kazdin, A.E. 75, 170, 175
Keane, T.M. 142, 200, 293
Kendall, P.C. 75–6
Keyes, C.L. 30, 43, 45, 184
King, L. 41
Kolcaba, K. 292
Koons, C.R. 227
Kopp, R.R. 126, 128, 130, 132
Kovecses, Z. 124–5

Lackoff, G 125
Lampman, C. 76
"Land of I'm Sorry" exercise 281–2
"Land of Sorrow" exercise 48, 189
"Land I Wish" exercise 256–7
Lang, P. 91, 107, 293
language acquisition 82
Layard, R. 60
Lazarus, A. 92–3, 94, 97, 103, 125, 263
LeClerc, G. 65
LeCroy, C.W. 244
Lemieux, C.A. 130
Levitt, E.E. 73–4
Lietaer, G. 141
limitations of imagery therapy
    evidence base for 291–4
    importance of therapist expertise 294–5
    necessity of ending sessions positively
        119
    obstacles 100–3
    with psychotic patients 120
Linehan, M.M. 23, 24, 142, 227
Linley, P.A. 38
Lopez, S.J. 47
Ludwig, A. 60
Luria, A.R. 82
Lyubomirsky, S. 43–4, 47–9

Magaletta, P.R. 252
Mahoney, Michael 12, 30, 58, 116, 277
    creative psychotherapy 68, 69
    meditation and imagery 141, 182
    on metaphors 130–1
    "The Pilgrim in Process" poem 295–6
    pretreatment client contact 185
Mannix, L.K. 292
marital therapy 225–7
Markova, D. 64

Marks, I.M. 26, 292
Marlatt, G.A. 141
Marshall, I. 92
Mason, R. 170
May, R. 65
McClure, J.M. 130, 170, 171
McNiff, S. 68
meaning
    attributed to imagery 164
    searching for 117–18
mediated vs. automatic thoughts 19, 20,
        33, 213–14, 233
meditation 140–1
Meichenbaum, D.H. 109
memories
    active 98
    eliciting/working through 114–15,
        207–10
    multiple factors influencing 93–4
    real and fantasized 152–3
    retrieving childhood 121–2
    therapist practice for eliciting own
        104–5
    use of imagery to recall test material
        236–8
mental imagery 96–7
metaphor therapy 131
metaphors 123–4
    for child therapy 74, 77, 81
    client-generated 132–3
    dreams and ladders 7–8
    and emotions 124–5
    happiness and positivity 37, 42
    limitations of using 135
    for meditation 140–1
    therapeutic role of 125
        as a natural language 125–6
        along the therapy phases 129
        applied to different therapeutic
            orientations 129–31
        as therapy's routine or main tool
            127–9
        to express specific ideas 126–7
    therapist-generated 133–4
    therapist guidelines 135
middle childhood, case studies
        267–71
mind-body connections, using imagery to
        find 117
mindfulness 22–4

mirrors
  in fictional literature 50, 125, 132
  therapeutic use of 50, 209, 220, 229
Mischel, W. 82
mood disorders 39–40
Moore, E.K. 142
Moreno, J.L. 108
mothers of at-risk children, group therapy
  224–5
motivations of client, assessment of 190–2,
  196
mourning 113, 208
muscle relaxation 143–7

negative affects 33, 39–40, 44, 45–6
negative thoughts 38–9, 42, 46, 200, 231,
  233
Neimeyer, R.A. 15, 21–2, 125, 182, 184,
  186, 254–5
Nietzsche technique, assertiveness
  248–9
Niven, D. 45
noncreative imagery in therapy 69–70
Norcross, J.C. 278
Nowicki, G.P. 60

obstacles arising during therapy 100–2
Oliver, J.M. 252
ongoing assessment of therapy 25, 26, 185,
  193–4, 197
optimism
  definitions of 251–2
  future planning 253–5
  practice aimed at developing 255

pacing clients, importance of 119, 158–9
past events
  forgetting, skills for therapists 281–2
  using imagery to treat traumatic
  199–215
Pauling, Linus 64
performance anxiety, skills for coping with
  236
  execution phase 238–9
    eliciting positive images 239–40
    gradual exposure to feared situation
    240–2
    using humor and role reversal 242–3
  preparation phase, use of visualization
  236–8

Perry, K.J. 200
Peterson, C. 252
Pettletier, A.M. 108
phobias 171–2
physical abuse 231–3
physical health, imagery therapy helping
  117
Piaget, J. 21, 78–9
Pink, D.H. 60
pleasure, fostering through imagery 118
positive emotions 255–9
positive psychology
  a recognized theory and therapy 38
  on being a positive therapist 37–8
  defining 41–2
  guidelines for applying 51–3
  and happiness 42–4
  positive view of clients and therapeutic
    processes 38–41
  subjective wellbeing 44–7
  training in 47–51
positive qualities as a therapist, focusing on
  282–5
positive thinking 30, 118
positivity 41
  facilitating positive emotions and
    sensations 255–9
  increasing relationship 259–62
  self-help skills for therapists 286–7
  skills for developing 251–5
Positivity (Fredrickson) 39
posttraumatic stress disorder (PTSD) 31,
  40, 114–15, 199–201
  combat trauma, treating with imaginal
    exposure 204–5
  preliminary imaginal exposure for
    treating 201–4
Power, M. 82–3
pre-imagery practice of client relaxation
  153–4
pretreatment phase of therapy, assessment
  184–5
problems
  analysis of, SDT model 33
  childhood 75
  of client, assessment of 186–7, 195
  finding flexible solutions to 116–17
process imagery 99
profile of client, guidelines for developing
  34–5

progress, ongoing assessment of 185,
193–4, 197
progressive muscle relaxation 143–7
psychodrama 108
psychosomatic complaints 97–8, 267–9
psychotic patients, dangers of imagery 120

rational-emotive behavioral therapy 18–19
recall, using visualization to aid 236–8
receptive imagery 97–8
reflection, follow-up 163–4
relationships 221–7
assessment skills 221–7
client-therapist 29, 197
increasing happiness in 259–62
relaxation 139, 141–2
effectiveness of in therapy 143
meditation 140–1
pre-imagery practice of 153–4
preliminary preparations 139–40
self-relaxation exercises for therapists
147–8
summary 147
techniques
autogenic relaxation 143
deep muscle relaxation 143–7
visualization 143
role-reversal imagery 242–3
Ronen, T. 29, 264–6, 270
rope images, relationship assessment
224–7
Rosenbaum, M. 29, 270
Rosner, R.I. 96
Rothenberg, A. 67
Rowling, J.K. 50, 187–8
Ryff, C.D. 42, 45

Safran, J.D. 29, 66–7, 181
Schaffer, H.R. 75, 84
Schatz, D.M. 278
Schefft, B.K. 29–30
schemata 19, 81
schizophrenia 31, 120
SDT *see* skills-directed therapy
Segal, Z.V. 23, 24, 29, 66–7, 140, 160,
162, 181, 228
selective mutism 264–6
self-assessment skills 218–21
self-control models 20, 33–4
self-efficacy 18, 192, 252, 291–2

self-help skills for therapists 277–8, 286–8
focusing on positive abilities 282–5
leaving things behind 281–2
planning future therapeutic processes
285–6
self-supervision 278–81
self-relaxation exercises for therapists
147–8
Seligman, Martin 38, 41, 199, 251, 252
sensations, facilitating positive 255–9
sensitivity to internal stimuli, skills for
increasing 227–31
setting, therapeutic 28
arrangement of 150
sexual abuse 210–11
Sheldon, B. 30, 66
Sheldon, K.M. 41
Shorr, J. 117–18
Singer, J.L. 93, 107, 286, 293
skills for coping *see* coping in the present
skills-directed therapy (SDT) 32–4
Smith, R. 64
Snyder, C.R. 251
social contacts, skills for initiating 244–6
social development 84
social learning 17–18, 79
social relationships, skills for improving
243–4
social support 221–2, 243
stories
distorting memories 94
of dreams and visions 96
enhancing information processing 130
for treating anxiety 126–7
see also metaphors
Stott, R. 124, 126, 130
stressful performance situations, using
positive imagery 239–40
Strosahl, K.D. 131, 135
stuttering, relaxation technique for 172–3
subjective wellbeing 44–7
supervision, therapist skill 278–81
survivor guilt 211–13
symbolic versus concrete imagery 98–9

targets for conducting assessment 186
clients' emotions, thoughts, and
behaviors 187–90
clients' motivations, strengths and
expectations 190–2

targets *(Cont.)*
 clients' problems 186–7
 ongoing progress 193–4
 outcome at termination 194–5
 therapist guidelines for main questions
  195–7
 treatment needs 192–3
Tbnsager, M.E. 185
Teasdale, J.D. 23, 24, 140, 160, 162, 181,
 228
techniques of CBT 28–9
television phobia, relaxation technique for
 171–2
termination of therapy
 on a positive emotion 119
 assessment of change 194–5, 197
 imagery phase of sessions 160–2
 outcome evaluation 185
 travel and transition metaphors 131
test anxiety
 noncreative imagery example 69
 relaxation technique for 173–4
 skills for coping with 236–40
 using humor and role reversal 243
therapists
 creativity 66–72
 journey towards becoming 3–13
 obstacles with using imagery 101–2
 preparation of 150
 role of 29–30
 self-help skills 277–88
 self-relaxation exercises 147–8
 techniques used by 28–9
 therapeutic process and setting 27–8
 therapeutic relationship 29, 197
 way of thinking 29–30
Thoresen, C.E. 182
Torrance, E.P. 62

trauma 199
 using imagery for cognitive restructuring
  210–14
 see also posttraumatic stress disorder
  (PTSD)
treatment needs, assessment of 192–3, 196

visualization
 eliciting positive emotions 256–9
 learning and memorizing materials
  through 236–8
 relaxation technique 143
Vygotzky, L. 79, 82

Wallas, G. 64
Ward, C.H. 96
Ward, T. 64
warning signals 229–30, 254
Watson, J.C. 141, 142
Weisberg, R.W. 57–8, 64, 70
Weisz, J.R. 75, 170, 175
White, B. 200
Williams, J.M.G. 23, 24, 140, 160, 162,
 181, 228
Wilson, K.G. 131, 135
Winnicott, Donald 59
Wolpe, J. 141
words
 assessment limitations 183
 using positive 50
working alliance 29, 197
Wright, B.A. 47

Yanai, Yehuda 25
young children, using imagery with 264–7

Zimmerman, B.J. 175
Zohar, D. 92